A Bibliography of the *Romance* and Related Forms in Spanish America

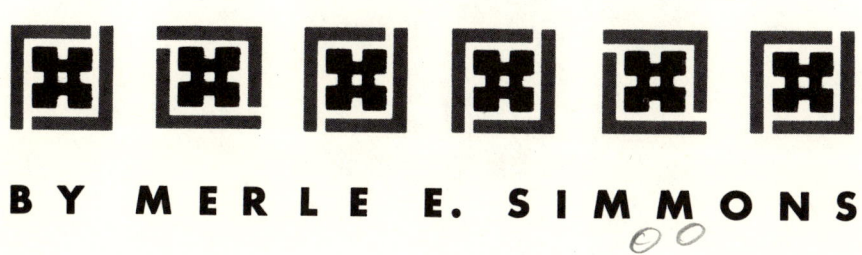

BY MERLE E. SIMMONS

A Bibliography of the *Romance* and Related Forms in Spanish America

INDIANA UNIVERSITY PRESS
BLOOMINGTON   1963

Indiana University Folklore Series Number 18
Indiana University, Bloomington, Indiana

Publication Committee

Editor: Richard M. Dorson
Consulting Editor: John W. Ashton

Assistant Editors: Jerome R. Mintz, Felix Oinas,
Thomas A. Sebeok, Erminie Wheeler-Voegelin

The Indiana University Folklore Series was founded in 1939 for the publication of occasional papers and monographs by members of the faculty.

This volume was composed at the Indiana University Research Center in Anthropology, Folklore, and Linguistics.

Copyright 1963 by Indiana University Press ©
Library of Congress Catalog Card No. 63-62501

To My Wife

PREFACE

    This bibliography stems from my work on the Mexican corrido. Before progressing very far into study of the ballads of Mexico, I was struck by the lack of bibliographical guides to the whole field of Mexican popular literature; and as my investigations carried me farther afield into other areas of Spanish America, I soon became aware that Mexico was not alone in her need; that, with the notable exceptions of Argentina and Chile, there were only isolated and fragmentary bibliographies to which folklorists and others might turn. To fill part of this void I have set out here to supply a working bibliography in one fairly restricted area of popular literature in America.
    My subject is the ballads of Spanish America — at least this is my point of departure — and since my search for the origins of American narrative songs led inevitably to the romances of Spain, I have entitled my work: A Bibliography of the Romance and Related Forms in Spanish America.
    But much has happened during the four and a half centuries since the conquerors brought their narrative poems and songs to America. Though there are a few regions where the traditional romance still enjoys considerable vogue in popular literature, in most countries it is no longer the principal metric form used in narrative compositions. In some cases it has evolved into other similar but structurally quite different genres (e. g., the corrido in Mexico) or its narrative function has been taken over by other distinct meters (e. g., the décima so frequently used in the Antilles and elsewhere). Hence, the "related forms" to which I refer in my title are often metrically quite unrelated to the romance, their only point of contact with the latter being the uses to which they are put.
    Had it been possible to limit my subject by considering only purely narrative compositions, my task would have been greatly simplified. But this was out of the question, for predominantly narrative genres, like the corridos of Mexico, also serve other ends; very frequently they abandon narration completely in order to comment on political and social matters or on human foibles in general. This being true, what of other similar commentaries such as pasquines, whose long history extends all the way back to the conquest? Admittedly these often scurrilous poems tend to be mere doggerel and they seldom pass into popular tradition, but in their attention to current affairs, usually political events, they are so closely akin to many corridos that they demanded a place in my bibliography. A further complication arises from the close relationship between romances and coplas in Hispanic tradition. In view of Francisco Rodríguez Marín's belief, which I

share, that the copla must be considered a derivative of the romance, coplas too had to be counted among the many "related forms" treated in this study, though at the expense of greatly broadening my work. For these reasons my principal problem has been where to stop. On the one hand, a work of this kind should not become so unwieldly as to be difficult to use; on the other, it should give ample assistance to any investigator desirous of blazing new trails into fringe areas of the subject under study.

My attempted solution of these problems has been to employ different criteria in dealing with the diverse forms and types of compositions herein studied. I have been as exhaustive as possible in treating all popular poetry written in romance meter and all narrative or topical poems, whatever their form. Likewise, I have made a special effort to attain substantial completeness in dealing with the corridos of Mexico and all compositions known by that name throughout Spanish America. In the case of the ubiquitous copla, on the other hand, I have set for myself no such unattainable goal, for the field is so vast that it defies even an approach to completeness by one whose principal interest lies elsewhere. I have, nevertheless, consistently incorporated all the items I encountered which contained texts of coplas or information about them, and I am hopeful that scholars interested in studying this genre of popular literature will find my listings of value.

As I have moved farther out into the fringe areas of my subject, my procedure has been dictated by eminently practical considerations. Closeness in form or tone to romances or corridos has generally determined whether or not pasquines or other compositions of doubtful pedigree have been admitted into this study. But my criteria have not always been constant, for in the case of countries whose popular poetry and songs have been little studied (i.e., Bolivia, Paraguay, Ecuador, and certain others), not infrequently I have included entries which I would have eliminated as of negligible interest had they dealt with Mexico, Argentina, or other regions whose popular literature has been the subject of intensive investigation.

From the inception of this work my intention has been to provide investigators with an annotated bibliography wherein, by means of brief but reasonably complete commentaries, I would indicate the contents of each entry. This I have done in all cases where I have been able to consult works listed; items which appear without descriptions are those which I have been unable to locate and examine, albeit in some instances where I lack personal acquaintance with a book or article, I have filled the void by citing other critics' comments. But any descriptive material not specifically attributed to others is to be taken as my own and indicates personal consultation of the work cited.

Those items which I have not been able to examine and for which I have found no critical descriptions have, quite naturally, posed bothersome problems. It is often difficult to know whether or not they should be included here. There is no problem, of course, when an explicit title describes clearly the character of a volume or an article. But difficulties arise where contents are less clearly revealed: e.g., works about folklore in general whose titles do not indicate whether they contain material about the specific subjects of interest to me here. At considerable risk of error I have generally adopted a lenient attitude, particularly in treating those countries whose popular literature has been studied only superficially. My policy in these cases could be aptly described as grasping at straws. A similarly benign attitude has led me to admit certain vague titles which I judge, on the basis of my general knowledge of the field, to offer promise of possibly useful information about ballads or subjects treated in ballad literature. An example is Dantel Argandoña's "El bandido en la literatura chilena." Also, certain works which, after consultation, I found to be lacking in any specific mention of narrative poetry or song, I have sometimes included if their generalized comment could be applied profitably to the study of ballad literature (e.g., Angélico Chávez, "The Inter-Relation of History and Folklore").

Another problem relative to titles arises in the case of certain other works actually consulted. A considerable number of these have deceptive titles; that is to say, they promise much but prove, upon examination, to be of negligible value. The best examples, perhaps, are the works of Sánchez y Fuentes in Cuba. These, while they profess to deal with folklore, in reality have little to do with truly popular literature. Almost all of the material classified therein as folklore turns out to be semiartistic or completely learned in character. Unfortunately, Sánchez y Fuentes is not alone in this, and many investigators have included practically anything of a nationalistic or regional character under the heading of folklore. The problems which this practice creates are obvious. Still other works with "deceptive" titles, though quite estimable studies of genuine popular literature, contain nothing germane to my restricted subject. To omit either the latter or the pseudo-folkloric studies, where their titles look promising, would, I believe, be a disservice to scholars who, upon finding reference to them elsewhere, would feel obliged to seek them out on the assumption that I had probably missed them in compiling this bibliography. Hence, my usual practice has been to list such titles with appropriate comment in the belief that it is as helpful to users of this study to be led away from unrewarding sources as it is to be guided to the productive ones.

In the interest of narrowing somewhat the scope of my work, there are a few limits which I have arbitrarily placed upon it. Without underestimating the possible influence of Indian literature and music upon the ballads in Spanish in certain areas of Latin America (the subject has not received the attention which it deserves from folklorists), I have not made any serious attempt to compile the bibliography of Indian poetry and songs in America. To scholars with competence in Indian tongues

I leave the task of careful inquiry into this subject. For my part I have tried only to list some of the most important sources in this field of study.

Nor have I attempted to deal here with the popular literature of Brazil. My decision to confine myself to Spanish America was prompted by the necessity of keeping my subject from mushrooming, not by my failure to appreciate the extreme importance of ballads in Portuguese to the general history of the romance tradition in America. A bibliographical study of Brazilian counterparts of the compositions treated here is indispensable to the completion of my work. Perhaps at some later date I, or someone else, will be able to supply this need.

Another limitation to be noted is my decision not to attempt to cover intensively the field of gaucho poetry in Argentina and Uruguay. I have tried, it is true, to include the most important sources of information about gaucho literature, especially those works concerned with truly popular poetry as opposed to the "gaucho" school of stylized semi-artistic or artistic compositions of which Martín Fierro is the best example. But the excellent bibliographies of Madaline Nichols have covered the whole field of both types of gaucho poetry so thoroughly that I felt it best to devote my own efforts primarily to other less explored areas, particularly in view of the impossibility of my locating in the United States many of the extremely numerous titles listed by Nichols. In her work will be found ample material to guide any scholar who desires to investigate in libraries of the Río de la Plata region the relationship between gaucho poetry and the romances or other narrative poems of Argentina and Uruguay.

In order further to keep the scope of my work within reasonable bounds I decided, finally, not to attempt to list commercial phonograph recordings of ballads and other songs related to my subject. Instead of broadening my own work to include such a vast body of material, I have chosen merely to list a few bibliographical sources of information about recordings of this type.

In organizing my study I have divided my listings into sections based on geographical areas. In all cases save two I have grouped titles by countries; the exceptions are the Río de la Plata area, where I have considered Argentina and Uruguay as a single region, and Mexico, which for my purposes embraces the southwestern part of the United States and anywhere else in the latter country where Spanish-speaking communities exist. Though there are other areas in America which might have been combined in like manner, nowhere else do the essential cultural ties between two adjacent political regions seem to be so commonly recognized. Considering Mexico and the United States together will, I am confident, arouse no protest from any quarter. And lest Uruguayan readers take exception to my decision to treat their country along with Argentina in a single section, I feel compelled to remind them that scholars of both countries often follow the same

Preface xi

practice. Indeed, it is precisely because there are so many works which cut across political boundaries in treating the literary history of the Plata region that an attempt on my part to separate the two countries here would have necessitated numerous double listings or cross references. To avoid these needless repetitions I have adopted the policy indicated above.

In addition to these groupings by geographical areas, I have included at the beginning of my study one section listing works of a general character which seemed not to belong to any single region. I have tried to keep this section within modest limits by placing here only those titles which could not be reasonably classified as belonging <u>predominantly</u> to some one specific region. Scholars interested in any area of America would do well to consult this general section in addition to the specialized bibliographies of individual countries, since some exceedingly important works about Spanish American popular literature in general are to be found in it.

The history of the <u>romance</u> in America at all periods developed on two levels, the artistic and the popular. In this bibliography I am concerned primarily with truly popular and with semipopular compositions, not with the work of learned poets. Though many of the latter use <u>romance</u> meter, I do not include in this study modern cultivators of <u>romances</u> or <u>corridos</u> if their work is intended primarily for a select audience of cultivated literary tastes. Hence, the work of such estimable poets as Miguel N. Lira, Arturo Capdevila, and many other talented artists who have adapted popular poetic forms to literary purposes are not included; consideration of their works would entail study of an aspect of the <u>romance-corrido</u> tradition in America other than the popular current which concerns me here.

In treating the colonial period, however, I have used another criterion. Few of the truly popular songs of two or three centuries ago, which existed for the most part in oral tradition, have survived in printed documents, and any attempt to trace the development of popular <u>romances</u> in America will inevitably be tied in with the study of more or less artistic compositions. Since the bibliography of literary <u>romances</u> which date from the period before independence is not voluminous in any case, I have included as many references as I have found to artistic as well as to popular <u>romances</u> in the period before about 1830. My choice of this date is arbitrary. I choose it because it represents a time after most countries in Spanish America had achieved political independence but before the strong surge of romantic interest in ballad literature had led artistic poets, following in the footsteps of the Duque de Rivas and Zorrilla, to produce a large volume of artistic <u>romances</u>. I should state further that even during the period before 1830, I have made no attempt to include references to dramatists or dramatic works, though playwrights like Juan Ruiz de Alarcón naturally cultivated the <u>romance</u>, and I have omitted all references to the most illustrious cultivator of the artistic romance in colonial times, Sor Juana Inés de la Cruz. Numerous scholars have gathered the voluminous bibliography of and about the famous Mexican poetess, thus precluding any necessity of my treating her here. In a few other cases of well known writers (Juan del Valle y Caviedes for example), I merely refer the reader to a source of general information.

Let it be stated at once that in my attempts to deal with the innumerable genres of popular poetry and song which grace the immense area known as Spanish America, my frame of reference is always the romances of Spain and the corridos of Mexico. With these I can claim some degree of personal familiarity, while my acquaintance with the popular literature of other areas is relatively much more limited. So it is that when I declare that a composition is like or unlike the romances of Spain or the corridos of Mexico, I am merely availing myself of comparisons with the genres I know best. And when I refer to the "romance-corrido tradition," I am again using a Spanish-Mexican frame of reference, not because it is better or more worthy of esteem than any other parallel that might have been drawn but only because it represents the current in Hispanic-American popular literature with which I am familiar. The fact that the corrido of Mexico has been studied perhaps as extensively as most comparable genres of poetry and song from other areas probably makes this choice as logical as any other from the standpoint of most if not all of the users of my bibliography.

I should add that my study includes all the items which have come to my attention down to the very moment of completing my manuscript. Although I am aware that my listings for the last year or two are necessarily incomplete because of the time lag which inevitably occurs between the publication of books and articles and their appearance in bibliographies and book lists where they might come to my attention (not to mention their availability for consultation on library shelves), I have, nevertheless, elected to include anything I have heard of down to the present moment. The admitted incompleteness of my list, my inability to provide comments on items which I have not yet been able to consult, and also the personal risk I run of being charged with carelessness for not including recent items which may be known to almost everyone except me, are, I feel, outweighed by the desirability of making my work as complete, and hence as useful, as possible to investigators who consult it. For that reason, down to the very moment of putting my manuscript into the hands of the publisher, I have incorporated last-minute items.

This bibliography could not have been prepared without the help of numerous people, many of whom I have never met. My greatest debt is to those bibliographers of Spanish American popular literature who have preceded me and afforded valuable leads to sources which I have consulted and used here. While some of their work left much to be desired, and there were times when my feelings of gratitude were more

than a little tinged by exasperation with obscure listings and flagrant
errors, I am deeply cognizant of the debt which I owe to all my predecessors, both the competent and the less able. Without their efforts
my own attempts would have been futile. And lest my criticism of
some of their work be wrongly interpreted, I must express my special
gratitude to and admiration for such able scholars as Ralph S. Boggs,
Raúl Silva Castro, Augusto Raúl Cortázar, Gilbert Chase, and Eugenio
Pereira Salas, to mention only a few of the most outstanding bibliographers in the field.

Among the personal friends who have aided me in the preparation
of this work, I wish to thank Professor Vicente T. Mendoza of the Universidad Nacional Autónoma de México for permission to use his excellent personal library wherein I was able to consult a considerable number of items that had eluded me elsewhere. To my esteemed friend
and colleague at Indiana University, Professor John M. Hill, go my
thanks and appreciation for having read my entire manuscript and for
having offered many judicious and timely suggestions.

Finally, I am grateful to the American Philosophical Society for
a financial grant from the Penrose Fund which in 1955 enabled me to
do research on this project in the libraries of Spain and Mexico.

Notwithstanding the excellent help which I have received, this bibliography undoubtedly contains its full share of errors. For these I
assume sole responsibility and beg the indulgence of all its users.

                                                      Merle E. Simmons
                                                      Bloomington, Indiana
                                                      January, 1961

TABLE OF CONTENTS

List of Abbreviations	1
General Section	11
Argentina and Uruguay	37
Bolivia	89
Chile	97
Colombia	129
Costa Rica	157
Cuba	161
Dominican Republic	181
Ecuador	189
Guatemala	195
Honduras	199
Mexico	203
Nicaragua	289
Panama	295
Paraguay	299
Peru	303
Puerto Rico	335
El Salvador	341
Venezuela	345
The Pacific Islands	369
Index	373

LIST OF ABBREVIATIONS

AACL	Anuario de la Academia Colombiana de la Lengua (Bogotá).
Abs	Abside (México).
ACA	Amazonia colombiana americanista, órgano semestral del "Cileac" (Sibundoy, Putumayo, Colombia).
AFA	Anales de la Asociación Folklórica Argentina (B. A.).
AFC	Archivos de folklore cubano (Habana).
AFCU	Archivos del folklore chileno (Santiago).
AIIE	Anales del Instituto de Investigaciones Estéticas (México).
AIL	Anales del Instituto de Lingüística (Mendoza, Argentina).
AIn	América indígena, órgano oficial del Instituto Indigenista Interamericano (México).
AJP	American Journal of Philology (Baltimore).
ALatPR	Alma latina (San Juan, Puerto Rico).
AmerH	América, revista de la Asociación de Escritores y Artistas Americanos (Habana).
Americ	The Américas (Washington, D. C.).
AndQ	Andean Quarterly (Santiago de Chile).
AnFFE	Anales de la Facultad de Filosofía y Educación, Universidad de Chile, Sección de Filología (Santiago).
AnMN	Anales del Museo Nacional de Arqueología, Historia y Etnografía (México).
AnSFA	Anales de la Sociedad Folklórica Argentina (B. A.).
Anthropos	Anthropos (Wien, Austria).
APF	Archivos peruanos del folklore (Lima).
ArizQuar	Arizona Quarterly (Tucson).
ASFM	Anuario de la Sociedad Folklórica de México (México).
Atenea	Atenea (Santiago de Chile).

AUCH	Anales de la Universidad de Chile (Santiago).
Aulos	Aulos, revista musical (Santiago de Chile).
AVF	Archivos venezolanos de folklore (Caracas).
Azul	Azul (República Argentina).
BAAL	Boletín de la Academia Argentina de Letras (B. A.).
Babr	Books Abroad (Norman, Okla.).
BACA	Boletín [de la] Asociación Cultural Ameghino (Luján, provincia de Buenos Aires, Argentina).
BAChH	Boletín de la Academia Chilena de la Historia (Santiago).
BAFA	Boletín de la Asociación Folklórica Argentina (B. A.).
BAGN	Boletín del Archivo General de la Nación (México).
BATF	Boletín de la Asociación Tucumana de Folklore Tucumán, Argentina).
BBAA	Boletín bibliográfico de antropología americana (México).
BBMP	Boletín de la Biblioteca Menéndez y Pelayo (Santander, España).
BCC	Boletín bimestral de la Comisión Chilena de Cooperación Intelectual (Santiago).
BCF	Boletim trimestral da Comissão Catarinense de Folklore (Florianápolis, Santa Catarina, Brasil).
BFM	Boletín de filología (Montevideo).
BGE	Boletín de la Sociedad Mexicana de Geografía y Estadística (México).
BHA	Boletín de historia y antigüedades, órgano de la Academia Colombiana de Historia (Bogotá).
BIBNC	Boletín de la Biblioteca Nacional de Caracas.
BICC	Boletín del Instituto Caro y Cuervo (Bogotá).
BIF	Boletín del Instituto de Folklore (Caracas).
BIFC	Boletín del Instituto de Filología de la Universidad de Chile (Santiago).
BIFL	Boletín del Instituto de Folklore del Litoral (Santa Fe, Argentina).
BIFP	Boletín del Instituto de Investigaciones Folklóricas (Panamá).

List of Abbreviations

BIMMF	Boletín del Instituto Mexicano de Musicología y Folklore (México).
BLAM	Boletín latinoamericano de música (Montevideo and other cities).
BMJH	Boletín del Museo de Motivos Populares Argentinos José Hernández (B. A.).
BNYPL	Bulletin of the New York Public Library (New York).
Bol	Bolívar (Bogotá).
BolMN	Boletín del Museo Nacional de Arqueología, Historia y Etnografía (México).
BPAU	Bulletin of the Pan American Union (Washington, D. C.).
Bro	Brotéria (Lisboa).
BSGL	Boletín de la Sociedad Geográfica de Lima (Lima).
BSS	Bulletin of Spanish Studies (Liverpool).
BUPan	Boletín de la Unión Panamericana (Washington, D. C.).
CCE	Casa de la cultura ecuatoriana (Quito).
CDC	Cuadernos dominicanos de cultura (Ciudad Trujillo).
CFQ	California Folklore Quarterly (Berkeley, California).
Clav	Clavileño (Madrid).
CMS	Correo musical sud-americano (B. A.).
ComerL	El Comercio (Lima).
Cri	Crisol, revista mensual publicada por el Bloque de Obreros Intelectuales de México (México).
CroL	La Crónica (Lima).
CuA	Cuadernos americanos (México).
Cuauh	Cuauhtémoc, revista de cultura y de actualidad (México).
Cub	Cubagua (Caracas).
CuC	Cuba contemporánea (Habana).
CuH	Cuadernos hispanoamericanos (Madrid).
CUn	Cultura universitaria (Caracas).
CV	Cultura venezolana (Caracas).
DdeG	Diario de Guerrero (Chilpancingo, Guerrero, México).

DH	Divulgación histórica (México).
EAfr	Estudios afrocubanos (Habana).
EstA	Estudios americanos (Sevilla).
EstBA	Estudios (B. A.).
EstCH	Estrella de Chile (Santiago).
Eurindia	Eurindia (México).
Ex	Excelsior (México).
FA	Folklore Américas (Chapel Hill, North Carolina, and Gainesville, Fla.).
FACI	Folklore americano (Lima).
FenL	Fénix, revista de la Biblioteca Nacional (Lima).
FICU	Folklore, boletín del Departamento de Folklore del Instituto de Cooperación Universitaria de los Cursos de Cultura Católica (B. A.).
FPL	Folklore, tribuna del pensamiento peruano (Lima).
FyL	Filosofía y letras (México).
Gaea	Gaea, anales de la Sociedad Argentina de Estudios Geográficos (B. A.).
HAHR	Hispanic American Historical Review (Durham, North Carolina).
HCPC	Hojas de cultura popular colombiana (Bogotá).
Hisp	Hispania (Stanford University, California, Washington, D. C., and Baltimore).
Ho	Humanismo (México).
HP	El hijo pródigo (México).
HR	Hispanic Review (Philadelphia).
Hu	Humanidades (La Plata, Argentina).
IAA	Ibero-Amerikanisches Archiv (Berlin).
IAm	The Inter-American (Washington, D. C.).
IAmBR	Inter-American Bibliographical Review (Washington, D. C.).
IAmM	The Inter-American Monthly (Washington, D. C.).
IAR	Ibero-Amerikanisches Rundschau (Hamburg).

List of Abbreviations

IL	Investigaciones lingüísticas (México).
Ipna	Ipna (Lima).
JAF	Journal of American Folklore (New York).
JIFMC	Journal of the International Folk Music Council (Cambridge, England).
Lasso	Lasso (B. A.).
LetE	Letras del Ecuador (Quito).
LetrasM	Letras de México (México).
LitAr	Literatura argentina (B. A.).
Lyceum	Lyceum (Habana).
LyP	El libro y el pueblo (México).
MAM	Memorias de la Academia Mexicana Correspondiente de la Real Española (México).
Merc	El Mercurio (Santiago de Chile; originally published in Valparaíso).
MF	Mexican Folkways (México).
MdS	Mar del Sur (Lima).
MLN	Modern Language Notes (Baltimore).
MP	Mercurio peruano (Lima).
MSMC	The Masterkey (Southwestern Museum, Los Angeles, California).
MusRM	Música, revista mexicana (México).
Nac	La Nación (B. A.).
Nacion	El Nacional (México).
NacionC	El Nacional (Caracas).
ND	La nueva democracia (New York).
NLB	The Newberry Library Bulletin (Chicago).
NMFR	New Mexico Folklore Record (Albuquerque).
NMHR	New Mexico Historical Review (Albuquerque-Santa Fe).
NMus	Neues Musikblatt (Mainz, Germany).
Nos	Nosotros (B. A.).
Nove	Novedades (México).

NRFH	Nueva revista de filología hispánica (México).
NuM	Nuestra música (México).
OTLV	Onza, tigre y león, revista para la infancia venezolana (Caracas).
PAB	Pan American Bulletin (Washington, D. C.).
Pal	El Palacio (Santa Fe, New Mexico).
PAM	Pan American Magazine (Washington, D. C.).
PanAm	The Pan American (New York).
PanAmB	The Pan American Book Shelf (Washington, D. C.).
Patria	Patria, órgano del Ejército Chileno (Santiago ?).
Ph	Phoenix, Zeitschrift für deutsche Geistesarbeit in Sudamerika (B. A.).
PhilQ	Philological Quarterly (Iowa City, Iowa).
PrBA	La Prensa (B. A.).
PrL	La Prensa (Lima).
PTFS	Publications of the Texas Folklore Society (Austin and Dallas).
PyS	Previsión y seguridad (Monterrey, Nuevo León, México).
QIA	Quaderni ibero-americani (Torino, Italy).
RABA	Revista americana de Buenos Aires (B. A.).
RABM	Revista de archivos, bibliotecas y museos (Madrid).
RABrM	Revista da Associação Brasileira da Música (Rio de Janeiro).
RAL	Revista das Academias de Letras, Federação das Academias de Letras do Brasil (Rio de Janeiro).
RAmer	Revista de América (Bogotá).
RAMSP	Revista do Arquivo Municipal (São Paulo, Brasil).
RAPE	Revista de la Asociación Patriótica Española (B. A.).
RBC	Revista bimestre cubana (Habana).
RBChE	Revista de bibliografía chilena y extranjera (Santiago).
RBM	Revista brasileira de música (Rio de Janeiro).
RBN	Revista de la Biblioteca Nacional (Habana).
RCAE	Revista del Círculo de Altos Estudios (Rosario, Argentina).

List of Abbreviations

RCEE	Revista del Centro de Estudios Extremeños (Badajoz, España).
RCF	Revista colombiana de folclore (Bogotá).
RChHG	Revista chilena de historia y geografía (Santiago).
RdE	Revista de las Españas (Madrid).
RDTP	Revista de dialectología y tradiciones populares (formerly Revista de tradiciones populares) (Madrid).
REM	Revista de estudios musicales (Mendoza, Argentina).
RepAm	Repertorio americano (San José, Costa Rica).
RevCat	Revista católica (Santiago de Chile).
RevCu	Revista cubana (Habana).
RevF	Revista filológica: Arquivo de Estudos de Filologia, História, Etnografia, Folklore e Crítica Literária (Rio de Janeiro).
RevIA	Revista del Instituto de Antropología de la Universidad Nacional de Tucumán (Tucumán, Argentina).
RevMM	Revista musical mexicana (México).
RevP	Revista del Pacífico (Valparaíso, Chile).
RFCC	Revista de folklore, órgano de la Comisión Nacional de Folklore (Bogotá).
RFCh	Revista de folklore chileno (Santiago).
RFE	Revista de filología española (Madrid).
RFH	Revista de filología hispánica (B. A. and New York).
RFLC	Revista de la Facultad de Letras y Ciencias (Universidad de la Habana).
RHis	Revista de historia (Pasto, Colombia).
RevIb	Revista iberoamericana (México).
RevInd	Revista de las Indias (Bogotá).
RevIndM	Revista de Indias (Madrid).
RevS	Revista sud-americana (B. A.).
RH	Revue Hispanique (Paris-New York).
RHM	Revista hispánica moderna (New York).
RCLA	Revista hispanoamericana de ciencias, letras y artes (Cádiz).

RINT	Revista del Instituto Nacional de la Tradición (B. A.).
RIPN	Revista del Instituto Pedagógico Nacional (Caracas).
RJav	Revista javeriana (Bogotá).
RJZB	Revista del Jardín Zoológico de Buenos Aires (B. A.).
RLin	Revista Linares (Linares, Chile).
RM	Revista de música (B. A.).
RMC	Revista musical chilena (Santiago).
RMM	Revista musical de México (México).
RMS	Revista mexicana de sociología (México).
RN	Revista nacional (Montevideo).
RNC	Revista nacional de cultura (Caracas).
Ru	Ruta (México).
RUCuzco	Revista universitaria (Cuzco, Perú).
RUnI	Revista universitaria, órgano oficial de la Universidad Popular (Iquique, Chile).
RR	The Romanic Review (New York).
RUBA	Revista de la Universidad de Buenos Aires (B. A.).
RUNC	Revista de la Universidad Nacional de Córdoba (Córdoba, Argentina).
RVF	Revista venezolana de folklore (Caracas).
SCCol	Selecciones culturales de Colombia (Bogotá).
Scrib	Scribners Magazine (New York).
Sen	Senderos (Bogotá).
SFQ	Southern Folklore Quarterly (Gainesville, Fla.).
Sig	El Siglo (Bogotá).
Sphinx	Sphinx, revista del Instituto Superior de Lingüística y Filología de la Universidad Mayor de San Marcos (Lima).
SRCS	Sustancia, revista de cultura superior (Tucumán, Argentina).
Sur	Sur (B. A.).
SWR	Southwest Review (Dallas, Texas).
TF	Tierra firme (Madrid).

TI	Tribuna israelita (México).
Tiem	El Tiempo (Bogotá).
TMS	Tlalocan, a Journal of Source Materials on the Native Cultures of Mexico (Sacramento, California).
Todo	Todo (México).
TradP	Tradición, revista peruana de cultura (Cuzco, Perú).
UA	Universidad de Antioquia (Medellín, Colombia).
UniversalCar	El Universal (Caracas).
UniversalGraf	El Universal Gráfico (México).
UniversalMex	El Universal (México).
UnivM	Universidad (México).
UnivA	Universidad de los Andes (Mérida, Venezuela).
UnivCB	Universidad Católica Bolivariana (Medellín, Colombia).
UnivMex	Universidad de México (México).
UnivSF	Universidad (Universidad Nacional del Litoral, Santa Fe, Argentina).
USFX	Universidad de San Francisco Xavier (Sucre, Bolivia).
WF	Western Folklore (Berkeley, California).
YA	Yeda-'am, Journal of the Folklore Society in Israel (Tel-Aviv).
ZRPh	Zeitschrift für Romanische Philologie (Halle, Germany).

An explanation of the style employed in making my entries is in order:

1. B. A. has been used throughout as an abbreviation for Buenos Aires. México, D. F. has been shortened in all cases merely to México. Names of cities like Santiago de Chile or Santiago de Cuba have been shortened to Santiago, provided they appeared in the section devoted to Chile or Cuba, as the case might be. If, however, a work listed in the section on Cuba was published in Santiago de Chile, the full name has been given. It may be assumed that any small or obscure cities or towns listed without further identification are located in the country in whose section they appear.

2. Wherever it has been possible to eliminate Vol., Tomo, No., Núm., etc. without creating confusion, this has been done. Numbers appearing before a colon refer to volume number (i.e., Volumen,

Volume, Tomo, Heft, etc.), while numbers immediately following a colon identify a given issue within a volume (i.e., Number, Número, etc.). Wherever possible, I have eliminated the abbreviation pp. in giving page numbers. But if confusion would have resulted, I have retained it in order to separate page numbering from the number of an issue or a volume. Thus an item listed as "BAAL, XV:57 (octubre-diciembre de 1946), 637-669" is to be interpreted as appearing in the Boletín de la Academia Argentina de Letras, Vol. XV, No. 57 (octubre-diciembre de 1946), pp. 637-669. In all cases where a publication employs an unconventional system of identifying issues or volumes (such as using entrega instead of número or numbering tomos within volumes), I have eschewed the use of cryptic devices and given a complete entry.

3. While this study is intended to be primarily a working bibliography for scholars and not a source of detailed descriptive data for bibliophiles, I have deemed it desirable to try to include in my entries the number of pages of each volume cited together with its approximate size in centimeters. A procedure that is commonly followed in bibliographies which come out of Spanish America, I have adhered to it wherever possible (i.e., in all cases where I have seen the volume in question or found it described on a Library of Congress card or elsewhere) in the belief that such information is useful to working scholars (particularly to those in one library I have heard of where cataloging and shelving are by a "sistema topográfico," i.e., in order of decreasing size).

4. Passages quoted in the annotations will sometimes contain inconsistencies of spelling and accentuation, according to varying usage in the original sources.

GENERAL SECTION

   In this general section are included those works which could not be assigned logically to any of the sections on specific countries. The most notable scholarly studies of this kind are undoubtedly those of Ramón Menéndez Pidal, though Luis de Santullano has recently made a significant contribution in the field. I have also listed here the most important bibliographical studies of a general character which deal with the popular poetry and song of Spanish America. Among these are the works of Ralph S. Boggs, Gilbert Chase, and others who have made lesser contributions.

GENERAL SECTION

1. Aguerrevere, A. D. "Bibliografía crítica del romance español en América." M. A. thesis, Stanford University, 1926.
[Lists with fairly detailed criticism a few of the early works on the romance in America.]

Aguilera, Francisco. See Handbook of Latin American Studies, entry no. 51.

2. "Algunos cuentos y cantos folklóricos en las Américas." BUPan, LXXXI:2 (febrero, 1937), 149-218.
[Mostly cuentos with only a few folk songs. None is narrative or related to the romance or the copla.]

3. Antología de poetas hispano-americanos publicada por la Real Academia Española. 4 vols. Madrid: Est. Tipográfico Sucesores de Rivadeneyra, 1893. 23 cm.
[Many artistic romances are contained in this work; some of them are popular in tone. The extensive introductions are by Marcelino Menéndez y Pelayo and have been reprinted in his Historia de la poesía hispano-americana.]

4. Arroyo, César E. "Romancero del pueblo ecuatoriano." Revista de la Sociedad "Jurídico-literaria" (Quito), XXIII:74-75 (enero-febrero de 1920), 1-32; also printed with the title "El romancero en América" in Arroyo's Retablo, figuras, evocaciones, escenas. Madrid: n. p., 1921. xiv, 221 pp. 19 cm.
[A very diffuse article, the first half of which is devoted to characterizing literature in America in general and differentiating it from that of Spain. The second half treats romances, but almost all of those studied are artistic and nonpopular compositions which date from the colonial period to the time of Juan Montalvo. The author apologizes for including the only compositions which are slightly popular in flavor, two fragments that "llegaron a cantarse en las iglesias de Lima y Quito, durante las misas, entre la Espístola y el Evangelio . . . ." One, not a romance, is a patriotic song from the period of Ecuadorian independence and sounds quite lively; the other is a romancillo which praises Simón Bolívar.]

5. Bayo, Ciro. "La poesía popular en la América del Sur." RABM, Tercera época, Tomo VI, enero de 1902, 43-49.
[A collection of popular poetry including some traditional romances. There is a brief introduction.]

6. _____, ed. Romancero criollo. Madrid, 1921. (Biblioteca universal, No. 178.)
[A collection of romances, corridos, coplas, and other types of poetry from America. Almost all are reprinted from the works of Vicuña Cifuentes, Chacón y Calvo, and others.]

7. Bayo, Ciro. Vocabulario criollo-español sud-americano. Madrid: Librería de los Sucesores de Hernando, 1910. 254 pp. 22.5 cm.

[In giving definitions the author occasionally quotes a strophe of a copla, a romance, a vidalita, or some other kind of popular poetry. But these cases are few in number.]

8. Bello, Andrés. "Uso antiguo de la rima asonante en la poesía latina de la edad media, i en la francesa; i observaciones sobre su uso moderno." In Vol. VI, Obras completas de don Andrés Bello. Santiago de Chile: Pedro G. Ramírez, 1883; also in Estudios filológicos, Vol. VI of Obras completas de Andrés Bello. Caracas: Ministerio de Educación, 1955. Pp. 351-364.

[An article published originally in Repertorio americano, January, 1827, pp. 21-33. It is a very illuminating discussion of the antiquity of assonantal rhyme, which Bello is able to trace back to Latin and old French texts of the twelfth century. Reference to romances in America is only incidental, as is passing mention of the use of assonance in yaravíes and other types of American popular songs.]

9. Berggreen, Andreas Peter. Folke-sange og Melodier, Faedrelandske og Fremede. 11 vols. Copenhagen: A. C. Reitzels, 1869-71.

[Chase (ref. 25, p. 34) comments: "Vol. 10 contains 2 Nicaraguan folk songs arranged for piano (Nos. 105-106); also 6 Mexican folk songs (Nos. 99-104) and 3 Peruvian folk songs (Nos. 110-112), with piano accompaniment."]

Berrien, William. See Handbook of Latin American Studies, entry no. 51.

10. Bertini, G. M. Romanze novellesche spagnole in America. Torino: Quaderni Ibero-Americani, 1957. xii, 75 pp.

[The author discusses the background of novelesque romances in America with particular attention to their peninsular origins. Then he offers a section of texts, eighty-three in all, which are variants of eight well known romances (e. g., La esposa infiel, Las señas del esposo, Delgadina, and others). In his copious notes he makes a comparative study of these texts. Included are many useful bibliographical references along with identification of the sources from which the texts are taken. There is also a glossary of Spanish Americanisms.]

11. Boggs, Ralph Steele. Bibliography of Latin American Folklore. New York: H. W. Wilson Co., 1940. x, 109 pp. 23.5 cm. (Publications of the Inter-American Bibliographical and Library Association, Ser. I, Vol. 5.)

[An extremely useful general bibliography which includes some entries that deal with popular poetry and song.]

12. _____. "Caribbean Ballads of the Spanish Conquest." In The Caribbean: Contemporary Trends, ed. by A. Curtis Wilgus. Gainesville, Fla.: University of Florida Press, 1953. Pp. 91-99.
[The author speculates on the reasons why the Spanish conquerors seem not to have inspired many truly popular ballads either in Spain or in America, notwithstanding the fact that their exploits coincided with a period in which the romance was flourishing.]

13. _____. "Folklore Bibliography for 1938." SFQ, III(1939), 45-57; ". . . for 1939." IV(1940), 23-50; ". . . for 1940." V(1941), 39-76; ". . . for 1941." VI(1942), 11-68; ". . . for 1942." VII(1943), 13-73; ". . . for 1943." VIII(1944), 27-100; ". . . for 1944." IX(1945), 13-88; ". . . for 1945." X(1946), 17-108; ". . . for 1946." XI(1947), 1-92; ". . . for 1947." XII(1948), 1-94; ". . . for 1948." XIII(1949), 1-104; ". . . for 1949." XIV(1950), 1-77; ". . . for 1950." XV(1951), 1-107; ". . . for 1951." XVI(1952), 1-78; ". . . for 1952." XVII(1953), 1-88; ". . . for 1953." XVIII(1954), 1-84; ". . . for 1954." XIX(1955), 1-75; ". . . for 1955." XX(1956), 1-88; ". . . for 1956." XXI(1957), 1-77; ". . . for 1957." XXII(1958), 1-68; ". . . for 1958." XXIII(1959), 1-77; with Roberts, Sarah Elizabeth, ". . . for 1959." XXIV(1960), 1-75.
[An extremely useful bibliography of folklore, particularly for the study of Latin America. Whenever possible, the bibliographer gives descriptions of the works listed. In every number there is a section of entries dealing with popular songs and poetry in Latin America. The work is indispensable for the study of Spanish American folklore. When I cite this work in the present bibliography, the date I give in parentheses or brackets refers in each instance to the date in Boggs' title, not to the year of publication. In 1961 Américo Paredes replaced Boggs as the compiler of this bibliography.]

14. _____. La poesía folklórica. Chapel Hill, N. C.: Orange Printshop.

15. _____. "La recolección de la música folklórica en el Nuevo Mundo." BLAM, V (octubre, 1941), 221-224.
[A discussion of the techniques to be followed in gathering and organizing musical folklore for analysis. The author points out errors which in the past have diminished the value of much collecting. There is no consideration of any specific genres, but the article is germane to the study of any type of popular song.]

16. _____. "Spanish Folklore in America." University of Miami Hispanic-American Studies (Coral Gables, Fla.). No. I (November, 1939), 122-136.
[A general discussion of folklore in America with cursory treatment of the romance and other forms of popular poetry.]

_____. See Handbook of Latin American Studies, entry no. 51.

17. Botsford, Florence Hudson [Topping]. Folksongs of Many Peoples. 2 vols. New York: Women's Press, 1921-22. 26.5 cm.; also, 3 vols. New York: G. Schirmer, n.d. 28.5 cm.

[Vol. II of the first edition contains (pp. 78-79) a version of El payo (Estaba un payo sentado/en las trancas de un corral).]

18. Brandão, Théo. "La condessa." RDTP, X(1954), Cuaderno 4.°, 591-641.

[In this study of a Portuguese children's game which is based on the romance, Hilo de oro, hilo de plata, the author cites a great many American versions of the Spanish romance. Most, if not all, are lifted from standard works like those of Mendoza, Cadilla de Martínez, and others.]

Brown, Elsie. See Handbook of Latin American Studies, entry no. 51.

19. Brown, Paul A., and Richmond, W. Edson. "Annual Folklore Bibliography 1954." JAF Supplement, 1955, pp. 26-46. This has become an annual feature of the JAF Supplement. Subsequent yearly bibliographies have appeared as follows: April, 1956, pp. 18-45; April, 1957, pp. 19-43; April, 1958, pp. 19-59; April, 1959, pp. 27-64; April, 1960, pp. 21-41; and April, 1961, pp. 28a-99.

[A yearly general bibliography of folklore which contains many listings of books and articles about Latin America, including works on popular poetry.]

Burgin, Miron. See Handbook of Latin American Studies, entry no. 51.

20. Cabrera, Ana S. Rutas de América; el folklore, la música, la historia, la leyenda, las costumbres. Buenos Aires: Peuser, Ltda., 1941. 242 pp. 24 cm.

[Chap. II, "Panorama de la música folklórica sudamericana," deals with the history of Latin American musical folklore and includes a few comments about the yaraví; Chap. III, "Del folklore chileno," treats the cueca, the tonada, and, incidentally, Chilean narrative songs, which are compared in passing with the Mexican corrido; Chap. IV, "La canción y la danza populares en México," includes a section of about three pages on the corrido and incorporates a few texts of coplas. The treatment of the corrido, like that of all subjects in the book, is superficial, but the general interest of the work is not to be denied.]

21. Cabrices, Fernando. "Mateo Rosas de Oquendo, poeta y escritor satírico de la conquista." RNCu, Año V:40 (septiembre-octubre, 1943), 10-16.

[A very informative article in which the author takes exception to Alfonso Reyes' crediting Rosas de Oquendo with being one of the first exponents of American picaresque literature. Cabrices considers the picaresque genre peculiar to Spain, hence feels that Rosas de Oquendo must be considered a Spanish, not an American, poet.]

Campaigns and Cruises in Venezuela and New Granada, and the Pacific Ocean; from 1817 to 1830. See Vowell, Ricardo Longeville, entry no. 122.

22. Cancionero popular americano; 75 canciones de las 21 repúblicas americanas. Washington, D. C.: Unión Panamericana, 1950. 128 pp. 23 cm.

[Includes several popular and semipopular songs which are historical or narrative or related to peninsular romance tradition. Such are El torito (p. 117), La zamba de Vargas (p. 127), Romance de mi destino (pp. 102-103), in romance form but not truly popular, and La Adelita (pp. 4-5). These songs are from Costa Rica, Argentina, Ecuador, and Mexico respectively.]

23. Carvalho Neto, Paulo de. "El romance (contribución a su planteamiento didáctico)." AVF, Años VI-VII, Tomos IV-V(1957-1958): 5, pp. 181-192.

[The article is concerned mostly with Brazilian romances, though with considerable attention to their relationships to Spanish counterparts. The author is concerned particularly with problems of classifying romances (i.e., romances de niños, romances de adultos, etc.).]

24. Chase, Gilbert. Bibliography of Latin American Folk Music. Washington, D. C.: Library of Congress, 1942. ix, 141 pp. mimeographed.

[A well-ordered and extensive bibliography of Latin American folk music. There are 1143 entries, counting a section of Addenda. Items are grouped by countries and in most cases there are the following subdivisions: "History, Criticism, Description"; "Collections of Music"; "Individual Songs"; and "Collections of Texts."]

25. _____. A Guide to Latin American Music. The Library of Congress, Music Division: U. S. Government Printing Office, n.d. xiii, 274 pp. 23.5 cm.

[An expanded version of Chase's earlier bibliography (see entry no. 24) and the best work that exists in the field. Following a general bibliography, there are specialized bibliographies, one for each country of the Americas.]

26. _____. The Music of Spain. New York: W. W. Norton, 1941. 375 pp. 22.5 cm.

[Chap. XVII, "Hispanic Music in the Americas" (pp. 257-272) provides good general treatment of the subject, including considerable attention to romances, corridos, and other types of popular songs. Corridos are treated in two subdivisions: "Spanish American Ballads" (pp. 264-266) and "Hispanic Music in the United States" (pp. 270-272). There is also an extensive bibliography in Chap. XVII (pp. 334-337).]

Chase, Gilbert. See Durán, Gustavo, entry no. 36.

_____. See Handbook of Latin American Studies, entry no. 51.

27. Chávez, Angélico. "The Inter-Relation of History and Folklore." NMFR, V(1950-1951), 1-3.

[An interesting brief discussion. The author believes pure history and pure folklore may come together and contribute to each other, though under such circumstances each must be prepared to resist the close scrutiny of research methods used in the other field.]

28. Colección general de canciones españolas y americanas con acompañamiento. Madrid, n.d.

29. Collection Phonothèque Nationale (Paris). Catalogue établi par la Commission internationale des arts et traditions populaires (C. I. A. P.). Unesco Paris, 1952. 254 pp. 24 cm.

[Among the holdings of the Phonothèque Nationale listed here are some recordings from Latin America. They are not numerous and only Argentina, Bolivia, Chile, and the United States are represented from Spanish-speaking areas.]

30. Coluccio, Félix. Antología ibérica y americana del folklore. Buenos Aires: Guillermo Kraft, 1953. 320 pp. 23 cm.

[According to a review by Rodolfo Holzmann (FA, Año I:1 [noviembre de 1953], 305), this is apparently an expanded version of Colcuccio's earlier anthology (see entry no. 31).]

31. _____. Folklore de las Américas; primera antología. Buenos Aires: Ateneo, 1949. 466 pp. 21 cm.

[Innumerable brief discussions about diverse aspects of the folklore of the Americas. Arranged by countries, and scores of individual contributors are represented. Ana S. Cabrera has a chapter entitled "Corridos o baladas" in the section devoted to Mexico (pp. 272-275); also, there is a chapter entitled "Corrido del caballo 'melao' y 'corrío' que empieza 'esta noche canto aquí'" by Raúl Olivares Figueroa in the section on Venezuela (pp. 449-451).]

32. Cometta Manzoni, Aída. El indio en la poesía de América Española. Buenos Aires: J. Torres, 1939. 290 pp. 20 cm.

[Contains a study of the Indian as a subject for poetry. It deals with his role in epic poetry and romances by artistic poets such as Ercilla, Rosas de Oquendo, Echeverría, and others.]

33. Cortijo, A. L. La música popular y los músicos célebres de la América Latina. Barcelona: Editorial Maucci, n.d. 446 pp. 21 cm.

[A survey of Latin American music, fairly thorough in some instances, very superficial in others. While there is occasionally some discussion of popular, usually Indian, origins, most attention is directed to semilearned composers and musicians. In some instances, however, there is some treatment of folkloric dances and music, and occasional texts of coplas are provided. Of the various sections of this extremely uneven book, that on Argentina seems to be the most thorough. Very little attention is given to narrative genres, though romances are mentioned in passing in the section on Argentina.]

34. Delgado Vivanco, Edmundo. "El caballo en los cantares populares." TradP, VIII:xvi-xviii (enero, 1954-junio, 1956), 22-35.

35. Devoto, Daniel. "Un ejemplo de la labor tradicional en el romancero viejo." NRFH, Año VII:3-4 (julio-diciembre, 1953), 382-394.

[A very fine study of the evolution of a romance, La hija del rey de Francia, from an artistic composition of the fifteenth century into a popular form which has remained alive in Spanish oral tradition. Though the author refers to Poncet y Cárdenas, Vicuña Cifuentes, et al., these references seem to be to their comments on the stylistic characteristics of romances in general and do not seem to indicate the existence of La hija del rey de Francia in American tradition.]

36. Durán, Gustavo. Recordings of Latin American Songs and Dances; An Annotated Selected List of Popular and Folk Music. Washington, D. C.: Panamerican Union, Music Division, 1942. 65 pp. 23 cm.; Second edition, revised and enlarged by Gilbert Chase. Washington, D. C.: Panamerican Union, Dep't. of Cultural Affairs, Division of Music and Visual Arts, 1950. xii, 92 pp. 23 cm.

[Lists by countries the types of songs and dances which are characteristic of each and then provides data on commercial recordings that illustrate each type. In the section on Mexico some corridos are listed.]

D'Eça, Raul. See Handbook of Latin American Studies, entry no. 51.

37. Espinosa, Aurelio M. "El romancero." Hisp, XII:1 (February, 1929), 1-32.

[The author summarizes in popular form the whole field of the study of the Spanish romance. He covers the subject in masterful fashion and includes, mostly in footnotes, much bibliographical information. Though he deals primarily with Spain, he has occasion also to touch on the romances of America.]

38. _____. "Sobre la importancia del romancero." RCu, XV(1941), 214-219.

[An answer to an article of Bruno Jacovella in Folklore (B. A.), I:3 (marzo, 1941). Espinosa defends Menéndez Pidal and other scholars in the field of folklore against Jacovella's attacks, and he criticizes the hispanophobia of those who seek to make popular literature in America entirely criolla.]

39. Espinosa, Aurelio M., Jr. "The Field of Spanish Folklore in America." SFQ, V:1 (March, 1941), 29-35.

[A general summary of the fields of folklore in Spanish America, the work that has been done, and that which remains to be done. One section deals with ballads.]

40. Folk Music of the United States and Latin America; Combined Catalog of Phonograph Records. Washington, D. C.: Library of Congress, Division of Music, 1948. 47 pp. 23 cm.; also, a later edition entitled Folk Music: A Selection of Folksongs, Ballads, Dances, Instrumental Pieces, and Folk Tales from the United States and Latin America; Catalog of Phonograph Records. Washington, D. C.: Library of Congress, Music Division, Recording Laboratory, 1959. iv, 103 pp. 23 cm.

[Lists recordings held and offered for sale by the Library of Congress. The southwestern part of the United States, Mexico, Puerto Rico, and Venezuela are represented. There are corridos from Mexico and Venezuela among many other types of folk songs.]

41. Fraser, Norman, ed. International Catalogue of Recorded Folk Music. Prepared and Published for Unesco by the International Folk Music Council. London: Oxford University Press, 1954. xii, 201 pp. 21.5 cm.

[Lists both commercial recordings and those held by institutions. There are sections on Latin America, though not all countries are represented.]

42. Gabriel, José. "El romancero criollo." RN, Año VII:75 (marzo de 1944), 396-401.

[The author extols the poetic worth of the peninsular romancero and then discusses the migration of the Spanish poems to Africa and America. Though written almost in newspaper style and with no pretense of erudite investigation, the article is stimulating.]

Gandía, Enrique de. See entry no. 275.

43. García de Diego, Pilar. "El testamento de la tradición." RDTP, IX(1953), Cuaderno 4.°, 601-666; X(1954) Cuaderno 3.°, 400-471.

[An excellent study of popular testamentos of all descriptions. The author traces their development from Greek and Roman times and she includes discussions of American compositions. Included are some versions of the "no me entierren en sagrado" romance.]

Garibaldi, Carlos Alberto. See Garibaldi, Verdad, entry no. 44.

44. Garibaldi, Verdad and Garibaldi, Carlos Alberto. Cancionero infantil; canciones, rondas y juegos folklóricos y populares de América y España. Montevideo: Departamento Editorial, 1946. 130 pp. 25.5 cm. (Colección Ceibo, Vol. XIII.)

45. Geiger, Paul, ed. Bibliographie internationale des arts et traditions populaires: International Folklore Bibliography: Volkskundliche Bibliographie. Volume publié avec le concours de l'UNESCO. Années 1939-1941. CIAP (Commission Internationale des Arts et Traditions Populaires), 1949. xxvi, 273 pp.; _____, and Wildhaber, Robert, eds. Bibliographie internationale des arts. Années 1942-1947 avec supplément d'années antérieures. Bâle, 1950. xxvi, 482 pp.; Wildhaber, R., ed. Internationale Volkskundliche Bibliographie. Années 1948 et 1949 avec supplément d'années antérieures. Bâle, 1954.

[Though this work is not very rich in listings of works on the popular poetry and song of Spanish America, it should not be ignored completely.]

46. Grases, Pedro. "La nomenclatura de bailes y canciones en Hispanoamérica." RVF, I:1 (enero-junio de 1947), 123-130.

[A discussion of the chaos which exists in the nomenclature of popular songs and dances in America. Though there is only minor mention of romances and corridos as such, the article is applicable and is important to the study of any aspect of folk songs or dances in America.]

47. Gray, Beryl. " 'Coplas' of Spain and Latin America." PAM, XLIV:4 (April, 1931), 298-303.

[A brief discussion of the copla in Hispanic tradition followed by a collection of texts with remarkably good English translations. Unfortunately, in keeping with the unscholarly purpose of the article, no sources are indicated for any of the compositions.]

Grismer, Mildred B. See Grismer, Raymond L., entry no. 48.

48. Grismer, Raymond L., and Grismer, Mildred B. A New Bibliography of the Literatures of Spain and Spanish America. Vol. I [Aa-Ans]. Minneapolis, Minn.: Perine Book Co., 1941; Vols. II [Ant-Azz], III [B-Biblioteca], IV [Biblioteca-By], V [Caa-Carc]. St. Louis, Mo.: John S. Swift, Inc., 1941, 1942, 1942, 1944; Vols. VI [Card-Casw], VII [Cat-Cez]. Dubuque, Iowa: Wm. C. Brown, 1945, 1946. [Mildred B. Grismer's name appears only on Vols. III and IV.]

[A very extensive list of titles and useful as far as it goes, though it contains no critical or descriptive material.]

49. Guichot y Sierra, Alejandro. Noticia histórica del folklore; orígenes en todos los países hasta 1890, desarrollo en España hasta 1921. Sevilla; Hijos de Guillermo Alvarez, 1922. 256 pp. 24.5 cm.

[Includes some bibliographical items on Mexico (p. 111), Central America (p. 112), and South America (pp. 112-114). Though only a brief list, the material contained therein is not to be overlooked.]

50. Hague, Eleanor. Latin American Music, Past and Present. Santa Ana, Cal.: The Fine Arts Press, 1934. 98 pp. 26 cm.

[A survey which contains a great deal of general information. It includes treatment of romances, corridos, and other types of popular poetry. There is a bibliography.]

51. Handbook of Latin American Studies. A Guide to the Material Published in 1935 on Anthropology, Archaeology, Economics, Geography, History, Law, and Literature, ed. by Lewis Hanke. Cambridge, Mass.: Harvard University Press, 1936. (With certain changes of title this publication has reached a total of 22 volumes, No. 22 being published in 1960. The first 13 volumes were published by the Harvard University Press; the last 9 volumes have been published in Gainesville, Fla. by the University of Florida Press. At various times the following persons have served as editor: Lewis Hanke, Raul D'Eça, Miron Burgin, Francisco Aguilera, Charmion Shelby, Elsie Brown, and Nathan A. Haverstock.)

[In this bibliographical guide there are many entries concerning all types of Latin American folklore. Beginning in 1938 there was an annual section entitled "Folklore" by R. S. Boggs. This series ended with the volume for 1945. Items of interest are to be found, however, in other sections. In the first volume of the Handbook, Robert Redfield edited a section on "Ethnology"; and a section on "Music," which is still appearing, has at various times been edited by William Berrien, Gilbert Chase, Charles Seeger, and Richard A. Waterman.]

Hanke, Lewis. See Handbook of Latin American Studies, entry no. 51.

52. d'Harcourt, Marguerite Béclard. "Las fuentes de inspiración musical popular en América del Sud." RM, II:1 (julio, 1928), 29-33.

Haverstock, Nathan A. See Handbook of Latin American Studies, entry no. 51.

53. Henius, Frank. Songs and Games of the Americas. New York: Charles Scribner's Sons, 1943. 56 pp. 26 cm.; edition in Spanish, Canciones y juegos de los niños de América. B. A.: Editorial Americales, 1946. 79 pp.

[The edition in English contains the Spanish texts with translations of thirty-eight games and songs. Among them is an Argentine version of the romance, Hilito de oro.]

54. Henríquez, Ureña, Pedro. "Música popular de América." Conferencias (Biblioteca del Colegio Nacional de la Universidad de la Plata), I(1930), 177-236.

55. _____. "Romances en América." CuC, III (diciembre, 1913), 347-367.

[The author believes that, at least in the countries of America with which he is familiar, the romance has been little used for local themes. He notes, however, that in the Antilles and Mexico it still exists in oral tradition, and he cites some texts and fragments of romances which he was able to gather from among members of his own family during a visit to the Dominican Republic. Among these are Delgadina, La niña convertida en árbol, Hilo de oro, Doña Ana, Don Gato, and others.]

56. Herrera Carrillo, Pablo. "La conquista musical de América por España." BGE, LXIII:3 (mayo-junio de 1947), 609-640; also, Anales de la Sociedad de Geografía e Historia de Guatemala (Guatemala), XXIV:1-2 (marzo y junio de 1949), 174-192.

[Contains an account of how Las Casas and other Dominicans wrote long narrative songs in Indian tongues in order to win over the natives of Central America to Christianity. The author refers to them, a bit loosely perhaps, as "corridos."]

57. Herzog, George. Research in Primitive and Folk Music in the United States. Washington, D. C.: American Council of Learned Societies, 1936. 97 pp. 22 cm. (Bulletin No. 24, American Council of Learned Societies.)

[A good summary of the state of research in 1936 and the problems facing investigators. Divided into two sections, one deals with primitive music, the other with folk music. Despite its title, the work includes a few references to Spanish American songs, not only in the southwest of the United States but also in Central America. Each section includes bibliographies and lists collections of recorded and transcribed music. Most of this material, of course, is now out of date.]

58. Hudson, Arthur Palmer. "La poesía folklórica." FA, X:1-2 (June and December, 1950). 41 pp.

[A good general synthesis which seeks to summarize present knowledge and theories about folk poetry throughout the world. A section entitled "El romance" (pp. 21-30) discusses the ballad in world literature, and the romance of Spain receives considerable attention. The corrido of Mexico is barely mentioned and is not treated at all on pp. 31-32 where the author deals with contemporary songs about current events. Here he discusses only the production of such ballads in the United States.]

International Catalogue of Recorded Folk Music. See Fraser, Norman, entry no. 41.

59. Jacovella, Bruno C. "Apuntes sobre tipos y retratos de los hechos culturales poéticos." BMJH, II(1950):11, 2-6.

[Boggs comments (ref. 13 [1950], p. 60): "On the nature of folk poetry and types of folksy poetry by poets who turn to the folk for form, style and content."]

60. Jijena Sánchez, Lidia Rosalía de. Poesía popular y tradicional americana. B. A.: Espasa-Calpe Argentina, S. A., 1952. 219 pp. 17.5 cm.

[Texts of popular songs of many types grouped by countries. There are coplas, romances, corridos, etc. and a bibliography which indicates the sources of the texts printed.]

61. Jijena Sánchez, Rafael, and López Peña, Arturo, eds. Cancionero de coplas; antología de la copla en América. B. A.: Editorial Abies, 1959. 266 pp. 19 cm.

[Following an "Estudio sobre el folklore, la poesía y la copla" (pp. 9-60), which discusses various sociological, psychological, and literary aspects of the copla and other popular poetry, the editors offer a fairly large collection of copla texts. Most are taken from standard collections from many parts of Spanish America. Bibliographical sources are given at the end of the volume.]

62. Jones, C. K. A Bibliography of Latin American Bibliographies. Second edition. Washington, D. C.: U. S. Printing Office, 1942. 311 pp. 23 cm. (Latin American Series, No. 2, of the Library of Congress, Hispanic Foundation.)

[A fundamental source of information about bibliographies on any subject pertaining to Latin America. Following a long general section covering Latin America as a whole, there are sections devoted to each country individually. In most cases entries are annotated. The total number of entries is 3016, not counting late entries which are identified with a, b, etc. within the original scheme of numbering. The entire volume is well indexed by author's names and by subject matter.]

63. Labastille, Irma, ed. Canciones típicas. New York, Chicago, etc.: Silver Burdett Co., 1941. 48 pp. 25 cm.

[Chase (ref. 25, p. 35) comments: "19 songs from 16 Latin American countries with descriptive notes and English translations of the texts."]

64. Leonard, Irving A. Books of the Brave. Cambridge, Mass.: Harvard University Press, 1949. xiii, 381 pp. 24 cm.

[A very fine study of the literature read in Spanish America during the colonial period. There is occasional mention of romanceros, particularly those which the author discovered in lists of shipments of books sent to the New World.]

65. _____. Los libros del conquistador. México: Fondo de Cultura Económica, 1953. 404 pp.

[A translation of Books of the Brave (see entry no. 64).]

66. _____. Romances of Chivalry in the Spanish Indies, with Some Registros of Shipments of Books to the Spanish Colonies.

In University of California Publications in Modern Philology (Berkeley), XVI(1932-1933):3, pp. 217-371.

[An excellent study of the book trade between Spain and America during the colonial period. Some romanceros are listed in some representative shipments of books which were sent between 1586 and 1605.]

67. Lima, Emirto. "A guitarra, instrumento romanceiro." RBM, V:1 (1938), 48-59.

[Chase (ref. 25, p. 33) comments: "Historical comments for a guitar recital by José Mazzila."]

68. _____. "Música española en América." RCLA, II (mayo, 1932), 164-165.

69. "List of Works in the New York Public Library Relating to the West Indies." BNYPL, XVI(1912):1 (January), 7-49; 3 (March), 231-278; 4 (April), 307-355; 5 (May), 367-440; 6 (June), 455-484; 7 (July), 503-546; 8 (August), 563-621; also published as a separate volume, New York, 1912. 392 pp.

[This excellent bibliography of seven installments is divided into sections entitled: "Bibliography" (p. 7), "General History, Description, etc." (pp. 7-43), and "Works Relating to Individual Islands and Colonies" (pp. 43 to the end of the bibliography). This latter section has twenty-seven subdivisions corresponding to different geographical areas. In the subdivision on Cuba there is a separate unit entitled "Literature, Art, and Folklore" (pp. 434-440).]

70. Luce, Allena. Canciones populares. Nueva York: Silver Burdett Compañía, 1921. vi, 138 pp. 26 cm.

[A collection of texts with musical accompaniments. There are seventy-five songs in all from Puerto Rico, Cuba, Mexico, Spain, and other countries. Although there is little of interest to the study of the romance or other narrative songs, see Hilo verde from Puerto Rico (p. 121), a version of Mambrú (p. 119), and El huérfano from Puerto Rico (pp. 22-23).]

71. Lumpkin, Ben Gray, and others, eds. Folksongs on Record, Compiled and Edited by Ben Gray Lumpkin with Norman L. ("Brownie") McNeil and Forty Other Collectors. Issue Three, cumulative, including essential material in Issues One and Two. Boulder, Colorado: Folksongs on Record, and Denver, Colorado: Alan Swallow, 1950. viii, 98 pp.

[Boggs (ref. 13 [1950], p. 48) says: "Lists nearly 4000 commercial phonograph recordings of folk and folksy ballads, songs, dances, and diverse music from U. S. A., Latin America, and various parts of the world."]

McNeil, Norman L. ("Brownie"). See Lumpkin, Ben Gray, entry no. 71.

72. Madrid, Miguel Angel. "The Attitudes of the Spanish American People as Expressed in Their Coplas or Folk Songs." Ph. D. diss., Columbia University, 1953. 139 pp.

73. Malaret, Augusto. "Los americanismos en la copla popular." Universidad Pontificia Bolivariana (Medellín, Colombia), XXI(1957): 77, pp. 402-438.
[Undoubtedly a supplement to ref. 74, though I have been unable to consult the work.]

74. _____. Los americanismos en la copla popular y en el lenguaje culto. New York: S. F. Vanni, 1947. 253 pp. 20 cm.
[A very useful list of Americanisms with definitions which are documented in many instances by popular coplas. The origins of the latter are given by countries, though not by specific localities within countries.]

75. _____. "Cancionero de americanismos." BFM, VI: 46-47-48 (mayo, junio y setiembre de 1951), 277-299.
[A supplement to ref. 74. There are more listings of words illustrated by coplas and some supplementary bibliography is included.]

76. Mann, W. Volk und Kultur Latein-Amerikas. Hamburg: Broschek and Co., 1927. 301 pp. 22 cm.
[Chase (ref. 25, p. 27) comments: "Folk elements and characteristics in the music of South America, p. 250-251."]

77. Martí, Samuel. "Música de las Américas." CuA, Año IX, Vol. LII (julio-agosto de 1950), 244-260.
[An excellent discussion of the pre-Hispanic music of America. Numerous passages are cited from chronicles that attest to the type of music which existed, and the author sustains the thesis that this music was a thriving art that had developed considerable complexity. While his discussion does not directly touch any significant point that might be considered to be related to the corrido or to other narrative poetry, his general summary of what is known about his subject is of significance to any study of music and song in America.]

78. Mattfeld, Julius. The Folk Music of the Western Hemisphere: A List of References in the New York Public Library, Reprinted with Additions from the Bulletin of the New York Public Library, November and December, 1924. New York, 1925. 74 pp. 25.5 cm.
[The section on Latin America (pp. 34-37) contains references to the folk music of many countries, particularly that of Mexico and areas of the United States where Mexican and Spanish folk music is still alive.]

79. Mélo, Veríssimo de. Curiosos aspectos da poesia tradicional. Sep. de Bando (Natal, Brazil), 1952.
[Pérez Vidal, in a review of the volume (RDTP, VIII(1952), Cuaderno 4.°, 704-705) indicates that the work deals with poetic contests such as the contrapuntos of Spanish America. He indicates that it contains many texts.]

80. Méndez, Concha. "El romancero español." PyS, XIII(1949), 257-260, 262.
[Boggs (ref. 13 [1949], p. 38) says: "General survey article on the Spanish ballad in folklore and literature, in Spain and America."]

Mendoza, Vicente T. "La cachucha." See entry no. 1440.

81. _____. "La décima (Sus derivaciones musicales en América)." NuM, Año II:6 (abril, 1947), 78-113.
[A survey of the literary and musical form of the décima in Spain and America. Mendoza finds examples with texts and music from almost all countries. An interesting aspect of his study is the many different names by which the décimas are known. The study concludes with a comparative analysis of the musical structure of the examples from Spain and America.]

82. Menéndez y Pelayo, Marcelino. Historia de la poesía hispanoamericana. 2 vols. Madrid: V. Suárez, 1911-13. 25 cm. (Vols. II and III of Obras completas); also, Santander: Aldus S. A. de Artes Gráficas, 1948. 21 cm. (Vols. XXVII and XXVIII of Edición nacional de las obras completas de Menéndez Pelayo. This is the edition which I have used in compiling the present bibliography and all references are to it.)
[A fundamental work, this study contains a vast store of information, both factual and bibliographical, mostly about artistic poets but with occasional references to popular or semipopular works. Each chapter is devoted to one of the countries of Spanish America. The material contained here appeared first in the Antología de poetas hispano-americanos publicada por la Real Academia Española (see entry no. 3).]

83. Menéndez Pidal, Ramón. L'Epopée Castillane à travers la Littérature Espagnole. Paris: Librairie Armand Colin, 1910. xxvi, 306 pp. 18 cm.
[Discusses (pp. 181-182) reasons why new romances were not produced in significant numbers during the Spanish conquest of America to celebrate the deeds of the conquerors.]

84. _____. "Las primeras noticias de romances tradicionales en América, y especialmente en Colombia." In Homenaje a Enrique José Varona. La Habana: Publicaciones de la Secretaría de Educación, 1935. Pp. 23-27; also, RevCu, I:1 (enero, 1935), 8-13.

[A very interesting discussion of the possibility of finding authentic traditional romances in America.]

85. Menéndez Pidal, Ramón. Romancero hispánico (hispano-portugués, americano y sefardí). 2 vols. Madrid: Espasa-Calpe, 1953. 23 cm.
[This masterful exposition of the definitive ideas and theories of the greatest scholar in the field of the Spanish romance contains in almost every chapter suggestive ideas of interest to students of the romance and its derivatives in America. Especially interesting are parts of several chapters of Vol. II, particularly Chap. XVI, "Difusión territorial del romancero; siglos XV al XVII," and Chap. XX, "La tradición moderna fuera de Castilla."]

86. _____. El romancero; teorías e investigaciones. Madrid: Editorial Páez, 1928. 229 pp. 17.5 cm.
[Contains the article "Los romances en América," (pp. 184-229). See entry no. 87.]

87. _____. "Los romances tradicionales en América." Cultura española (Madrid), 1906, No. 1, 72-111; also in Los romances de América y otros estudios. B. A.-México: Espasa-Calpe, 1939. Pp. 7-50.
[The earliest serious study of a scholarly nature about the romances of America. It contains much valuable material about the history of the romances and the texts of a large number of them.]

Morales, Ernesto. "La poesía popular española en América." See entry no. 826.

88. Morley, S G. "Are the Spanish Romances Written in Quatrains?" RR, VII(1916), 42-82.
[Offers a large body of evidence in support of the theory that until the last years of the sixteenth century romances were not generally written in quatrains. In discussing the problem of quatrain division and rhyme systems, the author has occasion to refer to some American compositions taken from Vicuña Cifuentes, Chacón y Calvo, and Espinosa.]

89. La música popular latino-americana. México, D. F.: Secretaría de Educación Pública, 192?. 28 pp. mimeographed.
[Chase (ref. 25, p. 27) writes: "Deals with the indigenous music of the Andean region; classification of Incan (Peruvian) melodies; rhythms of Indian music (Andean); folk dances of the Indians; folk music of Venezuela (p. 10-12), Colombia (p. 12), Bolivia (p. 12-15), Chile (p. 15-16), Argentina (p. 16-22), Antilles (p. 22-26)."]

90. Nettl, Bruno. "La música folklórica." FA, XIV:2 (December, 1954), 15-34.
[After considering briefly the general history of the study of folk and primitive music, the author outlines in concise and lucid terms

some of the problems involved in the analysis of melody, rhythm, scales, etc. of both types of music. The value of the article is enhanced by a bibliography (pp. 30-34). Although there is no specific treatment of romances or corridos, I include the work here because it is a good point of departure for the study of Spanish folk music of almost any type.]

91. Paredes, Américo. "Folklore Bibliography for 1960." SFQ, XXV:1 (March, 1961), 1-89.
[A continuation of the series begun by Ralph Steele Boggs (see entry no. 13).]

92. Pedrell, Felipe. Diccionario técnico de la música. Cuarta edición. Barcelona: Isidro Torres Oriol, n.d. 528 pp. 28 cm.
[A useful dictionary of musical terms. It includes careful definitions of romance, copla, and certain types of Spanish American songs such as yarabí, triste, etc. Corrido does not appear.]

93. Pereda Valdés, Ildefonso. "Personajes folklóricos." AVF, Años VI-VII, Tomos IV-V(1957-1958):5, pp. 219-229.
[Among several figures from folk tradition the author deals with Mambrú and gives the historical background of the song about him. The article contains nothing new, but the author cites numerous bibliographical sources of versions of the song from many countries.]

94. Pires de Lima, J. A. "As bebidas alcoólicas no folclore íbero-americano." RDTP, VI(1950), Cuaderno 2.°, 171-184.
[A fairly extensive collection of coplas about the drinking of wine and other alcoholic beverages. Most of the examples are Portuguese, Brazilian, or Spanish. But some are from Carrizo's collections of Argentine popular songs.]

95. Praesant, Hans. "Ibero-Amerikanische Bibliographie: Auswahl-Verzeichnis der deutschprachigen Literatur." Beilage zu Ibero-Amerikanisches Archiv (Berlin), IV(1930-31):2, through XVI (1942-43):3-4, a total of fifty-one bibliographies.
[An excellent series of bibliographies which must be considered a fundamental work in the field of Spanish American literature.]

96. Quiñones Pardo, Octavio. "Cancionero americano." RAmer, VIII:23 (noviembre de 1946), 284-288.
[A selection of coplas arranged by countries: Argentina, Brazil, Chile, Ecuador, Mexico, Colombia, Panama, Peru, and Venezuela. There is no commentary of any kind.]

Redfield, Robert. See Handbook of Latin American Studies, entry no. 51.

Richmond, W. Edson. See Brown, Paul A., entry no. 19.

97. Robe, Stanley L. "Selective Bibliography of the Folk Drama in Hispanic America." WF, XVI(1957), 287-289.
[A useful listing of twenty-five titles.]

98. _____. "Some Hispanic Equivalents of the Big Rock Candy Mountain." WF, XIII:1 (January, 1954), 34-39.
[A discussion of Hispanic ballads and stories which deal with Jauja or other fantastic places. The author traces the rise of the Jauja legend and mentions or quotes textually, but only in English translation, songs or romances from Panama, Spain, New Mexico, Mexico, and Chile.]

Roberts, Sarah Elizabeth. See Boggs, Ralph Steele, entry no. 13.

99. Rodríguez Marín, Francisco. El "Quijote" y Don Quijote en América (Conferencias leídas en el Centro de Cultura Hispano-Americana los días 10 y 17 de marzo de 1911). Madrid: Librería de los Sucesores de Hernando, 1911. 118 pp. 19.5 cm.
[In reporting on lists of book shipments made to America in 1600, the author mentions some coplas (p. 29).]

100. Rodríguez-Moñino, Antonio. "Cómo se publicaba un libro en Indias a principios del siglo XVII; andanzas inquisitoriales de La Ovandina, crónica de linajes coloniales." TF, Año II(1936):3-4, pp. 413-437.
[Relates the vicissitudes of a book on geneologies published in Lima with the title La Ovandina by D. Pedro Mexía de Ovando. When certain people took exception to its contents, an anonymous Romance a La Ovandina appeared to make fun of the book and the author. As a result, the work was made the subject of an investigation by the Inquisition. Rodríguez Moñino relates all that happened in detail and prints (pp. 416-417) the full text of the Romance. Actually it is a composition made up of twenty-eight redondillas of scant literary merit, but of interest as a kind of glorified pasquín.]

101. Rojas, Ricardo. Cosmópolis. Paris: Ed. Garnier, 1908. 205 pp.
[One chapter is said to be "Romances tradicionales en América" (see ref. 25, p. 28).]

102. Román, Marcelino M. Itinerario del payador. B. A.: Lautaro, 1957. 396 pp. 19.5 cm.
[This work is a veritable mine of information about the popular songs and poetry of Spanish America and Brazil, though there is particular emphasis upon Argentina. The bibliographical information contained in numerous footnotes is extremely valuable. The book suffers, however, from an overly rhetorical and cloying style, and its last few chapters are marred by biased expressions of the author's political prejudices.]

Romero, Emilia. El romance tradicional en el Perú. See entry no. 1877.

103. Santullano, Luis. "La poesía del pueblo en Hispanoamérica; algunas noticias sobre su expresión inicial." CuA, Año IX, Vol. XLIX:1 (enero-febrero, 1950), 165-180.

[Consideration of evidence about the dances and songs of pre-Hispanic America, mainly that contained in the better known chronicles. Though not exhaustive, the study is informative and interesting. There is very slight attention to the romance's relationship to Indian traditions.]

104. _____. La poesía del pueblo; romances y canciones de España y América. B. A.: Imprenta López, 1955. 994 pp.

[An excellent work which covers the whole field of ballad literature in America. Though the author frankly states that it is not intended for the specialist, and indeed there is little in his treatment of the subject which is new, the fact is that he summarizes very well the general knowledge which we have of the romance-corrido tradition in America. The author's procedure is to introduce each section of his book by a brief study of the subject being treated and then to offer texts that serve as representative types. There are hundreds of these texts (without music) in sections on La tradición española, El romance español llega a la tierra americana, Romances de España y América, Rondas infantiles, Romances originales de América, etc. There is a special section on the corridos of Mexico.]

105. Seeger, Charles. "The Importance to Cultural Understanding of Folk and Popular Music." In Conference on Inter-American Relations in the Field of Music; Digest of Proceedings, Principal Addresses. Washington, D. C.: Division of Cultural Relations, Department of State, 1940. Mimeographed with no pagination for the volume, though individual articles have numbered pages. 10 pp.

[After summarizing his personal views about acculturation and counter-acculturation in the field of music of the Americas, the author proposes careful study of folk and popular music because he feels that only these offer much opportunity for getting close to the masses, since both fine music and primitive music are media which are cultivated only by small minorities in all countries. His comments do not apply to any specific type of folk music, but some of the ideas expressed about the acculturation process during the colonial period in the New World are pertinent to the study of any genre of folk or popular music or literature.]

106. _____. "Notes on Music in the Americas; Oral and Written Traditions in the Americas." BPAU, LXXIX:5 (May, 1945), 290-293; 6 (June, 1945), 341-344.

[A discussion of the interplay between oral and written tradition. Though the article deals with the broad aspects of the subject and rarely with any specific area, it is quite stimulating. But there is no mention of romances, corridos, or other specified genres of popular songs.]

Seeger, Charles. See Handbook of Latin American Studies, entry no. 51.

107. Serís, Homero. Manual de bibliografía de la literatura española. Primera parte. Syracuse, N. Y.: Syracuse University, Centro de Estudios Hispánicos, 1948. xliii, 422 pp. 20 cm.
[An excellent bibliography which contains some entries on the romances and other popular poetry of the New World.]

Shelby, Charmion. See Handbook of Latin American Studies, entry no. 51.

108. Simmons, Merle E. "Pre-Conquest Narrative Songs in Spanish America." JAF, LXXIII:288 (April-June, 1960), 103-111.
[From numerous chronicles of the Spanish conquest of America the author extracts evidence that the Indians sang and danced narrative songs in the period before the Spanish conquered the New World.]

109. Slonimsky, Nicolas. "The Folklore of Latin America's Music." Christian Science Monitor's Weekly Magazine Section, July 18, 1942, pp. 8-9; also printed as "El folklore musical de la América Latina." RMM, II:4 (21 de agosto, 1942), 79-82.
[A brief survey of Latin American musical folklore. Country by country the author mentions the most important investigators and lists some of their works. Though a good survey of its kind, it is, of course, intended only for the general reader who is completely uninformed.]

110. Spell, Lota M. "Notes on Music in South America." Southwestern Musician (Arlington, Texas), IV:2 (1937), 4, 12.
[Chase (ref. 25, p. 28) says: "Brief comments on the chief popular songs and dances."]

111. Suannes, S. "Poesía popular e tradicional americana." BCF, VIII(1957-1958):23-24, pp. 32-36.
[Boggs (ref. 13 [1958], p. 49) says: "Portuguese translations of folk poetry from Nicaragua, Bolivia, Mexico, and Peru."]

112. Torre Revello, José. El libro, la imprenta y el periodismo en América durante la dominación española. B. A.: Talleres S. A. Casa Jacobo Peuser, Ltda., 1940. 269, ccxxxviii, 19 pp. 28 cm. (Facultad de Filosofía y Letras, Publicaciones del Instituto de Investigaciones Históricas, No. LXXIV.)
[Contains much documentary information about books sent to America. Some of them were romanceros and other works which contained popular literature.]

113. Torres, María de Guadalupe. "Los romances españoles en América." Ph. D. diss., Stanford University, 1951. ix, 247 pp.
 [The author seeks out all the versions she can find in America of certain Spanish romances (Delgadina, Las señas del marido, En el portal de Belén, etc.) and provides very useful bibliographical references to places where they can be located. She provides the texts of a considerable number of versions of each romance.]

114. Traversari-Salazar, Pietro P. "L'arte en América: Storia dell'arte musicale indigena e populare." Atti del Congresso Internazionale di Scienze Storiche (Roma, 1-9 Aprile, 1903). VIII, Sezione 4 (1905), 117-129.
 [Chase (ref. 25, p. 28) comments: "Covers Mexico, Cuba, Central and South America. A musical supplement contains 17 tunes from Mexico, Argentina, Peru, Bolivia, Ecuador and Venezuela."]

115. Urquieta, Felipe. "Breve reseña histórica de la música americana." Estudio (Barcelona), Año VIII, Tomo XXXI:92 (agosto, 1920), 188-192.
 [A cursory attempt to survey the development of American music from pre-conquest Indian music to opera. The article is of no importance.]

116. Valle, Rafael Heliodoro. "Bibliografía americana, 1936-1937." BBAA, I:4 (octubre a diciembre, 1937), 267-287; ". . . , 1937-1938." BBAA, II:4 (octubre a diciembre, 1938), 161-191; ". . . , 1937-1939." BBAA, III:2 (mayo a agosto, 1939), 195-219; ". . . , 1938-1940." BBAA, IV:2 (mayo a agosto, 1940), 165-215.
 [The above numbers were all that were published of this excellent bibliography. Although it is only rarely annotated and is not divided according to regions or subjects, it is notable for the completeness and accuracy of its entries.]

117. _____. "El folklore en la literatura de Centro América." JAF, XXXVI:140 (April-June, 1923), 105-134.
 [Includes a "Bibliografía del folklore centroamericano" (pp. 110-134). It is very useful, though not always well annotated. Few of the entries deal with popular poetry.]

118. Vara Reyes, Víctor. "Humor en la copla española e hispano-americana." Revista de la Universidad Juan Misael Saracho (Tarija, Bolivia), II(1950):5, pp. 18-28.

119. Vega, Carlos. "Panorama de la música popular sud-americana." PrBA, 30 de enero, 1938, Segunda sección, p. 2.
 [Chase (ref. 25, p. 29) says: "Reprinted in Ars, Vol. I, No. 2 (Sept., 1940), pp. 9-11. Includes music."]

120. Vega López, Carlos. La poesía popular de la América Española. Madrid: Editorial Marineda, 1924. 46 pp. 23.5 cm.

[A somewhat romantic treatment of the popular poetry collected by
Ciro Bayo, which is interpreted in the light of the theories of
Menéndez Pidal. Though there is little that is original, the author
synthesizes well the broad history of the entry into America of
popular poetry from the Iberian Peninsula and its development in
the New World, with special reference to the Chilean corrido. Many
texts are quoted, most of them taken from Ciro Bayo, and there is
a bibliography of thirty-nine items.]

121. Vergara y Martín, Gabriel María, comp. Algunos refranes,
modismos y cantares geográficos que se emplean en la América
Española o se refieren a ella. Madrid, 1931. 20 pp.
[The cantares geográficos are probably coplas.]

122. [Vowell, Richard Longeville.] Campaigns and Cruises in
Venezuela and New Granada, and the Pacific Ocean, from 1817 to
1830. 3 vols. London: Longman and Co., 1831.
[Chase (ref. 25, p. 119) comments: "Vol. I: Chilean national
dances, p. 310; words of a revolutionary song of Bolívar's troops
(translated), p. 467; also mention of music in the following pages,
116, 173, 177, 187. Vol. II: music, p. 35; words of La montonera
(a serenade) and La zambullidora, pp. 35-38 (with translations of
these songs in the Notes at the back of the book); dancing, musical
instruments, p. 103." Machado (ref. 2021, p. 118) prints some songs
taken from this source. Also, see Medina, José Toribio, entry no.
622.]

Waterman, Richard A. See Handbook of Latin American
Studies, entry no. 51.

123. Webster, Persis Marie Johnson. "The Traditional Spanish
Ballad in Modern Tradition." M. A. thesis, Stanford University,
1944. lll, 343, ix pp.
[An attempt to gather as many versions as possible of Spanish
ballads which are still alive today in Spanish and Spanish American
tradition. The author's collection totals 247 ballads grouped
according to themes: e. g., Carolingian Ballads, Historic Ballads,
Religious Ballads, etc. Her bibliography indicates that she has
drawn upon only the most important printed collections. Representative versions are given for each ballad and bibliographical references
are then provided to sources of other versions. There is considerable
descriptive material about content and form, but there is little
critical analysis.]

Wildhaber, Robert. See Geiger, Paul, entry no. 45.

Wilgus, A. Curtis. See Boggs, Ralph Steele, entry no. 12.

124. Ximénez, Fray Francisco. Historia de la provincia de San
Vicente de Chiapa y Guatemala. 3 vols. Guatemala: Tipografía

Nacional, 1929. (Biblioteca "Goatemala" de la Sociedad de Geografía e Historia, Vols. I, II, and III.)
[In Vol. I (p. 280) there is a reference to the singing of romances on shipboard during a voyage from Spain to America in 1544.]

125. Zanzig, Augustus D. "Some Collections of Folk Songs in the Library of the Pan American Union." In Conference on Inter-American Relations in the Field of Music, Report of the Committee. Washington, D. C., 1940. Pp. 92-93.

ARGENTINA AND URUGUAY

The musical folklore of the Río de la Plata region has been studied by more competent scholars than that of any other region of America with the possible exception of Chile. Although Argentine investigators have in recent years been divided, to the detriment of their work, into warring factions, whose differences were as much political and personal as scholarly, much meritorious work has been done. After the early efforts of Ventura R. Lynch, Ciro Bayo, Ricardo Rojas, and other lesser figures, the more recent investigations and compilations of texts by scholars like Jorge M. Furt, Juan Alfonso Carrizo and his school (Juan Draghi Lucero, Orestes di Lullo, et al.), Ismael Moya, and Ildefonso Pereda Valdés in Uruguay have greatly enriched our knowledge of the abundant literary folklore of the Plata area. Meanwhile, primarily in the field of music but with important attention also to the literary aspects of folklore, Carlos Vega, Josué Teófilo Wilkes, Isabel Aretz-Thiele, and others have produced very scholarly works of outstanding merit.

Argentina and Uruguay offer special problems to the investigator of the romance tradition in that narrative genres in romance meter or closely related to the Spanish romance in form, style, or purpose are known under a variety of names. For this reason I have had to include references to such songs and dances as the cielo and cielito, the triste, the gato, the vidala and vidalita, and others. As in all other sections of my work, I admit, of course, references to coplas and décimas, genres which are found in great abundance in the Río de la Plata region.

Besides the useful though sometimes frustrating bibliographical listings which are provided by Carrizo and his followers in their cancioneros, the most competent work on the bibliography of Argentine folklore has been done by Augusto Raúl Cortázar. At the time of this bibliographer's greatest activity about a decade and a half ago, he made invaluable contributions, and his work has aided me immeasurably in my study. Likewise Madaline Nichol's bibliographies of gaucho literature are basic to any study of gaucho poetry and song. I have tried to extract from her listings and include here all those titles which seemed to deal with genuinely popular narrative poetry, while omitting those which appeared to treat the poetry of the learned or semilearned gaucho poets such as Ascasubi, Hernández, and their followers. But not having been privileged to work in Argentine libraries, and hence unable to consult many titles listed by Miss Nichols, I have undoubtedly made mistakes in following this admittedly precarious procedure. Users of this bibliography who, with better library facilities, may be working intensively in the field of Argentine-Uruguayan folklore would do well to consult Miss Nichols' important works.

126. A la venida de la expedición española contra el Río de la Plata. B. A.: Prensas de Alvarez, 1819.
 [An hoja volante which Rojas cites (ref. 387 [1924 ed.], Vol. VIII, pp. 455-456). He prints the text and indicates that this cielito is the work of the same poet who wrote a Cielito de Maipú (see ref. 226). Although on p. 455 Rojas gives the date as 1819 and later on p. 465 he speaks of the work as "aquella inimitable de 1819," he also says on p. 465 that "La primera edición de este cantar salió en Buenos Aires de la imprenta de Alvarez, sin fecha." He says that its original title was A la venida de la expedición (cielito).

127. Aguirre, Julián. Música popular argentina. B. A., 1912.

128. Alais, Octavio P. Libro criollo. B. A., 1903.

129. _____. Vida de campo. B. A., 1904.

130. Alcorta, Amancio. Obras musicales. 2 vols. Paris, 1869, 1883.
 [Furt (ref. 272, Vol. I, p. 461) lists this work in a bibliography of música gauchesca.]

131. Alsina, Adolfo, and López y Planes, Vicente F. Colección de documentos relativos a sucesos del Río de la Plata desde 1806.
 [Said by Medina (ref. 339, p. 224) to contain Rivarola's Romance heroico . . . de la reconquista, pp. 72-98; also, Adiciones y correcciones to the Romance herioco, pp. 98-103; also, Romance de la gloriosa defensa, pp. 406-440. Masciopinto (ref. 335) indicates that it also contains a romance real by Miguel Belgrano about the English attack on Buenos Aires (see Belgrano, Miguel, entry no. 165).]

132. Alvarez, Juan. "Orígenes de la música argentina." Revista de derecho, historia y letras (B. A.), Año XI, Tomo XXXII (enero de 1909), 26-27.
 [A survey of Argentine popular music. Spanish, African, and Indian influences are ranked in that order of importance. Alvarez considers the Indian elements very minor, but he attributes more importance to African influences than do most investigators. Some of the texts of coplas are still of interest, but most of the work, despite its merit at the time of publication, has been superseded. There is no mention of romances, corridos, or any other popular narratives on topical subjects.]

133. Ambrosetti, Juan Bautista. Apuntes para un folklore argentino. B. A., 1893.
 [Cortázar indicates (ref. 244, p. 82) that the work deals with gaucho literature.]

134. _____. "Materiales para el estudio del folklore misionero." RJZB, I:Entrega 5 (mayo 15 de 1893), 129-160.

[This early article is devoted almost exclusively to legends and superstitions with only very minor mention of poetry (two texts of coplas are given).]

135. Andreu, R. "El payador y el milonguero; artículo sobre la poesía nacional de Chile y Argentina." El Mercurio (Valparaíso, Chile), 21 de marzo, 1888.

136. Angeles Caballero, César. "Bibliografía folklórica da la Argentina." FACI, Año I:1 (noviembre, 1953), 316-322.

[A brief bibliography which, though useful, is marred by numerous obvious errors.]

137. Antología folklórica argentina para las escuelas de adultos [published by the Consejo Nacional de Educación]. B. A.: Guillermo Kraft, Ltda., 1940. 239 pp. 21 cm.

[Along with many other types of folklore (legends, tales, riddles, etc.) there are texts of romances, décimas, coplas, and other genres of popular poetry. The romances are Camina la Virgen Santa and Entre San Pedro y San Juan, both religious in nature. Also to be noted are a narrative poem written in a style very similar to that of Mexican corridos, De la muerte de Quiroga y de la suerte que cupo a Santos Pérez (pp. 168-180), a political commentary in the form of a glosa in décimas (pp. 181-182), and an account of a contrapunto which took place in a military encampment during the war between Lavalle and Estanislao López (pp. 92-93). Unfortunately, the value of the entire work is limited because no sources are given for any of the texts provided.]

138. Antología folklórica argentina para las escuelas primarias [published by the Consejo Nacional de Educación]. B. A.: Guillermo Kraft, Ltda., 1940. 244 pp. 21 cm.

[A collection of many types of children's folklore. There is a chapter on "Rimas infantiles y canciones de cuna" (pp. 167-220) and another on "Villancicos" (pp. 221-230) which contain the texts of several traditional romances and historical songs such as Don Gato, Hilo de oro, and Mambrú. Also, there are coplas scattered through several chapters. Unfortunately, no sources are given for the texts printed in the collection; hence, its value is limited.]

139. Anzalaz, Alfredo. "La alimentación popular argentina a través de sus coplas." FPL, Núm. 30 (junio y julio de 1953), 982-983.

[A collection of some popular coplas which deal with food and drink. Reprinted as indicated below in entry no. 141.]

140. _____. "El amor en la copla popular argentina." BCC, V(1953-1954):17-19, pp. 75-80.

141. _____. Folklore argentino: cantares, leyendas y tradiciones de tierra adentro. La Rioja, Argentina: Ediciones Biblos, 1952. 61 pp. 20.5 cm.

[A volume of short chapters on various topics related to folklore in Argentina. The first two are the most extensive and the only ones related to romances and narrative or topical poetry in general. The first (pp. 7-31) is entitled "Origen histórico de la Zamba de Vargas" and is an excellent treatment of the background of the famous battle at Pozo de Vargas in La Rioja in 1867 and of the songs which it inspired. A total of twenty-two versions of the Zamba de Vargas are given. Though not romances, some are narratives. The second chapter is the article cited above in entry no. 139.]

142. _____. "Música tradicional argentina: 'La zamba de Vargas.'" AVF, Año II-III(1953-1954), Tomo II:3, pp. 53-69; also, BCC, VI(1956):22, pp. 95-111.

[After narrating the historical events which gave rise to the Zamba de Vargas, the author gives the texts of ten versions of the song from La Rioja, nine from Santiago del Estero, and seven from other regions. At the end he provides a bibliography of twenty-two items concerning the famous battle and those who participated in it. The song, of course, is not a part of the romance tradition, but it should not be omitted from any study of popular narrative poetry.]

143. Aprile, Bartolomé R., and Sierra, Apolinario. Relaciones; canciones criollas. B. A., 1938.

144. Aramburu, Julio. El folklore de los niños; juegos, corros, rondas, canciones, romances, cuentos y leyendas. B. A.: "El Ateneo," 1940. 147 pp. 19 cm.; also 1944. 203 pp. 18.5 cm.

[Contains many children's songs and dances, including a number of romances and other narrative songs: Delgadina; Blanca Niña; Las señas del esposo; El conde niño; Dónde vas, Alfonso Doce; Luis Ortiz; and many others. The commentaries and criticism are sketchy.]

145. Araoz de La Madrid, Gregorio. Memorias del general Gregorio Araoz de La Madrid. 2 vols. B. A.: Guillermo Kraft, 1895. 26.5 cm.; also, an abridged edition: Madrid: Editorial-América, n.d. 416 pp. 22.5 cm.

[Contains a décima of nonpopular tone which the author says was recited to him by a priest as a greeting on his return from a campaign in 1826 (Vol. I, p. 315 [pp. 325-326 of the Madrid edition]). Also, there are references to the singing of vidalitas in the 1820's by the general and his troops, and some texts are given (Vol. I, pp. 320, 354-356; Vol II, p. 167 [pp. 331, 366-368 of the Madrid edition]).]

146. Araucho, Manuel de. Cancionero popular argentino. N. p., n. d.

Archivo capitular de Jujuy. See Rojas, Ricardo, entry no. 386.

147. Aretz, Isabel. Costumbres tradicionales argentinas. B. A.: Editorial Raigal, 1954. 221 pp. 22.5 cm.
[A good description of many folkloric customs having to do with music and dancing. There are musical transcriptions and literary texts of many compositions from Argentina and other areas of Spanish America. Some are romances (mostly religious songs) and a great many are coplas.]

148. _____. El folklore musical argentina. B. A.: Ricordi Americana, 1952. 271 pp. 24 cm.
[A basic work for the study of Argentine musical and poetic folklore. Included are discussions of the types of songs and dances which are cultivated, the instruments which are used, and the scales which are employed. There are excellent definitions with many musical and literary examples of such genres as vidalas, tristes, tonos, décimas, yaravíes, milongas, and others. Also, there are bibliographies at the end of each chapter. The romance (with mention of the corrido, though without relating it specifically to Argentina) is discussed, albeit very briefly (p. 95).]

149. Aretz-Thiele, Isabel. Música tradicional argentina; Tucumán, historia y folklore. Tucumán: Universidad Nacional de Tucumán, 1946. 743 pp. 28.5 cm.
[A superb musical-literary study of the popular songs and dances of the Tucumán area. After treating Spanish and Indian contributions to the music of the region, the author, using the methods of Carlos Vega, analyzes the various genres of popular music and dance which she collected in extensive field work. There are exhaustive sections on the vidala, the cielito, the tono, the milonga, canciones religiosas, arrullos y villancicos de navidad, canciones históricas, and other types of songs and dances too numerous to mention here. Many texts given are coplas and there are some geniune romances included. There is music for all compositions. Also, there is an excellent bibliography of 188 items.]

150. _____. Primera selección de canciones y danzas tradicionales argentinas para escolares. B. A.: Ricordi Americana, n.d. 62 pp.
[Of the twenty-two compositions, which are all given with music and literary text, one entitled Estaba la Margarita is a romance and is a version of Las señas del esposo. It was collected from oral tradition by the author.]

151. _____. Unpublished collections in the Archivo Fonográfico de la Sección de Musicología del Museo Argentino de Ciencias Naturales, Buenos Aires.

152. _____. "El velorio del angelito." FICU, I:3 (mayo, 1941), 27-28.
[The author gives useful bibliography of sources where the velorio del angelito is mentioned and she gives with music one of the songs which are sung at such velorios.]

Arosteguy, Abdón. See Podestá, Antonio D., entry no. 368.

153. Autenchlus Maier, Olga Francesca. "El folklore de Casabindo (Puna de Jujuy, Argentina)." RDTP, XVI(1960): Cuadernos 1° y 2°, 115-127.
[Includes the texts of a few coplas.]

Avellaneda, Félix F. See Lafone Quevedo, Samuel A., entry no. 308.

154. Ayestarán, Lauro. La música en el Uruguay, Vol. I: primera parte, la música primitiva; segunda parte, la música culta hasta 1860. Montevideo: Servicio Oficial de Difusión Radio Eléctrica, 1953. xx, 818 pp. 30 cm.
[Boggs (ref. 13 [1954], p. 40) comments: "Of folklore interest are the first 2 chapters: Indigenous music, p. 3-49 (first reference, 1531, Charrúa and Chaná masses sung in 1624, 18. century Indian musicians of Soriano, Indian dances of 1816, the musical bow . . .), and Negro musical, p. 51-111 (Comparsas of 1760, negro dances, festivals, candombe . . .). Even certain sections of the culta part of this fine work will interest the folklorist."]

155. _____. "Temas bíblicos en el folklore musical uruguayo." Escritura (Montevideo), Año I:1 (octubre de 1947), 61-65.
[The author offers the text and music of an estilo consisting of four décimas which was collected from oral tradition. It is a popular expression in poetic form of a portion of the book of Proverbs. The author analyzes the compositon's musical and literary characteristics and cites sources where Argentine variants of the Uruguayan version of the poem can be found.]

Azara, Agustín de. See Azara, Félix de, entry no. 156.

156. Azara, Félix de. Descripción é historia del Paraguay y del Río de la Plata, ed. por Agustín de Azara. 2 vols. Madrid: Imprenta de Sánchez, 1847. 22 cm.
[Azara, a royal official who went to the Plata region in 1781, finished his manuscript in 1806. He writes (Vol. I, p. 309): "En cada pulpería hay una guitarra, y el que la toca bebe á costa agena. Cantan Yarabis ó Tristes que son cantares inventados en el Perú, los mas monótonos y siempre tristes, tratando de ingratitudes de amor, y de gentes que lloran desdichas por los desiertos."]

157. Baqueiro Foster, Gerónimo. "Los 'cielos', 'cielitos' y 'cielitos lindos' de América." Nacion, suplemento dominical del 9 de noviembre de 1952, p. 14; 16 de noviembre, p. 14; 23 de noviembre, p. 14; 30 de noviembre, p. ?.

[The author considers various theories about the cielo and cielito of Argentina (its origins, the possible Spanish, Indian, and English elements which may have entered into it, and the like). In following up these topics he traces relationships with the Spanish seguidilla, the son of various regions, the zamacueca of Chile, etc. Because I have been unable to consult the last installment of the article, I cannot report its conclusions. In the main the author seems to be trying to tear down many previously accepted ideas, particularly that of the relationship of the cielo to the English country dance (contradanza).]

158. Baratta, María de. "Origine e motivi della poesia argentina popolare e d'arte." Il Tesaur (Udine, Friuli, Italia). Anno III(1951): 4-6, pp. 21-24.

159. Barbieri, Vicente. "Enterrado en campo verde." CUn, No. 46 (noviembre-diciembre, 1954), 80-87.

[The author points out that Rafael Obligado in his Santos Vega uses in the third part of the poem, El himno del payador, some lines lifted from a well known Spanish romance ("No me entierren en sagrado").]

160. Barreda, Ernesto María. Nuestro parnaso; colección de poesías argentinas. 4 vols. B. A.: J. L. Dasso y Cía., [1914]. 22.5 cm.

[Morales (ref. 346, p. 27) seems to indicate that this work contains something about the Romance en que canta un guaso en estilo campestre .... It may incorporate the text. See Maziel, Juan Baltasar, entry no. 338.]

161. Bauzá, Francisco. Historia de la dominación española en el Uruguay. 3 vols. Montevideo, 1895-1897.

[In Vol. II, p. 193, of the above work there is said to be reference to the gauchos' singing of coplas.]

162. Bayo, Ciro. "Cantos populares americanos." RH, XV(1906), 796-809.

[A collection of traditional romances along with other popular poetry from Argentina and Bolivia. There is a brief introduction.]

163. _____. Romancerillo del Plata; contribución al estudio del romancero rioplatense. Madrid: V. Suárez, 1913. 238 pp. 18.5 cm.; also, B. A.: Institución Cultural Española, 1943. 197 pp. 15.5 cm.

[An excellent early study of various forms of popular poetry with examples from Argentina and other countries as well. There is a discussion of romances, romancillos, corridos, and other genres.]

164. Becker, Zahara Z. Poesía folklórica infantil del Uruguay. Montevideo: Ediciones CEFU, 1956. 19 pp.

165. Belgrano, Miguel. Rasgo poético a los habitantes de Buenos-Ayres, en obsequio del valor y lealtad con que expoliaron a los ingleses de la América Meridional. El 5 de julio de 1807. Reimpreso en Buenos Ayres, En la Real Imp. de Niños Expositos [sic], 1808. 8 pp.

[Masciopinto (ref. 335, pp. 105-106) prints a few lines of this endecasyllabic romance and indicates that it can be found in Adolfo Alsina's and Vicente F. López y Planes' Colección de documentos relativos a sucesos del Río de la Plata desde 1806 (entry no. 131). It is not a florid composition in the usual neo-classical style of the times; in fact, it is quite sober and unadorned.]

166. Benítez, Juan Jesús. "Cantares de la tradición oral bonaerense." RINT, Año I, Entrega primera (enero-junio, 1948), 102-115.

[Songs collected from oral tradition by Benítez in 1945. Most, though not all, of this first installment of a proposed series are nonnarrative décimas. None is a romance or corrido. More installments are promised, but the review apparently suspended publication.]

167. Berdiales, Germán. "La Pascua de Reyes de 1805, en pergamino, relatada por el payador Santos Vega." Revista de educación (La Plata, Argentina), III(1958):4, pp. 171-175.

168. Berón, Sebastián C. Décimas variadas para cantar con guitarra. B. A.: Editores Llambias y Pardo, 1887. 31 pp.; also, Valparaíso, Chile: Imp. Valparaíso, 1896. 30 pp.

169. _____. Truco y retruco; segunda payada de los célebres payadores León Robles y Pedro González. B. A.: Llambias y Pardo, 1887.

170. Blanco Amor, Eduardo. "Intimidad de España. Romances de ciegos." Nac, 17 de noviembre de 1935, cuarta sección, p. 2.

171. Blaya Alende, Joaquín. "El folklore musical argentino." Alma latina (San Juan, P. R.), X:208 (25 de noviembre, 1939), 17, 55.

[Chase (ref. 25, p. 238) comments: "Touches also on Venezuelan folk music."]

172. Borges, Jorge Luis. "Las coplas acriolladas." Nos, Año XX, Tomo LII:200-201 (enero-febrero, 1926), 75-79.

[An excellent little article wherein the author, by comparing Argentine and Spanish versions of coplas which have passed from the Peninsula to the New World, shows that the criollo spirit seems to have wrought changes of text and of tone which Borges considers significant to the study of the essence of "criollez."]

173. Bosco, Eduardo Jorge. Obras. 2 vols. B. A.: Angel Gulab, 1952. 24 cm.

[Boggs (ref. 13 [1952], p. 52) says: "Includes poetic texts of cielitos of Maypo, Bañado, Restaurador, Olivos, and Marca de Ancona, and media caña Constitucional, with notes, a study of folk poetry and verses only of cancionero popular porteño, and notes on the gaucho."]

174. Breve recuerdo del formidable ataque del exercito inglés a la Ciudad de Buenos Ayres, y su gloriosa defensa por las legiones Patrioticas el día 5 de julio de 1807. Buenos Ayres, En la Imp. de los Niños Expósitos, 1807. 8 pp.

[Menéndez Pelayo (ref. 82, Vol. II, p. 331) indicates that it contains a romance endecasílabo entitled Canto de reconocimiento al Dios . . . (etc.). It is said to be the work of Joseph Gabriel Ocampo, a priest from Tucumán, Argentina.]

175. Bunge, Carlos Octavio. La poesía popular argentina. Vol. XVIII of Biblioteca internacional de obras famosas.

176. Bustamante, Perfecto P. Girón de historia; leyendas, tradiciones regionales y relatos históricos. B. A.: Talleres Gráficos J. Crovetto y M. Carrio, 1922. 278 pp. 18 cm.

[Furt (ref. 272, Vol. I, p. 446) cites coplas from pp. 64-93 of the above.]

177. Caballero Farfán, P. Influencia de la música incaica en el cancionero del norte argentino. B. A.: Comisión Nacional de Cultura, 1946. 148 pp. 26 cm.

178. Cabrera, Ana S., comp. Cantos nativos y danzas del norte argentino. 3rd. ed. B. A.: G. Ricordi, n.d. 10 leaves without pagination. 31 cm.

[An Album para canto y piano, it contains six compositions with texts and music arranged for piano. None is narrative or related to romances, but there are some coplas.]

179. _____. "El folklore musical argentino." Anales del Instituto Popular de Conferencias (B. A.), VIII(1922), 226-231.

180. Cáceres Freyre, Julián. "Fabricación del patay en los algarrobales del campo de Palcipas (La Rioja y Catamarca) (República Argentina)." FACI, Año III:3 (noviembre, 1955), 5-30.

[The author frequently cites coplas as he writes about patay, "una especie de pan o galletas que se fabrica con la fruta del algarrobo negro (Prosopia nigra) una vez molida hasta reducirla a fina harina." All texts are taken from Carrizo's cancioneros.]

181. Calvo, Mercedes. "Jujuy y sus canciones." Nac, 5 de febrero de 1939.

182. Campo, Luzán del. Cancionero del mate; folklore de Argentina, Brasil, Chile, Uruguay y Paraguay. 2.ª ed. B. A.: Editorial Tupa, 1944. 123 pp. 21.5 cm. (First ed. 1942, according to the L. of C. catalogue.)

[A collection of literature about mate, some of it learned, some of it popular. There are included a few romances. One entitled El mate y la religión is expecially interesting as a true romance with popular flavor. The author refers to it as an "Antiguo romance popular en el Paraguay durante el coloniaje," but he doesn't say where he got it or on what he bases his statement.]

183. Canal Feijóo, Bernardo. Ensayo sobre la expresión popular artística en Santiago del Estero. B. A.: Compañía Impresora Argentina, 1937. 134 pp. 29 cm.

[A general study of various types of folklore, including coplas and vidalas. There is no mention of romances or other narrative genres.]

184. _____. El norte. B. A.: Emecé Editores, 1942. 109 pp. 18 cm. (Colección Buen Aire.)

[Included here is a "Cancionerillo de Santiago" which contains popular poetry from Santiago del Estero, mostly cuartetas glossed by décimas. Some of these are narrative poems about historical events. There is also a section of "Canciones para el velorio del 'Angelito'," which are songs to be sung upon the death of children. There are no romances in the volume.]

185. _____. "La voz secreta de la raza en el folklore argentino." In Proceedings of the Eighth American Scientific Congress, Held in Washington, May 10-18, 1940, Vol. II (Anthropological Sciences). Washington, D. C.: Department of State, 1942. Pp. 265-269. 24.5 cm.

[Contains an interesting discussion of the use of Quechua words and phrases in the coplas of Santiago del Estero, a region whose Indian population has disappeared through mestizaje. The author concludes that the use of the Indian tongue is not capricious, that it is used to express satire or to state bold truths which should ethically not be said in Spanish. Unfortunately, this intriguing hypothesis is stated without supporting evidence, as no textual examples of any coplas are given.]

186. Cancionero anónimo.

[Carrizo (ref. 199, Vol. I, p. 292) mentions this volume and says: "Tiene 17 por 10 centímetros, está roto y conserva las páginas de la número 7 a la 44."]

187. Cancionero de las invasiones inglesas.

[A collection of canciones and letrillas which appeared in Buenos Aires at the time of the English invasion. Morales (ref. 346, p. 37) cites Ricardo Rojas as the source of his information about the existence of this cancionero.]

188. Cano, Rafael. Del tiempo Ñaupa (folklore norteño). B. A.: Talleres Gráficos Argentinos L. J. Rosso, 1930. 475 pp. 20 cm.

[A series of brief chapters about customs, beliefs, dances, and the like from the northern part of Argentina. Romances or other narrative poetry are not treated as such, but there are some essays on popular dances which contain many texts of coplas, vidalas, and other genres. A chapter on the Zamba de Vargas also is valuable for the several versions of this narrative song-dance which it contains.]

189. Cano Vélez, F. Ramón. Amaicha del Valle. Tucumán: Imprenta E. T. A., 1943. 150 pp. 24 cm.

[Cortázar (ref. 237, p. 77) quotes some strophes of a chilena which deals with Felipe Varela, a caudillo from Catamarca. He says that it appears on pp. 43-44 of the above.]

190. El canto popular, documentos para el estudio del folklore argentino. B. A.: "Coni," 1923. 29 cm.

[Contains a discussion of pre-Hispanic music as related to folklore genres of Argentina. Some musical transcriptions are included.]

191. Carpena, Elías. "Dos nuevas versiones del romance de Delgadina." BAAL, XIV:53 (octubre-diciembre de 1945), 685-698.

[After presenting two prose versions of the story of Delgadina (one is very unusual since it seeks to justify the father), the author offers two versions of the romance of Delgadina. Though both were collected near Buenos Aires, the first and more conventional version was sung by some Spanish girls; the second, a thoroughly criollo adaptation, contains some very interesting changes in details of the story.]

192. _____. Romances del Pago de la Matanza. B. A., 1958.

193. Carrizo, Juan Alfonso. "Algunos aspectos de la poesía popular de Catamarca, Salta y Jujuy." Hu, XXI(1930), 195-232.

[A good general treatment of Argentine popular poetry. In the first portion of the article, a discussion of the problem of Spanish vs. Indian influences, several texts, mostly décimas, are provided in order to show how old Spanish themes still live in Argentine tradition. Traditional romances are passed over rather lightly, though the author records his success in collecting such compositons (e. g., Camino de Belén, Las señas del esposo, Delgadina, and others), and he prints the text of a colonial romance of the year 1630 first discovered by Ricardo Rojas. Carrizo points out that it is an old Spanish romance which Menéndez Pidal found in Tangiers among the Jews. Next, the texts of several historical songs of the nineteenth century are given. Some are décimas, some are romances, some are redondillas, and several are very close to the Mexican corrido in tone and style (e. g., Don Facundo Quiroga [pp. 221-222] and Voy a cantar la agonía [p. 224]). The article closes with a discussion of some religious poetry, mostly décimas.]

194. _____. Antecedentes hispano-medievales de la poesía tradicional argentina. B. A.: Estudios Hispánicos, 1945. 864 pp. 27.5 cm.
[A fundamental work on the subject indicated and one which is applicable to the popular poetry of the entire Hispanic world. It traces the history of the development of medieval themes in coplas, décimas, romances, and other genres. Thousands of texts are given and there is an extensive bibliography.]

195. _____. Antiguos cantos populares argentinos. B. A.: Silla Hermanos, 1926. iv, 258 pp. 28 cm.
[A collection of popular songs and poetry preceded by an explanation of the system employed in dividing them into romances, canciones, and coplas, each with subdivisions. There are many historical songs and coplas in the collection and there is a bibliography.]

196. _____. "La blasfemia y los cantos populares." BAAL, IV:13 (enero-marzo, 1936), 56-57.
[An investigation into the reasons why the coplas of Argentina, unlike those of Spain, are free of profane language. The author believes the difference can be attributed to the very stern policies of the Church in Argentina.]

_____. Cancionero de Catamarca. Alternate title of Antiguos cantos populares argentinos.

197. _____. Cancionero popular de Jujuy. Tucumán: M. Violetto, 1934. 529 pp. 28 cm.
[An introductory section studies the geography, the history, and the social structure of Jujuy and treats the Spanish and Indian influences which have contributed to the formation of the popular songs and poems of the area. The extensive collection of popular poetry which follows includes romances, canciones históricas (some very similar to Mexican corridos), coplas históricas, and many other types of compositions. There is a bibliography.]

198. _____. Cancionero popular de Jujuy-Tucumán. B. A.: Roldán, 1935.

199. _____. Cancionero popular de La Rioja. 3 vols. B. A.: A. Baiocco y Cía., 1942. 28 cm.
[Vol. I contains a general study of geographical, social, and historical data of significance to an understanding of La Rioja. Vol. II contains texts of popular poetry. There are sections which contain romances, romancillos, and canciones históricas (some very similar to Mexican corridos). Vol. III contains a large collection of coplas along with a few romances of interest. There is an extensive bibliography.]

200. _____. Cancionero popular de Salta. B. A.: A. Baiocco y Cía., 1933. 707 pp. 28 cm.
[Contains a large collection of popular songs and poetry, including

romances, coplas, romancillos, canciones históricas, and the like. There is a bibliography.]

201. Carrizo, Juan Alfonso. Cancionero popular de Tucumán. 2 vols. B. A.: A. Baiocco y Cía., 1937. 27.5 cm.

[This work follows the general pattern of the other cancioneros compiled by Carrizo. Because it is typical, I have chosen it for detailed description in order to provide those not familar with these cancioneros a fair idea of their character. Vol. I includes 341 pages of background material concerning the history, customs, and geography of Tucumán, along with a discussion of the nature of its popular poetry. On p. 343 begins the section entitled "Cancionero propiamente dicho," which comprises the rest of Vol. I and all of Vol. II. In Vol. I there are sections on "Romances" (pp. 343-368), "Rimas infantiles" (including some romances) (pp. 369-424), "Canciones históricas" (pp. 425-479), and "Canciones religiosas" (pp. 481-536). In the Appendix (pp. 537-550) melodies are given for a few of these compositions and there is an "Indice alfabético de autores citados" (pp. 551-556). Vol. II contains a wide variety of different types of songs and poetry, some compositions resembling Mexican corridos rather closely. In this connection, a section entitled "Matonescas" (pp. 377-391) is particularly interesting. The largest section of Vol. II is "Coplas" (pp. 407-587).]

202. _____. Cantares históricos del norte argentino. B. A.: Centro de Instrucción de Infantería, 1939. 124 pp. (Biblioteca del suboficial, Vol. 94.)

203. _____. "Los cantares tradicionales de La Rioja en su relación con el teatro." In Cuaderno de cultura teatral, No. 17. B. A., 1942. Pp. 29-38.

204. _____. Cantares tradicionales del norte; antología breve. B. A.: Talleres "Optimus" de Cantiello y Cía., 1939. 49 pp. 24 cm.

[An anthology of texts taken from Carrizo's long cancioneros. A preliminary note explains that the volume is intended as a popularization of these more scholarly works. Included are a number of glosas in décimas, the narrative poem entitled Don Juan Facundo Quiroga, and a large number of coplas.]

205. _____. Cantares tradicionales del Tucumán; (antología) de los cancioneros de Catamarca, Salta, Jujuy, Tucumán y La Rioja. B. A.: Espasa-Calpe Argentina (A. Baiocco y Cía.), 1939. 208 pp. 23 cm.

[As the author indicates in his prologue, this is a collection lifted from his long cancioneros and is intended for the nonspecialist. Like the more extensive works, this volume has sections on "Romance," "Romancillos y rimas infantiles," "Canciones históricas," "Coplas," and the like. There is a bibliography of fifty-four items.]

206. _____. "Dos antiguallas tradicionales." FICU, Año 1940:2 (diciembre), 13-14.
[Reports the discovery in Jujuy of some fragments of the old sixteenth-century Spanish romance of Fonte frida.]

207. _____. "Filiación hispánica de la poesía tradicional del Tucumán." Primer Congreso de la Cultura Hispano-Americana; acta inaugural (Salta). Vol. I. B. A.: Talleres "Optimus" de Cantiello y Cía., 1942. Pp. 79-96.
[A note to the title says: "Esta conferencia fue dicha de memoria y reconstruida en parte por su autor." In it Carrizo points out the powerful influence of Spain in Argentine life and quotes the texts of numerous coplas, romances, and décimas by way of illustrations. There is, of course, nothing in this lecture that cannot be found in the author's cancioneros.]

208. _____. Florilegio — El cristianismo en los cantares populares — (de los cancioneros populares de Catamarca, Salta, Jujuy y Tucumán). Tucumán: M. Violetto, 1934. 118 pp. 18 cm.
[In the prologue the author explains that this volume is a selection of compositions, mostly of a religious nature, taken from his long cancioneros and intended for the nonspecialist. There are forty-two texts, almost all cuartetas glossed by décimas, along with some discussion of the characteristics of popular poetry. The volume may be ignored by anyone familar with Carrizo's more serious works.]

209. _____. Historia del folklore argentino. B. A.: Ministerio de Educación, Instituto Nacional de la Tradición, 1953. 187 pp. 20 cm.
[An excellent survey of the history of folklore studies in Argentina. Though there is no formal bibliographical section, there is an index, and in the text of his work the author describes almost all the most important works on Argentine folklore. Hence, the volume is valuable to the study of any aspect of Argentine folklore because of the information which it contains on bibliographical sources.]

210. _____. "Juan Domingo Díaz, su vida y su obra." SRCS, Año II:7-8 (septiembre, 1941), 516-551.
[A study of a semipopular poet of Tucumán who was born in 1805. Though there is no indication that he used romance meter, many of his poems, which are usually cuartetas glossed by décimas, are topical and narrative in nature.]

211. _____. "Nuestra poesía popular." Hu, XV(1927), 241-342.
[An excellent and very stimulating study of popular poetry in Argentina. In reality it is a long commentary on the author's Cancionero de Catamarca. Among the many interesting sections of the article are discussions of Spanish and Indian influences in popular poetry, including extensive treatment of romances in Spain

and in America; the development of poesía matonesca or romances de valentones into American poems, both popular and artistic, the best example of these being Martín Fierro, which Carrizo considers a modified romance de valentón; the reasons why lyric, not epic, romances from Spain have survived in American tradition; and many other challenging problems. In a section on "Canciones históricas" there are some representative texts which are of interest, particularly a poem on the death of a Gobernador Cubas, which Carrizo collected from oral tradition and which is very similar to the corridos of Mexico.]

212. Carrizo, Juan Alfonso. "La poesía popular y el Martín Fierro, sobre la edición crítica de Eleuterio F. Tiscornia." Nos, Año XXII, Tomo LIX:224 (enero de 1928), 41-60.

[Essentially a very favorable review of Tiscornia's book, though the author takes the occasion mainly to criticize Ricardo Rojas and others who have considered Martín Fierro to be popular poetry worthy of being classfied as an Argentine epic poem. Carrizo offers much linguistic evidence from the poem to prove that it is a learned composition and he suggests that Tiscornia has performed a great service in providing a critical edition which will serve as a starting point for further scientific linguistic research.]

213. _____. La poesía tradicional argentina; introducción a su estudio. La Plata, Argentina, 1951. 325 pp.

214. _____. "El tema del labrador de amor y la mala cosecha." In Homenaje a Fritz Krüger, Tomo I. Mendoza, Argentina: Universidad Nacional de Cuyo, 1952. Pp. 295-301.

[Contains texts of some popular décimas and coplas from Puerto Rico and Argentina which are derived from a Spanish work, El pastor de Filida (1582), by Luis Gálvez de Montalvo.]

215. _____. "Tucumán, jardín de la poesía popular argentina." PrBA, 9 de julio, 1936.

216. _____. "El viejo tema poético de la imposibilidad de disponer del alma, aunque sí de la vida." TradP, Año I, Vol. I (enero-febrero, 1950), 9-12.

[The theme is traced from Gonzalo de Berceo through Lope, Calderón, and other writers of the Golden Age to Spanish and Spanish American popular coplas. American texts are given from Chile, Argentina, and Peru.]

217. _____, and Jacovella, Bruno C. "Cantares de la tradición bonaerense." RINT, Año I, Entrega 2.ª (julio-diciembre, 1948), 258-294.

[A discussion of the cuadernos manuscritos of country people who have made collections of popular songs. Carrizo considers these to be written collections of true folklore. The present article is based on a cuaderno made by Justo P. Rodríguez, sixty-five years of age, whose collection extends back into the nineteenth century. Mostly it consists of décimas, mainly glosas, and what Carrizo calls "romances consonantados." Some texts taken from Rodríguez' cuaderno are given, and one on the death of Juan Facundo Quiroga (pp. 271-272) is very similar to Mexican corridos. The other textual examples are romances and décimas of various types, but they are not narratives.]

218. Carrizo Valdés, Jesús María. Los refranes y las frases en las coplas populares. B. A.: Departamento de Folklore, Instituto de Cooperación Universitaria, 1941. 54 pp.

Casá, Agustín Guillermo. See House, Guillermo, entry no. 293.

219. Castex, Eusebio R. Cantos populares; apuntes lexicográficos. B. A.: Talleres Gráficos "La Lectura," 1923. 156 pp. 19.5 cm.

[Furt (ref. 272, Vol. I, p. 458) cites an amorous copla taken from this volume, which he criticizes rather severely.]

220. Castro, Américo. "Romancerillo del Plata." Nosotros (México), No. 6 (1913).

[An elusive reference which I have been unable to consult. It is undoubtedly a review or an essay inspired by Ciro Bayo's Romancerillo del Plata. I list it only because of the prestige of the author.]

221. Catálogo de la colección de folklore donada por el Consejo Nacional de Educación. 6 vols. B. A.: Imprenta de la Universidad, 1925-1938. 23.5 cm.

[This work lists by name the teachers who contributed to the collection of folklore gathered under the direction of the Consejo Nacional de Educación in 1921. Arranged by regions, the material of each individual is catalogued. Included are all kinds of folklore such as riddles, narraciones, superstitions, songs, poetry, and the like. Some of the entries refer to romances.]

222. Chazarreta, Andrés. Album santiagueño de piezas criollas. 1916.

223. _____. Colección de bailes nacionales para piano.
[Furt (ref. 272, Vol. I, p. 451) cites the work.]

224. _____. Segundo álbum musical santiagueño de tonadas y bailes criollos para piano y canto.
[Furt (ref. 272, Vol. I, p. 451) lauds it as a source of popular songs.]

225. _____. Tercer álbum musical de tonadas, vidalas y bailes criollos para piano y canto. Buenos Aires, n.d.
[Furt (ref. 272, Vol. I, p. 451) quotes a number of coplas taken from the above.]

226. Cielito de Maipú. B. A.: Prensas de Alvarez.
[Rojas (ref. 387 [1924 ed.], Vol. VIII, pp. 451-454) gives the text of this very interesting historical cielito.]

227. Cielitos que con acompañamiento de guitarra cantaban los soldados del ejército patriota frente a las murallas de Montevideo.
[Rojas (ref. 387 [1924 ed.], Vol. VIII, p. 436) calls this the first document of genuine popular poetry and says that it probably dates from 1813. He doesn't indicate where he found it but he quotes a few strophes textually.]

228. Coluccio, Félix. Diccionario folklórico argentino. B. A.: "El Ateneo," 1948. 203 pp. 21 cm.; also, 2.ª edición aumentada y corregida. B. A.: "El Ateneo," 1950. 503 pp. 23.5 cm.
[The second edition, which I have examined, is a useful listing of words related to folklore studies, with definitions and examples of usage. It also includes a biographical index of folklorists, a list of folklore organizations in America, and a bibliography of authors and works cited. Many coplas are used as illustrative examples. Romance is listed only in connection with the Romance del pobre y del rico, which is defined as a "Romance tradicional religioso," and the Romance del señor gato, of which one version is given. The word corrido is not listed.]

229. ———. "El velorio del angelito." AVF, Año I:1 (enero-junio, 1952), 153-156.
[Describes the velorio del angelito as it is found in Argentina and gives the texts of the songs which are sung and danced. They are coplas. There is also brief attention to the velorios in Venezuela, Colombia, Mexico, and Santo Domingo.]

230. Composiciones poéticas de la epopeya argentina. B. A., 1910.
[A large collection of topical poetry divided by years from 1810-1822. The subjects treated are the events of the wars of independence in Argentina and elsewhere in Spanish America. The poems are artistic in tone and only a few compositions, notably some cielitos, employ romance form.]

231. Concolorcorvo (Calixto Bustamante). El Lazarillo/de ciegos caminantes/desde Buenos-Ayres, hasta Lima/con sus Itinerarios según la más pun/tual observación, con algunas no/ticias útiles a los Nuevos Comercian/tes que tratan en mulas; y otras/Históricas./ Sacado de las Memorias que/hizo Don Alfonso Carrió de la Vandera en/este dilatado viage y Comisión que tubo/por la Corte para el arreglo de Co/rreos y Estafetas, situación y/ajuste de Postas, desde/Montevideo/ Por Don Calixto Bustamante, Carlos/Inca Alias, Concolorcorvo. Natural/del Cuzco, que acompañó al referido comisio/nado en dicho Viage y escribió sus extractos./

Con licencia. / En Gigón, en la Imprenta de Rovada, Año de 1773.;
also, El lazarillo de ciegos caminantes desde Buenos Aires hasta
Lima, 1773. Vol. IV of Biblioteca de la Junta de Historia y
Numismática Americana. B. A., 1908. 324 pp.; also, B. A.:
Ediciones Solar, 1942. xix, 430 pp. •20.5 cm.
 [Contains a few references to popular music of the areas indicated
(e.g., the gauchos' singing of coplas (p. 27 [1908 ed.]). However,
it contains nothing specific about romances or narrative forms of
poetry.]

   Consejo Nacional de Educación. See Antología folklórica
argentina para las escuelas de adultos and Antología folklórica
argentina para las escuelas primarias, entries nos. 137 and 138.

   Consejo Nacional de Educación, Comisión de Folklore y
Nativismo. See Música argentina nativa, entry no. 354.

  232. Contrapunto entre los famosos payadores, Pablo Vázquez
y Gabino Ezeiza, tomado taquigráficamente por un testigo presencial.
6.ª ed. Rosario, n.d.

  233. Contreras, Segundo N. Disertaciones musicales. B. A.:
Librería "La Cotizadora Económica" de E. Perrot, 1931. 126 pp.
18.5 cm.
 [Chase (ref. 25, p. 51) comments: "Several of the essays deal with
folk music, both indigenous and Creole."]

  234. "Coplas de nuestro cancionero anónimo." BIFL, No. 7
(1945), 4.

  235. "Coplas del Litoral." BIFL, No. 5 (1945), 3.

  236. Cortázar, Augusto Raúl. "Bibliografía folklórica argentina."
Libros i revistas, boletín bibliográfico de la revista Waman Puma,
Año I, Vol. I:1 (julio de 1944), 105-109. (Published as part of Waman
Puma, Año IV, Vol. III:16 [julio de 1944].)
 [Eighteen entries, some of which concern folk songs and poetry.
Though not of much significance because of its brevity, it is an
annotated bibliography and of value as far as it goes.]

  237. _____. El carnaval en el folklore calchaquí, con una
breve exposición sobre la teoría y la práctica del método folklórico
integral. B. A.: Editorial Sudamericana, 1949. 286 pp. 20.5 cm.
 [A very thorough study of the European origins of Carnival and of
the celebrations which occur in Calchaquí. Many coplas are scattered
throughout the volume. Of most interest is a brief section entitled
"La historia en las tradiciones" (pp. 74-79), which contains some
historical coplas that are closely related to the romance-corrido
tradition. The most important of these is a fragment which deals
with a border raid in 1869 led by the caudillo Felipe Varela. It is
taken from F. Ramón Cano Vélez, Amaicha del Valle (pp. 43-44).]

238. Cortázar, Augusto Raúl. Confluencias culturales en el folklore argentino. B. A.: Artes Gráficas Sebastián de Amorrortu e Hijos, 1944. 100 pp. 21 cm.
[A very well documented essay on the broad subject indicated. Passing mention of the romance and other popular poetry is, however, unimportant to the study of these genres; the author merely refers the reader to the standard works in the field.]

239. _____. "Contribuciones a la bibliografía folklórica argentina." FACI, VI-VII:6-7 (1959), 38-68.

240. _____. "Del folklore calchaquí; caminos de los valles." Chasquí (B. A.), I(1945):1, pp. 6, 8, 16.

241. _____. "Las fiestas en el folklore chalchaquí." AFA, III (1947-1948).
[The bibliography of RDTP, VII(1951), 714, says it contains "ejemplos poéticos."]

242. _____. Folklore argentino, el noroeste. B. A.: Librería "El Ateneo," 1950. 63 pp. 21 cm.
[In describing the life of the people of northwestern Argentina, the author has occasion to quote many copla texts. Romances are mentioned only in passing and no texts are given.]

243. _____. Folklore literario y literatura folklórica. In Vol. V of Historia de la literatura argentina, ed. by R. A. Arrieta. B. A.: Peuser, 1959. Pp. 17-395. 23.5 cm.
[An extremely rich source of information. Though necessarily extensive rather than intensive as it deals with each general topic, the treatment is notable for all the suggestions and leads which it offers for further study. Following a fine section on the numerous cancioneros which Argentine folklorists have compiled, the author divides Argentina into eight geographical regions and deals with the folklore of each area separately. There are innumerable bibliographical leads in every section. This work is a basic source for any study of Argentine folklore.]

244. _____. Guía bibliográfica del folklore argentino; primera contribución. B. A.: Universidad de Buenos Aires, 1942. 291 pp. 23 cm.
[An excellent bibliographical contribution. After a fairly lengthy introduction explaining the author's problems and the procedures employed, there follows the bibliography proper, which includes 897 items and is divided into eleven sections according to the general subjects treated (e. g., "Bibliografía de bibliografías," "Colecciones," "Obras folklóricas," "Obras de carácter literario," "Obras de carácter histórico," and the like). There is a brief appendix about the organization of the studies which led to the publication of this bibliography.

Finally, there is an alphabetical index of authors, organizations, and reviews cited. This is a fundamental work for any study of Argentine folklore.]

246. . "El paisaje en los cancioneros bonaerense y salteño." Gaea, V(1937), 423-427; reprinted B. A.: Coni, 1937.

[The author attempts to synthesize some of the attitudes revealed in the coplas of two quite different regions of Argentina, the province of Buenos Aires and the Valles Calchaquíes of Salta. The gauchos of the pampean region are more attracted to animals, especially the horse, while the mountaineers of Salta display more attention to details of landscape, particularly those related to the botanical world.]

246. , ed. Renca; folklore punteano. B. A., 1958. 198 pp.

247. . "La vida tradicional en las viejas fincas calchaquíes." UnivSF, No. 22 (invierno-primavera, 1949), 149-171; reprinted Santa Fe, 1950. 27 pp.

[Deals with the history, traditions, customs, etc. of the Valle de Calchaquí near the city of Salta. A few texts of historical coplas are given.]

248. Cufré, Angela G. de. El folklore argentino. B. A.: Imprenta Balmes, 1949. 135 pp. 23 cm.

[A rather ingenuous survey of Argentine folklore. There is, however, a brief section entitled "La poesía popular" (pp. 116-120) which contains a few copla texts and a romance fragment. Apparently all of them come from Carrizo's cancioneros. The entire book may be safely ignored.]

249. Daireaux, Emile. La vie et les moeurs à La Plata. Deuxième edition. 2 vols. Paris: Hachette et Cie, 1889. 24 cm.; also, Vida y costumbres en La Plata. 2 vols. B. A.: F. Lajouane; Paris: C. Bouret, 1888. 25 cm. [The L. of C. card for this volume says: "The author's translation of 'La vie et les moeurs à la Plata', which was published in Paris in 1887."]

[Furt (ref. 272, Vol. II, p. 349) quotes from Vol. I, p. 35, of the above work (1889 ed.): "Le soir, autour d'une bouteille de genièvre, pendant qu'un des assistants touche l'eternelle guitare, le payador, sur un ton monotone, débite quelques vers où se reflète l'heure actuelle, et, peu à peu s'echauffant, se hausse à des accents vraiment poètiques, où l'idée et la peinture à traits accentués, à (sic) plus de valeur que l'harmonie, généralement un peu nomotone et languissante."]

250. De punta y hacha; payada memorable entre los famosos payadores J. Betinotti y F. Bianco. B. A.: Ed. Olimpo, 1949.

[Román (ref. 102, p. 206) indicates that this is a stenographic transcription of a famous payada which took place in the Teatro Argentino in Buenos Aires on May 25, 1913.]

251. Décimas variadas. B. A., 1909.
[Listed by Nichols (ref. 356, p. 37), this work may be an edition of Sebastián C. Berón's Décimas variadas para cantar con guitarra.]

252. Décimas variadas para cantar con guitarra. B. A., 1906.
[This work, listed by Nichols (ref. 356, p. 37), is probably an edition of the work of the same name by Sebastián C. Berón.]

253. De María, Isidoro. Tradiciones y recuerdos; Montevideo antiguo. 3 vols. Montevideo: Imprenta de Turenne, Varzi y C^a, 1888-1890. 24.5 cm.; another edition: Montevideo antiguo. Selección y prólogo de Armando D. Pirotto. 2 vols. Montevideo-B. A.: Talleres Gráficos "Colombino Hnos.," 1938.
[The work is listed in Nichols' bibliography of folklore about the gaucho. In the 1938 edition, which is the only one I have been able to consult, there is little about the gaucho or anything else of a popular nature, except for two copla texts. This edition, however, is not complete.]

254. Draghi Lucero, Juan. Cancionero popular cuyano. Mendoza: Talleres Gráficos de Best Hermanos, 1938. cxlvii, 632 pp. 26 cm.
[In an extensive general introduction the author discusses the history of Cuyo and characterizes the popular poetry of the region. The main body of the work is a large collection of popular poetry and songs of all kinds. Of interest are sections entitled: "Romances-tonadas" (pp. 1-6), which includes versions of some traditional Spanish romances (Delgadina, Catalina, and others); "Tonadas noticieras" (pp. 187-239) and "Tonadas históricas" (pp. 265-272), which includes several topical compositions that closely resemble Mexican corridos in form and style along with others that are in décimas; "Cantos infantiles" (pp. 313-335), which contains versions of Mambrú and the romance, Hilo de oro; and "Versitos y dichos" (pp. 291-312), which is a collection of coplas. A section entitled "Poesía vulgar chilena de fines del siglo XIX referida a sucesos de la Argentina" (pp. 337-371) contains several historical compositions about Argentina, mostly glosas in décimas, along with some songs unrelated to the theme indicated. In an appendix (pp. 547-582) there are additional examples of the types of compositions treated in the body of the study. The volume concludes with a section of "Temas musicales" (pp. 583-626) and a bibliography (pp. 627-632).]

255. Duayen, César. Stella (novela de costumbres argentinas). Barcelona: Tipografía de la Casa Editorial Maucci, 1909. x, 391 pp. 21 cm.
[A novel about Argentine life which occasionally reflects popular customs. The singing of coplas is mentioned in several places, and some texts are quoted. With two possible exceptions, they are, I suspect, the creations of the novelist; hence, the importance of the work is negligible.]

256. Echevarría de Lobato Mulle, Felisa Carmen. Romancero de la villa de Luján. Luján: Librería de Mayo, 1957. 67 pp. 24 cm.

257. Espejo, Gerónimo. El paso de los Andes; crónica histórica de las operaciones del ejército de los Andes. B. A.: Imprenta y Librería de Mayo, 1882. 710 pp. 22.5 cm.
[The author quotes (pp. 594-595) fourteen lines of a song which an anonymous soldier of San Martín composed about the Battle of Chacabuco. The very interesting text contains a quatrain and one décima of the four which undoubtedly made up the original composition.]

258. Ezeiza, Gabino. Canciones del payador argentino. B. A., 1896.

259. _____. El cantor argentino. N. p., n. d.

260. _____. Cantores criollos. N. p., n. d.

261. _____. Colección de canciones. N. p., n. d.

262. _____. Mi guitarra. N. p., n. d.

_____. See Contrapunto entre los famosos payadores . . . , entry no. 232.

263. Falcão Espalter, Mario. "La poesía gauchesca." In Reyles, Carlos. Historia sintética de la literatura uruguaya, Vol. I. Montevideo: Alfredo Vila, Editor, 1931. 51 pp. [Each of the eight articles which make up the volume is numbered separately.]
[The author traces the development of the gaucho as a type and also of artistic and semipopular gaucho literature through Delgado, Ascasubi, Lussich, Bermúdez, Regules, El Viejo Pancho (Alonso y Trelles), Alcides de María, Cuadri, and others. Though all this is literary criticism, not scholarly investigation, the essay is packed with information about the gaucho poetry of Argentina and Uruguay and is admirably done. There is, however, only brief and unimportant mention of romances or other narrative poetry. There is more attention to décimas, though not to historical or narrative compositions.]

264. Fernández, Horacio. El poema campesino. B. A., 1918.

265. Ferreyra Videla, Vidal. "Cancioneros populares argentinos." EstBA, No. 360 (agosto, 1941), 51-56; No. 363 (noviembre, 1941), 345-349.
[An unimportant discussion of the spirit of Argentine popular songs, including romances, with a plea that a cancionero be made for the province of Córdoba.]

266. _____. "Del folklore del Río Segundo de Córdoba." EstBA, Año XXXII(1942), Tomo LXVIII:372, pp. 230-234.

267. Finot, Alfonso. Chaullunquía (cristales de hielo); versos del altiplano y la montaña. B. A., 1950. 145 pp.

268. Folklore argentino, proyecto del vocal doctor Juan P. Ramos, resolución del H. Consejo; instrucciones a los maestros. B. A., 1921.

[Contains a section on romances and narrative poetry of other types along with some bibliographical references.]

269. Forte, Vicente. La zamba de Vargas, canto y piano, tomada de los señores D. V. Lombardi y A. Beltrame. B. A., 1923. (Biblioteca de la Sociedad Argentina de Arte Nativo, Núm. 1.)

_____. See Lynch, Ventura R., entry no. 328.

Freitas, Pablo. See Ziegler, Federico, entry no. 453.

270. Furt, Jorge M. Arte gauchesco; motivos de poesía. B. A.: Imprenta y Casa Editorial "Coni," 1924. 203 pp. 17.5 cm.

[A literary evocation of the life and character of the gaucho as revealed in coplas, vidalas, and other types of gaucho popular poetry and song. Many texts are quoted, but their provenience is never indicated. It should be noted, however, that the author states that this is a nonscientific work which he felt impelled to write after finishing his more pretentious Cancionero popular ríoplatense. The work is interesting reading, but of little value to serious study of popular poetry.]

271. _____. "Bibliografía de la música folklórica argentina." BACA, sección Arte argentino, pp. xi-xxviii.

272. _____. Cancionero popular ríoplatense; lírica gauchesca. 2 vols. B. A.: Imprenta y Casa Editora "Coni," 1923, 1925. 22.5 cm.

[In Vol. I, following an excellent detailed introduction (pp. 15-88), there is a large collection of 1366 coplas (pp. 91-442). They are grouped according to subject matter, but none deals with historical or topical themes. There are notes and valuable bibliographical data (pp. 445-466). Vol. II adds over a thousand coplas to the collection (pp. 13-286). Again there are extensive notes (pp. 289-342) and an appendix (pp. 343-374), which is a bibliographical study of gaucho poetry with good treatment of the standard works in the field. A complete index of the coplas contained in Furt's collection follows (pp. 377-407).]

273. _____. Coreografía gauchesca; apuntes para su estudio. B. A.: "Coni," 1927. 78 pp. 23 cm.

[A study of choreography with a few texts of songs which accompany dances. Some of these are in romance meter, though they are not narratives.]

274. _____. Lo gauchesco en "La literatura argentina" de Ricardo Rojas. B. A.: Coni, 1929. 304 pp. 18.5 cm.
[A very harsh criticism of Rojas' book, Los gauchescos. Some of Furt's comments take issue with Rojas' discussion of the romance and its derivatives in gaucho literature.]

275. Gandía, Enrique. Cultura y folklore en América. B. A.: "El Ateneo," 1947. 375 pp. 20 cm.
[A collection of very fine essays about Argentine cultural and literary life. A few of them touch on folklore, most notably Chap. VI, "Música y músicos de los rincones perdidos" (pp. 119-127) and Chap. VII, "Ideas y notas de la música indígena" (pp. 129-148). The latter is a particularly good treatment of pre-Hispanic Indian music, with revealing passages from Fernández de Oviedo about Indian songs which recorded the lives and deeds of leaders and heroes. In other chapters the author occasionally touches on themes related to popular song and poetry: e.g., his very interesting discussion of gaucho poetry (Martín Fierro and other poems) which he considers completely learned and artistic.]

276. _____. Luis de Miranda, primer poeta del Río de la Plata. B. A.: Librería y Editorial "La Facultad," 1936. 161 pp. 20.5 cm.
[A biography of the soldier-priest-poet which includes in the appendix a careful edition of his poem on the suffering of the colony at Buenos Aires in 1537. The composition, which is in the Archivo de Indias in Seville, is entitled Romance, but it is not in romance meter. It is, however, genuinely narrative and belongs in the history of the artistic romance-corrido tradition.]

277. García, Serafín. Panorama de la poesía gauchesca y nativista del Uruguay. Montevideo: Editorial Claridad, 1941. 312 pp. 20.5 cm.
[An anthology which contains a large number of important artistic poems which are related to the romance tradition for reasons of form, narrative purpose, or satirical intent. Most date from the latter part of the nineteenth century to the present, a period not covered by this bibliography, but there is a section on Bartolomé Hidalgo which includes texts of several of his compositions from the early part of the nineteenth century that are not readily available in recent editions. These compositions are: Cielito contra los españoles (p. 17); El gaucho de la Guardia del Monte contesta al manifiesto de Fernando VII y saluda al Conde de Casa-Flores con el siguiente cielito en su idioma (pp. 17-20); Diálogo patriótico interesante entre Jacinto Chano, capataz de una estancia en las islas del Tordillo y el gaucho de la Guardia del Monte (pp. 20-25); Nuevo diálogo patriótico entre Ramón Contreras, gaucho de la Guardia del Monte, y Chano, capataz de una estancia en las Islas

del Tordillo (pp. 25-28); Al triunfo de Lima y el Callo (Cielito patriótico que compuso el gaucho Ramón Contreras) (pp. 29-31); and Relación que hace el gaucho Ramón Contreras a Jacinto Chano de todo lo que vió en las fiestas mayas de Buenos Aires (pp. 31-35). There is also a very useful bibliography which lists numerous editions of Hidalgo's works.]

278. Garzón, Tobías. Diccionario argentino. Barcelona: Imprenta Elzeviriana de Borrás y Mestres, 1910. xv, 519 pp. 26.5 cm.
[A dictionary of Argentinisms with examples to document usage. Most citations are from artistic writers and poets, but some examples are lifted from popular poetry of various kinds.]

279. Gennero, S. "Cantos y danzas de Santiago del Estero." Ensayos (Santiago del Estero), Núm. 6 (1938), 190-192.

280. Giménez Rueda, Julio. "Música y bailes criollos de la Argentina." Música de América (B. A.), II:8 (1921).

Gobernación del Tucumán. Papeles de gobernadores en el siglo XVI. See Levillier, Roberto, ed., entry no. 319.

281. Gómez Carrillo, Manuel. Colección de motivos, danzas y cantos regionales del norte argentino. B. A.: Breyer, 1924 [?].

282. González, Joaquín V. Mis montañas. B. A.: Ediciones Estrada, 1944. xxiv, 264 pp. 19 cm. (Biblioteca de clásicos argentinos, Vol. XVI); also in Vol. XVI of Obras completas de Joaquín V. González. B. A.: Imprenta Mercatali, 1936. Pp. 369-612. (Earlier editions, according to the preface of the 1944 edition, were in 1893, reprinted in 1895; second edition, 1905; and third edition, 1914.)
[Costumbristic sketches about life in La Rioja. Two chapters are of interest: Chap. V, "La vidalita montañesa," describes the singing of vidalitas; Chap. XIII, "La trilla — Los novios," describes the wedding of a local payador, who is described as "el de las décimas llorosas y de los romances melancólicos."]

283. _____. Música y danzas nativas. B. A.: S. Glusberg, 1920. 64 pp. 20 cm.; also in Vol. XX of Obras completas de Joaquín V. González. B. A.: Imprenta Mercatali, 1936. Pp. 21-48.
[Four chapters entitled "Naturaleza y arte," "Música y danzas indígenas," "Evolución de la raza y la expresión musical," and "El alma de la raza" are of interest. The first and last are impressionistic personal notes about music, but the second deals specifically with the yaraví and includes the text of one from Ollantay. Chapter III treats the vidalita and includes two texts, one of them a political song written in opposition to Facundo Quiroga. It costs the author his life when the famous caudillo apprehended him.]

284. Grenón, Pedro. Nuestra primera música instrumental; datos históricos. B. A.: Librería "La Cotizadora Económica" de E. Perrot, 1929. 106 pp. 28 cm.

[Aretz-Thiele (ref. 149) cites this work (pp. 56, 70) for some early information about the singing of coplas, the use of guitars, etc. The references are to the middle and latter part of the seventeenth century.]

285. Grossmann, R. "'Volksliteratur' am Río de la Plata." Philologisch-Philosophische Studien. Festschrift für Eduard Wechssler zum 19. Oktober 1929. Jena and Leipzig: Verlag von Wilhelm Gronau, 1929. Pp. 34-44. (Berliner Beiträge zur Romanischen Philologie, Band 1.)

[The author makes an attempt to distinguish between truly popular literature (coplas, romances, vidalitas, and the like) and the artistic poetry of writers like Echeverría and Hernández. The work is a good general treatment, though the romance receives only the barest passing mention.]

286. Groussac, Paul. "El gaucho; costumbres y creencias populares de las provincias argentinas." In El viaje intelectual; impresiones de naturaleza y arte. Primera serie. Madrid: Librería General de Victoriano Suárez, 1904. Pp. 47-75. (Originally appeared as Popular Customs and Beliefs of the Argentina Provinces. Chicago: Donohue, Henneberry and Co., 1893. 27 pp. 21 cm. A note at the end of the Spanish edition says that the translation first appeared in La Nación [B. A.].)

[Discusses the history, way of life, and character of the gaucho. There is mention of the trovador, the singing of romances, the contrapunto, etc. A few copla texts are given. But the article is no longer of importance and may be ignored.]

———. Popular Customs and Beliefs of the Argentine Provinces. See entry no. 286.

287. Gudiño Kramer, Luis. "Noticias sobre el folklore argentino y sus expresiones en la literatura gauchesca." Ideas (Paraná), julio, 1942, 13-17.

288. Guerrero Cárpena, Ismael. "Santos Vega y Poca Ropa, payadores ríoplatenses." BAAL, XV:57 (octubre-diciembre de 1946), 637-669.

[Seeks to correct many misconceptions that have grown up around the Santos Vega legend with information supplied by the author's father, who knew Poca Ropa. The article is illuminating not only with regard to the two principals but also because it is replete with information about payadas in general.]

———. See Wilkes, Josué Teófilo, entry no. 448.

289. Gutiérrez, Juan María. "La literatura de mayo." In Críticas y narraciones. B. A.: El Ateneo, 1928. Pp. 121-146.

[Contains some comments about cielitos and also some patriotic poetry, semipopular in character, from the period of Argentina's wars for independence.]

290. Hahn, Bolko von. "Argentinische Nationaltänze und Volkslieder." Lasso, VII(1939): 4 (Oktober), 203-209.

Henius, Frank. See entry no. 53.

Hidalgo, Bartolomé. See García, Serafín, entry no. 277.

291. Hidalgo, Félix. Décimas amorosas para cantar en guitarra. N.p., n.d.

292. Hölzer, V. Argentinische Volksdichtung. Ein Beitrag zur hispano-amerikanischen Literaturgeschichte. Bielefeld: Progr. Gymnasium und Realgymnasium, 1912. 32 pp.

293. House, Guillermo [Agustín Guillermo Casá]. Del llano y la montaña; linduras provincianas. B. A., 1922.

[Furt (ref. 272, Vol. I, p. 454) quotes some amorous coplas which he attributes to a newspaper article by Guillermo House, "Antes de irse . . ." (La Nación [B. A.], 5 de marzo de 1922. Then he refers to the above work, meaning apparently that the article also appeared there.]

294. Hudson, W. H. W. H. Hudson's Letters to R. B. Cunninghame Graham. [London]: The Golden Cockerel Press, 1941. 128 pp. 19.5 cm.

[According to Leslie (ref. 1393, p. 290) W. H. Hudson makes reference to the "no me entierren en sagrado" theme of Spanish romance tradition and quotes one text from Argentina (pp. 31-33).]

295. Ibáñez, Avelina M. Unitarios y federales en la literatura argentina. B. A.: Imprenta López, 1933. 595 pp. 25 cm.

[Carrizo (ref. 209, p. 109) says: "En tanto nosotros publicábamos los cancioneros ya citados, la señorita Avelina M. Ibáñez, en su tesis para obtener el doctorado en Filosofía y Letras, titulada Unitarios y federales en la literatura argentina (Buenos Aires, 1933), reunió un centenar de cantares popularizados en el país, de mediados del siglo pasado . . . ."]

296. Ibarguren, Carlos. "El espíritu y la cultura hispánica en la expresión popular argentina." BAAL, VII:28 (octubre-diciembre de 1939), 561-576; also, RAPE, XII(1939):138, pp. 8-12.

[An attempt to show that the spirit of Spain still lives in Argentina in popular poetry. The author cites coplas, romances, etc., and he points out Spanish influences upon Martín Fierro. Though interesting, the article is of negligible importance.]

297. _____. "La música popular." Preludios (B. A.), IV:13-14 (abril-septiembre, 1941), 457-458.

298. Inchauspe, Pedro. "La copla popular." Comentario (B. A.), V(1958):20, pp. 63-67.

299. _____. Voces y costumbres del campo argentino. B. A.: Santiago Rueda, 1942. 265 pp. 22.5 cm.
[The subject of this work is the gaucho, and the method used is to define in dictionary style important words and terminology. In Chap. 9, "Bailes y canciones," there are definitions of several types of popular songs such as the triste, the vidalita, and others. Also, earlier in the work there is a brief description of the payador. Such texts as the author quotes are taken from the collections of Carrizo and others. Nothing he deals with is true narrative poetry.]

300. Jacovella, Bruno. "Una escuela folklórica superada y un 'romancero' en que intenta sobrevivirse." FICU, 2.° trimestre, 1942:6, pp. 57-60.
[A violent attack on Ismael Moya's Romancero. Moya's material, his methods, and, ultimately, his intellectual honesty are questioned.]

_____. See Carrizo, Juan Alfonso, entry no. 217.

301. Jahn-Ruhnau, Romuald. "Das argentinische Volkslied." IAR, III:6 (1937), 174-175.

302. Jijena Sánchez, Rafael. De nuestra poesía tradicional. B. A.: Ediciones Buenos Aires, 1940. 59 pp. 21 cm.
[A brief discussion of popular and semipopular poetry with special attention to the work of José Domingo Díaz, Apolinar Berber, and Juan Alfonso Carrizo.]

303. _____. "Expresiones de folklore argentino, con relación al espíritu tradicional." RDTP, XV(1959): Cuaderno 3°, 259-273.
[Contains several texts of popular poetry and song including some coplas and romances.]

304. _____. Hilo de oro, hilo de plata. B. A.: Ediciones Buenos Aires, 1940. 189 pp. 21 cm.
[A collection of sixty-seven traditional children's songs, some of them romances from Spanish tradition.]

305. _____. La luna y el sol; letras que dicen y cantan los niños cristianos. B. A.: Ediciones Buenos Aires, 1940. 123 pp. 21 cm.
[A collection of children's religious poetry and songs from Latin America and, to a lesser extent, from Spain. Included are the texts of a number of romances such as Camino del Calvario, La Virgen se está peinando, and others. There are also many texts of coplas and a bibliography of works consulted (pp. 121-122).]

306. Jijena Sánchez, Rafael. Vidala; letras para cantar con la caja. B. A.: Talleres Gráficos San Pablo, 1936. 84 pp. 18 cm.
[Chase (ref. 25, p. 52) comments: "With an introduction on the vidala."]

307. Labardén, Manuel José de. "Al Paraná." In El telégrafo mercantil, rural, político, económico e historiógrafo del Río de la Plata (B. A.).
[An oda which Menéndez y Pelayo (ref. 82, Vol. II, p. 325) calls a "romance endecasílabo" and a "Poesía descriptiva americana." The representative strophes which he prints are neo-classical in tone.]

308. Lafone Quevedo, Samuel A. Tesoro de catamarqueñismos. Tercera edición complementada con palabras y modismos usuales en Catamarca por Félix F. Avellaneda. B. A.: Imprenta y Casa Editora "Coni," 1927. 375 pp. 25.5 cm. (The earlier editions of this work appeared in 1895 and 1898.)
[A listing of localisms used in Catamarca preceded by some introductory chapters about the region and its language. The only thing of importance to the study of popular literature is a short section about the vidalita which contains a few texts.]

309. Lanuza, José. Cancionero del tiempo de Rosas. B. A.: Emecé Editores, 1941. 100 pp. 18 cm. (Colección Buen Aire, No. 2.)
[A collection of poems, some popular, some artistic, about the period of Rosas. There are romances, décimas, and octosyllabic quatrains which are like corridos in form and spirit. Some of the texts are lifted from well known collections by Carrizo, Lynch, Furt, et al.]

310. _____. Coplas y cantares argentinos; notas sobre poesía popular. B. A.: Emecé, 1952. 210 pp. 18 cm.
[A commentary on Argentine life, history, and customs based upon all kinds of popular and semiartistic poetry. There are texts of many kinds of coplas and a few fragments of romances, décimas, and other poems. All the texts apparently come from collections by Carrizo and others, though the author rarely cites sources. There are, however, interesting, though superficial and unoriginal, chapters entitled: "Cielito, cielo y más cielo" (pp. 18-24), "Los cielitos de Contreras" (pp. 25-31), "El romance de la muerte de Facundo Quiroga" (pp. 42-50), "Cancionero de pobres" (pp. 66-88), and a subdivision of a chapter, "El romancero se traslada" (pp. 170-176).]

311. Latorre, Mariano. "El huaso y el gaucho en la poesía popular." Atenea, XXXVI:137 (noviembre de 1936), 184-205; 138 (diciembre de 1936), 380-400.
[A formless essay on the huaso of Chile and the gaucho of Argentina as human types. Though the title is misleading, since popular poetry is only one of many sources of information, there is considerable

attention to poetry, some of it popular, more of it the gaucho poetry of Delgado, Ascasubi, Hernández, and others. The author discourses upon the rise of the gaucho as a literary and national hero and examines reasons why the huaso did not develop in a similar way. In the defeat of Taguada in the Contrapunto de Taguada y don Javier de la Rosa he sees symbolized the defeat and decline of the huaso as a type.]

312. Lavalle, Enrique Richard. "Origen de la vidalita." CMS, I:9 (25 de mayo, 1915), 6.
[Chase (ref. 25, p. 53) comments: "Attempts to demonstrate that the vidalita is of indigenous origin."]

Lavín, Carlos. See entry no. 607.

313. Leguizamón, Martiniano. Calandria; costumbres campestres. B. A.: Ivaldi y Checchi, 1898. 281 pp. 17.5 cm.
[Furt (ref. 272, Vol. I, p. 451) quotes a copla taken from the above work.]

314. _____. "Coplas de la tierra; petenera y vidalita." Nos, Año IV, Tomo VI:30 (julio de 1911), 85-95; reprinted in Páginas argentinas; crítica literaria e histórica. B. A.: Librería Nacional, J. Lajouane y Cía., 1911. Pp. 307-330.
[In a volume of verses entitled Tras los mares, the Sevillian poet Juan Antonio Cavestany included a poem which he called Petenera y vidalita. In it he sang of the unity of the Spanish world as evidenced by the similarities between the Andalusian petenera and the Argentine vidalita. Leguizamón objects that the vidalita is of American origin, and in support of his conclusion he sets forth convincing evidence based upon subject matter, strophic form, musical accompaniment, and the like.]

315. _____. El gaucho: su indumentaria, armas, música, cantos y bailes nativos. B. A.: n. p., 1916. 43 pp.; one chapter reprinted as "Música, cantos y bailes nativos." Música de América (B. A.), Año III:1, pp. 10-11.

_____. "Música, cantos y bailes nativos." See entry no. 315.

316. _____. Recuerdos de la tierra. B. A.: F. Lajouane, 1896. xxxvii, 392 pp. 18 cm.
[Furt (ref. 272, Vol. I, p. 450) prints some coplas taken from the above work (pp. 104, 106).]

317. _____. El trovero gauchesco. B. A., 1922.

318. Lehmann-Nitsche, Robert. Collection of phonograph recordings of Argentine popular music made about 1905 by Lehmann-Nitsche and, according to Furt (ref. 272, Vol. I, p. 447), housed in the Psychological Institute of the University of Berlin.

319. Levillier, Roberto, ed. Gobernación del Tucumán. Papeles de gobernadores en el siglo XVI. 2 vols. Madrid: Imprenta de Juan Pueyo, [1920 (according to Palau y Dulcet).]. 24 cm.

[Moya (ref. 353, Vol. I, p. 121) versifies a paragraph from this book to show how prose writers of the period tended to write in octosyllabic romance form. Moya's reference, however, is inaccurate; the passage he quotes is in Vol. II, p. 438, of Levillier's work.]

320. Lizondo Borda, M. "'Vidala' y 'vidalita'." Nos, LII(1926), 143.

[A short article about the origin of the words vidala and vidalita.]

321. Lo que canta el pueblo; cancionero popular. B. A.

[Palau indicates that it was published during the early years of the present century. He comments: "He visto Año VI, número 90, 32 p., gran 8.°"]

322. López Osornio, Mario A. Oro nativo; tradiciones bonaerenses, poesía popular y antología del payador en la pampa. B. A.: "El Ateneo," 1945. 286 pp. 20 cm.

[A very fine study which consists of three parts: I. "Diversiones," II. "La poesía popular en la pampa," III. "Antología del payador." In section II (pp. 49-201) the author discusses practically all types of popular poetry and gives innumerable texts of décimas, cielitos, vidalitas, and the like. He offers only one romance with the explanation that this genre was little cultivated among the gauchos. The very interesting third section contains the works of many Argentine payadores. They are dealt with individually by name, and in most cases some biographical data and some texts are given.]

López y Planes, Vicente F. See Alsina, Adolfo, entry no. 131.

323. Lozano, Pedro. Historia de la conquista del Paraguay, Río de la Plata y Tucumán. 5 vols. B. A.: Casa Editora "Imprenta Popular," 1874-1875. 23 cm.

[With reference to the Indians of the valley of Londres, Lozano says (Vol. I, p. 429) that when they came together to mourn the death of some relative, ". . . al modo que los antiguos romanos, pagaban á las preficas para celebrar con sus forzadas lágrimas las exequias, asi aquí alquilaban plañideras, que entre fingidos suspiros refiriesen las hazañas del difunto, cantándole tristes endechas . . . ."]

Lugones, Leopoldo. See entry no. 405.

324. Lugones, Lorenzo. Recuerdos históricos sobre las campañas del ejército auxiliador del Perú en la guerra de la independencia en esclarecimiento de las memorias póstumas del brigadier general Don José María Paz, por el coronel Don Lorenzo

Lugones. Pub. en Buenos Aires en el año de 1855. 2. ed. B. A.: Imprenta Europea, 1888. 159 pp. 21.5 cm.

[Rojas (ref. 387 [1924 ed.], Vol. VIII, pp. 443-444) quotes a passage from this work about an incident that occurred in the encampment of General Belgrano during Argentina's war for independence and gives some lines of a cielito which the event inspired.]

325. Lullo, Orestes di. Cancionero popular de Santiago del Estero. B. A.: A. Baiocco y Cía., 1940. viii, 524 pp. 27 cm.

[A large collection of popular poetry and songs which contains romances, canciones históricas, coplas, décimas, and other genres along with background material about the area studied. The work follows the procedures employed by Carrizo in his famous cancioneros.]

326. _____. El folklore de Santiago del Estero (material para su estudio y ensayos de interpretación). Tucumán: Imprenta López, Perú 666, Buenos Aires, 1943. 446 pp. 24 cm.

[This extensive work treats almost every aspect of folklore, including popular songs and poetry. Most of the information and texts about these subjects are in the sections entitled "Danzas populares" (pp. 91-111) and "Cantos populares" (pp. 113-157), though there are scattered texts in several other sections. Included are coplas, canciones históricas, décimas, etc. A subheading entitled "Poetas y cantores populares de Santiago del Estero" (pp. 122-136) is of particular interest.]

327. _____. "Villancicos recogidos en La Rioja y Santiago del Estero." FICU, No. 2 (diciembre, 1940), 19-20.

328. Lynch, Ventura R. Cancionero bonaerense. B. A.: Imprenta de la Universidad, 1925. xiv, 64 pp. 29 cm.

[A re-editing of part of Lynch's book, La provincia de Buenos Aires hasta la definición de la cuestión capital de la república (B. A., 1883). It is a study of gaucho folklore, including some historical narratives in verse which belong to the romance-corrido tradition. This new edition contains an "Estudio preliminar" by Vicente Forte which deals with the folk songs of Buenos Aires.]

329. _____. Folklore bonaerense. B. A.: Lajouane, 1953. 92 pp. 18 cm.

[A popularization of Lynch's Cancionero bonaerense. Some changes have been made in the interest of clarity and there are some omissions.]

330. Machado, José E. El gaucho y el llanero. Caracas: Tip. Vargas, 1926. 30 pp. 20 cm.

[An essay on the life of the gaucho and the llanero, whom Machado considers kindred types. Almost all phases of their lives are touched upon, including their songs and manner of singing porfías or contrapuntos. But the whole work is superficial and contributes nothing not already known to any investigator who is even vaguely familiar with the subject.]

331. Madueño, Raúl R. El árbol en el cancionero popular argentino. B. A.: Ed. del autor, 1942. 16 pp.

332. ———. "Valores plásticos en la poesía popular norteña." SRCS, IV(1943):15-16, pp. 610-618.

333. María, Alcides de. Cantos tradicionales. B. A., 1920.

334. Mariluz Urquijo, J. M. "Aires populares en la noche salteña." Historia, revista trimestral de historia argentina, americana y española (B. A.), Núm. 2 (1955), 93-96.
[Described as follows (Revista de historia de América [México, D. F.], No. 43 [junio de 1957], p. 274): "Artículo basado en las diligencias practicadas en 1805 por el alcalde de primer voto de Salta, Manuel Antonio de Tejada, en averiguación de ciertos excesos, cometidos con motivo de unas reñidas elecciones municipales. Como dice el autor, estos documentos 'nos permiten asomarnos a la vida nocturna — familiar y alegre — de la ciudad norteña . . . Conocemos así el nombre de algunos de sus músicos populares y el título de las canciones en boga, dejando a los folkloristas la tarea de precisar con exactitud la procedencia de éstas o la de clasificar las influencias exteriores reflejadas en el repertorio de los músicos criollos.'"]

335. Masciopinto, F. Adolfo. "El ideario de los hombres de mayo en el cancionero popular." UnivSF, Núm. 23 (verano-otoño, 1950), 87-125.
[An excellent article which shows in the poetry of the time the spirit of the epoch of Argentine independence. Not many of the poems, except for those of Pantaleón Rivarola, are true romances, and almost all are semipopular (some are, in reality, pasquines). But all are of interest.]

336. Massini Ezcurra, José María. El cancionero argentino. Santa Fe: Ed. del autor, 1957.
[Said to be a study of El cancionero argentino published by José Antonio Wilde between 1837 and 1838.]

337. ———. "El cancionero argentino: Permanece desconocida en su mayor parte la recopilación efectuada por José Antonio Wilde en 1837 y 1838." UnivSF, Núm. 33 (1956), 95-120.
[This may be the same study as ref. 336.]

338. Maziel, Juan Baltasar. "Romance en que canta un guaso en estilo campestre los triunfos del Excmo. señor Don Pedro de

Ceballos." In Barreda, Ernesto María. Nuestro parnaso. 4 vols. B. A.: J. L. Dasso y Cía., [1914]. Pp. 21-22.
[An early Argentine romance written about 1777 to honor the Viceroy. Its first strophe as quoted by Morales (ref. 346, p. 27) sounds much like popular narrative poems: "Aquí me pongo a cantar." Morales seems to indicate that the complete text appears in Barreda's book as indicated above. Puig (ref. 371, Vol. I, p. 49) says that the original text is to be found in the Colección Segurola of the Biblioteca Nacional.]

339. Medina, José Toribio. Historia y bibliografía de la imprenta en el antiguo Vireinato del Río de la Plata; historia y bibliografía de la imprenta en Buenos Aires. La Plata: Taller de Publicaciones del Museo de La Plata, 1892. 4 parts in 1 vol. 46 cm.
[Contains the texts of Pantaleón Rivarola's Romance heroico . . . de la gloriosa reconquista (Part III, pp. 224-231) and his Romance de la gloriosa defensa (Part III, pp. 235-247). Also, Medina gives bibliographical notice of the Adiciones y correcciones to the Romance heroico.]

Mendoza, Vicente T. "La canción del novio desairado." See entry no. 1445.

340. Miranda, Manuel. Contrapunto entre un oriental y un argentino. Rosario, 1914.

341. Miranda de Villafañe, Luis de. Romance; versiones paleográfica y moderna, con noticia preliminar de José Torre Revello. B. A.: Coni, 1952. 31 pp. facsimile. 23 cm. (Colección de textos críticos americanos, 2.)

_____. See Morla Vicuña, Carlos, entry no. 351.

342. Moglia, Raúl. "La poesía tradicional en la Argentina." Nos, Año XX, Vol. LIII:206 (julio, 1926), 421-422.
[A short note on some Spanish antecedents of a strophe of a popular copla sung in Argentina.]

343. _____. "Romances porteños." Revista del profesorado (B. A.), Nos. 18, 19, 20, 21, 22, and 24.

344. Molins, W. Jaime. "Nuestra música aborigen, payador o pallador." Música de América (B. A.), I (julio, 1920), 2 pp.

345. Monguió, Luis. "Un rastro del romance de Fontefrida en la poesía gauchesca." RevIb, X:20 (marzo de 1946), 283-285; reprinted in Estudios sobre literatura hispanoamericana y española. México: Ediciones de Andrea, 1958. Pp. 58-61.
[The author believes that Fontefrida inspired some lines which he quotes from Bartolomé Hidalgo's Diálogo entre Jacinto Chano . . . y el gaucho de la Guardia del Monte. He is unable to determine,

however, whether the romance exists in popular Argentina tradition or whether Delgado learned it from a printed source.]

346. Morales, Ernesto. Lírica popular ríoplatense; antología gaucha. B. A.: El Ateneo, 1927. 244 pp. 19 cm.
[A collection of poetry including popular coplas, along with a cielito and a vidalita. The body of the work, however, is made up of selections from Hidalgo, Ascasubi, El Viejo Pancho, and others.]

347. _____. Los niños y la poesía en América. Santiago de Chile: Ediciones Ercilla, 1936. 152 pp. 22 cm.
[The Library of Congress card reads: "Contents. — Los niños. — Poesía en América. — Literatura folklórica."]

348. _____. Niños y maestros. B. A.: "El Ateneo," 1939. 180 pp. 20.5 cm.
[Chase (ref. 25, p. 53) comments: "Includes: Romances, canciones y rondas de niños."]

349. _____. El sentimiento popular en la literatura argentina. B. A.: "El Ateneo," 1926. xii, 256 pp. 18 cm.
[In the first portion of his work entitled "Poesía" the author offers a rapid survey of the role of popular songs like the cielos, vidalas, and romances in Argentine poetry. He gives a number of fragmentary texts by way of illustration, though he does not indicate their sources.]

350. Moreno, J. El cancionero mendocino (álbum de canciones regionales para canto y piano). Mendoza: J. Peuser, 1936. 49 pp.

351. Morla Vicuña, Carlos. Estudio histórico sobre el descubrimiento y conquista de la Patagonia y de la Tierra del Fuego. Leipzig: F. A. Brockhaus, 1903. v, 304, 223 pp. 23.5 cm.
[Contains (pp. 274-275) a narrative poem which, notwithstanding Morla Vicuña's description of it as a romance, is not of that genre. It concerns the expedition of Pedro de Mendoza into the area of the Río de la Plata in 1535-1536 and is the work of Luis de Miranda.]

352. Moya, Ismael. Didáctica del folklore. B. A.: "El Ateneo," 1948. 294 pp. 20.5 cm.
[A general treatise on folklore designed as a guide for the uninitiated as well as for the more advanced investigator. Among many other things there is a section entitled "Las formas poéticas del folklore" (pp. 120-135) wherein the author deals with the romance, the corrido, the décima, and other popular forms. In addition to romances of Spanish origin, he describes native types of romances known as romances históricos criollos and corridos criollos. He gives the text of a song about one Tomás Paredes as an example of the latter. It is very similar to the corridos of Mexico. Also, there are some comments on the role of popular singers as purveyors of history (pp. 151 ff.). In a bibliography at the end of the work there is an

interesting list of traditional Spanish romances which schoolteachers discovered in Argentina in a single year, 1921.]

353. _____. Romancero. 2 vols. B. A.: Imprenta de la Universidad, 1941. 22 cm.

[Vol. I of this important work includes a very comprehensive study of the romance in America with particular consideration of the various types to be found in Argentina and of the role they play in Argentine tradition. The last section, "Romances tradicionales de la Argentina," contains texts of numerous versions of Spanish romances. Vol. II contains many more texts of romances and other types of popular poetry. Some of the compositions are from Spanish tradition; some are of Argentine origin.]

354. Música argentina nativa; cantares y canciones danzadas. B. A.: Consejo Nacional de Educación, Comisión de Folklore y Nativismo, 1947.

355. Nichols, Madaline W. "The Argentine Gaucho." BPAU, LXXV:5 (May, 1941), 271-275.

[A popularization of the author's more profound investigations of the gaucho. Included are a few coplas translated into English. There is no mention of true narrative poetry.]

356. _____. "Der Gaucho als literarische Figur: Eine bibliographische Studie." IAA, XII:1 (April, 1939), 22-43.

[A bibliography of 806 entries divided into three large groupings: I. Bibliographisches Material, II. Kritische Werke, III. Gaucholiteratur. These sections are in turn divided into subgroups dealing with gaucho poetry, gaucho theater, the gaucho novel, etc. The bibliography is not annotated and listings are not detailed (publisher, number of pages, etc. are lacking). It is, however, a very useful list of source materials.]

357. _____. The Gaucho, Cattle Hunter, Cavalryman, Ideal of Romance. Durham, North Carolina: Duke University Press, 1942. ix, 152 pp. 23 cm. (Series I, Vol. 7, of Interamerican Bibliographical and Library Association Publications.); translated as El gaucho, el cazador de ganado, el jinete, un ideal de novela. B. A.: Peuser, 1953. 235 pp. 28 cm.

[A very fine brief study of the gaucho, his history, his way of life, his role in Argentine life, etc. In Chap. VIII, "The Gaucho of Romance," there is passing mention of some gaucho folklore, including a few coplas. The main importance of the work, however, lies in its fine bibliography (pp. 65-144 of the edition in English). It contains 1431 entries classified under several headings to make for easy consultation. Almost all listings include brief annotation.]

358. Obligado, Pastor S. Tradiciones de Buenos Aires.
10 [i.e., 9] séries [i.e., vols.]. B. A.: several publishers, 1888-1920. 25.5 cm. (The titles vary: Séries I-V [II was never published] are called Tradiciones de Buenos Aires; Séries VI, VIII, IX, and X are called Tradiciones argentinas; and Série VII is called Tradiciones y recuerdos.); also an abbreviated edition, Tradiciones argentinas. Selección y estudio preliminar de Antonio Pagés Larraya. B. A.: Librería Hachette, 1956.
 [A collection of sketches obviously written under the influence of Ricardo Palma. In all volumes there are occasional fragments of popular poetry, mostly coplas. Some of them are political pasquines. In Vol. VIII there is a fragment of a popular romance (p. 64).]

Ocampo, Joseph Gabriel. See Breve recuerdo del formidable ataque, entry no. 174.

359. Onís, Federico de. "El 'Martín Fierro' y la poesía tradicional." In Homenaje ofrecido a Menéndez Pidal, Vol. II. Madrid: Librería y Casa Editorial Hernando, 1925. Pp. 403-416.
 [A study of the popular and learned elements in Martín Fierro with some interesting comments on the payadores. The author concludes that, despite its being the work of an individual, José Hernández, the poem is extremely popular in inspiration, vocabulary, sources, etc.]

360. d'Orbigny, Alcide Dessalines. Voyage pittoresque dans les deux Amériques, résumé général de tous les voyages de Colomb, Las-Casas, Oviedo . . . Humboldt . . . Franklin . . . etc., par les rédacteurs du Voyage pittoresque autour du monde; publié sous la direction de m. Alcide d'Orbigny . . . Paris: L. Tenré, 1836. xvi, 568 pp. 27.5 cm.
 [Furt (ref. 272, Vol. II, p. 347) quotes a reference to the singing of "romances" called "yaravis" by the gauchos. It is taken from p. 249 of the above work.]

361. Page, Frederick Mann. Los payadores gauchos. The Descendants of the Juglares of Old Spain in La Plata; A Contribution to the Folk-lore and Languages of the Argentine Gaucho. Darmstadt: G. Otto, 1897. 88 pp. 23.5 cm.
 [Treats the general history of the romance in Spain and studies Santos Vega, Martín Fierro, and other gaucho poems as evidence of the development of the romance spirit among the payadores.]

362. Palma, Athos. Ocho canciones salteñas. [B. A. (?)]: G. Ricordi y Cía., n.d.

363. Pampa Viejo, Don. Fogón de las tradiciones. 2 vols. 5.ª ed. of Vol. I; 2.ª ed. of Vol. II. B. A.: Editorial Bell, 1945. 19 cm. and 20 cm.
 [A curious hodgepodge of popular and semipopular literature of all kinds: anecdotes, sketches, poetry, riddles, etc. Most of it is

semilearned, but some, as in the case of numerous coplas, is truly popular. Besides coplas, there are some décimas, romances, and the like; but none of these latter appears to be genuine traditional poetry, though many compositions are without doubt widely known. "Fogón de las tradiciones" is a regular section of the periodical Pampa argentina (B. A.).]

364. Peña, Enrique. El inca Bohorquez. B. A., 1921.
[Aretz-Thiele (ref. 149, pp. 56-57) quotes from this work some coplas (as she calls them, though literarily they are a romance) which were sung in 1657.]

365. Pereda Valdés, Ildefonso. Cancionero popular uruguayo (materiales recogidos en los departamentos de Montevideo, Cerro Largo, Durazno, Canelones y Lavalleja, y ensayo de interpretación de los mismos con una introducción al estudio de la ciencia folklórica). Montevideo: Editorial Florensa y Lafon, 1947. 202 pp. 23.5 cm.
[After some introductory chapters, the author offers several interesting sections: "Cancionero de Cerro Largo" (pp. 41-47); "Cancionero del Río Negro" (pp. 49-55), both of which are collections of coplas; "Versos populares" (pp. 57-68), which includes some poems inspired by historical events, one or two of them being close to the corrido tradition; and "Romances" (pp. 69-74), which contains Uruguayan versions of several Spanish romances (Delgadina, Las señas del marido, and others).]

366. _____. Raza negra; cancionero afro-montevideano. Montevideo: Edición del periódico negro La Vanguardia, 1929. 79 pp. 19 cm.

367. Pirotto, Armando D. Silva de varios romances. Montevideo: Jerónimo Sureda, 1935. 200 pp. 18 cm.
[A collection of Spanish romances. However, in the appendix, "Los romances españoles en el Río de la Plata" (pp. 193-198), there are three romances from Argentina: Santa Catalina, Delgadina, and Romance de don Francisco (a version of La esposa infiel). The author gives no data about them or their sources.]

368. Podestá, Antonio G. Música criolla: gato, tango, minué, hueya, adagio, estilo, triste, pericón. B. A., 1900.
[Furt (ref. 272, Vol. II, pp. 362-363) indicates that this work first appeared as part of Abdón Arosteguy's Ensayos dramáticos in 1896.]

369. Podestá, José J. Canciones populares del Gran Pepino 88. N. p., n. d.

370. Pradere, Juan A. Juan Manuel de Rosas; su iconografía. B. A.: J. Mendesky e Hijo, 1914. 271 pp. 31.5 cm.
[Contains the well known cielito on the death of Dorrego, a poem of popular flavor written in corrido form. The volume also contains

other poems of a political nature, though they are not romances or corridos.]

371. Puig, Juan de la C. Antología de poetas argentinos. 10 vols. B. A.: M. Biedma é Hijo, 1910. 22.5 cm.
[Vol. I contains Pantaleón Rivarola's Romance heroico . . . de la gloriosa conquista and his Romance de la gloriosa defensa (pp. 83-165); also the romance entitled Canta un guaso en estilo campestre, which Puig attributes to Baltasar Maziel.]

372. Quesada, Ernesto. La época de Rosas. B. A.: Casa Jacobo Peuser Ltda., 1923. xcvii, 240 pp. 27 cm. (Publicaciones del Instituto de Investigaciones Históricas, No. XVIII.); also, Nueva edición corregida y aumenta. B. A.: Artes y Letras Editorial, 1926. 240 pp. 19.5 cm.
[Wilkes (ref. 444, p. 298) indicates that on p. 12 there is something about the "contenido espiritual de algunas de nuestras músicas."]

373. Quesada, V. G. "El harpa en Santiago del Estero (costumbres argentinas)." RevP, V(1861), 105; also RevS, I, 154 ff.

374. Quiroga, Adán. El cantar de las montañas. Almanaque de Fra Diávolo. Catamarca, 1891.

375. _____. "El folk-lore argentino." RABA, VII:9 (junio, 1918), 70-91.
[Chase (ref. 25, p. 53) comments: "Music, dance, song and musical instruments, pp. 81-82."]

376. _____. "Folklore calchaquí." RUBA, marzo, 1929.

377. Quiroga, Carlos B. Alma popular. B. A.: "Buenos Aires", Cooperativa Editorial Limitada, 1924. 222 pp. 19 cm.
[A source of many texts of coplas with consideration of the psychology of the people of Catamarca as revealed in these songs. There is also one composition entitled Aventuras de un jilguero, which is a corrido in form, though not so named.]

378. _____. "El carnaval de Belén." Nos, Año XIII, Tomo XXXIII:125 (octubre de 1919), 219-239.
[A description of the celebration of Carnival in Belén. Many popular coplas are quoted textually. This sketch is reprinted in Cerro nativo (see the reference which follows).]

379. _____. Cerro nativo; el hombre y la naturaleza (espíritu de la región). B. A.: Ediciones de "Nuestra América," 1924. 254 pp. 19 cm.; also, Tercera edición definitivamente corregida por el autor. B. A.: Talleres Gráficos Argentinos L. J. Rosso, 1934. 278 pp. 18.5 cm. (In this third edition the author indicates that the first edition appeared in 1921.)
[In several places there are texts of popular corridos, especially in

a sketch entitled "El carnaval de Belén" (pp. 85-118 [pp. 82-119 of the 1934 ed.]).]

    Rael, Juan B. "Un cantar hallado en Tucumán." See entry no. 1560.

380. Ramos, Juan P. "Das argentinische Volkslied." Ph, VII(1921), 8-29.

_____. See Folklore argentino, entry no. 268.

381. Recuerdos de la patria. Paraná, 1902-1903.
[Furt (ref. 272, Vol. II, p. 313) says that this work contains some coplas in Quichua. The examples he gives in both Quechua and Spanish show that they come from Hispanic tradition.]

    Reyles, Carlos. See Falcão Espalter, Mario, entry no. 263.

382. Rivarola, Pantaleón. La gloriosa defensa de la cuidad de Buenos-Ayres, capital del Vireynato del Río de la Plata: Verificada del 2 al 5 de julio de 1807. Brevemente delineada en verso suelto, con notas: Por un fiel vasallo de S. M. y amante de la patria . . . . Buenos Aires, En la Real Imprenta de los Niños Expósitos, año de 1807.
[Medina (ref. 339, p. 235) prints the text of this poem. Menéndez y Pelayo (ref. 82, Vol. II, p. 330) says: "Son nuevos romances de ciego, compuestos por el doctor Rivarola."]

383. _____. Romance heróyco, en que se hace relacion circunstanciada de la gloriosa reconquista de la ciudad de Buenos Ayres, capital del vireynato del Rio de la Plata, verificada el dia 12 de agosto de 1806, por un fiel vasallo de S. M. y amante de la Patria, quien lo dedica y ofrece al muy noble y leal cabildo y Regimiento de esta ciudad. Impreso en los reales talleres de la Casa de Expósitos. 39 pp. 20.5 cm.; Adiciones y correcciones a la dedicatoria que el autor del Romance Heroyco sobre la reconquista de Buenos-Ayres hizo al M. I. Cabildo de Buenos Aires. En la Imprenta de los Niños Expósitos, Año, 1807. 8 pp.; according to Medina (ref. p. 234) the Romance and the Adiciones were reprinted: Romance heroyco en que se hace relacion circunstanciada de la gloriosa reconquista de la ciudad de Buenos Ayres capital del Rio de la Plata, verificada el dia 12 de Agosto de 1806. Por un fiel vasallo de S. M. y amante de la patria. Impreso en Buenos Aires y ahora nuevamente reimpreso en Lima con algunas notaciones. MDCCCVIII, Acosta de D. Guillermo del Río.
[Menéndez y Pelayo (ref. 82, Vol. II, p. 330) comments upon the Adiciones y correcciones: "Versa principalmente sobre los errores históricos del romance, y se atribuye a D. José Joaquín de Araujo. Romance y adiciones fueron reimpresos en Lima, al año siguiente 1808."]

Rivarola, Pantaleón. See Puig, Juan de la C., entry no. 371.

384. Rodríguez, Alberto. Cancionero cuyano; canciones y danzas tradicionales. B. A.: Numen, 1938. 180 pp.

[A collection of popular songs and dances with a study of the same. Though it does not treat romances or other narrative forms, a discussion of folk singers and their art is of interest.]

385. Rodríguez Molas, Ricardo. La primitiva poesía gauchesca anterior a Bartolomé Hidalgo. B. A., 1958. 29 pp. 23 cm.

386. Rojas, Ricardo. "Los archivos de provincia." Prologue of Vol. I of Archivo capitular de Jujuy. B. A.: Imprenta de Coni Hermanos, 1913. Pp. vii-lxxxi.

[Rojas publishes a romance (pp. lxxix-lxxx) of which he says: "La [poesía] encontré humildemente escondida en el margen de un legajo así caratulado: 'n° 1916, f. 36. C. C. Mandamiento de prisión y embargo de bienes contra Andrés (Cacique de Humahuaca) y Alonso Chorro, por apalear unas muchachas.' Es us legajo de 1630, pero la letra del romance, sobre la vuelta en blanco de la página 9, paréceme posterior, — quizá de fines del siglo XVII. Narra la fiera historia de una Francesca jujeña. El romance podría titularse: La piedad de un vengador, para avenirse á su asunto calderoniano." The composition is a genuine romance, probably of peninsular origin.]

387. _____. La literatura argentina; ensayo filosófico sobre la evolución de la cultura en el Plata. 4 vols. B. A.: Imprenta de Coni Hermanos, 1917-1922. 22.5 cm. (Vol. I, Los gauchescos; Vol. II, Los coloniales; Vol. III, Los proscriptos; Vol. IV, Los modernos.); also, Vols. VIII-XV of Obras de Ricardo Rojas. B. A.: Librería "La Facultad", J. Roldán y Cía., 1924-1925. 19.5 cm. (Vols. VIII-IX, Los gauchescos; Vols. X-XI, Los coloniales; Vols. XII-XIII, Los proscriptos; Vols. XIV-XV, Los modernos.); also, Historia de la literatura argentina. Vols. I-VIII of Obras completas. B. A.: Editorial Losada, 1948. 22 cm. (Vols. I-II, Los gauchescos; Vols. III-IV, Los coloniales; Vols. V-VI, Los proscriptos; Vols. VII-VIII, Los modernos.)

[Los gauchescos is a comprehensive study of gaucho literature, both popular and artistic. Los coloniales deals with learned literature, but two chapters are of interest: Chap. XII, "Cancionero de las invasiones inglesas," which deals with poems inspired by historical events, and Chap. XIV, "Cantos de la epopeya americana." Los proscriptos, which deals with the period of independence, the epoch of Rosas, and the years between the fall of Rosas and 1880, contains nothing about popular literature. Los modernos, which covers the period after 1880, contains nothing about true popular poetry, but it does include treatment of a few artistic poets who cultivated the romance or who sought inspiration in popular themes.]

388. _____. El país de la selva. Paris: Garnier Hermanos, 1907. xii, 268 pp. 18 cm.; also, B. A.: Librería "La Facultad," J. Roldán y C.ª, 1925. xii, 284 pp. 19.5 cm.

[The book is rich in descriptions of fiestas, dances, and other occasions where popular songs are sung in the northern part of Argentina. Also, there is attention to the singers of such compositions. Of particular interest are Chapter V, "Las fiestas," and Chapter VII, "El trovador," but there is material scattered through other parts of the book as well. Some of the texts given are coplas, some are historical songs which resemble corridos, some are yaravíes, and some are of other genres.]

_____. See Tejeda, Luis de, entry no. 409.

389. Rojas Paz, Pablo. "El arte popular." Azul (República Argentina), Año I:4 (mayo de 1930), 113-127.

[An excellent subjective essay on the nature of popular art with almost exclusive reference to popular songs. The essayist analyzes the role of popular songs and singers in society and the interrelationship between popular and learned art. He is particularly concerned with the importance of popular songs as a reflection of the history of a people.]

Román, Marcelino. See entry no. 102.

Romance que canta un guaso en estilo campestre los triunfos del Excmo. señor Don Pedro de Ceballos. See Maziel, Juan Baltasar, entry no. 338.

390. Rosemberg, Tobías. El alma de la montaña; folklore del Aconquija. Edición anotada. B. A.: Editorial Raigal, 1953. 129 pp. 20.5 cm.

[Among many other folklore materials the author gives a number of copla texts and one romance about the sailor who refuses to sell his soul to the devil for three ships laden with gold and silver.]

391. Sánchez, Ricardo. "El payador, sus afinidades con el milonguero." El Tiempo, 6 de febrero, 1896.

392. Sandoval de Estigarribia, María Jerónima. "Literatura popular guaraní de Corrientes." BFM, VI:43-44-45 (marzo, junio y setiembre de 1950), 142-183.

[An extremely interesting collection of poems and songs gathered from oral tradition. Many are Spanish coplas or décimas which have been translated totally or in part into Guaraní. Though none of the compositions are true romances, the collection is of value to the study of the relationship between Spanish and Indian folklore.]

393. Sarmiento, Domingo Faustino. Facundo; edición crítica y documentada. La Plata: Universidad Nacional de la Plata, 1938. xxiv, 474 pp. 24 cm. (Biblioteca de autores nacionales y extranjeros

referente a la República Argentina, Vol. I.) [There are, of course, innumerable editions of this classic work.]
[Includes a section entitled "El cantor" (pp. 60-63) which treats the gaucho as a folk singer. Also, there is a discussion of the types of gaucho poetry (pp. 51-53).]

394. Sarmiento, Manuel. "Folklore del altiplano de Jujuy." BATF, Año II, Vol. I(1951):15-16, pp. 145-164.
[Boggs (ref. 13 [1951], p. 25) says: "Describes the region, people, dwelling, food, occupations, coca vice, customs, beliefs, Carnival songs (words only), festivals of St. John, Santiago, All Saints, rodeos, vocabulary."]

395. Schaeffer Gallo, Carlos. "La leyenda del Kacuy, poema trágico en tres actos y en prosa." Nos, Año VIII, Vol. XIV:60 (abril de 1914), 34-80.
[The dramatist incorporates a number of popular coplas into his play.]

396. Schianca, Arturo C. Historia de la música argentina, origen y características. B. A.: Establecimiento Gráfico Argentino, n.d. 202 pp. 22 cm.
[Impressionistic and unscholarly, this work is concerned exclusively with popular dances and songs. After tracing briefly the history of music in Argentina down to the period of independence, the author offers brief sections on such dances as the gato, the cielo, the cuando, and the zamba and on such songs as the décima, the triste, and the vidalita. The latter part of the volume contains some musical transcriptions and very brief consideration of gaucho literature. There is no mention of romances and the décimas treated are not narratives. There are, however, a few coplas scattered through the work.]

397. Silva Valdés, Fernán. "El canto platense." PrBA, 26 de agosto, 1934.

398. _____. "Consideraciones sobre el canto popular." PrBA, 22 de agosto, 1937.

399. _____. "Payadores." PrBA, 2 de agosto, 1936.

400. Sordelli, V. O. " 'Mis arreos son las armas'." Nac, 23 de marzo, 1941.
[The bibliography of RHM, VIII(1942), contains a note: "Reminiscencia poética entre un pasaje del Martín Fierro y el romance llamado de La constancia."]

401. Sperotti Piñero, Emma Susana. "La poesía gauchesca: Su parentesco con la poesía popular mexicana." Letras potosinas (San Luis Potosí, México), XVI(1958):128-129.

402. Suriguez y Acha, Carlos. En la pampa. B. A.-Milan, 1908.
[Furt (ref. 272, Vol. I, p. 455) quotes a copla taken from this source.]

403. Talamón, Gastón O. "Acerca de la canción argentina." Nos, Año XX, Vol. LIII:206 (julio, 1926), 381-391.
[Refutation of an article by Carlos Vega with the same title (see entry no. 418) in which the latter doubts the existence of a unique, regional Argentine art. To prove the contrary, Talamón cites the tango (Vega had called it "nuestro pobre tango") which he considers a unique product of Argentine culture. In addition, he mentions zambas, tristes, vidalitas, and gatos as other manifestations of a truly Argentine national art.]

404. _____. "El cancionero popular y la música culta argentina." Azul, Año II:8 (enero-febrero, 1931), 15-25.
[The author calls for breaking down the separation which the Renaissance brought between the literature, art, music, etc. of the elite and those of the masses. He notes the richness of Argentine popular traditions, but in his discussion he deals almost exclusively with popular dances, and there is only the barest mention of poetry and songs. There is nothing about romances, corridos, or other narrative compositions.]

405. _____. "Leopoldo Lugones y el 'folklorismo'." Azul, Año II:10 (junio, 1931), 87-94.
[Takes issue with an article of Leopoldo Lugones that appeared in La Nación in which doubt is expressed about the value of folklore as a source of inspiration for a composer of artistic music. There is nothing about romances, corridos, or other narratives.]

406. _____. "Por el folklore." Nos, Año X, Vol. XIII:89 (septiembre, 1916), 290-297.
[An appeal to Argentines to study their folk music as a patriotic duty.]

407. A Tale of Tucumán. London, 1831.
[Rojas (ref. 387 [1924 ed.], Vol. VIII, pp. 439-440) indicates that Zeballos (see ref. 451) prints some coplas found in English translation in the above work. They were gathered and translated by English prisoners taken during the English invasions of Argentina and interned in the south of that country.]

408. Tejeda, Luis José de. Coronas líricas, prosa y verso. Córdoba: Imprenta de Bautista Cubas, 1917. lv, 340 pp. 26 cm.
[Among the compositions contained herein are two romances of Tejeda: En la jura de la Inmaculada Concepción (pp. 1-5) and Romance sobre su vida (pp. 20-57).]

409. Tejeda, Luis José de. El peregrino en Babilonia; con un estudio por Ricardo Rojas. B. A., 1916. vi, 287 pp. 18.5 cm. (Biblioteca Argentina, Vol. X.)

[An autobiographical poem in romance meter by Tejeda, whom Ricardo Rojas calls Argentina's first poet.]

410. Telégrafo mercantil rural, político-económico, e historiógrafo del Río de la Plata, 1801-1802. Vols. VI and VII of Biblioteca de la Junta de Historia y Numismática Americana. B. A., 1914. 22.5 cm.

[Contains several romances and romancillos. None is popular, though some are relatively simple in style for the period at which they appeared. From Vol. VI see: from Tomo I of El Telégrafo, Conversata entre un Palangana y un Estudiante (pp. 228-231), and from Tomo II of El Telégrafo, El águila, el león y el cordero (p. 129), El comerciante y la cotorra (pp. 143-144), Historia del doctor Buñuelos, escrita en francés por Mr. Boudein y traducida al Castellano por D. Sancho Rabioles (pp. 218-223), and Los papagayos y la lechuza (pp. 249-251). From Vol. VII see: from Tomo III of El Telégrafo, Al buen gusto (pp. 35-36), Satirilla festiva (pp. 39-40), Satirilla festiva, por D. Narciso Fellobio Canton, Filosofo indiferente (pp. 54-55); from Tomo V of El Telégrafo, El indio, el cisne y el cuervo (p. 7). El Telégrafo also contains other poems of a topical nature, though they are not romances.]

411. Terrera, Guillermo Alfredo. Primer cancionero popular de Córdoba; investigación científica folklórica. Córdoba: Imprenta de la Universidad, 1948. 475 pp. 29 cm.

[A long study of the popular songs of Córdoba. In a section of romances the author lists some that are of interest: Don Gato, La esposa infiel, and others. Also, there is a short section devoted to versos históricos. Despite the author's insistence on the "scientific" character of his work, it is far from being so.]

412. Tiscornia, Eleuterio. Martín Fierro. B. A.: Imprenta y Casa Editora "Coni," 1925. xx, 501 pp. 26 cm.

[A masterful critical edition of the poem with numerous notes which link it to earlier works of gaucho literature and to the poetry of oral tradition. There is a bibliography and a vocabulary.]

―――――. See entry no. 901.

413. Torre Revello, José. "El clérigo Luis de Miranda de Villafañe; su romance sobre la conquista y población de Buenos Aires." PrBA, 26 de enero, 1936, suplemento dominical.

414. ―――――. "Los orígenes de la danza, la canción y la música populares argentinas." CV, No. 99 (noviembre-diciembre, 1929),

310-324. (This must be a reprint of the author's book with the same title: Sevilla: Bergali, 1926. 15 pp.)

[A cursory examination of popular songs and dances, including the romances sung by the conquerors.]

_____. See Miranda de Villafañe, Luis de, entry no. 341.

415. Trejo Lerdo y Tejada, Carlos. El folklore argentino. México, D. F.: Editorial "Cultura," 1941. 62 pp. 18 cm.

[Chase (ref. 25, p. 54) comments: "A rather rambling essay on Argentine folk songs and dances."]

416. Tuñón, Fernando. "Don Máximo Herrera a los 102 años, fue 'glorificado' por sus amigos." PBT [title of a review] (B. A.), 19 de septiembre de 1952.

[Román (ref. 102, p. 150) indicates that this article deals with a popular singer who later died in 1953 at the age of 103.]

417. Unamuno, Miguel de. "La literatura gauchesca." La ilustración española y americana (Madrid). Año XLIII:XXVII (22 de julio de 1899), pp. 44, 46.

[A short but very penetrating commentary on gaucho literature and its relationship to popular poetry. Unamuno expresses great admiration for several of the gaucho poems like Martín Fierro and declares that Spanish American poets should seek inspiration in the popular poetry of their area.]

418. Vega, Carlos. "Acerca de la canción argentina." Nos, Año XX, Vol. LIII:204 (mayo, 1926), 84-90.

[The author develops the thesis that regionalism in songs and in art in general should not be sought in a country like Argentina where the influx of immigrants, along with other influences, has prevented the development of cultural unity. A very challenging article, its thesis is applicable to romances and other genres of popular poetry, though the author is not writing specifically about them.]

419. _____. "Algo más sobre la canción argentina." Nos, Año XX, Vol. LIV:210 (noviembre, 1926), 351-367.

[A rejoinder to criticism by Gastón Talamón (see entry no. 403) of an article (see entry no. 418) in which Vega sought to show that a real "Argentine" music does not exist because of the presence in Argentina of so many heterogeneous influences. A large part of this discussion centers around the tango.]

420. _____. "Contradanza y cielito." PrBA, 26 de marzo, 1939.

[The author holds that the Argentine cielito is merely the gaucho version of the English contradanza introduced into Argentina during the first half of the eighteenth century. Vega is concerned only with choreography in this discussion, not with the literary aspects of the verses which accompany the dance.]

421. Vega, Carlos. "La creación en estilo popular." PrBA, 18 de julio, 1937.

422. _____. Danzas y canciones argentinas; teorías e investigaciones. B. A.: Establecimiento Gráfico de Eugenio Ferrero, 1936. 309 pp. 22.5 cm.

[A very thorough study of various types of Argentine dances (gato, cielito, cuando, pericón, etc.). Also, there is a section on "Canciones criollas" (pp. 275-302) which contains treatment of the triste, the vidala, and the vidalita. Scattered through the book are coplas which accompany dances. There are no romances or other narratives, but in the section on cielitos there are some strophes based on historical events.]

423. _____. "Eliminación del factor africano en la formación del cancionero criollo." Cursos y conferencias (B. A.), X:7 (1936), 765-779.

424. _____. "En torno a las tradiciones orales." PrBA, 13 de junio, 1937, sección segunda, p. 2.

[A most illuminating little article about the way in which so-called "oral" tradition often can be traced back to printed or written sources. Vega uses as an example a Trisagio which he himself found in oral tradition in Santiago del Estero, and he shows how it clearly derives from a Gozos a la Santísima Trinidad, first published in Madrid in 1786 and reprinted in Cuzco in 1845. He provides texts and music. There is no treatment of romances or corridos, but coplas are mentioned, including one based on the religious poem in question and adapted to amorous style.]

425. _____. "La forma del cielito." PrBA, 8 de enero, 1939, sección segunda.

[A study of the nature of the dance known as the cielito. Some of the texts which accompany it would be of interest to students of the copla.]

426. _____. "Música popular argentina." PrBA, 29 de septiembre, 1935.

427. _____. La música popular argentina, canciones y danzas criollas. Tomo segundo: Fraseología, proposición de un nuevo método para la escritura y análisis de las ideas musicales y su aplicación al canto popular. 2 vols. B. A.: Imprenta de la Universidad, 1941. 32 cm.

[An extremely important study of both popular and artistic music. The author is primarily preoccupied with the problem of transcribing popular music accurately. A very technical treatise, it should be consulted by anyone studying any type of popular music.]

428. _____. Música sudamericana. B. A.: Emecé Editores, 1946. 117 pp. 18 cm. (Colección Buen Aire, No. 6.)
[A collection of articles written by Vega between 1935 and 1938. "Un trisagio santiaguino" (pp. 47-54) is the article treated in entry no. 424 of this bibliography. Also, there is a chapter on the vidala, "La forma poética de la vidala" (pp. 85-102). This is probably the same article listed below in entry no. 431.]

429. _____. Panorama de la música popular argentina, con un ensayo sobre la ciencia del folklore. B. A.: Editorial Losada, 1944. 361 pp. 22 cm.
[A study of musical techniques observed in various kinds of popular music, which Vega treats by regions.]

430. _____. Unpublished collections in the Archivo Fonográfico de la Sección de Musicología del Museo Argentino de Ciencias Naturales, Buenos Aires. The materials were collected from 1931-1945.

431. _____. "La vidala; su forma poética." PrBA, 1 de enero, 1937.

Vega López, Carlos. La poesía popular de la América Española. See entry no. 120.

432. Velázquez, Rafael P. Ensayos de historia y folklore bonaerense, en el centenario de la creación del partido de Tuyú (hoy General Juan Madariaga). B. A.: Talleres Gráficos "La Argentina," 1939. 385 pp. 23.5 cm.

433. Viana, Javier de. Campo. Montevideo: A. Barreiro y Ramos, 1896. 278 pp. 19.5 cm.; also, other editions: Montevideo, 1910; Madrid: Editorial América, [1918?]. 280 pp. 19 cm.; 3.ª ed. Montevideo: C. García, 1921. 154 pp. 18.5 cm.
[Furt [ref. 272, Vol. I, p. 448) quotes some coplas taken from this novel.]

434. _____. Yuyos (cuentos camperos). 2.ª ed. Montevideo: Tip. y Edit. O. M. Bertani, 1912. 218 pp. 19.5 cm.
[Furt (ref. 272, Vol. I, p. 452) quotes some coplas taken from the above.]

435. Vidal de Battini, Berta E. "El folklore en la escuela." Monitor de la educación común (B. A.), julio de 1932.
[Carrizo (ref. 200, p. 44) refers to a historical copla taken from this source.]

436. Vidart, Daniel D. La vida rural uruguaya; escenario geográfico, proceso histórico, caracteres socioculturales. Montevideo: Talleres Gráficos "33," 1955. 211 pp. 24 cm.
[Chapter XII, "El payador," is of interest and has some texts, though there is really nothing new. A great deal of the material

presented is from Martín Fierro, Cantaclaro, and other well known sources.]

437. Videla, Heriberto. Canciones de mi tierra; quince canciones y danzas mendocinas: refundición y armonización. Mendoza, 1943. 101 pp. 29 cm.

438. Viglietti, Cédar. Folklore en el Uruguay; la guitarra del gaucho, sus danzas y canciones. Montevideo: Yi, 1947. 168 pp.
[Boggs (ref. 13 [1948], p. 69) says: "Including 12 musical texts of native songs and dances by Luis Alba. On the Indians and their music, the gaucho and his guitar, music in city and country, the cielito, triste and estilo, pericón y media caña, vidalita, milonga and cifra, gato, huella and malambo, polka, and the payadores, with il. verses."]

439. _____. "La guitarra en la época artiguista." RN, XLVII (1950):139, pp. 54-59.

440. Villafañé Casal, María Teresa. Elementos para una geografía folklórica argentina. La Plata, 1945. 149 pp.

441. Villafuerte, Carlos, ed. El cantar de las provincias argentinas; melodías y coplas recogidas por el autor. B. A.: El Ateneo, 1951. 105 pp. 29 cm.
[A collection of thirteen songs with texts and musical accompaniment. Each song is representative of a province of Argentina and each is preceded by a short introduction which evokes the area it represents. The compositions are of various genres. Some are coplas and there is a version of the Zamba de Vargas.]

442. Wilkes, Josué Teófilo. "La antigua tonada tucumana." REM, Año I:3 (abril de 1950), 11-39.
[A very exhaustive analysis of the music and text of the Vidala de la Virgen Generala. The author seeks to prove that it is of recent origin and not a true vidala in the traditional sense of the term.]

443. _____. "De algunos aspectos y particularidades rítmicas del cancionero musical popular argentino." BLAM, Año V(1941), 565-584.
[A study of rhythms of various types of Argentine popular music, though not specifically of the romance.]

444. _____. "Ensayo para una clasificación rítmica del cancionero criollo según la rítmica clásica." BLAM, Año II, Tomo II (abril de 1936), 297-313.
[An attempt to classify the music of Argentine songs and dances according to the system and terminology of the Greeks. A technical study with a number of musical illustrations, it is admirably documented. Though there is no specific mention of romances or corridos, the vidala and several dances receive attention. Quite interesting

also is a discussion of the song of Mambrú. Though the material is not original with Wilkes and he cites his sources, it is a good summary of what is known about this composition.]

445. _____. "La rítmica específica del cantar nativo; noticia preliminar." REM, Año II:4 (agosto, 1950), 11-42. (The author indicates that with slight modifications this article is the same one that appeared in BAAL, XIII(1945), 389-432).

[A very fine study of rhythms of Spanish music and the influence of the latter on American, particularly Argentine, songs and dances. The romance in Spain is mentioned only in passing and the author's comments on American music do not deal with narrative types as such, since he is not concerned with literary themes. But his comments would be of extreme interest to students of the musical aspects of any kind of popular songs.]

446. _____. "Los senderos sonoros de la música argentina popular y culta." UnivSF, No. 20 (1948), 89-117.

447. _____. "Sintaxis sonora del cantar vernáculo." AFA, 1945, 85-87.

448. _____ and Guerrero Cárpena, I. Formas musicales río-platenses (cifras, estilos y milongas); su génesis hispánica. B. A.: Imp. Patagonia, 1946. 312 pp. 24 cm.

449. Williams, Alberto. "La vidala chayera." La quena (B. A.), II:10 (1922), 14-16.
[Furt (ref. 272, Vol. I, p. 452) quotes a copla from the above.]

450. Zaffaroni Bécker, Zahara. Poesía folklórica infantil del Uruguay (contribución). [Montevideo]: Centro de Estudios Folklóricos del Uruguay, 1956. 19 pp.
[Boggs (ref. 13 [1956], p. 46) says: "Texts of various types of folkverse of Children from Uruguay, from memory of author."]

451. Zeballos, Estanislao S., ed. Cancionero popular de la Revista de derecho, historia y letras. B. A.: Imprenta de J. Peuser, 1905. 22.5 cm.
[Contains a large collection of patriotic poetry, but few truly popular poems. There is an occasional poem in romance form and a great many glosas in décimas; also, there are some coplas.]

452. _____. "El espíritu popular en la poesía." Caras y caretas (B. A.), Año XIII:607 (25 de mayo de 1910).

453. Ziegler, Federico, and Freitas, Pablo. El carnaval de 1871, colección de canciones de las comparsas que saldrán este año. B. A., 1871.
[Furt (ref. 272, Vol. I, p. 459) quotes a copla taken from the above.]

BOLIVIA

Folklore studies in Bolivia have been very sketchy up to the present time. The only work of note in the field of folk poetry and song is M. Rigoberto Paredes' El arte folklórico de Bolivia, source of many of the bibliographical data which I offer here. It will be noted that almost all the items I list are concerned with coplas and pasquines, there being almost no information up to the present time about true romances or other narrative genres of poetry or song.

BOLIVIA

454. Aires bolivianos. Primera serie: Cuecas, bailes, huayños criollos de palpitante actualidad. La Paz: Imprenta de la Librería "Cervantes," 1931.
[Paredes (ref. 480, p. 109) cites the work as a source of coplas.]

455. Anaya de Urquidi, Mercedes. Tradiciones y leyendas del folklore boliviano. Segunda edición. La Paz: Gilbert y Casanovas, 1946. 206 pp. 22 cm. (The prologue of the first edition, which is reprinted in the second edition, is dated 1936.)
[A collection of traditions and legends in prose. There are a few coplas which were sung by a payador (p. 68).]

456. Aponte, José Manuel. Tradiciones bolivianas. La Paz: Imp. Velarde, 1909. xv, 434 pp. 17.5 cm.
[A volume of sketches obviously written in imitation of the work of Ricardo Palma. Occasional coplas are scattered through various chapters. Also of interest is one sketch entitled "Mataron a Cañoto" (pp. 222-273) about Cañoto, a "trovador de la campaña" who, during Bolívar's war for independence about 1820-1821, harassed the Spanish with impudent and daring songs. Those quoted here, however, are pasquines in the form of coplas, not romances or corridos.]

457. Autenchlus Maier, Olga Francisca. "Entre mineros." RDTP, XVI(1960): Cuaderno 3°, 249-286.
[Included in this long article about the folklore of Bolivia's miners via is one text of a romance (p. 267) on a religious subject. There are also a few copla texts.]

458. Ballivián y Roxas, Vicente. Archivo boliviano; colección de documentos relativos a la historia de Bolivia, durante la época colonial, con un catálogo de obras impresas y de manuscritos, que tratan de esa parte de la América Meridional. Tomo I. Paris: A. Franck (F. Vieweg), 1872. xiv, 535 pp. 24 cm.
[Paredes (ref. 480, p. 114) quotes two pasquines from this work (pp. 394-396). They date from about 1650.]

Bayo, Ciro. "Cantos populares americanos." See entry no. 162.

Beltrán Avila, Marcos. Capítulos de la historia colonial de Oruro. See entry no. 1748.

Caballero, Jorge Giacoman. See Nuevo cancionero, entry no. 479.

459. Cancionero amor y patria. La Paz: Editorial "Claridad," septiembre de 1933.
[Paredes (ref. 480, p. 110) cites the work as a source of coplas.]

460. Cancionero boliviano. La Paz, marzo de 1934.
[Paredes (ref. 480, p. 110) cites the work as a source of coplas and comments: "Dedicado a los soldados que actuaron en la guerra con el Paraguay."]

461. Cancionero chapaco. Tarija: Librería e Imprenta "Renacimiento," 1945.
[Paredes (ref. 480, p. 110) cites the work as a source of coplas and says: "Comprende 365 estrofas numeradas, que son independientes unas de otras."]

462. Cancionero; honor y gloria a los soldados bolivianos. La Paz: Tip. "El Illimani," 1933.
[Paredes (ref. 480, p. 110) cites this work as a source of coplas.]

463. Cancionero 1931. La Paz: La Librería Mundial.
[Paredes (ref. 480, p. 109) cites the work as a source of coplas.]

464. Cancionero moderno. La Paz: Imprenta Universo.
[Paredes (ref. 480, p. 109) cites the work as a source of coplas.]

465. Cancionero patriótico. Primera serie. Cochabamba: Imprenta S. Cuenca. 8 pp. unnumbered.
[Paredes (ref. 480, p. 110) cites the work as a source of coplas and says that it is dedicated to the soldiers of the War of the Chaco.]

466. Cancionero popular, con las últimas canciones de moda. Edición mensual. Editores R. San Martín and V. C. Pérez. La Paz: Editorial América, 1932.
[Paredes (ref. 480, p. 109) cites the work as a source of coplas. He indicates that he has seen three cuadernillos of the series.]

467. Cancionero selecto. Edición exclusiva del "Bayer y Editorial Musical" Víctor Loayza. La Paz: Imprenta Fénix.
[Paredes ref. 480, p. 109) cites the work as a source of coplas.]

468. Cancionero "Studium"; últimas novedades de canciones para la juventud. Editores Alanor Hermanos. La Paz: Imprenta "La Nacional," 1932. 18 pp. unnumbered.
[Paredes (ref. 480, p. 109) cites the work as a source of coplas.]

469. El chaqueño. Cancionero No. 1. La Paz: Editorial "Claridad," febrero de 1934.
[Paredes (ref. 480, p. 110) cites the work as a source of coplas and says: "Cancioneros de esta edición y con el mismo título aparecieron hasta 7, con distintas páginas cada cuadernillo, dedicados a los soldados del Chaco."]

470. Cortés, José Domingo. Bolivia, apuntes jeográficos, estadísticos, de costumbres descriptivos e históricos. Paris: Tip. Lahure, 1875. 172 pp. 29 cm. (This book is a revised edition of the author's La República de Bolivia. Santiago de Chile, 1872.)
[Contains an elementary discussion of the Indian music and poetry of Bolivia (pp. 75-81). Also, there is a description (p. 73) of quainos (sic), "composiciones musicales en que se cantan cuartetas de versos de siete a ocho sílabas, con un mismo estribillo . . . ." Ismael

Moya (ref. 353, Vol. II, pp. 131-132) gives a Quechua translation of a romance entitled La viuda which he says he found in this work. I have been unable to locate it. I have not been able to consult the 1872 edition, however, and it may appear there.]

471. Costas Arguedas, José Felipe. "Folklore de Yamparáez." USFX, XVI(1950):37-38, pp. 287-387.

[An interesting work about many types of folklore from the Chuquisaca region of Bolivia. But although there is some discussion of dances and music, there is nothing about narrative songs or poems, and a section on coplas contains only Indian verses translated into Spanish. They seem to be unrelated to the coplas of Hispanic tradition.]

472. El eco de la guerra. Cancionero No. 10. La Paz: Editorial "Claridad," 1934.

[Paredes (ref. 480, p. 109) cites the work as a source of coplas.]

473. Fortún, Julia Elena. "La música folklórica." La Razón (La Paz ?), 18 de julio de 1948.

Harcourt, Raoul, and d'Harcourt, Marguerite. See entry no. 1812.

474. Jáuregui Rosquellas, Alfredo. [Article]. Boletín de la Sociedad Geográfica "Sucre" (La Paz ?), Nos. 411-412.

[Paredes (ref. 480, pp. 127 ff.) quotes some very interesting pasquines from the period around 1827 which reveal Bolivian animosity against Bolívar, Sucre, and the other "colombianos" who helped gain Bolivian independence. They come from the above source, but Paredes gives no other bibliographical data.]

475. Lira popular; colección de cantares populares de Bolivia.

[Carrizo (ref. 197, p. 149) says: "El ejemplar que conozco y poseo no tiene año ni pié de imprenta; está falto de algunas hojas. Por los cantares consignados no es anterior a este siglo, su formato es de 8 x 15 centímetros."]

476. Mallo, Nicanor. Tradiciones bolivianas. Primera serie. Sucre, 1918.

[Paredes (ref. 480, p. 120) quotes some pasquines from the period of Bolivian independence (p. 141 of Mallo's work).]

477. Mendoza, Jaime. "Jula-julas; sobre el folklore musical boliviano." RCAE, IV:12-14 (1938), 36-38, also, Kollasuyo (La Paz), Año V:45 (enero-febrero, 1943), 26-30.

[The author relates how many years ago he heard a melody sung by some Indians on a lonely road in Bolivia. Later he had the song transcribed by a musician. Though there is nothing specific about narrative poetry or coplas, there is comment upon possible Spanish influence upon the musical aspects of the composition which the author heard.]

478. Mendoza, Jaime. "Motivos folklóricos bolivianos." USFX, abril-junio, 1939; also, RABA, XVI:186 (octubre, 1939), 99-110; also, Revista de la Universidad de Chuquisaca (Sucre), No. 20 (1939), 177-193.
[An unpretentious but informative article about the Indian music of the Andes region and the instruments — the erkje, the quena, the charango, the guitarrilla, and the guitarra — used by the Indians. There is no attention to singing or texts of any kind of song. But the author's observations — particularly his criticism of those who consider the Indian humorless and depressed — are of interest to any folklorist studying the Bolivian region.]

479. Nuevo cancionero. De la Circulación Industrial, etc. Editor don Jorge Giacoman Caballero. Oruro: Editorial "La Patria," 1932.
[Paredes (ref. 480, p. 109) cites this work as a source of coplas.]

Paredes, M. Rigoberto. El arte en la altiplanicie. See entry no. 480.

480. _____. El arte folklórico de Bolivia. Segunda edición corregida y aumentada. La Paz: Talleres Gráficos de Armando Gamarra Dick, 1949. 151 pp. 25 cm. (First published as El arte en la altiplanicie, 1913. The author explains that the change of title was necessary because in the second edition he includes folklore from many sections of Bolivia.)
[A quite respectable study of a great many aspects of Bolivian musical, literary, and choreographic folklore. Most of the data given are taken from written sources such as chronicles, newspapers, and the like. The treatment of music is purely descriptive, since the author offers no transcriptions of any kind. Also, it should be noted that many works of learned poets are included along with some poems, mainly coplas, of truly popular origin. Chap. V, "Coplas y composiciones políticas populares," is of particular interest since it includes several historical coplas in the nature of pasquines which are not too far removed from the tone and style of Mexican corridos.]

481. Paredes Candia, Antonio. Literatura folklórica (recogida de la tradición oral boliviana). La Paz: Talleres Gráficos A. Gamarra, 1953. 132 pp. 22 cm.
[The volume is made up of legends, tales, riddles, jokes, etc. But there are no songs except for a few children's rhymes.]

Pérez, V. C. See Cancionero popular, entry no. 466.

482. Pinto, Manuel M. La revolución y la intendencia de La Paz en el virreynato del Río de la Plata con la concurrencia de Chuquisaca. B. A.: Tip. A. Cantiello, 1909. 290, cclxxxviii pp. 26 cm.
[Paredes (ref. 480, pp. 119-120) quotes some pasquines of Pedro Domingo Murillo, a famous writer of pasquines during the period of the war for independence in Bolivia. They are taken from the above work (pp. 65-66).]

483. Rivera, Felipe V. El último cancionero, con poesías escogidas, bailes, cuecas, pasacalles, tristes, huainos y koluyos, grabados en discos Víctor por Felipe V. Rivera y su conjunto boliviano. La Quiaca [Argentina], 1933. 36 pp.

484. Ruiz, Bernardino [?]. Fiestas triunfales — Que consagró el 2 de agosto de 1812. La fidelísima Imperial Villa de Potosí. Al invicto General Americano. El sr. Mariscal de Campo DON JOSE MANUEL DE GOYONECHE. Las dirige y dedica al Público el Coronel de Ejército D. Mariano Campero de Ugarte, Gobernador Intendente de la provincia de Potosí. Lima: Imprenta de los Huérfanos, 1812.
[Paredes (ref. 480, p. 123) quotes a royalist poem from the period of Peruvian-Bolivian independence which appears in the above work (p. 22). His footnote reference does not make it entirely clear, however, whether Ruiz is the author or the editor of the work.]

San Martín, R. See Cancionero popular, entry no. 466.

Santa María, F. Apuntes biográficos. See entry no. 1881.

485. Schallehn, Hellmut. "Die Grundlagen der Volksmusik in Bolivien und Paraguay." Die Brücke zur Heimat, Jg. 33 (1933).

486. Sotomayor y M., Ismael. "Romancero y miscelánea del arte nativo." Antología "Génesis" (La Paz), II(1948), 215-218.
[Boggs (ref. 13 [1949], p. 25) says: "General observations on Bolivian folklore, work done and to be done. Says little about ballads but rather folklore in general."]

487. Testamento de Potosí (romance anónimo). Notas de José Enrique Viaña. Potosí: Edit. Potosí, 1954. 77 pp. (Cuadernos de la Colección de la cultura boliviana, No. 2.)

488. Vargas, Teófilo. Aires nacionales de Bolivia. [?] vols. Cochabamba-Santiago de Chile: Impreso en los Talleres "Casa Amarilla," [1940-?]. 32.5 cm.
[Lara (ref. 1824, p. 81) refers to Vol. I of this work. The Library of Congress catalogue makes reference to Vol. IV, but doesn't indicate how many volumes there are.]

Vellard, Jen Albert. "Folklore de los pescadores del Lago Titicaca." See entry no. 1908.

Viaña, José Enrique, ed. See Testamento de Potosí, entry no. 487.

489. Zárate, Belisario. Folklore boliviano; 12 piezas vernaculares típicas, piezas para piano. Cochabamba: Imp. Segura, 1938.

490. Zinny, Antonio. Historia de los gobernadores de las provincias argentinas. 5 vols. B. A.: Administración General "Vaccaro," 1920-1921. 23 cm.
[Contains a copla written to celebrate the founding of La Paz (Vol. I, p. 113).]

CHILE

The popular poetry and song of Chile have been studied by many talented scholars and bibliographers. In the two editions of his Estadística bibliográfica de la literatura chilena, Ramón Briseño, upon giving the first impulse to Chile's long history of excellent bibliographical investigation, did not fail to list a great many hojas sueltas from the middle years of the nineteenth century. Some of these, I suspect, probably contained narratives in poetic form, though I have not been able to prove this with the library facilities at my command. Later two distinguished successors among Chilean bibliographers, Ricardo E. Latcham and Carlos E. Porter, turned their talents toward anthropological and ethnological subjects and contributed useful guides to the folklore research of their day. In recent years Eugenio Pereira Salas and Raúl Silva Castro have continued to provide their country with better bibliographical aids to the systematic study of its national folklore than are possessed by any other country in Spanish America up to the present time.

Nor has Chile lacked assiduous collectors and compilers of folklore materials or scholars competent to study and interpret their country's poetry and song. Some talented investigators, beginning with Rodolfo Lenz in the late nineteenth century, have been interested primarily in the works of those semilearned but still quite earthy poets (Bernardino Guajardo, Nicasio García, Juan Rafael Allende, et al.) whose poetic narratives and commentaries on the events of their day lie somewhere between the realm of genuine folklore and that of the more academic poetry of true literary artists. Chile, alone among the countries of Spanish America, has produced a vast amount of poetry and song on this peculiar level; i.e., compositions which are less popular in character than the vast majority of Mexico's corridos but less literary than the compositions of most of Argentina's "gaucho" poets. Were it not for the efforts of Rodolfo Lenz, Domingo Amunátegui Solar, and, in more recent times, Inés Valenzuela, the works of this type of Chilean popular poet would have been much less known and appreciated than is the case today.

A respectable number of Chile's good folklorists, on the other hand, have preferred to study their country's strong romance-corrido tradition. Foremost among these, of course, is Julio Vicuña Cifuentes, whose scholarly compilation of romance and corrido texts in the early years of the twentieth century has served since then as the inevitable point of departure for all investigations. Ramón A. Laval, Francisco J. Cavada, Abdón Andrade Coloma, Lucila Dufourq, Elisa Figueroa, Cremilda Manríquez, Lucila Muñoz, Antonio Acevedo

Hernández, and Lina Vargas Andrade, to mention only a few of the more outstanding figures in the field, have made significant contributions of varying merit. It is notable, however, that while the musical aspects of Chilean folklore are not entirely ignored by some of the scholars mentioned, this field has been slighted. Certainly Chile has produced no musicologists in the field of folklore studies comparable to Vega and Wilkes in Argentina.

In expanding upon the field of the romance-corrido tradition in Chile to include allied genres, I have been most concerned with the décimas, particularly in the works of the semipopular poets already mentioned, and with tonadas, payas, and a few other minor types which sometimes serve narrative purposes. The subgroups are less important in Chile, however, than in some other Spanish American countries because the romance tradition is strong, and narrative poems known as corridos or logas are also widely cultivated. No country in America save Mexico has a stronger corrido tradition, and the possible relationship between the corridos of Chile and those of Mexico, like a great many curious similarities which can be detected between the musical and poetic folklore of the two countries, remains to be studied systematically.

Finally, I refer users of my bibliography to the "Guía" bibliográfica para el estudio del folklore chileno" by Eugenio Pereira Salas for additional references to certain hojas sueltas containing Chilean popular poetry. Here I have not attempted to incorporate the single hojas sueltas listed by Pereira Salas since no possibility existed of my being able to examine them in the libraries where I have been able to work; hence I should have been unable to elaborate upon the information provided about them by Pereira Salas in his work.

CHILE

491. Acevedo Hernández, Antonio. Canciones populares chilenas; recopilación de cuecas, tonadas y otras canciones acompañada de una noticia sobre la materia y sobre los que han cantado para el público chileno. Santiago: Ediciones Ercilla, 1939. 193 pp. 17.5 cm.

[In two preliminary chapters the author surveys Latin American music in general, though he makes little distinction between true folklore and what is merely in vogue among the masses. Although they are not in romance or corrido form, the texts of some songs inspired by Chilean history are of interest. Slightly more than the latter half of the volume is taken up by a collection of texts. There are some cuecas inspired by the war against Spain in 1865 (pp. 69-102). Most, however, are satirical, not narrative. A section entitled "Versos a lo humano y a lo divino" (pp. 103-193) contains songs of many types. Many are cuartetas glossed by décimas, but few are of great interest.]

492. ———. Los cantores populares chilenos. Santiago: Nascimento, 1933. 296 pp. 19 cm.

[A discussion of popular poetry, popular poets, and singers of the pueblo. Though a collection of popular verse is included, little of it is in romance form, most of it being cuartetas glossed by décimas. Some of these compositions, however, are topical and narrative in character.]

493. ———. El libro de la tierra chilena; lo que canta y lo que mira el pueblo de Chile. Santiago: Ediciones Ercilla, 1935. 136 pp. 19 cm.

[A series of short chapters written in popular style but containing much information. "La tonada chilena" (pp. 9-16) contains many coplas; "Los payadores clásicos" (pp. 17-22) relates the payada between Taguada and Don Javier de la Rosa; "Noticias sobre los cantores populares chilenos" (pp. 29-36) and "Los escenarios en que actuaron los cantores: La fonda popular, la de la Peta Basaure" (pp. 37-40) describe the puetas and the places where they performed; "Romances que el pueblo repite" (pp. 41-48) contains the texts of several composiciones, some the work of puetas, some truly popular romances. There are coplas scattered through other sections of the work.]

494. Alba, Antonio. Cantares del pueblo chileno, arreglados para canto y guitarra. Santiago: Casa Niemeyer, 1898.

495. "El album de aires tradicionales y folklóricos de Chile." RMC, Año 1:1 (1 de mayo de 1945), 40-41.

[Merely a notice of the appearance of an album of ten records under the R. C. A. label. It does not indicate the contents of the album.]

496. Aldava, Fray. El poeta Pircano o sea el roto Pancho Poroto. Santiago: Imp. Aurora, 1903. 32 pp.

497. Alegría, Fernando. "Chilean Troubadors." Americ (English ed.), V:8 (August, 1953), 16-19, 46; "Payadores bajo la Cruz del

Sur; poetas populares del siglo XIX que simbolizan el espíritu de su época." Americ (Spanish ed.), V:9 (septiembre de 1953).

[A popularization of the essential facts about the history of Chilean popular poetry, with particular reference to Guajardo and other poets who thrived at the end of the nineteenth century. Texts and translations are given of several strophes from the contrapunto between Taguada and Don Javier de la Rosa. Also, there are representative texts taken from the works of Guajardo and his school of poets.]

498. Allende, Humberto. "Chilean Folk Music." BPAU, LXV:9 (September, 1931), 917-924.

[Some informative comments about Chilean folk music and its Indian and Spanish background. There are passing references to romances (in Spain), zamacuecas, tonadas, and other types of folk literature, but a tendency toward doubtful generalizations unsupported by evidence can be detected.]

———. See also Allende, Pedro Humberto, entry no. 502.

499. Allende, Juan Rafael. Obras completas. Poesías populares de El Pequén. Tomo I. Santiago: Imp. y Encuadernación El Comercio, 1903. 160 pp.

[Pereira Salas (ref. 645, p. 54) says: "Hay tomos I a XIII." It is not clear, however, whether he means that there are thirteen volumes in the Obras completas or whether this first volume contains the thirteen volumes of the Poesías populares of Allende, which had been appearing separately for several years. See my next entry.]

500. ———. Poesías populares. 10 vols. Santiago de Chile: Impreso por Pedro G. Ramírez, 1883.

[This entry comes from Palau. Though I have been unable to find reference elsewhere to the ten-volume work which apparently was published in 1883, I have found the following bibliographical data for Vols. IX-XIII of the same series: Tomo IX. Santiago: Impreso por Pedro G. Ramírez, 1886. 96 pp.; Tomo X. Santiago: Impreso por Pedro G. Ramírez, 1886. 96 pp.; Tomo XI. Santiago: Imprenta de P. Ramírez, 1889. 32 pp.; Tomo XII. Santiago: Imp. de P. Ramírez, 1889. 32 pp.; Tomo XIII. Valparaíso: Imp. de P. Ramírez, 1893. 16 pp. These data are from Anuario de la prensa chilena publicado por la Biblioteca Nacional.]

501. ———. [Popular poetry].

[Pedro Pablo Figueroa (ref. 570, p. 25) says: "En 1879, en el curso de la guerra del Pacífico — contra el Perú i Bolivia — el espiritual poeta i periodista don Juan Rafael Allende, publicó una serie de poesías populares suscritas con el seudónimo de El Pequén (sic), nombre de una ave nocturna de los campos. Estas poesías estaban destinadas al ejército i el Ministro de la Guerra, don José Francisco Vergara, hizo distribuir cinco mil volúmenes, de pequeño formato, entre los soldados en campaña. Estas obritas son hoi mui escasas."]

_____. For some information about Allende, see Silva Castro, Raúl, ref. 689; also, Amunátegui Solar, Domingo, entry no. 508.

502. Allende, Pedro Humberto. "Música popular chilena." In Vol. I of Chile y sus riquezas. Santiago, n.d. Pp. 804-805.

503. _____. "La musique populaire chilienne." In Vol. II of Art populaire, travaux artistiques et scientifiques du 1er Congrès International des Arts Populaires, Prague, 1928. Paris: Editions Duchartre, 1931. Pp. 118-123.

504. _____. "Los orígenes de la música popular chilena." Antártica (Santiago), No. 2 (octubre, 1944), 77-79.

505. _____. "Sobre la música popular." Revista Ercilla (Santiago), 16 de septiembre, 1938.

_____. See also Allende, Humberto, entry no. 498.

506. Ampuero, Galvarino. "Repertorio folklórico de Chiloé." AFCU, Fascículo No. 5 (1954?), 5-96.
[Contains three strophes of some popular songs (pp. 34-36). One is taken from a jarana ("Aquí me pongo a cantar"); the other two are in the nature of coplas. The remainder of the study deals with legends, food, beliefs, etc.]

507. Amunátegui, Miguel Luis. "Camilo Henríquez." In La alborada poética en Chile después del 18 de setiembre de 1810. Santiago: Imprenta Nacional, 1892. Pp. 3-216.
[An extensive study of the poet Henríquez and his works, with many texts, some of them directly inspired by events of Chile's war for independence. Several are romances reales, others are in romance form with seven and ten-syllable lines, still others are décimas. All are artistic compositions, of course.]

508. Amunátegui Solar, Domingo. "Bosquejo histórico de la literatura chilena." RChHG, Año V, Tomo XIII:17 (primer trimestre de 1915), 17-34; Año IX, Tomo XXX:34 (segundo trimestre de 1919), 240-270; also reprinted in book form: Santiago, 1915 (or 1920). 669 pp. 23 cm. [Silva Castro (ref. 691, p. 83) says that the date is given as 1915 on the title page and 1920 on the outer cover.]
[RChHG published Amunátegui's complete work in installments over a period of several years. The first installment here cited as relevant to my subject is Chap. V of the longer work and it deals with literature of the eighteenth century. The author discusses popular poetry (pp. 21-23) and suggests that many Chilean romances, tonadas, pallas, and corridos appeared during this century, though their remote origins go back to the soldiers who conquered America. He cites Vicuña Cifuentes and the chronicle of Mariño de Lovera in

support of his thesis. Also, he discusses the nature of the corrido in Chile. The second installment cited above is Chap. XXIII of the complete work and is devoted almost entirely to popular poetry (romances, corridos, cuartetas glossed by décimas, tonadas, zamacuecas, coplas, and the like). The author leans heavily upon Lenz and Vicuña Cifuentes in his discussion. Finally, he turns his attention to two popular poets, Juan Rafael Allende and Carlos Pezoa Veliz. He gives textual examples of their works, some of them true romances. In summary, Amunátegui's treatment of popular poetry is very good. There is little that is original — for the most part he quotes Lenz, Vicuña Cifuentes, and Lizana — but the work is a useful synthesis.]

509. Amunátegui Solar, Domingo. Bosquejo histórico de la literatura chilena; período colonial. Santiago: Imprenta Universitaria, 1918. 106 pp. 18 cm.

[This is the first part only of the long work listed above. It contains the section on the eighteenth century which has been described in my previous entry.]

510. Andrade Coloma, Abdón. "Folklore de Valdivia." AFCU, Fascículo No. 1, pp. 7-117; also, entitled "Contribución al estudio del folklore de Valdivia." BIFC, V(1947-1949), 267-377.

[A compilation, with a few brief commentaries, of various types of folklore from the region of Valdivia. Among other things, there are sections on "El contrapunto" (pp. 23-29), wherein the author deals with the contrapunto of Taguada and Don Javier de la Rosa, "Romances, logas y corridos" (pp. 29-45), and "La tonada, la canción, la décima" (pp. 45-64). Several texts are given, but the most interesting aspect of the study is the lyrical and amorous nature of the compositions known as corridos in Valdivia. The comments about the rhetorical character of the corrido are of particular interest.]

Andreu, R. "El payador y el milonguero; artículo sobre la poesía nacional de Chile y Argentina." See entry no. 135.

511. Angulo A., José. "El improvisador, verdadero precursor de la poesía nacional." ASFM, II(1941), 117-123.

[A discussion of improvisation among some Chilean poets.]

512. _____. "Música folklórica chilena." ASFM, II(1941), 125-131.

[An attempt merely to define and give examples of the cueca, the tonada, the esquinazo, the estilo criollo, the canción, and other types of popular compositions. The work is not of great importance.]

513. Anuario de la prensa chilena publicado por la Biblioteca Nacional (1886). Santiago: Imprenta Gutenberg, 1887. vii, 155 pp. (The first volume of a series which was published annually by various printers for each year from 1886 to 1915.)

[An attempt to list annually all printed material published in Chile and all that published in foreign countries about Chile or by Chilean writers. In the early numbers there are many entries for hojas sueltas of various kinds, some of them containing popular poetry. None of the compositions, however, is called a romance or a corrido. The listings of hojas sueltas declines markedly after 1887.]

514. Araneda, Rosa. Poesías populares; el cantor de los cantores. Libro I. Santiago: Imp. Cervantes, 1893. 64 pp. 11 cm.; Libro II. 1893. 48 pp.; Libro III. 1894. 48 pp.; Libro V. 1895. 48 pp.
[There undoubtedly was a Libro IV of this series, though Pereira Salas (ref. 645, p. 54) fails to list it. Nor is it listed in The Anuario de la prensa chilena publicado por la Biblioteca Nacional for the years 1893, 1894, and 1895, wherein the other volumes appear. The series was apparently continued by Daniel Meneses (entry no. 626).]

515. Arce, Magda. Huasos chilenos; folklore campesino. Santiago: Editor Carlos del Campo L., 1943.

516. Baeza, Mario. Cantares de Chile. Santiago: Editorial del Pacífico, 1956. 257 pp. 13 cm.
[A collection of texts of poems and songs of various kinds, some being folklore (coplas, décimas, and romances are included), while others are not true folklore. The work has no scholarly pretensions and the provenience of the texts is not indicated.]

517. Balmaceda, Jorge, and Klos, Carlos. Cantares chilenos. B. A., n.d.

518. Balmaceda Toro, Pedro (A. de Gilbert). Estudios y ensayos literarios. Santiago: Imprenta Cervantes, 1889. xxxviii, 384 pp.
[Silva Castro (ref. 691, p. 76) says that it contains an article entitled "Guajardo" (pp. 241-245) about the famous vulgar poet.]

519. Barahona Vega, Clemente. "Folklore chileno." Porvenir intelectual (B. A.), Nos. 149 and 150, 3 de enero, 16 de marzo, 1901.

520. Barros, Raquel, and Dannemann, Manuel. "La poesía folklórica de Melipilla." RMC, Año XII:60 (julio-agosto de 1958), 48-70.
[A very good descriptive treatment of the décimas which are sung in the department of Melipilla, province of Santiago. Strophic, thematic, and musical characteristics are carefully described, and there are interesting observations about the manner in which texts are kept in small notebooks.]

521. _____. "Los problemas de la investigación del folklore musical chileno." RMC, Año XIV:71 (mayo-junio de 1960), 82-100.
[An excellent survey of folklore studies in Chile along with a great deal of bibliographical data. Included are some comments about popular poetry and song.]

522. Barros, Raquel, and Dannemann, Manuel. "El guitarrón en el Departamento de Puenta Alto." RMC, Año XIV:74 (noviembre-diciembre de 1960), 7-45.

[Describes the guitarrón and the kinds of songs which are sung to its accompaniment. Several texts of various kinds of versos are given: e.g., versos por historia, versos a lo divino, versos a lo humano, versos por literatura, etc. The bibliography is also quite extensive.]

Barros Arana, Diego, ed. See Núñez de Pineda y Bascuñán, Francisco, entry no. 636.

523. Briseño, Ramón. Estadística bibliográfica de la literatura chilena. Santiago: Imp. Chilena, 1862. xiv, 546 pp.; Vol. II (1860-1876). Santiago: Imp. Nacional, 1879. xiii, 508 pp. 32 cm.

[A most useful listing of publications printed in Chile and of those printed elsewhere about Chile or by Chilean authors. Vol. I covers the years 1812-1859; Vol. II embraces the years 1860-1876 and is divided into more precise groupings than Vol. I. Briseño lists a considerable number of hojas sueltas, some of which may be of popular poetry. Their nature is often unclear since there is no description of any of the items listed.]

524. Bustos, Pedro. "El poeta popular Juan Bautista Peralta." Verdad y bien (Santiago), No. 364 (abril de 1930), 126-128.

[According to Silva Castro (ref. 691, p. 85), this is a biography of Peralta, a popular poet (1875-1933).]

525. Cabrera, Ana S. "Del folklore chileno." Nac, 10 de enero, 1937.

―――. Rutas de América. See entry no. 20.

526. Campo, S. del. "Algunas observaciones sobre el folleto de Don Desiderio Lizana 'Cómo se canta la poesía popular'." RevCat, Año 14:296 (6 de diciembre de 1913), 870-888.

[The author seeks to correct Lizana on such matters as his treatment of the contrapunto, the canto a dos razones, the paya, and the like. Particularly interesting are his account of the contrapunto between Taguada and Don Javier de la Rosa and his discussion of the payadores of Chile.]

―――. See also Un Colchagüino, entry no. 548.

527. El cancionero popular. 4 cuadernos. Santiago: Imprenta Santiago, 1894. 10.5 cm.

528. El cancionero popular; colección escogida de cantos, tonadas, romanzas, zarzuelas, zamacuecas, habaneras, danzas y versos populares. Primera parte. Valparaíso: Imp. de la Librería del Mercurio, 1896. 94 pp. 11 cm.; Segunda serie. 1896. 95 pp.; El cancionero popular; colección de décimas amorosas para cantar con guitarra. Tercera serie. 1896. 96 pp. (This series was reprinted in 1900.)

529. Canciones populares, danzas i zarzuelas. Iquique: Establecimiento Tipográfico de R. Beni, 1889. 93 pp.

530. Cantares de mi patria; recopilación completa de las mejores y más modernas canciones, tonadas, abaneras, cuecas, brindis, coplas, tristes, tonadas de pata en quincha, tangos, polcas y romanzas. Primera edición, 30,000 ejemplares. Valparaíso: Imp. Lit. Universo, 1908. 95 pp.

531. El cantor santiaguino. Santiago: La Esperanza, 1902. 32 pp.

532. Cantos militares. Talca: Imprenta Talca, 1902. 14 pp. 14 cm.

533. Casas Cordero, Hipólito. El encanto de la vida. Santiago: Imp. Barcelona, 1898. 48 pp.

534. _____. Poesías populares. Libro III. Santiago: Imp. Cervantes, 1894. 48 pp. 11 cm.
[This third book is listed in the Anuario de la prensa chilena publicado por la Biblioteca Nacional (1894). I have found no references to earlier or later volumes in the series.]

535. Castillo, V. El festivo; primer cuaderno de poesía popular. Santiago: Ed. La Prensa, 1900. 48 pp.

536. Cavada, Francisco J. Apuntes para un vocabulario de provincialismos de Chiloé (República de Chile), precedidos de una breve reseña histórica del archipiélago. Punta Arenas: Imprenta de El Asilo de Huérfanas, 1910. 155 pp. 17.5 cm.
[Contains an interesting definition: "Romancear (v.n.) Canturriar, especialmente hablándose de ebrios."]

537. _____. Chiloé y los chilotes; estudios de folklore y lingüística de la provincia de Chiloé. Santiago: Imprenta Universitaria, 1914. xvi, 448 pp. 25 cm.; first appeared in RChHG, 7 installments between Año II, Tomo III:7 (3.er trimestre de 1912), 362-463, and Año IV, Tomo IX:13 (1.er trimestre de 1914), 246-287.
[Contains a study of the folklore of Chiloé, including some valuable versions of Spanish romances (such as Delgadina, Conde Arcos [Alarcos], and many others) and local romances which belong to the romance-corrido tradition (such as El temblor del año 1837, La muerte de Juan José Colín, and La quema de Chacao).]

538. Centenario del folklore, 22 de agosto de 1946; festividades de la semana del folklore chileno. Santiago de Chile: Universidad de Chile, Instituto de Investigaciones del Folklore Musical, 1946. 28 pp. 24 cm.
[The program of the folklore week which was celebrated at the time indicated. Brief program notes deal with cuecas, tonadas, cuandos, and romances, but they are of scant value.]

539. Chacón del Campo, Julio. "Folklore linarense: Poesía popular." RLin, Año X:4 (octubre-diciembre, 1942).

540. _____. "Folklore linarense: El poeta, poesía popular." RLin, Año II:5 (enero-marzo, 1934).

541. _____. "Folklore: Palla entre don Javier de la Rosa y el mulato Taguada." RLin, Año X:4 (octubre-diciembre, 1942).

542. _____. La provincia de Linares. Santiago: Imp. Excelsior, 1926.
[Pereira Salas (ref. 645, p. 28) indicates that there is a chapter entitled "Romances y canciones."]

543. El chercán; nueva recopilación de cantos, canciones y arabies, romanzas, etc. Valparaíso: Imp. Nacional, 1902. 42 pp.

544. El Chonchón. "Romance de los bandidos Mendoza." Revista del sur (Concepción), 1882.

545. Clapier, Pedro J. La alegría; canciones históricas y amorosas. Santiago: Imp. y Encuadernación Barcelona, 1894. 31 pp. 11 cm.

546. _____. Poesías populares; concierto recreativo. Santiago: Imp. Alvión, 1894. 31 pp.

547. _____. El preferido; recopilación de poesías, canciones amorosas. Cuaderno primero. Quinta edición. Santiago: Imp. Barcelona, 1897. 31 pp.; Cuaderno segundo. Santiago: Imp. Barcelona, 1897.

548. Un Colchagüino (Juan Ramón Ramírez, known also by the pseudonym of S. del Campo). "La poesía popular en la provincia de Colchagua." RevCat, V(1903?), 22- , 85- , 259- , 478- , 625- , 739- ; VI(1904):61 (6 de febrero), 39-49; 62 (20 de febrero), 106-115.
[Vol. VI is the only one I have been able to consult. In No. 61 appears Chap. II of the longer work. It is concerned almost exclusively with the duel in song between Taguada and D. Javier de la Rosa and it contains a very complete resumé of the events and a great many verses of the contrapunto. In No. 62 appears Chap. III. It deals with the influence of the famous torneo and discusses some of the famous popular poets of the nineteenth century, whom the author considers imitators of Taguada and D. Javier de la Rosa. He provides some examples of their work. Some are cuartetas in contrapunto form, some are décimas, and there is one very interesting romance (p. 108). It is a long narrative about the poet's unfortunate experiences in marriage to a beata with exaggerated religious ideas.]

549. Los copihues, nuevo cancionero popular. La Serena: Imp. Moderna, n.d. 98 pp.

550. "Coplas de los chinos de Andacollo." La estrella de Andacollo (Santiago), diciembre de 1909, 760-762.

551. Cossío, J. M. de. "Romances sobre la Araucana." In Estudios dedicados a Menéndez Pidal, Vol. V. Madrid: Consejo Superior de Investigaciones Estéticas, 1954. Pp. 201-230.
[The author studies the various adaptations of Ercilla's poem in romances intended for circulation among the masses. Cossío is concerned with the nine romances which appeared in 1593 in Pedro Flores' edition of Ramillete de flores and six others to be found in the Romancero general (four in the first part, Flor de varios romances, 1589, and two in the sixth part).]

Custodio González, Angel, ed. See Núñez de Pineda y Bascuñán, Francisco, entry no. 636.

552. Dannemann R., Manuel. "El 'canto a dos razones' en la poesía popular chilena." Revista de la Agrupación Folklórica del Instituto Chileno de Cultura Hispánica (Santiago), No. 2 (1955), 22-28.
[Boggs (ref. 13 [1956], p. 43) says: "Studies this type of 2 different metrical structures, used by folk poets of Chile in their poetic duels, with some examples."]

553. _____. "Variedades formales de la poesía popular chilena." Atenea, Año XXXIII:372 (septiembre-octubre de 1956), 45-71.
[A very useful discussion of the author's concept of what constitutes "popular" poetry in Chile followed by a series of short sections in which he describes various types of popular poetry and provides examples. Included here are such genres as corrío, palla, verso, canto a dos razones, and others.]

554. _____. "La voz paya como título de una modalidad poética folklórica chilena." FACI, VI-VII:6-7 (1959), 69-84.

_____. See Barros, Raquel, entries nos. 520, 521, and 522.

555. Dantel Argendoña, Elvira. "El bandido en la literatura chilena." BAChH, Año III:6 (1935?), 241-301.

556. "De las costumbres en la poesía." La bolsa (Valparaíso), 25 de septiembre de 1840.

557. Décimas populares. Santiago: Imp. Unión Americana, 1869. 2 lvs.

Díaz C., Fernando. See F. D., entry no. 565.

558. Díaz Casanueva, Humberto. Poemas para niños. Santiago, 1928.

Díaz Gana, Pedro. La condición del minero. See Figueroa, Pedro Pablo, entry no. 570.

_____. Historia de Sebastián Cangalla. See Figueroa, Pedro Pablo, entry no. 570.

559. Dufourcq, Lucila. "Estudio del folklore de Lebu." AnFFE, III(1941-1943), 225-294.

[A study which includes long sections on dichos, refranes, supersticiones, and adivinanzas, along with shorter chapters on romances, coplas, and some other genres of folklore. A few of the romances are significant additions to those contained in the collections of Vicuña Cifuentes and others.]

560. E. de V. "El negrito; poesía popular." RLin, Año I:3 (julio-septiembre, 1933).

561. Echeverría Reyes, Aníbal, and Cannobio, Agustín. La canción nacional de Chile. Valparaíso, 1904.

[Pereira Salas (ref. 647, p. 348) cites this work. Alegría (ref. 497, p. 16) says that there are two important collections of printed popular poetry from Chile, those of Rodolfo Lenz and A. Escheverría Reyes.]

562. Escudero, Alfonso. Romancero español. Santiago: Editorial Nascimento, 1939. lxxx, 348 pp. 14.5 cm. (Colección de clásicos, Nos. 2-7.)

[Pereira Salas (ref. 645, p. 53) says: "P. 257 y siguientes contienen: Romances recogidos de la tradición oral en Hispanoamérica, especialmente en Chile."]

563. Espinosa, Aurelio M. "Sobre un libro chileno." RChHG, Año III, Tomo VIII:12 (4.° trimestre de 1913), 396-407; appeared originally in Bulletin de Dialectologie Romane (Hamburg), July 31, 1913, pp. 49-55.

[A review of Julio Vicuña Cifuentes' Romances populares y vulgares recogidos de la tradición oral chilena. Though at the time of its appearance the reviewer's comments added considerable knowledge to the subject treated, the article is, of course, quite dated and no longer of importance.]

564. _____. "Una versión española del romance Las glorias de Teresa." AFC, IV:2 (abril a junio de 1929), 153-156.

[By way of commenting upon Ramón A. Laval's discovery in Chile of a romance sung by children, Las glorias de Teresa (see ref. 603), Espinosa prints a Spanish version of the song which he heard sung by some children in Avila.]

565. F. D. (Fernando Díaz C.). Poesías populares; reminiscencias elquinas. La Serena, 1913. 44 pp.

[According to Silva Castro (ref. 691, p. 81), it is a collection of poems by Díaz, a famous popular poet born in La Serena about 1831. They are mostly satirical compositions in romance meter, careless in form but imaginative. Silva Castro comments: "Tienen más interés folklórico que literario."]

566. F. H. H. El cantor popular. Santiago, 1865.

567. Fernández, Manuel. Romance jocoso-serio, en que se refieren los principales milagros i sucesos de la vida i muerte de San Antonio de Padua, escrito por el chileno Manuel Fernández en 1812 i publicado por el padre franciscano frai Gregorio Mazquez. Santiago: Imprenta Independencia, 1846. 32 pp.

568. Figueroa, Elisa. "Apuntes folklóricos de Malleco." AUCh, Año CVIII:79 (tercer trimestre de 1950), 87-111; also, AFCU, Fascículo No. 2, pp. 87-106.

[A study of all types of folklore from Malleco, including two popular poems which are related to the narrative romance tradition: Bartolillo (a version of the "No me entierren en sagrado" theme) and Mambrú. In the AUCh edition there are some "Notas de la redacción" (pp. 107-111) which are not included in the AFCU edition. They contain many bibliographical data about compositions cited, with particular reference to sources where variants may be found. Also, there is a bibliography of "Obras citadas" consisting of eighteen entries.]

569. Figueroa, Pedro Pablo. Locas de amor; romances nacionales. Santiago: Imprenta Victoria, 1887. 74 pp.

570. _____. El poeta popular Pedro Díaz Gana; poesías y memorias de Sebastián Cangalla. Santiago de Chile: Imprenta Moderna, 1900. 69 pp. 22 cm.

[Two introductory chapters, "El poeta popular Pedro Díaz Gana" and "La poesía popular en Chile" (pp. 9-36), treat the life and works of the popular artist. A work of his, Historia de Sebastián Cangalla, follows (pp. 37-65). In prose and verse (mostly romance meter), it is a bitter protest against the exploitation of the poor by the rich, the government, and the Church. The volume ends with another work of the poet, La condición del minero (pp. 66-69), also a romance which inveighs against the exploitation of miners.]

571. Figueroa Fernández, Amelia. Repertorio de poesía infantil. Santiago, 1947.

[Pereira Salas (ref. 645, p. 111) indicates that Chap. I (pp. 25-93) is devoted to Chilean folklore.]

572. García, Nicasio. Contrapunto de Taguada con don Javier de la Rosa, en palla a cuatro líneas de preguntas con respuestas. Recogida una parte y compuesto lo demás por el que suscribe, venciendo don Javier de la Rosa. Santiago: Imp. La Victoria, 1886. 1 p.

573. _____. Poesías populares. Tomo III. Santiago: Impreso por Pedro G. Ramírez, 1886. 96 pp.; Tomo V. Santiago: Imp. Cervantes, 1894. 95 pp. 9 cm.

[I have been unable to locate bibliographical data for the rest of the volumes in this series.]

574. _____. Versos. Santiago: Imp. Sud-América, 1873. 1 p.

García, Nicasio. See Silva Castro, Raúl, entry no. 690.

575. Garrido, Pablo. "El alma musical del pueblo chileno." Conferencia, III(1948):10-11, pp. 96-100.

576. _____. "El folklore musical de Chile." Las últimas noticias (Santiago), 11 de septiembre, 1944.

577. Garrido Avalos, Cirilo. Poesías populares acomodadas y arregladas por medio de un pensamiento con una pequeña instrucción al pueblo de más pequeña inteligencia que yo desde el anciano al mancebo, mozo y niño. Santiago: Imp. Instituto, 1907. 24 pp.

Gilbert, A. de. See Balmaceda Toro, Pedro, entry no. 518.

578. Guajardo, Bernardino. Poesías populares.
[Pereira Salas (ref. 645, p. 56) describes this work as "Nueve tomitos de 96 páginas cada uno." He gives no dates of publication or other bibliographical data. However, in the Anuario de la prensa chilena publicado por la Biblioteca Nacional (1886) there are entries for the following volumes in the series (pp. 79-80): Tomo VII. 3.ª ed. Santiago: Impreso por Pedro G. Ramírez, 1886. 96 pp.; Tomo IX. Santiago: Impreso por Pedro G. Ramírez, 1886. 96 pp.; Poesías populares: Testamento del poeta popular. Santiago: Impreso por Pedro G. Ramírez. 96 pp.]

579. _____. Versos con motivo del cólera. Santiago: Imp. de P. Ramírez, 1887.

_____. See Silva Castro, Raúl, entry no. 690.

580. Guerra, Bernardo de. Romance de los siete ladrones que a un tiempo murieron en la mina de la señora Muchástegui en Petorca, el año 1779. Santiago: Imprenta Valles, 1824. 8 pp.

581. Guerra P., Misael (Ismael Parraguez). "Los payadores: Santa Cruz." La lectura popular (Santa Cruz), Año II:144 (16 de mayo de 1909).

582. Guevara, Tomás. Folklore araucano; refranes, cuentos, cantos, procedimientos industriales, costumbres prehispanas. Santiago de Chile: Imprenta Cervantes, 1911. 288 pp. 24.5 cm.
[Chap. III, "Los cantos" (pp. 119-134), treats Araucanian songs. Some interesting texts without music are provided. Though the possible relationship of Araucanian songs to the romance or, indeed, to any kind of modern Chilean song is not studied, the author describes various kinds of Indian songs, including some which are narratives about heroes or historical events. Very interesting examples are the texts in Spanish of a Canto de Caupolicán (p. 122) and a Canto del cacique (pp. 122-123).]

583. Hanssen, Frederick, "Chilean Popular Songs." AJP, XIV (1893), 90-92.
[A small collection of Chilean coplas and other forms of popular poetry. One or two strophes might be fragments of corridos.]

Henríquez, Camilo. See Amunátegui, Miguel Luis, entry no. 507.

584. Hernández Cornejo, Roberto. El roto chileno; bosquejo histórico de actualidad. Valparaíso: Imprenta San Rafael, 1929. 651 pp. 19 cm.
[Silva Castro (ref. 691, p. 84) says that the work contains some data about popular poetry and the artists who compose it.]

585. Hernández Lagos, Julia. "Contribución al folklore de San Carlos." Studium, Año I:4 (marzo, 1927), 313-320; reprinted in BCI, Año V(1942), octubre-diciembre, 38-47.
[A collection of texts of popular poetry, including some coplas, a fragment of Las señas del marido, and a poem about the bandit Juan de Dios López, which bears no name but is in corrido form.]

586. Herreros Véliz, Ramón.
[Figueroa (ref. 570, p. 20) says: "Escribiendo romances sobre temas políticos, sociales o mineros, se hizo notable en Copiapó el viejo i espiritual poeta don Ramón Herreros Véliz, hijo de Vallenar, a quien conocimos en nuestra niñez, anciano ya, lleno de achaques, pero siempre festivo e injenuo como un niño." He goes on to indicate that Herreros Véliz used the pen name Taguada.]

587. Improvisadores chilenos. Santiago: Imp. Universitaria, 1902. 31 pp. (Vol. I of the Biblioteca económica, ed. by Domingo Urzúa Cruzat.)

588. Instituto de Extensión Musical de la Universidad de Chile. Chile. Santiago: Imprenta Afra, 1943. 53 pp. 23.5 cm.
[The Library of Congress catalogue indicates that the work contains a program of Chilean folk music presented at the Teatro Municipal in 1943. According to a long index of the volume which Pereira Salas prints (ref. 645, p. 81), it includes brief articles or comments which might touch on the romance-corrido tradition. It also contains twelve songs with texts and music, though apparently none is a corrido or a romance.]

589. Instituto de Investigaciones Folklórico-Musicales de la Universidad de Chile, Facultad de Bellas Artes. Prospectus entitled: Aires tradicionales y folklóricos de Chile; el cuando, danza nacional de Chile. 1928.

590. _____. Aires tradicionales y folklóricos de Chile; grabaciones R. C. A. Victor. 2a. serie. Santiago: Imprenta "Casa Amarilla," n.d.

591. Isamitt, Carlos. "Apuntes sobre nuestro folklore musical." Aulos, I:1 (octubre, 1932), 8-9; 2 (noviembre, 1932), 4-6; 4 (enero-febrero, 1933), 3-6; 6 (junio-julio, 1933), 6-8.

592. Jones, Earle K. "Folksongs of Chile." Chile (New York), July, 1926.

Klos, Carlos. See Balmaceda, Jorge, entry no. 517.

593. Krautmacher, Robert. "Chilenische Volksdichtung." Bundes-Kalender (Santiago?), 1933, pp. 23-30.

594. Larrañaga, Rómulo, (El Negro Peluca). El criminal; crímenes y episodios sangrientos nacionales. 12 cuadernos. Santiago: Imp. Económica, 1904. 32 pp. each cuaderno.

595. _____. El diablo alegre; versos pícaros y no pícaros. Tomo I. Santiago: Imp. Económica, 1911.

596. _____. El gran crimen de Talca; un hijo mata al padre. Debates completos por el Negro Peluca. Santiago: Imprenta Andrés Bello, 1895. 15 pp.

597. _____. El guitarrero popular; risas y carcajadas del Negro Peluca. 2 tomos. Santiago: Imp. Andrés Bello, 1894. 10.5 cm.

598. Latcham, Ricardo E. "Bibliografía chilena de antropología y etnología (1909-1913)." RBChE, Año II:1-2 (enero-febrero de 1914), 49-52.
[A listing of books and articles without descriptions or critical material. It is based primarily upon Publicaciones del Cuarto Congreso Ciéntifico (1.° Pan Americano) celebrado en Santiago de Chile del 25 de diciembre de 1908 al 5 de enero de 1909, the Revista de folklore chileno, and the Revista chilena de historia y geografía. Though it was useful when it appeared, it has been superseded by better bibliographies.]

599. _____. "Bibliografía chilena de las ciencias antropológicas, primera serie." RBChE, Año III:6 (junio de 1915), 148-185; "Segunda serie." Año III:7 (julio de 1915), 229-261.
[The "Primera serie" is a listing of 625 titles covering diverse branches of anthropology in the broad sense of the term. The list is entirely alphabetical with no grouping by subject matter or by any other criteria. A few entries have some descriptive commentary, though the vast majority do not. The bibliography is very carefully done, however, and is notable for the completeness of its entries. The "Segunda serie" incorporates 547 titles.]

600. _____. "La fiesta de Andacollo i sus danzas." AUCh, CXXVI (enero a junio, 1910), 663-685; also, RFCh, I:5 (1910), 197-219.
[Contains a description of the fiesta and an account of its history along with some verses sung on the occasion (pp. 676-677 in AUCh). They are religious coplas.]

Latorre, Mariano. See entry no. 311.

601. Laval, Ramón. Contribución al folklore de Carahue (Chile). 2 vols. Madrid: Librería General de Victoriano Suárez (Imprenta Clásica Española), 1916-1920. 28 cm.
[In Vol. I there are many romances and corridos which are of extreme interest. Also, there is considerable scholarly comment of great value. Chilean versions of a large number of traditional Spanish romances are included. Vol. II deals only with legends and tales.]

602. _____. Del latín en el folk-lore chileno. Santiago: Imp. Cervantes, 1910. 25 pp.; 2.ª edición. Santiago de Chile: Imprenta Cervantes, 1927. 42 pp. 23.5 cm.; first appeared in AUCh, CXXV (julio a diciembre, 1909), 931-953.
[In studying the appearance of Latin words and phrases in Chilean tradition, the author frequently quotes the texts of popular verses and songs. Some are coplas.]

603. _____. "Nuevas variantes de romances populares." AFC, III:4 (octubre a diciembre de 1928), 16-26.
[Contains the texts of some hitherto unpublished Chilean versions of romances from Hispanic tradition (La dama y el pastor, Don Gato, Camino del Calvario, and others).]

604. _____. Oraciones populares, ensalmos i conjuros del pueblo chileno comparados con los que se dicen en España. Santiago de Chile: Imprenta Cervantes, 1910. 132 pp. 25 cm.; first appeared in AUCh, CXXVI (enero a junio, 1910), 203-322.
[A collection of various types of popular religious literature. Included is a large body of verse, some of it being romances. This is an important source for the study of religious romances or coplas. Also, there are some décimas.]

605. _____. "Sobre dos cantos chilenos derivados de un antiguo romance español." RChHG, LXIII:67 (octubre-diciembre, 1929), 40-47.
[Contains two Chilean versions of the romance of La dama y el pastor. These are additions to the collection of Vicuña Cifuentes.]

606. Lavín, Carlos. "Reivindicación del folklore musical." Zigzag, 23 de junio de 1944.

607. _____. "La vidalita argentina y el vidalay chileno." RMC, Año 8:43 (septiembre de 1952), 68-75.
[Recounting how he was able in the 1940's to record some versions of a Chilean vidalay which he had first heard in 1894, the author finds general musical similarities (he offers seven musical transcriptions) between the vidalay of Chile and the vidalita of Argentina.]

Lenz, Rodolfo. Diccionario etimolójico de las voces chilenas derivadas de lenguas indíjenas americanas. See Los elementos indios del castellano de Chile, entry no. 608.

608. Lenz, Rodolfo. Los elementos indios del castellano de Chile; estudio lingüístico i etnolójico, primera parte. Diccionario etimolójico de las voces chilenas derivadas de lenguas indíjenas americanas. Santiago de Chile: Imprenta Cervantes, 1904. 448 pp. 23.5 cm.; Segunda entrega. Santiago de Chile: Imprenta Cervantes, 1910. xv, 449-938 pp. (continues pagination of the first part).

[Zambo and its derivatives (zambacueca, zamacueca, cueca, etc.) are defined (pp. 784-788) and a text is given and analyzed. Yaraví is also defined (p. 781).]

609. _____. Sobre la poesía popular impresa de Santiago de Chile; contribución al folklore chileno. Santiago de Chile: Sociedad Imp. Universo, 1919. 112 pp.; first appeared in AUCh, CXLIII (mayo i junio de 1919), 509-622; also RFCh, VI(1919), entregas 2 and 3.

[A loose translation with some re-editing of the pioneer study which Lenz prepared in 1894, only the first chapter of which was published (see entry no. 610). This edition in Spanish is the entire study along with some new data which were gathered during the years that intervened between the two editions. All this is explained in an "Advertencia al lector" (pp. 511-516 of the AUCh edition). The work itself is the first systematic study of popular poetry in Chile. It consists of an introduction and three chapters entitled: "Los poetas i cantores, sus instrumentos i sus formas poéticas"; "Las hojas sueltas de 'versos'"; and "Los temas de los poetas populares." Besides studying pratically all aspects of the subjects indicated, the author provides the texts of a great many compositons of all types, including a number of historical narratives written mostly in décimas.]

610. _____. "Über die gedruckte Volkspoesie von Santiago de Chile." Abhandlungen Herrn Prof. Dr. Adolf Tobler sur Feier seiner fünfundzwanzigjährigen Thätigkeit als ordentlicher Professor an der Universität Berlin von dankbaren Schülern in ehrerbietung Dargebracht. Halle: Max Niemeyer, 1895. Pp. 141-163.

[The first editing of the author's famous study of Chilean popular poetry. This first version was superseded by the greatly expanded work which appeared in Spanish in 1919 (see entry no. 609). Only the first part (through p. 567 of the AUCh edition of ref. no. 609) appeared at this time.]

611. _____.

[Diego Múñoz (ref. 632, p. 35) says: "Se editaron numerosas liras populares (toward the end of the nineteenth century) y el sabio investigador don Rodolfo Lenz logró reunir una colección de cerca de quinientos ejemplares, adornados todos ellos con hermosos grabados, algunos de ellos directamente ejecutados en madera por artistas del pueblo. Esta valiosa colección se halla actualmente en la Sección Chilena de la Biblioteca Nacional bajo el cuidado y guarda del escritor y folklorista Raúl Silva Castro."]

612. La lira popular. Santiago: Imp. Lagos, 1928. 2 pp.

Lira popular. See Valenzuela, Inés, entry no. 702.

613. Lizana, Desiderio. Cómo se canta la poesía popular. Santiago de Chile: Imprenta Universitaria, 1912. 73 pp. 25.5 cm.; first appeared in RChHG, Año II, Tomo III:7 (3.er trimestre de 1912), 244-310; also, RFCh, IV(1912), entregas 1 y 2.

[A very important study of the subject. After a brief introduction there are these sections: I. Los puetas; II. Organización del torneo; III. Canto a lo divino; IV. Canto a lo humano de verso hecho; V. Canto componiendo; VI. Del canto a dos razones; VII. De la paya propiamente tal; VIII. Canto de coleo; and Apéndice: El poeta Juan Agustín Pizarro. Lizana indicates that he is familiar only with the style of singing used in the provinces of O'Higgins and Colchagua. The real body of his study treats the characteristics of the puetas, the way in which torneos or contrapuntos are arranged and conducted, and the characteristics of the compositions which are sung in such contests. His discussions deal mostly with décimas, usually glosas, some of which are narratives about Chilean history, and cuartetas, usually in the nature of improvised coplas. In the appendix the author treats Juan Agustín Pizarro, whom he considers the best of the puetas who flourished in the department of Cachapoal during the middle of the nineteenth century. He provides some texts of poems, mostly décimas, by Pizarro.]

614. _____. "Poesía popular." Pacífico Magazine (Santiago), I(1913), 703.

615. Llantos del reino de Chile.

[Menéndez y Pelayo (ref. 82, Vol. II, p. 268) indicates that it is a poem written "con motivo de la partida del gobernador Amat en 1762." It is not clear that it is a romance. However, the composition listed just before this one is described as a "romance anónimo," so this may also be one.]

616. Lo que se canta en Chile. Santiago: Imp. Renacimiento, 1913. 84 pp.

617. M. "Nuestra contribución al estudio del folklore regional." RUnI, Año I:1 (septiembre de 1927).

M. V. C. See Villalobos C., Max, entry no. 714.

618. Madzen, Lorenzo. Cánticos populares. Santiago: Imprenta de "El Correo," 1886. 47 pp.

619. Manríquez, Cremilda. "Estudio del folklore de Cautín." AnFFE, III(1941-1943), 7-131.

[A study of various types of folk poetry, including coplas, cogollos, esquinazos, and the like, and including also a section on romances.

Most of these are variants of compositions which Vicuña Cifuentes printed in his collection.]

620. Mariño de Lovera, Pedro. Crónica del reino de Chile. Santiago: Imprenta del Ferrocarril, 1865. 456 pp. 25 cm. (Vol. VI of Colección de historiadores de Chile.)

[In relating the Spaniards' reactions to an approaching battle with the Araucanians of Lautaro in 1553, the chronicler records a conversation between two soldiers which, though written in prose, is in the form of three quintillas as though it well might have been lifted from a versified narrative of the event. Amunátegui (ref. 508, p. 90) calls it a "verdadero ejemplo de corrido." Though this is probably an overstatement, it indicates the general nature of the passage.]

621. Medina, José Toribio. Historia de la literatura colonial de Chile. 3 vols. Santiago: Imp. de la Librería del Mercurio, 1878. 25 cm.

[Contains very little about popular poetry. However, one short section, Chap. XIX, "Poesía popular," is reprinted from Valderrama's Bosquejo histórico de la poesía and deals with the Chilean contrapunto.]

622. ———. trans. Memorias de un oficial de marina inglés al servicio de Chile durante los años de 1821-1829. Santiago: Imprenta Universitaria, 1923. xi, 248 pp. 22 cm.

[A translation of a part of Richard Longeville Vowell's Campaigns and Cruises in Venezuela and New Grenada and the Pacific Ocean (see entry no. 122). There are some brief comments about dances of the huasos (pp. 67-68), including mention of the cuando. There is some attention to Chilean repentistas and two lines of a copla are quoted (p. 206).]

623. ———. Los romances basados en La Araucana, con su texto y anotaciones, y un estudio de los que se conocen sobre la América del Sur anteriores a la publicación de la primera parte de aquel poema. Santiago: Imprenta Elzeviriana, 1918. lxxvi, 52 pp. 20 cm.

[A study of the romances written in America before the publication of La Araucana and of those written afterwards which the poem of Ercilla inspired. See also Varias relaciones del Perú y Chile, entry no. 1905.]

Mendoza, Vicente T. "La canción chilena en México." See entry no. 1442.

624. ———. "La música popular en Chile." Andean Quarterly (Santiago), Spring, 1944, 27-32.

[A cursory general survey of the influences, both Spanish and Indian, which have played upon Chilean musical folklore. Romances and corridos receive passing mention in the rather extensive and useful listing of songs and dances found in Chile.]

625. Meneses, Daniel. Poesías populares: Los amores de la juventud. Tomo I. Santiago: Imp. del Comercio, 1899. 32 pp. 11.5 cm.; Tomo II. Valparaíso: Lit. e Imp. Gmo. A. Rohde y Cía., 1902. 32 pp. 12 cm.

626. _____. Poesías populares: El cantor de los cantores. Libro VI. Santiago: Imp. Cervantes, 1895; Libro VII. Santiago: Imp. Barcelona, 1896. 48 pp. 11 cm.

[This series seems to be a continuation of that of Rosa Araneda which bears the same title. See entry no. 514.]

627. _____. Poesías populares: Las glorias literarias. Valparaíso: Imp. y Litografía Gustavo Weidmann, 1902. 32 pp. 11 cm.

628. _____. Poesías populares: El guía de los cantores. Tomo I. Valparaíso: Imp. y Litografía Gustavo Weidmann, 1902. 32 pp. 11 cm.; Tomo II. Santiago: Imp. Chile, 1905. 32 pp.; Tomo III. Santiago: Imp. Europea, 1907. 32 pp.; Tomo IV. Santiago: Imp. Calle Gálvez, 1908. 32 pp.

629. _____. Poesías populares: La lira poética. Tomo I. Santiago: Imp. América, 1905. 32 pp.; Tomo II. Santiago: Imp. El Correo, 1906. 32 pp.

630. El mulato Taguada. Santiago: Casilla 3.570, No. 1 (diciembre, 1950); No. 2 (enero, 1951), No. 3 (marzo, 1951); No. 4 (abril, 1951).

[Pereira Salas (ref. 645, p. 59) describes this publication as a "periódico en hojas sueltas." He further declares: "Contiene: una parte antológica de la poesía vulgar y colaboraciones de Manuel Morillo, Benito Canela, Miguel Pino Piña y María Carrera."]

631. Muñoz, Diego. Brito, poeta popular nortino, cantor de la patria, del pueblo y de la democracia. Santiago: Imp. Gutenberg, 1946. 175 pp.

[The Brito referred to is Abraham Jesús Brito (1874-1945), a popular poet.]

632. _____. "La poesía popular chilena." AUCh, Año CXIII:93 (primer trimestre de 1954), 31-48

[A very interesting history of the popular poetry of Chile. Divided into three parts, the first deals with the romance as brought from Spain and as developed around Chilean subjects; the second is concerned with the décima; and the third traces the decline and decadence of popular poetry after World War I. There are texts of three romances (Blanca Flor y Filomena, La adúltera, and El huaso Perquenco) and many décimas, including some about historical subjects. Also, there are some contrapuntos.]

633. Muñoz, Lucila. "Estudio del folklore de San Carlos." AnFFE, III(1941-1943), 133-183.

[A study prepared in 1927 under the direction of Julio Vicuña Cifuentes.

Included are sections on romances and other popular poetry. Most of the romances are variants of compositions already printed by Vicuña Cifuentes.]

634. Muñoz R., José María. Don Zacarías Encina. Santiago: Imprenta Nascimento, 1932. 249 pp. 24 cm.

[A so-called "novela folklórica," this work is replete with proverbs, coplas, and other folkloric elements of popular origin. There seem to be no romances or other kinds of narratives.]

635. Navarro, Alfonso. "D. José Rosas Herrera, versificador popular." Revista cultura (Santiago), noviembre-diciembre, 1924, 288-294.

[According to Silva Castro (ref. 691, p. 84), this is a study of a popular poet born in Peñablanca in 1856 and still living when the article was written. Some of his compositions (décimas) are said to appear in this article.]

El Negro Peluca. See Larrañaga, Rómulo, entry no. 594.

Nercasseau y Morán, Enrique, ed. See Valderrama, Adolfo, entry no. 700.

636. Núñez de Pineda y Bascuñán, Francisco. Cautiverio feliz del maestro de campo, jeneral Don Francisco Núñez ne [sic] Pineda y Bascuñán, y razón individual de las guerras dilatadas del reino de Chile, ed. by Diego Barros Arana. Santiago: Imprenta del Ferrocarril, 1863. vi, vii, 560 pp. 25 cm. (Colección de historiadores de Chile, Vol. III.); also, El cautiverio feliz de Francisco Núñez de Pineda y Bascuñán, ed. by Angel Custodio Gouzález. Santiago: Zig-Zag, 1948. 440 pp., 11 lvs. 20.5 cm.

[A work dated 1673 which contains several intercalated artistic romances (pp. 46, 467, 470, 533, and 537 of the 1863 edition). Other shorter compositions or fragments are found in other parts of the volume. Most of the poetry has been omitted from the 1948 edition, but there remain a few lines in romance meter (pp. 43-44, 397-398).]

637. O. M. S. El cantor popular; colección escogida de zamacuecas, coplas, seguidillas, canciones, etc., etc. 4 vols. Concepción: Librería Serrato, Imp. El Comercio, 1893. 40 pp. each vol.

638. Otaiza de Estrada, Aída. Alhué (ensayo de monografía regional). Santiago: Imprenta y Litografía Universo, S. A., 1944. 18.5 cm.

[Listed by Pereira Salas (ref. 645, p. 29) in a section on Folklore.]

Parraguez, Ismael. See Guerra P., Misael, entry no. 581.

639. Pavés P., Francisco A. "Poetas populares e improvisadores." In Desarrollo intelectual de Curicó, publicaciones de la Comisión de Historia, Arte y Literatura del Segundo Centenario de Curicó. Curicó: Imp. La Prensa, 1913. Pp. 72-80.

El Pequén. See Allende, Juan Rafael, entry no. 499.

640. Peralta, Juan Bautista. El cantor santiaguino. Santiago: Imprenta Esperanza, 1902. 32 pp.

641. Peralta de Gaeta, Juan Bautista. La lira popular; poesía. Santiago: Imp. Nueva República, 1928. 2 pp. 37 cm.

642. Pereira Salas, Eugenio. "Consideraciones sobre el folklore en Chile." RMC, Año XIII:68 (noviembre-diciembre de 1959), 83-92.
[Surveys the development of numerous forms of Chilean popular songs and dances including the romance, the cuando, the cueca, and many others. A few texts are given, including one fragment of a romance from the time of Almagro.]

643. _____. "Danzas y cantos populares de la patria vieja." AnFFE, II(1937-1938):1 (Homenaje a la memoria del Dr. Rodolfo Lenz), 58-76.
[Chase (ref. 25, p. 118) notes that the material contained here has been incorporated into Los orígenes del arte musical en Chile (entry no. 647).]

644. _____. "Los estudios folklóricos y el folklore musical en Chile." RMC, Año I:1 (1 de mayo de 1945), 4-12.
[A valuable summary of the development of folklore investigations and related studies in Chile. The author traces the history of such activity and mentions the most outstanding names and works. Much of this is useful bibliography, though it would be more helpful if more bibliographical details were given.]

645. _____. "Guía bibliográfica para el estudio del folklore chileno." AFCU, Fascículo No. 4, pp. 1-112; also published in book form under the imprint of the Instituto de Investigaciones Musicales, 1952. 112 pp. 24 cm.
[A very valuable bibliography. After tracing the history of the study of folklore in Chile, the author offers a bibliography divided into eighteen sections plus a section of addenda. Practically all types of folklore are treated. Of particular interest are sections XI, "La literatura popular en verso," and XV, "La música folklórica tradicional y popular." In these there is much bibliography about popular poetry and song of all kinds.]

646. _____. Historia de la música en Chile (1850-1900). Santiago: Publicaciones de la Universidad de Chile, 1957. 379 pp. 27 cm.

647. _____. Los orígenes del arte musical en Chile. Santiago: Imprenta Universitaria, 1941. xvi, 373 pp. 25 cm.
[A fundamental study of the music of Chile with extensive treatment of popular music and dances, including discussion of romances and corridos in Chap. XVII, "El desarrollo histórico de la danza y de la música popular." There is a great deal of bibliography in the book.]

648. Pereira Salas, Eugenio. "El rincón de la historia: El arpa . . . que en dulce nota." RMC, Año I:4 (agosto de 1945), 41.

[A brief history of the Chilean harp from colonial days, when it was an ecclesiastical instrument, to its present-day acceptance as an instrument of the people.]

649. _____. "El rincón de la historia: La vihuela en la colonia." RMC, Año I:6 (octubre de 1945), 40.

[A romantic evocation of the introduction of the vihuela into Chile from Spain and its development into the fine guitars of Chile and the rest of America. The article is of no real importance.]

650. _____. Un romance inédito del siglo XVII. Santiago: Imprenta Universitaria, 1944. 18 pp. 24.5 cm.

[A paleographic edition of an artistic historical romance entitled Relación que hizo Butapichún, Capitán General de los yndios de guerra a Anganamón. It contains 240 lines and exists in manuscript form in a volume entitled Iglesias de Indias (1639) in the Newberry Library in Chicago. The event treated is the defeat of the Indians under Butapichún at the Battle of El Albarrada (known also by the names of Petaco or Arauco) on Jan. 13, 1631, by the forces under Governer Francisco Laso de la Vega. For the full title of the romance see entry no. 670.]

651. El picaflor; recopilación escogida de versos para bailes, canciones populares, décimas de notables autores, tonadas. Valparaíso: Imp. Nacional, 1902. 73 pp.

652. Pino Saavedra, Y. "Tres fonogramas de canciones populares chilenas." Vox, Internationales Zentralblatt für experimentelle Phonetik (Berlin), XVII(1931), 125-129.

653. Pinto F., Manuel A. Poesías populares. Tomo I. 2.ª ed. Valparaíso: Tipografía Nacional, 1896. 16 pp.; Tomo II. Valparaíso: Tipografía Nacional, 1896. 16 pp.

654. Plath, Oreste. Folklore chileno; aspectos populares infantiles. Santiago: Prensas de la Universidad de Chile, 1946. 119 pp. 26.5 cm.; this is a reprint of an article in AUCh, Año CIV:61-62 (primero y segundo trimestres de 1946), 203-317.

[A collection of many types of children's folklore. In the section entitled "Canciones de corro" (pp. 12-20) there are some songs which have their origin in Spanish romances (Don Gato, Hilo de oro, and others).]

655. Poesías populares. Santiago: Imp. de P. Ramírez, 1889. 32 pp.

[This work, listed by Pereira Salas (ref. 645, p. 58) and by the Anuario de la prensa chilena publicado por la Biblioteca Nacional, may well be one of the volumes of the work by Juan Rafael Allende which bears the same name (see entry no. 500).]

656. Poesías populares. 1. er tomo. Chillán: Imprenta y Encuadernación Moderna, 1906. 36 pp.

657. Porter, Carlos E. Bibliografía chilena de antropología y etnología. B. A.: Imprenta Juan A. Alsina, 1910. 44 pp. 24 cm.; a reprint from the Anales del Museo Nacional de Buenos Aires (B. A.), XX, 145-188.

658. _____. Bibliografía chilena de ciencias antropológicas. Santiago: Imprenta Santiago, 1912. 62 pp. 21 cm.

659. _____. Literatura antropológica y etnológica de Chile. Santiago: Imp. Universo, 1906. 36 (28?) pp. 23 cm.; a reprint from the Revista chilena de historia natural (Santiago), X(1906).

660. Porter de la Barrera, Ricardo. "El canto chileno." Patria, agosto de 1936.

661. _____. "El canto popular en Chile." Revista Hoy (Santiago), 13 de marzo de 1943.

662. _____. "Cantos de mi tierra." Patria, No. 276 (noviembre de 1944).

663. _____. "El folklore musical chileno." Patria, No. 295 (junio de 1946).

664. _____. "El ingenio en el canto popular." Revista En viaje, órgano de los Ferrocarriles del Estado (Santiago), junio de 1946.

665. _____. "Los payadores de antaño." Revista En viaje, órgano de los Ferrocarriles del Estado (Santiago), noviembre de 1941.

666. "Primer Congreso Nacional de Poetas y Cantos Populares de Chile." AUCh, Año CXIII:93 (primer trimestre de 1954), 5-27.
[A report on the Congress held April 15-18, 1954. The history of the Congress and the Unión de Poetas y Cantores Populares is sketched in some detail and a membership list is given.]

667. Ramillete de Flores, Quarta, Quinta, y Sexta parte de Flor de Romances nueuos, nunca hasta agora impressos, llamado Ramillete de Flores: De muchos, graues y diuersos Autores. Recopilado no cõ poco trauajo: Por Pedro Flores Librero: Y a su costa impresso. Y demas desto, va al cabo la tercera parte de el Araucana, en nueue Romances, excepto la entrada de este Reyno de Portugal, q̃ por ser tan notoria a todos no se pone. Con licencia y Priuilegio. En Lisboa. Por Antonio Aluarez Impresor, Año de 1593. Vendese en casa de el mismo Flores, al Pelorinho Velho. 444 pp.
[Medina (ref. 623) prints nine artistic romances inspired by La Araucana of Ercilla which were published in this work.]

Ramírez, Juan Ramón. See Campo, S. del, and Un colchagüino, entries no. 526 and 548.

668. Rela, Walter. "Un documento poético-popular chileno del siglo XIX." RN, IV(1959), 391-405.
 [Paredes (ref. 91, p. 58) says: "Two variants of singing contest in mid-19th century Chile, one from manuscript, one from oral tradition of 1933."]

669. Relación de la inundación, que hizo el Río Mapocho de la Ciudad de Santiago de Chile, el día 16 julio de 1783. Escrita en verso octosilavo [sic] por una Religiosa, etc. (Lima, 1783). 6 lvs.
 [Palau, in a poorly punctuated comment, says: "Escribió éste opusculo Sor Tadea de San Joaquin, y se reimprimió en Santiago do Chile [sic], 1862, 8.° 22 págs. y Id. 1877, 8.° 26 págs." Menéndez Pelayo (ref. 82, Vol. II, p. 268) lists the work as "otro romance anónimo."]

670. Relazión que hizo Butapichún, Capitán General de los yndios de guerra a Anganamón, persona a quien todos respetan y le dan quenta de los suzessos y batallas y asaltos que tienen con los españoles, por hauer sido el de más nombre entre ellos y hauer consiguido [sic] muy grandes vitorias en su tiempo, de la pérdida que tubo en el estado de Arauco peleando con don Francisco Lasso de la Vega Aluarado, Cauallero del háuito de Santiago, Presidente, Governador y Capp (it) án Jeneral del Reyno de Chile por su Mag (esta) d.
 [This is the full title of the romance which Pereira Salas edits in entry no. 650.]

671. Rivadeneira, Ester. "Folklore de la provincia de Bío-Bío." RChHG, LXXXVII:95 (julio-diciembre de 1939), 95-161; also published as a reprint, Santiago: Imp. Universitaria, 1940. 71 pp. 25 cm.
 [Folklore gathered around Los Angeles, capital of the province of Bío-Bío. Included are alabanzas, oraciones, games, riddles, etc. Some alabanzas are coplas, some are romance fragments (e. g., En el portal de Belén), but there is no attention to popular poetry as such.]

672. Roco del Campo. Antonio. Notas del folklore chileno. Santiago: Talleres Gráficos Gutenberg, 1939. 64 pp. 18.5 cm. (Ediciones populares, Caja de Seguro Obligatorio. Folletos de divulgación cultural, No. 2.)
 [Boggs (ref. 13 [1940], p. 52) says: "General observations and examples of various types of folklore, as found in Chile."]

673. _____. Panorama y color de Chile. Santiago: Ediciones Ercilla, 1939. 318 pp. 17.5 cm.
 [An anthology of literature about Chilean customs and the Chilean landscape. Included are a fairly respectable number of fragments of popular songs (there are some coplas) and several artistic composiciones written in romance form.]

674. Rodríguez, Zorobabel. "Apuntes sobre la poesía indígena de América." EstCh, I(1867-1868), 231, 243, 255, 266, 278.

675. _____. "Dos poetas de poncho: Bernardino Guajardo y Juan Morales." EstCh, Año VI(1873):304, p. 763; 305, p. 775; 307, p. 823; 308, p. 309, p. 856; reprinted in Vol. III of the author's Miscelánea literaria, política i relijiosa. Santiago: Imprenta de "El Independiente," 1876.

[Silva Castro (ref. 690, p. 73) calls this work the earliest study of vulgar poetry that he is acquainted with. It deals with two poets, Guajardo (whom Rodríguez calls Gallardo) and Juan Morales. According to Silva's rather lengthy description, it describes their appearance, their manner of composing, etc.]

676. Román Guerrero, Rebeca. "Folklore de la antigua provincia de Colchagua." RChHG, LX:64 (enero-marzo de 1929), ?-?; LXI:65 (abril-junio de 1929), 150-190; LXII:66 (julio-septiembre de 1929), 206-239.

[According to Pereira Salas' description (ref. 645, p. 29), there is a section called "Versos que dicen los niños." This is apparently in Vol. LX, which I was not able to consult; it does not appear in Vols. LXI or LXII. There is a bibliography of thirty-six items at the end of the last installment in Vol. LXII.]

677. El romancero; colección de romances de batallas célebres, poesías populares, canciones y zamacuecas, tonadas y esquinazos, versos para canto y cantos de amor en verso, con láminas. Valparaíso: Imp. y Encuadernación Victoria, 1896.

678. Romancero general (1600, 1604, 1605); edición, prólogo e índices de Angel González Palencia. Madrid: Consejo Superior de Investigaciones Científicas, 1947. lxvii, 402 pp. 26 cm. (Clásicos españoles, Vol. III.)

[A modern edition which incorporates the three Spanish editions of 1600, 1604, and the 1605 edition of the Segunda parte del romancero general. Medina (ref. 623) prints six romances based on La Araucana which appeared in this Romancero general. Four are from Part I (nos. 44, 45, 48, and 49) and two are from Part VI (nos. 492 and 493). In the critical introduction to this edition there are extensive notes about the various editions of the Romancero general.]

679. Romances del desafío de Oliveros y Montesinos. Valparaíso: Imprenta Nacional. 32 pp. 11 cm.

680. [Ruschenberger, William Samuel]. Three Years in the Pacific; Containing Notices of Brazil, Chile, Bolivia, Peru, etc. in 1831, 1832, 1833, 1834, by an Officer in the United States Navy. 2 vols. London: Richard Bentley, 1835 23 cm.; an earlier edition, Philadelphia: Carey, Lea and Blanchard, 1834. xi, 441 pp. 22 cm.; translated in part with the title, Noticias de Chile (1831-1832). Santiago: Editorial del Pacífico, 1956. 120 pp.

[In Vol. I (1835 edition) there is a description of the singing and dancing of the cuando (pp. 117-180). In Vol. II there is mention of several types of popular songs and dances along with the text of a rather lengthy letrilla containing some historical allusions to San Martín (pp. 362-363). None of these songs are corridos or romances, but because of the early date of the book I mention it here.]

681. Sabella, Andrés. "Abraham Jesús Brito, poeta popular nortino." Las últimas noticias (Santiago?), 30 de abril, 1947.

682. _____. "Pezoa Véliz, el poeta del pueblo chileno." Espiral (Bogotá), VIII(1958):74.

683. Salas Viu, V. "La música popular de Chile y la española." Insula (B. A.), II(1944), 64-66.

San Joaquín, Sor Tadea de. See Relación de la inundación, entry no. 669.

684. Sandoval, Luis. Selección de canciones populares chilenas. Santiago, 1937.

685. Sepúlveda, José Tadeo, and Waldemar, Franke H. Cantos populares. Primera serie, edición A i B. Chillán, 1890.

686. Sepúlveda Maira, María Luisa. Cancionero chileno; canciones y tonadas chilenas del siglo XIX para canto y guitarra. Segunda serie. Santiago: Casa Amarilla, n.d. [1945?]. ii, 14 pp.

687. Sererini, Pedro. El trovador moderno; colección de canciones, cuecas, brindis, décimas, cantos, zarzuelas, tangos y otras yerbas. Santiago: Imp. L. V. Caldera, 1906. 23 pp.

688. Silva A., Adolfo. Canciones, cantares y tonadas nuevas. Segunda serie precedida de un modo práctico para aprender la guitarra. La compilación más completa y variada de las últimas zarzuelas, cuecas, tonadas, tangos, coplas, versos para la novena del Niño Jesús, a lo divino, etc. Santiago, 1911. 61 pp.

689. Silva Castro, Raúl. "Nociones históricas sobre la décima glosada." AUCh, Año CXIII:93 (primer trimestre de 1954), 49-59.
[Silva Castro describes the collection of printed popular poetry gathered by Lenz and now housed in the Biblioteca Nacional de Chile. Then, after tracing the Spanish origins of the décima and its development in Chile, he gives the texts of several décimas by Bernardino Guajardo, Juan Rafael Allende, Nicasio García, and other popular poets.]

690. _____. "Notas bibliográficas para el estudio de la literatura chilena." AUCh, Año II, 3.ª serie, cuarto trimestre de 1932, 309-457; Suplemento a 1932, 703-823; also published separately, Santiago: Prensas de la Universidad de Chile, 1933. ix, 269 pp.
[An excellent bibliography with critical annotations of many entries. Some concern Chilean folklore.]

691. _____. "Notas bibliográficas para el estudio de la 'poesía vulgar' de Chile." AUCh, Año CVIII:79 (Tercer trimestre de 1950), 69-86; also, AFCU, Fascículo No. 2, pp. 69-86.
[A very useful bibliography which is arranged chronologically by years from 1866 to 1938. It has sometimes extensive descriptions of the books and articles listed and is an indispensable work on the subject of Chilean popular poetry.]

_____. See Torres-Ríoseco, Arturo, entry no. 694.

692. Soustelle, Georgette and Jacques. Folklore chilien; textes choisis et traduits, avec des annotations. Paris: Institut International de Cooperation Intellectuelle, n.d. [1938?]. 230 pp. 20 cm.
[Silva Castro (ref. 691, p. 86) indicates that the last section of the book is entitled "Poésie populaire" (pp. 189 ff.).]

693. Sundt, Roberto. "Bibliografía araucana." RBChE, Año V:11-12 (noviembre-diciembre, 1917), 300-315; Año VI:1-2 (enero-febrero, 1918), 3-20; 3-4 (marzo-abril, 1918), 87-101; 5-6 (mayo-junio, 1918), 182-213; 7-8 (julio-agosto, 1918), 269-286; 9-10 (septiembre-octubre, 1918), 345-360; and subsequent numbers. [I have been able to consult only the numbers listed. They include part of the entries for the letter L.]
[An excellent bibliography which annotates many of the items listed. It deals very broadly with its subject, the Araucanian Indians; hence it includes many works about Chile in general. Many listings have to do with anthropology, ethnology, and folklore, and while only a few deal obviously with romances, corridos, and other popular poetry (and these would probably all be found in other bibliographies), this work should not be overlooked by any student who might be investigating intensively the narrative poetry of Chile.]

694. Torres-Ríoseco, Arturo, and Silva Castro, Raúl. Ensayo de bibliografía de la literatura chilena. Cambridge, Mass.: Harvard University Press, 1935. x, 71 pp. 23.5 cm.

695. Türke, Juan. Pequeño cancionero militar. Núm. I. Santiago: Imprenta del Comercio, 1895. 8 pp. 20 cm.

696. Ulloa C., F. La penitenciaría de Santiago; lo que ha sido, lo que es y lo que debiera ser. Santiago, 1878. v, 122 pp.
[Silva Castro (ref. 691, pp. 74-75) says it contains some glosas written by inmates of the penitentiary (Chap. VIII, pp. 58 ff.). One is a décima a lo adivino; the other is a composition a lo humano.]

697. Uribe Echevarría, Juan. "Contribución al estudio de la literatura de costumbres en Chile." Prologue of Tipos y costumbres de Chile by Pedro Ruiz Aldea. Santiago: Ed. Zig-Zag, 1947. Pp. ix-lxxxvi.

698. Urrutia Blondel, Jorge. "Brief Notes on Chilean Folk Music." Andean Monthly (Santiago), II:8 (October, 1939), 23-29.
[A short article which deals with tonadas and more learned forms of music. There is nothing on romances or corridos.]

699. Valderrama, Adolfo. Bosquejo histórico de la poesía chilena. Santiago: Imprenta Chilena, 1866. 270 pp. 22 cm.; reprinted in Obras escogidas (see entry no. 700).
[Part IV, "Poesía popular," is an important early study of Chilean popular poetry. It treats the payadores and defines three classes of songs: tonada, corrido, and paya. The appendix contains examples of the corrido and the paya.]

700. _____. Obras escogidas en prosa de don Adolfo Valderrama; colección hecha por don Enrique Nercasseau y Morán y precedida de una biografía del autor. Santiago: Imprenta Barcelona, 1912. xvii, 544 pp. 22 cm. (Biblioteca de escritores de Chile, Vol. VIII).
[Silva Castro (ref. 691, p. 73) indicates that the "Bosquejo histórico de la poesía chilena" (see entry no. 699) is reprinted here.]

701. Valenzuela, Inés. "Acerca de la vida de los actuales poetas populares." AUCh, Año CXIII:93 (primer trimestre de 1954), 60-79.
[The author recalls the childhood influences that created the interest in popular poetry which led her to publish La lira popular. Then, after characterizing the publication and the poets who contribute to it, she offers a commentary on a recital by poets who were present at the Primer Congreso Nacional de Poetas y Cantores Populares de Chile. She provides a great many data about contemporary popular poets and prints a number of their compositions here. Most are in décimas, though some are in cuartetas, and a few deal with historical themes.]

702. _____, Director. Lira popular. Enero de 1950-?.
[A monthly publication which is described as follows (AUCh, Año CXIII:93 (primer trimestre de 1954), 5): "Esta lira siguió el modelo de gran tamaño que fué característico de las liras populares del período más brillante del desarrollo de la poesía popular chilena. Desgraciadamente, esta publicación, realizada cuidadosamente y en cuyas columnas se hicieron valiosas revelaciones, no pudo prosperar por falta de recursos económicos."]

703. Vargas Andrade, Lina. "Contribución al estudio de la literatura popular de Chiloé." AUCh, 2.ª serie, Año V, 1.ᵉʳ trimestre, 1927, 123-221.
[An important collection of folklore materials from Chiloé, including a goodly number of corridos, romances, and other popular poetry. Some of it is of peninsular origin, some is exclusively Chilean in character. There is a short bibliography.]

704. Vega, Carlos. "Música folklórica de Chile." RMC, Año XIII:68 (noviembre-diciembre de 1959), 3-32.
[A detailed study of the music of the cueca with numerous musical examples. The author also considers related genres such as the nave, the resbalosa, the cielito, and other songs and dances. He compares Argentine and Chilean forms.]

Vega López, Carlos. La poesía popular de la América Española. See entry no. 120.

705. Vial, Román. Costumbres chilenas. 2 vols. 2.ª ed. Santiago: Imprenta Cervantes, 1907. 18 cm.
[Costumbristic sketches and plays about Chilean life. In Vol. II there is an interesting description of a blind singer's rendition of a gloss of a cuarteta in décimas. The complete text is given.]

706. Vicuña Cifuentes, Julio. "Discurso de incorporación sobre la poesía popular chilena." Boletín de la Academia Chilena (Santiago), Vol. I(1915), Cuaderno III, 233-283; reprinted in the author's He dicho. Santiago, 1926. Pp. 17-76.
[A study of Chilean popular poetry, including romances, coplas, corridos, romances vulgares, and other genres. There are some texts of the different types treated.]

707. _____. "Estudios del folklore chileno." RChHG, I(1911): 1, pp. 100-109.

708. _____. Instrucciones para recoger de la tradición oral romances populares. Santiago: Imprenta E. Blanchard-Chessi, 1905. 43 pp.; reprinted in BCC, III:15 (mayo-junio, 1939), 12-23.

709. _____. "¿Qué es el folklore y para qué sirve?" RChHG, Año I:3 (3.er trimestre de 1911), 441-448; reprinted in BCC, III:15 (mayo-junio, 1939), 5-11.
[An elementary statement of the nature of folklore and how it can serve to impart understanding of the character of a people. By way of illustration, the author quotes a few coplas, though it is not clear whether they are from Chile.]

710. _____. Romances populares y vulgares recogidos de la tradición oral chilena. Santiago: Imprenta Barcelona, 1912. xxxiii, 580 pp. 22 cm. (Biblioteca de escritores de Chile, Vol. VII.)
[The fundamental and indispensable work on the romance and derived forms (corridos, logas, etc.) in Chile. It contains a voluminous collection of texts with valuable and very scholarly commentaries.]

711. Vidales, Pablo. Album de cantos escolares. Santiago: Imp. R. Brías, 1930. 96 pp.

712. Villablanca, Celestina. "Estudio del folklore de Chillán." AnFFE, III(1941-1943), 185-223.
[A report on an investigation made in 1927 at the suggestion of

Julio Vicuña Cifuentes. There are sections on romances, tonadas, coplas, and the like.]

713. Villalobos, L. "Folklore: El salteo a don Félix Méndez, romance vulgar." RLin, Año XI:44 (octubre-diciembre, 1943).

714. Villalobos C., Max (M. V. C.). El Cachafás; libro nuevo de lindísimas y variadas poesías y versos a la moda del día, canciones y arabíes, décimas y zamacuecas; recopilación hecha por la Librería de la Joya Literaria. Tacna: La Joya Literaria, 1911. 163 pp.

715. _____. El ruiseñor; nueva recopilación de versos, canciones nuevas, décimas y arabíes, cuecas. Segunda serie. Iquique: Imprenta R. Boni e Hijos, 1904. 109 pp.

716. "Violeta Parra, hermana mayor de los cantores populares." RMC, Año XII:60 (julio-agosto de 1958), 71-77.
[A biographical sketch with some dialogue from an interview which deals with the life of Violeta Parra, folk singer and investigator of folklore. The real purpose of the article is to announce the approaching appearance of two books by her, though their titles are not given.]

Waldemar, Franke H. See Sepúlveda, José Tadeo, entry no. 685.

717. Wegener, Elena. "Anotaciones folklóricas de Constitución." AFCU, Fascículo No. 8 (1957), 61-89.
[A collection of folk materials gathered in the town of Constitución. Included are some romances and other popular poetry. There are texts of Don Gato, Mambrú, Bernardina (a version of Delgadina), Blanca Flor y Filomena, Por el rastro de la sangre, etc.]

718. Zañartu, Sady. "El camino de la música chilena." Chile (New York), 1926.

719. _____. "Folk-lore chileno; procesión de la sangre, evocación de la semana mayor en Santiago de Chile, época colonial." CV, Año XIII:103 (mayo de 1930), 125-126.
[A narrative and descriptive poem which evokes the procession indicated. Written in octosyllabic cuartetas, rhymed abcb in either assonance or consonance, it is similar in form to the corridos of Mexico. But though it is not a particularly "artistic" composition, there is no real attempt to capture a truly popular tone either in style or vocabulary.]

COLOMBIA

Though J. M. Vergara y Vergara recorded the existence of traditional Spanish romances in Colombia in his Historia de la literatura en Nueva Granada published in 1867, the failure of folklorists to gather many romance texts since that time stands in contrast to their notable success in compiling voluminous collections of coplas, known usually as cantas. This leads inevitably to the conclusion that either the romance tradition has not been cultivated as extensively in Colombia as in many other regions of America or that Colombian folklorists have gathered one type of popular verse to the almost total neglect of another. While this latter is not likely, the general quality of folklore studies in Colombia has not been notably high, and the possibility exists that more careful collecting and research might reveal the presence of a romance tradition much stronger than present studies now lead us to believe.

In reality, such romance texts as we have from Colombia usually are to be found in collections of coplas, and most information about the role of narrative poetry in Colombian popular tradition appears in studies by investigators not primarily interested in romances. Among such collectors might be mentioned Juan de Dios Arias, Lucas de Batet, Pedro Fabo de María, Benigno A. Gutiérrez, Joaquín R. Medina, José Vargas Tamayo, Gustavo Otero Muñoz, Octavio Quiñones Pardo, and Antonio José Restrepo. But even in the field of their primary interest, the coplas, or cantas, a great many of these investigators have been eager aficionados rather than trained scholars, and folklore studies in Colombia still await the appearance of investigators akin to the several who have studied with marked competence the folklore of Argentina, Chile, Mexico, and a few other regions of Spanish America. This is not to say that the efforts of the aforementioned Colombians have not provided considerable data which will be of value to future investigators or that some scholars not mentioned, like those who have occasionally commented on the galerón, a variety of romance apparently found only in Colombia and Venezuela, have not performed useful service. I mean only to call attention to the generally unsystematic approach and fragmentary character of most studies of Colombian popular poetry and song; there is no intention of dismissing as unworthy all the work done by Colombian folklorists. Some of the latter, like Joaquín R. Medina, never laid claim to being scholars, and several of them worked at a time when the collecting and interpreting of folklore materials were in their infancy, not only in Colombia but elsewhere as well.

Likewise, in the field of folklore bibliography Colombia has not been marked by an abundance of competent scholars. To Gerardo

Enríquez Córdoba and Marcelino de Castellví must go an accolade for having made the only significant contribution in this field, though even their very useful bibliography, to which I myself am profoundly indebted, does not pretend to be a definitive work, but only a tentative attempt to fill a glaring gap.

Nor have the musical aspects of Colombian popular songs received the attention which they deserve, albeit Daniel G. Zamudio's brief but excellent study entitled "El folklore musical en Colombia" has much to offer scholars interested in either the musical or the literary aspects of folklore.

COLOMBIA

720. Abadía, Julio. El galerón llanero. Bogotá, 1944.
[Grases (ref. 2007, p. 131) indicates that this work studies the galerón "Como danza colombiana cantada con coplas, que determinan los pasos coreográficos del baile . . . ."]

721. Acuña, Luis Alberto. "Del folklore colombiano: Cantas del Valle de Tenza." RAmer, XVI:52 (abril de 1949), 278-284.
[Though essentially a review of Cantas del Valle de Tenza by Medina and Vargas Tamayo, the article attempts to survey some of the characteristics of the psychology of the people represented by the large collection of cantas (i.e., coplas) in question. The reviewer quotes textually thirty-seven of these.]

722. _____. "Folklore del departamento de Santander." RFCC, No. 5 (abril, 1949), 97-133.
[In his general survey the author includes a fairly extensive section on coplas grouped according to their subject matter. Some are "políticas." There are no romances or other true narratives.]

723. Alvarez de Velasco y Zorrilla, Francisco. Rhytmica sacra, Moral y Laudatoria, por Dn Francisco Alvarez de Velasco y Zorrilla, Gobernador y Capitan General de la Provincia de Neyba y la Plata, y Produrador General para esta Real Corte de Madrid por la Ciudad de Santa Fé, cabeça y corte del Nuevo Reyno de Granada. Compuesta de varias poesías, y metros, con una Epistola en prosa, y dos en verso, y otras varias Poesías en celebración de Soror Inés Juana de la Cruz, y vna Apologia, o discurso en proSa, sobre la Milicia Angelica, y Cíngulo de Santo Thomás. Dedícala su autor al Excelentissimo Dn Joseph Fernandez de Velasco y Tobar Condestable de Castilla y de Leon, Duque de la Ciudad de Frias, &.
Adviertesse que aunque van algunas Poesías a otros assumptos sin coordinacion de numeros, su legitima colocacion es por averse impreso las obras de que esta se compone, por distintos Impressores en diferentes lugares y tiempos.
[Alvárez de Velasco is a Colombian poet of the eighteenth century. Of this work Menéndez y Pelayo says (ref. 82, Vol. I, p. 426): "En la Biblioteca Nacional he examinado un voluminoso tomo colecticio, en que están juntos los papeles de Alvárez de Velasco, con este título general . . . ." He lists (pp. 426-431) the contents of the volume, which includes some romances and romances endecasílabos.]

724. Anuario bibliográfico colombiano, 1951-1956, compiled by Rubén Pérez Ortiz. Bogotá: Imprenta del Banco de la República, 1958. xx, 335 pp. 24 cm.; Anuario bibliográfico colombiano, 1957-1958, compiled by Rubén Pérez Ortiz. Bogotá: Prensas del Instituto Caro y Cuervo, 1960. xvi, 181 pp. 24 cm.
[Excellent bibliographies which represent the best work of their kind to come out of Colombia. Each contains brief sections on

folklore along with sections on literature, travel literature, and the like which contain references that would be of interest to folklorists.]

725. Aradía, Guillermo. "Glosas para tres danzas típicas colombianas: el bambuco, el galerón, la cumbia." HCPC, No. 18 (1952), 3 pp. unnumbered.

[Concerned exclusively with choreography, this article does not mention the singing of galerones or provide any texts.]

726. Arce, Margot. "La poesía popular colombiana." Atenea, Año XIII:132 (junio de 1936), 292-311.

[Good general treatment of the popular poetry of Colombia, with consideration of such matters as racial influences, meter, instruments, themes, and the like. Though mainly concerned with coplas, of which some texts are given, the article contains brief mention of galerones and corridos.]

727. Arciniegas, Germán. "La copla en Boyacá." Prologue to Cantares de Boyacá by Octavio Quiñones Pardo; also, in El Tiempo (Bogotá), 14 de noviembre de 1937.

[Enríquez Córdoba and Castellví (ref. 770, p. 152) refute some hypotheses expressed by Arciniegas in this work.]

728. Arciniegas, José Ignacio, comp. Cantares del Tolima Grande. Bogotá: Talleres de Italgraf, 1958.

729. Arcos, Dr. (Camilo S. Delgado). Historia, tradiciones y leyendas de Cartagena. 4 vols. Cartagena: Tip. "Mogollón," 1911-1914. 19.5 cm.

Arias, Juan de Dios. Folklore santandereano. See entry no. 781.

730. _____. "El romance en la tradición santandereana." Bol, No. 16 (enero-febrero, 1953), 137-165.

[An important collection of texts with commentary. The first part deals with old Spanish romances which have survived in Santander (Delgadina, Hilito de oro, Don Gato, etc.). The second and most valuable part deals with historical romances from Santander and includes some very fine texts.]

731. _____. "Romances y dichos santandereanos." RJav, XX:98 (septiembre, 1943), 116-123.

[Attests to the existence of romances in Colombian tradition and gives two Colombian versions of Hilito, hilito de oro.]

732. Batet, Lucas de. Cancionero huilense caqueteño.

[Batet, a Catalán priest, began to make this collection of about 2,000 cantares (coplas) in Colombia in 1930. Parts of it were published in the early 1940's in Amazonia colombiana americanista. For articles containing coplas from the collection or commentaries about it, see entries under Castellví, Marcelino; Enríquez Córdoba, Gerardo; and Igualada, Francisco de.]

733. _____. "Texto de las coplas del cancionero del P. Lucas de Batet." ACA, II:4-8 (1944), 133-137.
[The texts of thirty coplas of the thousands which Batet has collected in the Caquetá region of Colombia. Those in this collection deal with birds.]

734. Bose, Fritz. "Die Musik der Uitoto." Dissertation, Berlín, 1934.

735. Botero, Juan José. Lejos del nido; novela de costumbres. Bogotá, 1924.
[Otero Muñoz (ref. 842, p. 283) prints a copla taken from this work.]

736. _____. Mis cantares.
[Otero Muñoz (ref. 842, p. 278) prints an amorous copla taken from this work.]

737. _____. Poesías y comedias. Bogotá: Editorial Minerva, 1928. 328 pp. 17.5 cm.
[According to the Library of Congress card, this work contains a section of "Cantares y coplas," probably artistic poems influenced by popular poetry.]

738. Brisson, Jorge. Casanare. Bogotá: Imprenta Nacional, 1896. xiii, 318 pp. 24 cm.
[Otero Muñoz (ref. 842, p. 276) prints an historical copla taken from this work.]

739. Buenahora, Gonzalo. La guabina santandereana.
[In Folklore santandereano (ref. 781, p. 60) there is a citation from this work regarding the nature of the guabina, a type of Colombian copla.]

740. Caballero Sierra, Abimael. [La copla en el Magdalena]. Bogotá: Extensión Cultural de la Universidad Nacional, 1956. 7 lvs. 24.5 cm. (Entregas de poesía popular colombiana, No. 5.)

741. Caicedo Rojas, José. "El tiple." In Cuadros de costumbres de Rafael Eliseo Santander, Juan Francisco Ortiz y José Caicedo Rojas. Bogotá: Editorial Minerva, 1936. Pp. 129-139. (Biblioteca aldeana de Colombia, No. 22.)
[A very informative cuadro de costumbres about the tiple, a four-stringed instrument which the author calls a degeneration of the Spanish vihuela. It is used to accompany coplas by groups which vie with each other on street corners, a custom particularly characteristic of the hot country; also, it is used by traveling singers who perform in inns and other places where people gather. The author prints the texts of a dozen coplas typical of the kind sung to the accompaniment of the tiple.]

Camargo, Rafael María. See Pimentel y Vargas, Fermín de, entry no. 855.

742. Los cantos populares de mi tierra.
[Otero Muñoz (ref. 842, p. 244) cites the work, but I have been able to find no further information about it.]

743. Capdevila, José María. "Las cantas del Valle de Tenza." CUn, No. 42 (marzo-abril, 1954), 100-114.
[Despite its length, this is essentially a review of the book by Medina and Vargas Tamayo of the same title. Two-thirds of this article is a rambling introduction; the last third merely expresses high praise of the book and quotes some representative coplas from it.]

744. Carmona, Antonio. "Folklore colombiano; danzas, coplas y creencias del pueblo." AnSFA, II(1946), 20-21.
[An unimportant treatment of the subject which doesn't provide the text of even one copla.]

745. Caro, Víctor. "Informe sobre el concurso de cancioneros." RJav, XIV(1940):69, 230-235; also, AACL, VIII(1940-1941).
[Castellví (ref. 751, p. 22) mentions this report on a "concurso nacional de cancioneros," organized in 1940 by the Academia Colombiana de la Lengua, in which fourteen works were presented "correspondientes a la mayoría de regiones colombianas."]

Cartilla de folk-lore tolimense. See entry no. 762 under Dirección de Educación Pública [del Tolima].

746. Carvajal, Luis Gonzalo. "Epílogo de un amor campesino." Sig, 5 de febrero, 1944, p. 2 of "Páginas literarias."
[This and the three titles by Carvajal which follow are cited by Enríquez Córdoba and Castellví (ref. 769, p. 143).]

747. _____. "La fiesta de San Benito en Girón." Sig, 8 de enero, 1944, p. 3 of "Páginas literarias."

748. _____. "Folklore santandereano." Sig, 6 de noviembre, 1943, p. 3 of "Páginas literarias."

749. _____. "El velorio." Sig, 2 de octubre, 1943, p. 1 of "Páginas literarias."

750. Castellanos, Juan de. Historia de Cartagena. Bogotá: Talleres Gráficos Luz, 1942. 346 pp. 19.5 cm. (Biblioteca popular de cultura colombiana. Cronistas, Vol. II.)
[In Canto III, p. 66, an Indian captive relates to the Spaniards what happened upon the death of an important personage:

Pudiera daros cuenta mas menudo
De los lloros, areitos, borracheras,
Manera de llorar de la viuda,
Triste cantar de las endecheras;
. . . (etc.)

This work is merely a portion of the Elegía de los varones ilustres de Indias, written about 1569.]

751. Castellví, Marcelino de. "Algunos datos sobre la bibliografía y folkloristas colombianos." ACA, II:4-8 (1944), 21-23.
[A few notes about folklorists of Colombia. Though few in number, the descriptions of works mentioned are quite complete.]

752. _____. "Las investigaciones lingüísticas y etnológicas en la Misión del Caquetá." Boletín de estudios históricos (Pasto), V(1934):55, pp. 193-213.
[Enríquez Córdoba and Castellví (ref. 770, p. 152) indicate that this is an early report on the collecting of cantares begun by Lucas de Batet in 1930. It is said to cover about one thousand of these compositions.]

_____. See Enríquez Córdoba, Gerardo, entries no. 769 and no. 770.

753. Castilla Barrios, Olga. Breve bosquejo de la literatura colombiana. Bogotá: Aedita, 1954. 371 pp. 25 cm.

754. Castrillón Arboleda, Diego. "La verdad es lo popular." RFCC, No. 1 (noviembre de 1947), 79-87.
[In seeking to prove the idea expressed in the title, the author uses Colombian coplas as evidence.]

755. Chacón, Luis F. "La música popular colombiana." Colombia (Pamplona), No. 3 (febrero de 1923), pp. 67, 69; No. 4 (abril de 1923), pp. 96, 99.

756. Cifuentes, Santos. "Hacia el americanismo musical; la música en Colombia." CMS, I:22 (25 de agosto, 1915), 4-6, 10-11.
[Chase (ref. 25, p. 121) comments: "The first half of this article deals with folk music and includes about twenty musical examples."]

757. "Claver." "Cancionero poético-musical de Urabá-Chocó."
[Enríquez Córdoba and Castellví (ref. 769, p. 142) indicate that the work is mentioned by Víctor E. Caro in "Informe sobre el concurso de cancioneros." It is probably one of the cancioneros entered in the contest.]

758. Cuervo, Angel. En la soledad.
[Otero Muñoz (ref. 842, p. 297) cites this work as a source of a copla which he prints.]

759. Cuervo, Rufino. [Article or chapter.] AACL, 1874, p. 225.
[Menéndez y Pelayo (Romances populares recogidos de la tradición oral. Tomo X of Antología de poetas líricos castellanos [Madrid: Librería de Hernando y Compañía, 1900], p. 230) cites a passage about romances to be found at the place indicated above. A reprint of the Anuario (Bogotá, 1935) does not seem to contain the material in question. The reprint, however, appears to be incomplete and to contain only certain parts of the original, which I have been unable to consult.]

Delgado, Camilo S. See entry no. 729.

760. Díaz Castro, Eugenio. Manuela, novela de costumbres colombianas. 2 vols. Paris: Librería Española de Garnier Hermanos, 1889. 18.5 cm.; also, Bogotá: Editorial Kelly, 1942. 455 pp. 20 cm. (Biblioteca de cultura colombiana, No. 19.)
[There are popular coplas in Vol. I, pp. 34, 35, 53, and 115; and in Vol. II, pp. 14 and 17 (pp. 30, 32, 45, 104, 267, and 318 of the 1942 edition).]

761. _____. María Ticince.
[Otero Muñoz (ref. 842, p. 278) prints an amorous copla taken from this work.]

762. Dirección de Educación Pública [del Tolima]. Cartilla de folk-lore tolimense. Ibagué: Imprenta Departamental, 1935.
[Florez (ref. 780, p. 325) quotes some coplas taken from this source.]

763. _____. Mundo austral; publicación mensual. (Ibagué), Nos. 5-6 (octubre-noviembre de 1940).
[Florez (ref. 780, p. 326) quotes some coplas taken from this source.]

764. "Dobiarisa." "Cantos populares de los indios Cafíos."
[Enríquez Córdoba and Castellví (ref. 769, p. 143) indicate that the work is mentioned by Víctor E. Caro in "Informe sobre el concurso de cancioneros." It is probably one of the cancioneros entered in the contest.]

765. Domínguez Camargo, Hernando. A seventeenth-century poet of Colombia who wrote in romance meter.
[Menéndez y Pelayo (ref. 82, Vol. II, p. 11) indicates that some of his romances appeared in Jacinto de Evia's Ramillete de varias flores poéticas (see entry no. 773).]

766. Domínguez del Río, T. Romances viejos.
[Otero Muñoz (ref. 842, pp. 268 ff.) cites the work. Apparently it is a collection of Colombian poetry.]

767. Duque, Antonio de J. Cuadro sin marco.
[Otero Muñoz (ref. 842, p. 316) prints a copla taken from this work.]

768. Eloy, U. Miguel and Eloy, Rodulfo. Poesía popular del norte de Santander. Cúcuta: Imp. Departamental, 1940. xviii, 290 pp.

769. Enríquez Córdoba, Gerardo, and Castellví, Marcelino de. "Bibliografía sobre cantares folklóricos colombianos." [In table of contents: "Sobre cantares folklóricos de las diez áreas colombianas."] ACA, II:4-8 (1944), pp. 141-144.
[A very useful bibliography of seventy-six items which deals with all kinds of popular poetry and song. It is divided into sections corresponding to geographical areas of Colombia.]

770. _____. "El cancionero del P. Lucas de Batet y la etnoornitología." ACA, II:4-8 (1944), 145-159; with the addition of the name of J. R. Méndez Buendía to the authors of the article, III:9-10 (1945), 5-34.

[In reality an introduction to the publication of the Cancionero of P. Lucas de Batet. It explains the system used in studying and grouping the coplas and also the unusual scientific vocabulary employed. Apparently Castellví created most of these neologisms. The article is also of interest because of some biting criticism directed at certain hypotheses expressed by Germán Arciniegas about Colombian coplas in "La copla en Boyacá."]

771. Entregas de poesía popular colombiana, No. 1. Bogotá: Ministerio de Educación Nacional, División de Extensión Cultural, Escuela de Arte Folklórica, 1955. 16 pp. 24 cm.

[Boggs (ref. 13 [1955], p. 49) says: "Texts of coplas of Mercaderes and Florencia, Cauca, from the collection of Víctor Quintero R.]

772. Entregas de poesía popular colombiana, No. 2. Bogotá: Edit. Minerva, 1955. 10 lvs. 24 cm.

[Pérez Ortiz (ref. 724, p. 136) indicates that this is a collection of songs from the region of Zaizal. It was made by Gabriel Ramírez Serna.]

Entregas de poesía popular colombiana, No. 4. See Velásquez M., Rogerio, entry no. 913.

773. Evia, Jacinto de. Ramillete de varias flores poéticas, recogidas, y cultivadas en los primeros abriles de sus años. Por el maestro Xacinto de Evia, natural de la ciudad de Guayaquil, en el Peru. Dedicale al licenciado d. Pedro de Arboleda Salazar, prouisor, vicario general y gouernador deste obispado de Popayàn, por ausencia del ilustrissimo señor doctor don Melchor de Liñán de Cisneros, del consejo de Su Magestad, obispo dèl. Con licencia. En Madrid: En la imprenta de Nicolás de Xamares, mercader de libros. Año de 1676. 406 (i.e., 408) pp.

[Menéndez y Pelayo (ref. 82, Vol. II, p. 11) indicates that the work contains some romances written by Hernando Domínguez Camargo.]

774. Exbrayat, Jaime. Cantares de vaquería; del folclore cordobés y bolivarense. Medellín: Editorial Bedout, 1959. 115 pp.

[S. E. Ortiz, in a favorable review of this work (RCF, Segunda época, II:4 (1960), 176-177), indicates that it is a collection of copla texts taken from the oral tradition of cowboys from Córdoba and Bolívar.]

775. _____. "Del folklore sinuano y bolivarense." RFCC, No. 1 (noviembre de 1947), 49-60.

[A collection of coplas with commentaries. There is nothing about romances or other narrative genres. One interesting group of songs can be classified as a contrapunto, using the term in its Chilean and Argentine acceptation, though it does not appear in this article.]

776. Fabo de María, Pedro. Episodios de un misionero. Burgos: "El Siglo de las Misiones," 1930. Pp. 57-58.

[Enríquez Córdoba and Castellví (ref. 769, p. 144) list this reference, though in such unclear fashion that I am not sure that I have interpreted their data correctly ("El Siglo de las Misiones" may be a periodical instead of the publisher). In any case, they include the following note with their entry: "Refiere de una colección de romances, coplas y cantares de procedencia española que el pueblo colombiano conserva todavía'; la cual colección fue enviada por el colector a don Miguel A. Caro para que se cumpliese la invitación de don Ramón Menéndez Pidal a recoger 'romances históricos llevados a América por los colonizadores'." Apparently they mean that the passages quoted by them appear on pp. 57-58 of Fabo de María's work.]

777. _____. Historia de la ciudad de Manizales. 2 vols. Manizales: Tip. "Blanco y Negro," 1926.

[Said by Enríquez Córdoba and Castellví (ref. 769, p. 142) to contain a section entitled "Poesía popular y crítica literaria," pp. 479-486.]

778. _____. Idiomas y etnografía de la región oriental de Colombia. Barcelona: José Benet, 1911. 293 pp. 22.5 cm.

[In the appendix there is a chapter entitled "La poesía popular de la región de Casanare" (pp. 200-215). Fabo treats in a general way the poetry he has heard as a missionary and declares (p. 203) that "El romance es el único género que allí se cultiva . . . ." He goes on to compare the romances of Andalusia with those which he has heard, and he gives a rather detailed characterization of the popular poetry of the area and some romance texts (p. 205). Besides these, which are in some cases traditional romances of Spanish origin, Fabo also provides some texts of coplas, octavas, sextillas, and other forms as they are sung by the Colombian llaneros. Though not very scientific in character, the chapter is a valuable contribution.]

779. Fernández Piedrahita, Lucas. Historia general de las conquistas del nuevo reyno de Granada. Primera parte. N. p.: n. p., n. d. 599 pp. 27.5 cm.; also, Bogotá: Imprenta de Medardo Rivas, 1881. xxv, 412 pp. 24 cm.

[In the earlier of the two editions (which is of the seventeenth century), there is a report (pp. 21-22) on the Indians' singing of historical songs about present and past events and of their singing songs and dancing in preparation for battle. In another place (p. 40) the chief Zippa is reported as having been received in his court with dances and "cantos en que representaban sus hechos memorables . . . ."

Also, there is an account (p. 59) of how the Indians sang songs to memorialize the triumphs of their deceased ruler. These passages can be found between pp. 15-42 of the edition of 1881, though the transcriptions of this edition are frequently faulty.]

780. Florez, Luis. "El habla popular en la literatura colombiana." BICC, Año I:2 (mayo-agosto, 1945), 318-361.

[The author quotes many coplas by way of illustrating linguistic phenomena. Most of his examples, however, are taken from more or less well known printed sources.]

781. Folklore santandereano. Tomo I: Coplas populares. Bucaramanga: Imprenta del Departamento, 1942. 222 pp.; also, Segunda edición. República de Colombia, Departamento de Santander: Fondo Rotatorio de Publicaciones, n.d. [1943?]. 212 pp. 22 cm. Tomo II. Bogotá: Edit. Cosmos, 1954. 188 pp. 22.5 cm.

[Volume I is a collection of coplas made by the teachers of Santander under the direction of Dr. Horacio Rodríguez Plata, Director de Educación Pública. The coplas are divided and subdivided according to themes and subject matter. Each of the larger sections usually has some introductory comment, and the entire work is prefaced by an introduction by Juan de Dios Arias. I have not been able to consult the second volume.]

782. Forero, Manuel José. "Apuntes sobre el folklore de Colombia." Santafé y Bogotá (Bogotá), II(1924):10.

783. _____. "Para el folklore colombiano." Sen, I:4 (mayo de 1934), 190.

[Texts of nine coplas along with some trivial comments. The author does not give his sources nor indicate where he collected the songs.]

784. _____. "Un personaje francés en el folklore colombiano." BICC, Año I:1 (enero-abril, 1945), 154-159.

[A pointless article which begins with a discussion of some popular coplas and ends with mention of the fact that Mambrú is known in Colombia, though the only complete texts the author prints are Mexican versions taken from Mendoza's El romance español y el corrido mexicano.]

Grases, Pedro. "Galerón en tierra firme." See entry no. 2007.

785. Grillo, Max. Article in Trofeos.
[Otero Muñoz (ref. 842, p. 318) prints a copla taken from this work.]

786. Gruesso, José María. Las noches de Zacarías Geussor, socio de la Junta Privada del Buen Gusto . . . En la ciudad de Santa Fe de Bogotá.

[Menéndez y Pelayo (ref. 82, Vol. I, p. 436) mentions the composition as a romance endecasílabo. Gruesso was a member of a tertulia known as the Academia del Buen Gusto which existed in Bogotá toward the end of the eighteenth century.]

787. Guarín, José David. Cuadros de costumbres. Bogotá: Editorial Minerva, n.d. 163 pp. 19.5 cm.

[In a sketch entitled "Un día de San Juan en tierra caliente," there is an amorous copla (p. 132) which is apparently of popular origin.]

788. _____. Obras de J. David Guarín. Bogotá: Imprenta de Zalamea Hermanos, 1880. xiii, 320 pp.

[Otero Muñoz (ref. 842) in several places quotes coplas taken from works of this author. The titles of some of these are Las fiestas de julio o Las tres semanas, Los mordiscos, and ¡Qué molienda! I have been unable to locate these, but they may be in this collection of works by Guarín.]

789. Gutiérrez, Benigno A. Arrume folklórico: de todo el maíz; fantasía criolla, guachaqueada y psicológica, de trovas, levas y cañas . . .; nueva ed. notablemente aumentada y seguida de la memoria sobre el cultivo del maíz en Antioquia. Medellín: Imprenta Departamental, 1948. vii, 212 pp. (First ed., 1944 [see entries no. 790 and no. 791 below].)

[Boggs (ref. 13 [1948]), p. 28) comments: "Folk songs, tongue twisters, games, ballads, proverbs, omens, witchcraft, dances, legends, riddles, some music of folk songs, and miscellaneous folklore, writings inspired in folklore, etc., from Antioquia, Colombia." Boggs' description is confirmed in its most important details by Gutiérrez himself (ref. 792).]

790. _____. Arrume folklórico: de todo el maíz; suplemento. Medellín: Imprenta Departamental, 1949. 87 pp.

[Boggs (ref. 13 [1949], p. 21) says: "First ed. 1944. Rev. ed. 1948. The present Supplement contains music and words of 39 folksongs of various types, with notes, folksy narrative passages from literary authors treating different kinds of folklore, and text of a poem of 1866 on growing corn, with extensive notes on interpretation of words in it by Robert Jaramillo."]

_____. Contribución al estudio del folklore de Antioquia y Caldas. See Restrepo, Antonio José, El cancionero de Antioquia, 4.ª ed., entry no. 873.

791. _____. De todo el maíz; fantasía criolla, guachaqueada y pisicológica [sic], de trovas, levas y cañas. Medellín: Imprenta Departamental, n.d. 73 pp. + 8 unnumbered leaves containing an "Himno a Sansón" by Tomás Pérez and Bernardo Toro and a poem by Jorge Isaacs entitled "La tierra de Córdoba." [This probably is the 1944 edition of which Boggs speaks (see entry no. 790 above) because on the cover list of the author's works, titles are given down to this work

and 1944 is given as its date. The title page, however, bears no date.]

[A mélange of all kinds of poetry, traditions, and many other types of compositions from the area of Sansón. Learned and popular materials are mixed. Among things of popular origin are a number of coplas and décimas and some romances (Las señas del marido, Delgadina, and others). Also, there is some topical poetry which is very much in corrido tradition, though it is apparently more learned than popular, being written for special occasions in ten-syllable instead of eight-syllable lines.]

792. _____ Gente maicera; mosaico de Antioquia la Grande. Medellín: Editorial Bedout, 1950. 303 pp. 25 cm.

[A collection of literary works by many authors about the department of Antioquia. Besides many prose compositions, there are some poems, mostly artistic compositions, and several of these are in romance meter. There is some attention given to traditional songs, and a number of popular or semipopular compositions are quoted textually, mostly the works of repentistas of more or less popular background. Some of the coplas presented are truly popular and traditional. The volume contains much that is of interest, but its organization and presentation are chaotic. There is a very pedestrian artistic romance (pp. 162-163) entitled La silla y el sillón (Diálogo) by Francisco Ignacio Mejía, a repentista known as El tío Pacho. He was born in 1753 and lived into the nineteenth century. His romance is neoclassical in style, though not particularly lofty in tone.]

793. _____. Tonadillas típicas campesinas de la tierra antioqueña, recogidas y publicadas . . . a la mayor honra y gloria del Gallo Cantor Desconocido. Medellín, 1955.

794. Gutiérrez, Rufino. Monografías. Tomo I. Bogotá: Imprenta Nacional, 1920. lxxviii, 434 pp. 23.5 cm. (Biblioteca de historia nacional, Vol. XXVIII.)

[In the section entitled "Noticias sobre Pasto y demás provincias del Sur. De Tuquerres a Tumaco" (pp. 129-159), there are some coplas (pp. 131-133, 143-144) and some décimas (pp. 135-136). In the section entitled "Honda" (pp. 254-259), there are two strophes of a composition about an earthquake in 1805 which closely resemble corridos.]

795. Henao, Januario. Cuentos y cantares antioqueños.

[Otero Muñoz (ref. 842, p. 263) cites the work as the source of a learned or semilearned copla which has been adopted and sung by the pueblo.]

796. Hernández, Juan C. "Introducción al folklore boyacense." RAmer, IX:25 (enero de 1947), 118-127; also, "Introducción al folklore boyacense, primera parte." Revista cultura (Tunja), No. 96 (abril, 1947), 9-21; ". . . , segunda parte." La Gran Colombia (Medellín),

Año IV (noviembre-diciembre, 1947), 21 ff.
[In the Revista de América, which I have consulted, the author praises Antonio Morales, a poet from Boyacá, for his success in capturing in his artistic poetry the spirit of the Indian cantas of his native region. The strophes quoted do, indeed, show real popular flavor. A poem about one José Resurrición has much of the corridos about it.]

797. Hernández, Juan C. "Introducción a la poesía popular boyacense." RAmer, XVI:50-51 (febrero y marzo, 1949), 219-227.
[The author reports on an unpublished collection of cantas (coplas) gathered by the teachers of Boyacá under the direction of Inspector Luis A. Moreno. Hernández prints a considerable number of them and comments upon them and the popular poetry of Boyacá in general. He notes (p. 222): "Hay en muchas de las cantas una tendencia a salir de la copla para entrar en el romance." Some examples are given.]

798. Hernández de Alba, Gregorio. "En una noche de aquéllas." Sen, II:9 (octubre de 1934), 170-171.
[The author evokes a "noche de feria" in a village in the department of Santander. He provides texts of a number of coplas which he heard sung there.]

799. Igualada, Francisco de. "Informe sobre el Centro de Investigaciones Lingüísticas y Etnológicas de la Amazonia Colombiana (o Cileac) en 1933-1940." ACA, I(1940), 61-91.
[This (according to ref. 770) is a bibliographical report on the work of P. Lucas de Batet in collecting cantares. This is the second such report (for the first one, see Castellví's "Las investigaciones lingüísticas y etnológicas en la Misión del Caquetá"). This report of Igualada deals with about a thousand cantares not covered in Castellví's article.]

800. ———. "Musicología indígena de la Amazonia Colombiana." BLAA, IV(1938), 675-708.

Jaramillo, Roberto. See Gutiérrez, Benigno, Arrume folklórico: de todo el maíz; suplemento, entry no. 790.

801. Jaramillo G., Arturo. El alma popular.
[Otero Muñoz (ref. 842, p. 277) prints an amorous copla taken from this work.]

802. Keller, Jean P. "Popular Poetry in Colombia." Hisp, XXXV:4 (November, 1952), 387-391.
[The author quotes forty-three coplas lifted from various standard sources on Colombian popular poetry. The purpose of the article is merely informative and is intended to suggest the use of such poems in Spanish Club activities. All are amorous coplas.]

803. Lamo Arenas, Ramiro. "Notas sobre arriería." RCF, Segunda época, II:4 (1960), 55-56.
[Includes texts of several coplas and one romance.]

804. Lanao Loaiza, José Ramón. Las pampas escandalosas. Manizales: Ed. Arturo Zapata, 1936. Pp. 114, 127, 141, 145 (?), 146, 147, 152 (?). 190 pp. 17 cm.
[The page numbers given above are as Enríquez Córdoba and Castellví print them. Apparently they refer to places where cantares of some kind are to be found. The question marks in parentheses, however, seem to indicate uncertainty.]

805. León Rey, José A. Espíritu de mi oriente; cancionero popular, recogido, clasificado y anotado. 2 vols. Bogotá: Imprenta Nacional, 1951-[1953]. 25 cm.
[Capdevila (ref. 743, p. 101) says that this is a collection of coplas.]

806. _____. Tierra embrujada; tradiciones y leyendas. Bogotá: Editorial Centro, 1942. 238 pp. 17.5 cm.
[A series of prose sketches replete with popular coplas.]

807. Lescámez, Antón de. Romance de Ximénez de Quesada.
[A poem of eighty lines said to be the first poetry written in New Granada (see Otero Muñoz, Gustavo, entry no. 843).]

808. Lima, Emirto de. "La copla popular colombiana." ASFM, II(1941), 243-247.
[A minor contribution to the study of the nature of the copla in Colombia.]

809. _____. "Del folklore colombiano." BLAM, Año I, tomo I (abril de 1935), 47-55.
[A description of Carnival customs in Colombia. The author is concerned almost exclusively with dances, and in connection with these he offers a few coplas. Also, he describes some popular musical instruments and treats the characteristics of Colombian popular music. There is no mention of romances or other narrative genres.]

810. _____. Folklore colombiano. Barranquilla: [Lit. Barranquilla], 1942. 210 pp. 19.5 cm.
[According to a review by Bonifacio Gil (RDTP, IV(1948), Cuaderno 3.°, 486-487), it contains some chapters on the copla and one on "La guitarra, instrumento romancero."]

811. _____. "Varias manifestações folklóricas na costa colombiana do Atlántico." RABM, II:5 (1933), 45-47.

812. Lira Espejo, Eduardo. "Crónica del cantar colombiano." RMC, II:10 (abril de 1946), 16-25; also, RNC, Año VII:56 (mayo-junio de 1946), 89-101.
[An impressionistic rather than a scholarly treatment of Colombian popular music, dances, and songs. The bambuco, the galerón, coplas, and other genres are mentioned or discussed; and the article contains the texts of several coplas and one romance, a version of Caminan para Belén/ San José y Santa María (pp. 24-25 in RMC; pp. 100-101 in RNC).]

813. López Narváez, Carlos. "La copla en el Cauca." RFCC, 2.ª época, I:1 (diciembre, 1952), 213-227.

814. Luna, E. de. "La copla en el oriente de Colombia." RCLA, No. 117 (enero de 1933).

815. Marín, Abel. Polonia.
[Otero Muñoz (ref. 842, p. 297) prints a copla taken from this source.]

816. Martínez Mutis, Aurelio. Romancero del tabaco. Bucaramanga: Imprenta del Departamento, 1941. 230 pp. 23.5 cm.
[Juan de Dios Arias (ref. 730, p. 144) prints a text which he says he found in this work.]

817. Medina, Joaquín R., and Vargas Tamayo, José. Cantas del Valle de Tenza. 3 vols. Bogotá: Prensas del Ministerio de Educación, 1949. 20 cm. (Vols. III, IV, and V of Biblioteca del folklore colombiano.)
[A very fine collection of 4,488 cantas (coplas), almost all in octosyllabic cuartetas. The texts were gathered by Joaquín R. Medina, a parish priest, and arranged for publication by José Vargas Tamayo, who is author of a good preliminary study in which he discusses the collection made by Medina, the place of the copla in Spanish and American tradition, and its importance in the cultural life of the people of the Valle de Tenza. The collection itself is divided into thirteen large sections on the basis of themes treated, and these categories are extensively subdivided. There is also a very useful vocabulary in Vol. III.]

Mejía Angel, Carlos. See Mendia, Ciro, entry no. 819.

818. Mejía Robledo, Alfonso. "Improvisadores colombianos en poesía." UA, No. 44 (febrero-marzo de 1941), 589-603.

Méndez Buendía, J. R. See Enríquez Córdoba, Gerardo, entry no. 770.

819. Mendia, Ciro (Carlos Mejía Angel). En torno a la poesía popular. Medellín: Antonio J. Cano, 1927. xii, 121 pp. 18.5 cm.
[Part I treats various types of Colombian popular poetry with particular attention to its relationship to that of Spain, Mexico, Argentina, Venezuela, and other areas. The author depends mostly upon sources such as Restrepo, Otero d'Costa, and other standard works, but he has a sense of what is truly significant, so his selection of data is quite good. Among other things, he quotes the complete text of a "romance" taken from the novel El zarco by Tomás Carrasquilla. Though literarily undistinguished, it is interesting as a Colombian narrative in corrido form. Part II deals with coplas. The author describes the manner in which they are sung by a "cantador festivo," by arrieros, and by workers in sugar mills and on coffee planations.

Among many copla texts there is one derived from the romance of Spanish tradition, Camino de Belén. This is a good book of its kind. Popular in tone and with no pretensions of great erudition, it contains much information and many texts.]

Menéndez Pidal, Ramón. See entry no. 84.

820. Meré, Rafael. "Cantares asturianos y colombianos." RDTP, VIII(1952), Cuaderno 1.°, 148-153.

[Compares a number of coplas and two romances from Asturias and from Colombia. It is an interesting article, though the texts themselves come from already published sources.]

821. Merizalde del Carmen, Bernardo. Estudio de la costa colombiana del Pacífico. Bogotá: Imp. del Estado Mayor General, 1921. 248 pp. 24.5 cm.

[Otero Muñoz (ref. 842, p. 305) prints a copla taken from this work. Also, Enríquez Córdoba and Castellví (ref. 769, p. 143) refer to pp. 162-168 of the same volume.]

822. _____. "La poesía popular de los negros costeños." Boletín de la provincia de Nuestra Señora de la Candelaria de Colombia (Bogotá), I:1, pp. 37-40.

823. Monsalve Martínez, Manuel. "El Tolima y su poesía popular." UA, III:10 (junio y julio de 1936), 231-239.

[A brief article calling for the compilation of a Cancionero popular tolimense. The author cites several texts of popular poetry, mostly coplas, though they are not so labelled. One composition of four strophes, which is quoted from Tomás S. Restrepo's "Impresiones y recuerdos sobre Honda," is very close to Mexican corridos in form and style. It records an earthquake which occurred in 1805.]

824. Montoya Toro, Jorge. "Cuadernillo de poesía: Nacer y renacer del romance." UA, XXII(1948):88, pp. 635-639.

825. Mora Naranjo, Alfonso. "Cantares." La Patria (Manizales).
[Enríquez Córdoba and Castellví (ref. 769, p. 142) indicate that Fabo cites this collection in Historia de la ciudad de Manizales (p. 840).]

826. Morales, Ernesto. "La poesía popular española en América." CV, Año XII, Vol. XLI:100 (enero a abril de 1930), 123-137.

[An attack upon the Cancionero de Antioquia of Antonio José Restrepo, with particular censure of the nationalistic and regionalistic prejudices of its author. Morales, by quoting texts of popular poetry from Spain and Argentina, shows that many of Restrepo's verses, which he exalted as products of the popular genius of Antioquia, are merely part of Spanish tradition.]

Mundo austral (Ibagué, Colombia). See Dirección de Educación Pública del Tolima, entry no. 763.

827. Naranjo Martínez, Enrique. "Demosofía colombiana." Sen, II:10 (noviembre de 1934), 237-239.
[A hodgepodge of comments about various topics, including coplas, of which the author provides three texts. Two are of interest, having been inspired by one of Colombia's civil wars in 1876. Also, the texts of two chaotic galerones are given. The first has some lines which are from the popular song En el hato del sesenta and others which are derived from Echame ese toro afuera.]

828. Nel Ospina, Pedro. Río arriba.
[Otero Muñoz (ref. 842, p. 288) prints a copla taken from the above.]

829. Obeso, Candelario. Cantos populares de mi tierra. Bogotá: Ministerio de Educación de Colombia, 1950. 253 pp. (Biblioteca popular de cultura colombiana, No. 114.)

830. Olano, Ricardo. Apolinar.
[Otero Muñoz (ref. 842, p. 280) prints an amorous copla taken from this work.]

831. _____. Mirajes.
[Otero Muñoz (ref. 842, p. 283) prints a copla taken from here.]

832. Ortiz, Sergio Elías. "Coplas de la tierra de los comuneros." RCF, Segunda época, II:4 (1960), 39-54.
[Approximately one hundred copla texts without music from the region of Socorro, Colombia. They are grouped according to subject matter (coplas amorosas, coplas politiqueras, etc.).]

833. _____, and Ortiz, Laurencio. Cantares del departamento de Nariño (primera serie). Pasto: Edit. Cervantes, 1946. 25 pp. (Publicaciones del Instituto "Juanambú," No. 5.)

834. Ortiz C., Laurencio. "A propósito de los cantares de Soatá (Boyacá)." RCF, Segunda época, No. 3 (1959), 83-87.
[A collection of thirty-seven copla texts from the area of Soatá.]

_____. See Ortiz, Sergio Elías, entry no. 833.

835. Osorio, Juan C. "Breves apuntaciones para la historia de la música en Colombia." Repertorio colombiano, No. 15.

836. Ospina, Tulio. Caporrista y Mardoqueo.
[Otero Muñoz (ref. 842, p. 308) prints a copla taken from the above.]

837. _____. Mariquita la morena.
[Otero Muñoz (ref. 842, p. 288) prints a copla taken from this work.]

838. Ospina N., Francisco, comp. Coplas colombianas. Bogotá: Edit. Minerva, 1951. 216 pp. 24 cm.

839. Ossa, Peregrino. "Geografía de la Intendencia Nacional del Meta." Supplement to Revista agricultura (Bogotá), 1937.
[Enríquez Córdoba and Castellví (ref. 769, p. 144) cite this work.]

840. Otero d'Costa, Enrique. Cronicón solariego. Manizales, 1922.
[Angarita Arvelo (ref. 1949, p. 84) refers to the above for some commentary on a colonial romance which he prints.]

841. _____. Montañas de Santander. Bucaramanga: Imprenta del Departamento, 1932. vii, 185 pp. 23 cm.
[Chase (ref. 25, p. 122) comments: "The second part of this book, Apuntes sobre demosofía colombiana y música nacional, deals with various aspects of folk and national music in Colombia, quoting numerous texts of folk songs." Arias (ref. 781, p. 118) quotes a version of Jilito, jilito de oro which he took from this source.]

842. Otero Muñoz, Gustavo. La literatura colonial de Colombia, seguida de un cancionerillo popular. La Paz, Bolivia: Imp. Artística, 1928. 324 pp. 19.5 cm.
[Bk. III of the larger work is a "Cancionerillo popular" (pp. 239-320). After a very satisfactory general discussion of popular poetry, the author offers his collection of coplas, along with an occasional romance. These he has gathered from the works of various collectors, not from his own research into oral tradition. The collection, however, is quite useful, though bibliographical references are so sketchy as to be almost valueless.]

843. _____. "Los primeros poetas de la conquista." BHA, No. 217 (1932).
[Rodríguez Demorizi (ref. 1104, p. 10) indicates that Otero Muñoz discusses Antón de Lescámez, author of a Romance de Ximénez de Quesada, which Otero calls the first poem written in New Granada.]

844. Pabón Núñez, Lucio. Muestras folklóricas del norte de Santander. Bogotá: Ministerio de Educación Nacional, 1952. 177 pp. 21 cm. (Biblioteca de autores colombianos, Vol. XXI.)

845. Pardo Tovar, Andrés. "Experiencias de una excursión folclórica." RCF, Segunda época, II:4 (1960), 127-135.
[Reports on three romances collected in Quibdó and gives the text of one (Catalina, Catalina, which is a version of Las señas del esposo).]

846. _____. El folclore en la obra de Tomás Carrasquilla. Tunja: Ediciones del Centro de Divulgación Pedagógica y Cultural de Boyacá, 1959. 64 pp.
[S. E. Ortiz indicates in a review of the work (RCF, Segunda época, II:4 (1960), 177-178) that the volume deals in part with the famous novelist's use of traditional poetry in his works.]

"Pastrana, Hilarión." See "Trovador del Valle," entry no. 905.

847. Patiño, Víctor Manuel. "Fitofolklore de la costa colombiana del Pacífico." AVF, Año II-III (1953-1954), Tomo II:3, pp. 85-145.
[A valuable collection of 508 coplas, most of them eight-syllable

cuartetas, collected by Patiño in coastal Colombia while making botanical investigations. These selected texts from a larger collection are those which refer to plants in one way or another.]

848. Peñuela, Cayo Leonidas. "Cantos populares de la región de Soatá." Sen, I:4 (mayo de 1934), 191.
[A collection of twenty-five copla texts. No data about informants are provided.]

849. Perdomo Escobar, José Ignacio. "Esbozo histórico sobre la música colombiana." BLAM, Año IV, Tomo IV(octubre de 1938), 387-570.
[An attempt to outline the history of Colombian music in general. There is attention to popular songs and dances, and coplas are scattered through several parts of the study. Comments about romances, galerones, and corridos (pp. 532-533) are brief but quite informative, though they apparently refer only to the area of Casanare.]

850. _____. Historia de la música en Colombia. Bogotá: Imprenta Nacional, 1945. 348 pp. 19.5 cm.
[A good basic work which contains in Chap. XIV, "Folklore musical colombiano," some descriptive treatment of the type of song known variously as torbellino, galerón, or corrido.]

851. _____. "Música y músicos de la época colonial." BHA, XXIX:327 (enero de 1942), 53-65.
[Enríquez Córdoba and Castellví (ref. 769, p. 141) cite this work.]

852. Pérez Arbeláez, E. "Literatura popular de Magdalena." RAmer, IV(1945), 360-367; also, RepAm, II(1945):6, pp. 378-384.
[Texts of popular songs which the author collected in the department of Magdalena, mostly semipopular songs of the day. There are a few strophes, however, which sound like genuinely popular coplas.]

Pérez Ortiz, Rubén. See Anuario bibliográfico colombiano, 1951-1956, entry no. 724.

853. Pérez Ramírez, Elías. "Del folklore ocañero." RFCC, No. 1 (noviembre de 1947), 61-77.
[Coplas from the department of Ocaña, Colombia, with commentary.]

854. _____. "Más sobre folklore ocañero." RFCC, No. 3 (julio de 1948), 269-277.
[Additional coplas which supplement the collection given in entry no. 853.]

855. Pimentel y Vargas, Fermín de. (Rafael María Camargo). Escenas de la gleba.
[Otero Muñoz (ref. 842, p. 247) refers to this work as a source of coplas.]

856. _____. Vivaqueos.

[Otero Muñoz (ref. 842, p. 288) prints a copla taken from the above.]

857. Pinzón M., J. Odilio. "El carácter santandereano en la poesía popular." RJav, XV:74 (mayo, 1941), 217-226.

[A study of the character of the people of Santander as revealed in their coplas. The author gives no sources for the coplas that he quotes.]

858. Los poetas del amor y la mujer. Bogotá: Editorial Minerva, n.d. 284 pp. 20 cm. (Biblioteca aldeana de Colombia, No. 83.)

[In addition to many artistic poems, including some romances, there are seven coplas llaneras of popular origin (pp. 49-50).]

859. Pombo, Manuel. "De Medellín a Bogotá." In Obras inéditas. Bogotá: Librería Colombiana, 1914. lii, 312 pp. 23.5 cm.

[Enríquez Córdoba and Castellví (ref. 769, p. 142) say that Fabo cites the work in his Historia de Manizales. Their description of it: "Notas de viaje en forma de diario con unos pocos cantares; 'varios pertenecen indudablemente a los bogas del Magdalena'." The passage they include within their description is apparently from Fabo.]

860. _____. La niña Agueda y otros cuadros. N.p.: Editorial Minerva, 1936. 128 pp. 19.5 cm. (Biblioteca aldeana de Colombia, No. 27.)

[In the cuadro called "Los diablitos" the author quotes three strophes of a song in octyllabic cuartetas which are apparently of popular origin and belong to the copla tradition.]

861. Puig Campillo, Antonio. Cancionero popular de Cartagena. Cartagena: Impr. Gómez, [1953]. 298 pp.

862. Quiñones Pardo, Octavio. "El cancionero colombiano." RAmer, VIII:22 (octubre de 1946), 104-107.

[A selection of fifty-eight coplas from Colombia without commentary of any kind. At least one is a fragment of a romance ("No me entierren en sagrado").]

863. _____. "Cantares de Boyacá; descubrimiento de nuevas coplas." Tiem, 30 de enero, 1949.

864. _____. Cantares de Boyacá; libro de crónicas. Bogotá: Tipografía "Colón," [1937]. xxiv, 222 pp. 17.5 cm.

[Enríquez Córdoba and Castellví (ref. 769, p. 143) comment: "En esta obra interesan además de modo especial, las 'Anotaciones sobre el folklore del Litoral Pacífico', el registro de 'Cantares Nariñenses' y 'Apuntes sobre el folklore musical y poético del litoral Atlántico', p. 163, 189."]

865. _____. "La copla y la estampilla." SCCol, Año I:4 (1950), 15-19.

[A strained comparison between the folklorist and the philatelist followed by some "interpretations" of popular coplas. The work is of no importance.]

866. Quiñones Pardo, Octavio. "Diez coplas y un proyecto de ley." RFCC, No. 1 (noviembre, 1947), 35-41.
[A humorous article inspired by a proposal in the legislature to tax bachelors. By way of commentary on the single state, the author quotes several coplas from Colombia.]

867. _____. "Interpretación de algunos cantares de Boyacá." SCCol, Año I:1 (abril de 1950), 4-10.
[By way of characterizing the people of Boyacá, the author offers some unimportant commentaries in prose and in verse upon some of the coplas which are sung in that region. The texts of these are from printed sources (the author's Cantares de Boyacá and Otros cantares de Boyacá and the works of other collectors).]

868. _____. Interpretación de la poesía popular. Bogotá: Edit. Centro-Inst. Gráfico Ltda., 1947. 197 pp. 19.5 cm. (Biblioteca de folklore colombiano, Vol. I.)
[The "interpretation" consists of prose and verse commentaries upon songs, mostly coplas, taken from the author's collections of popular songs from Boyacá. The work is of little value.]

869. _____. "Interpretación de la poesía popular." SCCol, Año I:2 (1950), 5-9.
[More of the author's "interpretations" of popular coplas as described in previous entries.]

870. _____. "Orígenes de la poesía popular de Boyacá." SCCol, Año I:5 (1950), 15-22.
[A not dispassionate treatment of the development of popular music in Colombia. The author sustains the thesis that before the conquest the Indians already had songs about their heroes which were similar to the coplas and endechas of the Spanish conquerors. With evidence taken from chronicles, Quiñones Pardo seeks to prove that the coplas which still exist in Colombian tradition, and which are so revealing of the character of the masses, result from the amalgamation of these Indian and Spanish elements.]

871. _____. Otros cantares de Boyacá. Bogotá: Editorial ABC, 1944. 234 pp. 18 cm.

Quintero R., Víctor. See Entregas de poesía popular colombiana, No. 1, entry no. 771.

Ramírez Serna, Gabriel. See Entregas de poesía popular colombiana, No. 2, entry no. 772.

872. Restrepo, Antonio José. El cancionero de Antioquia. Barcelona: Editorial Lux, 1929. 473 pp. 20 cm.; also, 2.ª edición.

Barcelona: Núñez y Comp^a, 1930. 442 pp. 21 cm. [See the next entry also.]

[The core of this work is a large collection of texts of coplas and other types of popular poetry, including one corrido (pp. 464-466), a romance or relación (pp. 467-469), and a décima (pp. 469-471). This main section is preceded by several long preliminary chapters, the most important of these being "De la poesía popular en Colombia" (pp. 19-63), a florid and essentially superficial peroration, though some of the copla texts which it contains should not be ignored, and "Conviene a saber" (pp. 70-108), another long treatise that is of little value except for some of the copla texts which it contains.]

873. _____. El cancionero de Antioquia; also, Gutiérrez, Benigno A. Contribución al estudio del folklore de Antioquia y Caldas. Medellín: Editorial Bedout, 1955. 563 pp. 17.5 cm. (Colección popular de clásicos modernos, Vol. III.)

[This edition of Restrepo's work differs little from the first edition (see entry no. 872 above), though there is a section entitled "En defensa del 'Cancionero de Antioquia'" (pp. 403-421), written in 1929 to answer criticism of Ernesto Morales (see entry no. 826 above). The work of Gutiérrez (pp. 435-563) consists of two sections: "Tonadas típicas campesinas" (pp. 437-503) and "Relatos populares" (pp. 505-546). The treatment of popular songs is poorly organized, though a respectable number of texts and music are given. A few are related to the copla tradition and there is a fragment of El toro ("por ónde le metió el cacho/ el hiju'e la vaca negra?").]

874. Restrepo, Tomás S. Impresiones y recuerdos sobre Honda.
[Monsalve Martínez (ref. 823, p. 237) quotes some popular verses about an earthquake in Honda taken from the above source, which he identifies only by title. The composition quoted sounds much like a corrido.]

875. Revollo, Pedro María. Costeñismos colombianos o apuntamientos sobre el lenguaje costeño de Colombia. Barranquilla: Ed. Mejoras, 1942. xv, 320 pp. 23.5 cm.
[The lexicographer uses poetic examples of all kinds to document his entries. Some are popular coplas.]

876. Rivas, Medardo. Las fiestas de Piedras.
[Otero Muñoz (ref. 842, p. 277) quotes an amorous copla taken from this work.]

877. Robledo, Emilio. "De nuestro folklore." RJav, XX(1943), 266-269.
[Enríquez Córdoba and Castellví (ref. 769, p. 142) comment: "Sobre 3 romances antioqueños existentes también en otros lugares colombianos."]

878. Robledo, Emilio. "Papeletas lexicográficas." UA, II:6 (enero de 1936), 246-262; 7 (mayo de 1936), 419-448; 8 (abril de 1936), 585-600; III:9 (mayo de 1936), 95-110; 10 (junio y julio de 1936), 253-261. [Probably continues, but I have been unable to consult subsequent numbers.] (This work is a re-editing and amplification of an earlier work with the same title. An introduction to the first edition dated "Medellín, Agosto de 1934" is reprinted with this second edition.)
[A collection of Colombian provincialisms. Coplas are frequently cited by way of illustration.]

879. Robledo, Eusebio. El beso de la trilla.
[Otero Muñoz (ref. 842, p. 287) prints a copla taken from this work.]

880. _____. Un idilio.
[Otero Muñoz (ref. 842, p. 282) prints a copla taken from this work.]

881. Rochereau, P. E. "La poesía y los cantos mágicos de los Tunebos." Revista de misiones (Bogotá), No. 88 (1932), pp. 404, 413.

882. Rodríguez Mira, Pedro. "Aspectos de folklore: del libro inédito 'Coplas, trovas y cantares.'" Boletín del Instituto de Antropología (Medellín), II(1956):5, pp. 105-116.
[Boggs (ref. 13 (1957), p. 42) says: "General observations on ancient music."]

Rodríguez Plata, Horacio. See Folklore santandereano. Tomo I: Coplas populares, entry no. 781.

883. Rojas, Alfonso María. "Coplas populares colombianas: I. La constancia; II. La queja; III. Morenas y blancas." El obrero católico (Medellín), 12 de noviembre, 1938, p. 7; 3 de diciembre de 1938, p. 6; 28 de enero de 1939, p. 6.
[Enríquez Córdoba and Castellví (ref. 769, p. 142) cite the work.]

884. Romero, M. J. Sombra de martirio.
[Otero Muñoz (ref. 842, p. 296) prints a copla taken from this work.]

885. Rueda, Soledad Marina O. "Folklore de la costa del Pacífico en Barbacoas." RHis, IV(1949):23-25, pp. 247-259.

886. Ruiz M., Alberto. "Para el folklore colombiano; cantos populares de la región de Vélez." Sen, I:1 (febrero de 1934), 37.
[Ten copla texts.]

887. Sáenz, C. L. "Breves apuntes sobre la música popular colombiana." Cuadernos del Noticiario colombiano, No. 8 (1939), 17-26.

888. Salazar, José María. Arte Poética de Monsieur Boileau, traducida al verso castellano por el doctor José María Salazar, quien la dedicó al Sr. José Ignacio Pombo, en el año de 1810. Bogotá. Impresa por Valentín Martínez. Año de 1828.
[Menéndez y Pelayo (ref. 82, Vol. I, p. 437) quotes the first ten lines of this work. They are a romance endecasílabo.]

889. _____. La Colombiada; o, Colón, el amor a la patria y otras poesías líricas. Caracas: Oficinas Tipográficas de Briceño y Campbell, 1852. x, 192 pp. 20 cm.

[Menéndez y Pelayo (ref. 82, Vol. I, p. 437) quotes the first four lines of this work. They are a romance endecasílabo.]

890. _____. El Placer público de Santafé. Poema en que se celebra el arribo del excelentísimo Sr. D. Antonio Amar y Borbón, Caballero profeso del orden de Santiago, Teniente general de los Reales Ejércitos, Virrey, Governador y Capitán general del Nuevo Reino de Granada, por D. José María Salazar, colegial de San Bartolomé... Con licencia. En Santafé de Bogotá. En la Imprenta Real. Por D. Bruno Espinosa de los Monteros. Año de 1804. 28 lvs. 20.5 cm.

[This work may be a romance endecasílabo. Menéndez y Pelayo, who cites it (ref. 82, Vol. I, p. 437), does not make this clear, but the compositions of this poet which he prints are romances with eleven-syllable lines (see the other entries for this author).]

891. Samper, Darío. "Copla y guabina santandereanas." Bol, I(1951):5, pp. 965-974.

[Contains some coplas and some guabinas, a type of copla cultivated in Santander. The author evokes the area in nostalgic terms and characterizes the region and its people. Of interest is one fragment of a narrative poem which is similar to corridos, but it sounds like a non-popular composition.]

892. _____. "Coplas en el Valle de Tenza." Bol, I:3 (septiembre, 1951), 479-487.

[The author evokes his native Valle de Tenza in romantic terms and offers the texts of several coplas which he feels reflect the temperament of the people of the region.]

893. Samper, José María. El bambuco.

[Otero Muñoz (ref. 842, p. 286) prints a copla taken from this work.]

894. Samuel, S. J. "El canto popular en el Magdalena." RFCC, 2.ª época, I:2 (junio, 1953), 32-53.

895. Sánchez Montenegro, V. Los comuneros del sur; historia y folklore nariñenses. Pasto: Imprenta del Departamento, 1940. 42 pp. 24 cm.

[A very thorough study of a rebellion which occurred in Tuquerres in 1800 in protest against excessive taxation. Included are several popular poems inspired by the event. Though called coplas, most are very similar to Mexican corridos and are important to the study of narrative poetry in America.]

896. _____. "Panorama folklórico de Nariño." RFCC, No. 4 (febrero, 1949), 47-75.

[A treatise on the customs of the area of Nariño. There is only slight attention to popular music and poetry, though the author does mention "dejos de yaraví ecuatoriano," prints a few copla texts, and records the existence of El piojo y la pulga, from which he gives a two-line fragment.]

897. "La semilla colombiana." CV, IX:69 (enero-febrero, 1926), 99-101.

[Chase (ref. 25, p. 126) comments: "Popular songs of the first years of Colombia."]

898. Soffia, José A. Las dos hermanas; recuerdo del Magdalena. 1884.

[Otero Muñoz (ref. 842, p. 297) prints a copla by Soffia which appeared in the above work and which has become traditional.]

899. Stella, Luz. Los celos del río.
[Otero Muñoz (ref. 842, p. 297) prints a copla taken from the above.]

900. Téllez Camacho, Elberto. La copla santandereana en la provincia de Vélez.

901. Tiscornia, Eleuterio F. "Un discurso, un cancionero y 'Martín Fierro'." Azul, Año I:1 (febrero de 1930), 7-28.

[Tiscornia attacks Antonio José Restrepo's work, particularly his "Discurso sobre la poesía popular en Colombia," his Cancionero de Antioquia, and an appendix of this latter work in which Restrepo criticizes Ciro Mendia's ideas about Martín Fierro. Tiscornia censures Restrepo's romantic approach to Martín Fierro and to his own Cancionero de Antioquia.]

902. Tobón, Aurelio. Estudio sobre cantares y costumbres tolimenses.

[Listed by Enríquez Córdoba and Castellví as a folleto (ref. 769, p. 144), it is said to be "Consultable en la Biblioteca del Dr. Eduardo Martínez Esponda."]

903. Torres Torrente, _____. El cielo en la tierra.
[Otero Muñoz (ref. 842, p. 285) prints a copla taken from this work.]

904. _____. Lágrimas de amor.
[Otero Muñoz (ref. 842, p. 281) prints a copla taken from this work.]

905. "Trovador del Valle" and "Hilarión Pastrana." Cancionero del Valle de Tenza. Trabajo presentado para el concurso de cancioneros abierto por la Academia Colombiana.

906. _____. Tonadas del Valle de Tenza. Trabajo presentado para el concurso de cancioneros abierto por la Academia Colombiana.

907. Tuckman, William. "Folk Music in Colombia and Venezuela." PanAm, VI:8 (January, 1946), 48-49.

[Brief mention of several Colombian and Venezuelan songs and dances. It is of little interest except to a completely uninformed reader. The galerón is mentioned with reference to Colombia, though not in connection with Venezuela, and the corrido is mentioned in the discussion of Venezuela.]

908. El tuquerreño libre. Joaquín M. Pérez, director.
[From this source, apparently a newspaper, Sánchez Montenegro (ref. 895, p. 26) quotes some very interesting verses about a rebellion in Túquerre in 1800.]

909. Urueta, Rufo. La bruja.
[Otero Muñoz (ref. 842, p. 301) prints a copla taken from this work.]

910. Valencia, Reinaldo. "La música popular de Chocó." RevInd, I:4 (octubre-diciembre, 1936), 45-46.

911. Vargas Osorio, Tomás. La copla en Santander.

Vargas Tamayo, José. See Medina, Joaquín R., Cantas del Valle de Tenza, entry no. 817.

912. Velásquez, Samuel. Madre.
[Otero Muñoz (ref. 842, p. 315) prints a copla taken from this work.]

913. Velásquez M., Rogerio. El cancionero de Tres Ríos. Bogotá: Extensión Cultural de la Universidad Nacional, 1956. 8 lvs. 24 cm. (Entregas de poesía popular colombiana, No. 4.)

914. _____. "La canoa chocoana y el folclor." RCF, Segunda época, No. 3 (1959), 107-126.
[Contains several coplas and romances, though the latter are artistic imitations of popular poetry. The coplas are of popular origin.]

915. _____. "Cantares de los Tres Ríos." RCF, Segunda época, II:5 (1960), 9-99.
[A collection of 750 texts, mostly coplas, without music.]

916. _____. "Cuentos de la raza negra." RCF, Segunda época, No. 3 (1959), 1-63.
[Its title notwithstanding, this article contains quite a number of verses, most of them coplas and romances.]

917. _____. "La fiesta de San Francisco de Asís en Quibdó." RCF, Segunda época, II:4 (1960), 15-37.
[Contains a few copla texts along with other popular poetry. Of particular interest is some poetry by a popular singer known as el poeta chocoano.]

918. _____. "El folklore en la obra de Antonio José Restrepo." Bol, No. 42 (agosto de 1955), 309-329.
[A laudatory evaluation of Restrepo's work in the field of Colombian folklore. The author quotes copla and décima texts from Restrepo's collection.]

919. Velásquez, Samuel. "Leyendas y cuentos de la raza negra."
RCF, Segunda época, II:4 (1960), 67-120.
[Includes a few copla texts from the Chocó region of Colombia.]

920. Vergara y Vergara, J. M. Historia de la literatura en Nueva Granada, desde la conquista hasta la independencia (1538-1820).
Bogotá: Imprenta de Echeverría Hermanos, 1867. xxiv, 532 pp. 16.5 cm.; also, 2^{nda} edición con prólogo y anotaciones de Antonio Gómez Restrepo. Bogotá: Librería Americana, 1905. xxvii, 515 pp. 23.5 cm.; also, Vols. IV-V of Obras escogidas de don José María Vergara y Vergara. Bogotá: Editorial Minerva, 1931. 19.5 cm.
[Chap. XVIII, "Poesía popular — Carácter nacional — Conclusión," treats the origins of the popular poetry of New Granada with particular reference to the Spanish, Indian, and Negro elements that have entered into it. There are a few texts, including one romance and some coplas. In the second edition Gómez Restrepo adds an appendix containing some artistic romances by Hernando Domínguez Camargo which here appear for the first time in print.]

921. Wiesner, L. J. Psiquis rural.
[Otero Muñoz (ref. 842, p. 277) prints a copla taken from this work.]

922. Zamudio G., Daniel. "El folklore musical en Colombia."
RevInd, XXXV:109 (mayo-junio, 1949), suplemento No. 14. 30 pp. numbered independently of Vol. XXXV.
[A very important contribution to the study of Colombian musical folklore. The author traces the history of the development of music from pre-conquest times through the Spanish period, with special attention to what he considers to be Negro contamination of Spanish American music. Thereupon Zamudio analyzes some Colombian musical types. His first analysis of the galerón is both musical and literary, and he arrives at the interesting conclusion that it is related to liturgical music. In subsequent analyses he treats the bambuco, the guabina, the pasillo, the joropo, and otros aires. All in all, this is a valuable study, perhaps the best that has been made of Colombian folklore.]

923. Zapata Olivella, Delia. "El mestizaje, característica del folclor colombiano." Bol, No. 46 (1957), 153-159.

COSTA RICA

As is evident from the paucity of entries in this section of my bibliography, the popular poetry and song of Costa Rica remain almost untouched by folklorists and literary scholars.

924. Colección de bailes típicos de la provincia de Guanacaste. San José: Secretaría de Educación, 1929.
 [Said to contain (ref. 22, p. 117) a version of El torito. It is the "No me entierren en sagrado" theme.]

Dobles Segreda, Luis. See Fonseca, Julio, entry no. 925.

925. Fonseca, Julio. "Referencias sobre música costarricense." REM, Ano I:3 (abril de 1950), 75-97.
 [A survey of both popular and artistic music. Most of the first portion of the article entitled "Folklore" is quoted directly from comments of Luis Dobles Segreda, under whose direction collections of folk songs were published in 1929, 1934, and 1935. Though of interest, this discussion of popular music and most of the compositions printed here with music are alien to the romance-corrido narrative tradition. An exception is El torito (p. 83), which is a version of the "No me entierren en sagrado" romance of Spanish tradition.]

926. Gamboa, Emma. Canciones populares para niños. San José: Lehmann, 1941. 20 lvs. 30 cm. Reproduced from typewritten manuscript.
 [Chase (ref. 25, p. 129) comments: "Includes: Children's songs, folk songs and children's dances."]

927. Núñez, Evangelina de. Costa Rica y su folklore. San José: Imprenta Nacional, 1956. 395 pp.
 [Boggs (ref. 13 [1957], p. 19) comments: "Contains (p. 135-389) numerous short items in prose and verse by various authors on types, customs, legends, verse, music, festivals, dress, beliefs, arts, tales, Indians, and a great variety of aspects of local life."]

928. Reni, Aníbal. Recados criollos; folklore costarricense. San José: Edit. Tecolotl, 1944. 68 pp.

929. Umaña, Salvador. "Del folklore costarricense; trozos de un Cancionero nacional de cuna que se está recogiendo." RepAm, II:14 (1 de marzo de 1921), 196-197; II:21 (30 de mayo de 1921), 303-304.
 [A collection of children's poetry of various kinds. A few compositions are coplas. Though only a very minor contribution, the fact that it deals with a country which has been studied very little heightens its interest.]

CUBA

The predominance of the <u>décima</u> over all other types of popular poetry for all poetic purposes, narrative, lyrical, or satirical, is the most striking aspect of Cuban poetic folklore in general. From the eighteenth century, when José Rodríguez (El Padre Capacho) won popular acclaim as a <u>repentista</u> poet, through the appearance of such semipopular historical narratives as <u>La invasión de Cárdenas</u> and <u>La invasión de Vuelta Abajo</u> in the middle of the nineteenth century, and even down to the present day, popular poets and the Cuban <u>pueblo</u> have invariably displayed a marked preference for the <u>décima</u> over all other poetic forms. <u>Coplas</u>, to be sure, are widely sung and the <u>romance</u> is not moribund, but at no time in the history of Cuban folklore, as far as we know, have these forms ever challenged the supremacy of the <u>décima</u>.

The earliest investigators to direct their attention to Cuban musical and poetic folklore were two scholars who were active around the middle of the nineteenth century: Antonio Bachiller y Morales, whose disorganized but expansive literary and bibliographical interests encompassed folklore along with almost every other aspect of Cuban life, and Ramón de Palma y Romay, whose brief but informative pioneer study of Cuban popular poets and their works represents a first step in the direction of specialized folklore investigation in Cuba.

Nevertheless, the real flowering of serious research into Cuban popular tradition awaited the appearance in the early years of the twentieth century of several extremely competent scholars. To Carolina Poncet y Cárdenas and to José María Chacón y Calvo we owe most of our present knowledge of Cuban popular poetry, particularly of the <u>romance</u> which they unearthed in Cuban oral tradition; and to Fernando Ortiz we are indebted for the masterful and exhaustive research into Cuban musical folklore which has won for him a place of high honor among the most outstanding musicologists of Spanish America.

The efforts of these three important figures have been supplemented by the works of other scholars of merit such as Sofía Córdova de Fernández in the field of children's folk songs and Alejo Carpentier in the realm of musical history. But, unfortunately, not all those who have written about Cuban music and song have been scholars of such high calibre. Several self-styled students of "folklore," including some whose works have enjoyed considerable renown, have had only the haziest notion of their subject; and the promising titles of their books and articles are grossly misleading in that the subjects treated therein (learned poetry, operatic singers, concert guitarrists, and the like) are usually unrelated to genuine folklore.

Nor has Cuban folklore been favored by the attention of good bibliographers. The one specialized bibliography which we have (see entry no. 1062) is extremely unsatisfactory.

CUBA

930. Anfriso. Décima de Anfriso sobre los estragos que ha causado el cólera en esta ciudad. Habana: Imprenta Fraternal.
[Bachiller y Morales (ref. 936, Vol. III, p. 416) lists this composition in a section of works which appeared in 1833.]

931. ———. Bando, o sea, despedida del cólera, por el mismo y en la propia imprenta.
[Bachiller y Morales (ref. 936, Vol. III, p. 416) lists this composition immediately after the décima listed in entry no. 930.]

932. Arissó, Ana María. Estudio del folklore sagüero; investigación realizada durante los cursos 1938-1939 y 1939-1940 por los alumnos de gramática y literatura hispanocubana del Instituto de Segunda Enseñanza de Sagua la Grande.

933. Arrom, José Juan. "El negro en la poesía folklórica americana." In Miscelánea de estudios dedicados a Fernando Ortiz por sus discípulos, colegas y amigos con ocasión de cumplirse sesenta años de la publicación de su primer impreso en Menorca en 1895. Vol. I. La Habana: Ucar García, 1955. Pp. 81-106.
[Boggs (ref. 13 [1956], p. 42) says: "Cites copla verses from many parts of Spanish America showing attitudes and sentiments about the negro."]

934. Bacardí y Moreau, Emilio. Crónicas de Santiago de Cuba. 2 vols. Barcelona: Tipografía de Carbonell y Esteva, 1908, 1909. 22.5 cm. and 23 cm.
[In Vol. II the author frequently cites poems, ensaladillas, and other types of literature which were inspired by the events he records. Most are not popular, but some are. One poem in redondillas (the author calls it a romance) is very close to the style and tone of Mexican corridos (pp. 397-398). Also interesting are some political décimas (p. 411). Some coplas are also scattered through the volume.]

935. ———. Crónicas de Santiago de Cuba. [?] vols. Santiago de Cuba, 1923.
[A poem from the above source entitled La Bayamesa (Vol. IV, p. 319) is reprinted in a brief note entitled "La copla política en Cuba" in AFC, III:1 (enero-marzo, 1928), 84. Consisting of four coplas, the poem was inspired by the Ten Years' War in the eastern part of Cuba.]

936. Bachiller y Morales, Antonio. Apuntes para la historia de las letras y de la instrucción pública de la isla de Cuba. 3 vols. Habana: Imprenta de P. Massana (Vols. II and III, Imprenta del Tiempo), 1859, 1860, and 1861. 24 cm.; also, 3 vols. Habana: Imprenta de Cultural, S. A., 1936, 1936, and 1937. 20.5 cm. (Colección de libros cubanos, Vols. XXXIV, XXXV, and XXXVI.)
[A poorly organized work which is, however, of considerable merit. There are sections on poetry and on popular poetry, and occasionally nonpopular romances and décimas are quoted textually. The last part

of Vol. III is devoted to a bibliography of books and other material published in Cuba from 1724 to 1840. Though not very carefully done, the work lists some titles which apparently refer to popular narrative poetry.]

937. Bachiller y Morales, Antonio. Cuba: monografía histórica que comprende desde la pérdida de la Habana hasta la restauración española. Habana: Miguel de Villa, 1883. 214 pp. 22.5 cm.
[Besides containing an occasional strophe of topical but not popular poetry in the text, the volume has in the appendix some eighteenth-century compositions written to comment upon current affairs. They are semipopular in tone and are of historical interest. Some of them are décimas, some are coplas. The most interesting of this historical poetry deals with the English attack on Habana in 1762.]

938. _____. Cuba primitiva. Habana: Miguel de Villa, 1883. 214 pp.; also, 2.ª ed. corregida y aumentada: M. de Villa, 1883. 399 pp. 23 cm.
[Chase (ref. 25, p. 135) comments: "Words and music of an Antillean song, pp. 44-45. Vocabulary, pp. 185-395; see areito, maionauau."]

939. Barras y Prado, Antonio de las. La Habana a mediados del siglo XIX, Madrid: Imprenta de la Ciudad Lineal, 1925. 287 pp. 19.5 cm.
[There are three cuartetas of redondillas (pp. 195-196) about a political scandal in 1862. They are in the nature of political pasquines and resemble to some degree the satirical corridos of Mexico. See also, Ortiz, Fernando, ref. 1023.]

940. Berenguer y Sed, Antonio. Tradiciones villaclareñas. Habana: Imprenta y Papelería de Rambla, Bouza y Ca., 1929. 23.5 cm.
[Contains a section entitled "Ensaladillas villaclareñas" (pp. 197-203 [reprinted in AFC, IV:3 (julio-septiembre, 1929), 270-274]). It contains the texts of some décimas which circulated in Villaclara in manuscript form in answer to some sarcastic poems known as ensaladillas which, also in manuscript, had earlier criticized certain persons in the village. From the year 1848 the author also offers some poetic ensaladillas of similar character in octosyllabic rhymed couplets. They deal with the moral and physical defects of some of the people of the town. All of this is somewhat topical but is of scant interest except perhaps to investigators of the décimas in Cuba.]

C. G. V. See Valdés, Carlos Genaro, entry no. 1064.

Cabrera Paz, Manuel. See Guerra, Armando, entry no. 992.

941. Cáceres González, _____. Moderna colección de canciones y guarachas. Habana, 1900. 16 pp.

942. _____. Nueva lira criolla; guarachas, canciones y décimas. Habana, 1900. 256 pp.
[There is probably some relationship between this work and the Nueva lira criolla which I have found listed in several bibliographies. But I have not been able to consult enough of the works in question to unravel the mystery.]

943. Calero, José. Breves estudios musicales. La Habana: Imprenta "El Siglo XX," 1926. 194 pp. 20 cm.
[Chase (ref. 25, p. 135) comments: " 'El folklore musical cubano y el maestro Sánchez de Fuentes,' pp. 51-54."]

El Camarioqueño. See entry no. 1015.

Canción al propio objeto . . . . See Poesía heroica al feliz éxito de la expedición, entry no. 1031.

944. El cancionero cubano por un "Guajiro" de la Habana.

945. Canciones cubanas desde "La Bayamesa" hasta las más modernas. Madrid: Imprenta de Minuesa, 1879; also, 2.ª ed. Habana: J. Gutiérrez, 1880. 360 pp.; 3.ª ed. Habana: J. Gutiérrez, 1883. 362 pp.

946. Cantares de Vuelta-Abajo, recopilados por un Guajiro. 2.ª ed. Cuaderno I. Habana, 1876. 46 pp. (Trelles [ref. 1062, p. 106] indicates that the first edition was published in Havana in 1871.)
[A collection of décimas and glosas, some of which are apparently truly popular. They are, however, lyric rather than narrative.]

947. Canto a la expedición del señor Barradas. See Poesía herioca al feliz éxito de la expedición, entry no. 1031.

948. Cantos populares recopilados por un aficionado. Santiago: J. E. Ravelo, 1891.

949. Capdevila y Melián, Pedro. "Apuntes del folklore remediano." RBC, XLIII:2 (marzo-abril, 1939), 220-265.
[A very interesting collection of topical songs, mostly commentaries on politics, from Ciudad de Remedios. Though few are real folklore and most are the work of known authors, they are of value to the study of popular verse in general. Their importance specifically to the study of the romance-corrido tradition is limited.]

950. Carbonell y Rivero, José. La poesía lírica en Cuba, Tomo I. Vol. I of Evolución de la cultura cubana. La Habana: Imprenta "El Siglo XX," 1928. 328 pp. 25.5 cm.
[Contains information about several semipopular poets such as Fray José Rodríguez (El Padre Capacho). Also, the article "Cantares de Cuba" by Ramón de Palma y Romay (ref. 1026) appears in the appendix.]

951. Carpentier, Alejo. La música en Cuba. México: Fondo de Cultura Económica, 1946. 282 pp. 22 cm. (Colección "Tierra Firme," No. 19.)
[In Chap. I, "El siglo XVI," the author discusses at some length the

introduction of romances and coplas into Cuba. Particularly notable is his attempt to trace back to a Spanish romance the origins of a famous popular song, the Son de la Má Teodora. Also of great interest is a song of the nineteenth century which is literarily a genuine corrido about a guapo, one Juan Quiñones. Four strophes of the song are quoted (p. 182). Scattered through the book are several copla texts. There is also a good bibliography (pp. 279-282).]

952. Castellanos, Carlos A. "El tema de Delgadina en el folklore de Santiago de Cuba." JAF, XXXIII(1920), 43-46; also, AFC, II:2 (mayo de 1926), 131-136.

[Texts of two Cuban versions of Delgadina in verse and one in a combination of prose and verse.]

953. Chacón y Calvo, José María. "Cuestionario de literatura popular cubana." AFC, I:1 (enero de 1924), 9-37.

[After a short introduction which outlines the procedures which folklorists should use in gathering materials, the author offers partial texts of fifty-five romances which investigators should seek in Cuban tradition. Then there is a brief discussion of the décima and of other genres of folklore: children's games, tales, riddles, and the like.]

954. ———. "Figuras del romancero: El conde Olinos." AFC, II:1 (enero de 1926), 36-46.

[A lecture given at the Ateneo of Madrid on April 12, 1919. The author studies the romance of El conde Olinos, tracing its development from the Tristan legend into Spanish, Portuguese, and Cuban tradition. Besides Spanish and Portuguese versions of the romance, he offers a fragmentary Cuban text from his native town, Santa María del Rosario.]

955. ———. "El folk-lore cubano." Universal (Habana), 4 de enero, 1914.

956. ———. "Nuevos romances de Cuba." RBC, IX:3 (mayo-junio, 1914), 199-210.

[Contains the texts of Cuban versions of Gerineldo and Conde Olinos, along with a commentary and comparisons with versions from other regions. The two texts were collected by the author from oral tradition and are printed without music. The commentary, though good for its day, is based on much less information than is now available.]

957. ———. Los orígenes de la poesía en Cuba. Habana: Imprenta "El Siglo XX," 1913. 84 pp. 25.5 cm. ("Publicado en 'Cuba contemporánea'" appears on the title page [See entry no. 961].)

[The text of this study contains some brief comments on the romances of Cuba, but they are based on relatively little information since they antedate the work of Carolina Poncet y Cárdenas. In a section of the appendix entitled "Sobre los romances viejos conservados por la tradición oral en Cuba" (pp. 45-56) the author dwells at length upon the presence of romances in America and in Cuba, and while his comments are dated, he gives some interesting texts and comments about the Nau Catharineta in Portuguese tradition and its relationship to some Spanish romances and Cuban versions of Santa Catalina.]

958. _____. "El primer poema escrito en Cuba." RFE, VIII (1921), 170-175.
[A brief study of the Espejo de la paciencia of Silvestre de Balboa. Of no importance to the study of popular poetry but of significance to the history of narrative poetry.]

959. _____. "Romance de la dama y el pastor." AFC, I:4 (24 de junio de 1925), 289-297.
[Contains a Cuban version of La dama y el pastor and some variants of this romance from Spain and from Chile. The Spanish versions are from works of Fernán Caballero and of Wolf and Hoffman. Also, there are some unpublished versions sent to the author by Menéndez Pidal and Torner. The Chilean version comes from the collection of Vicuña Cifuentes.]

960. _____. "Romances tradicionales en Cuba; contribución al estudio del 'folk-lore' cubano." RFLC, XVIII:1 (enero de 1914), 45-121; also, in Ensayos de literatura cubana. Madrid: Editorial "Santurnino Calleja," 1922. Pp. 83-186.
[A fundamental work for study of the romance in Cuba and in America, though it is somewhat dated. It contains a collection of American romances, especially Cuban versions, with well documented comments and studies of their relationship to Spanish origins. Chase (ref. 25, p. 137) provides a detailed description of this work.]

961. _____. "Sobre los romances viejos conservados por la tradición oral en Cuba." CC, III(1913), 73-85. (This is an appendix of an article entitled "Los orígenes de la poesía en Cuba." CC, II(1913), 167-174, 238-252, 308-319; III(1913), 67-88, 151-176.)
[See entry no. 957.]

962. Colección de canciones y guarachas cubanas. N.d.

963. Colección de todas las poesías que se han publicado en esta ciudad en elogio del aeronauta don Domingo Blinó, con algunas inéditas. Habana: Imprenta Fraternal.
[Bachiller y Morales (ref. 936, Vol. III, p. 406) lists this work in a section devoted to publications which appeared in 1831. He comments: "Era Blinó, hijo de la Habana y excitó grande entusiasmo por su valor y arrojo."]

964. Colección escogida de canciones cubanas. Segunda parte. Habana: n.d.

965. Colección escojida de canciones, décimas y guarachas, en las que figuran las más selectas publicadas hasta el día. Habana: Se

vende en la calle de Aguacate núm. 48, Librería de E. Pazo é Hijo, 1904. 160 pp.

[A collection of popular poetry, most of which is topical. Though only two or three compositions concern real people, several are social satire similar to that of some Mexican corridos. There are many décimas, some of them being glosas, but there are very few romances and none of the latter is narrative. In addition to the 160 pages which apparently made up the book under the title given, two additional sections of sixteen pages each are bound in. These contain mostly satirical décimas.]

966. "La copla política cubana; décimas del año de 1762 acerca de la entrega de la Habana a los ingleses hasta su restauración, en que fué gobernador D. Sebastián Peñalver y el conde de Alvermar (sic.)." AFC, V:3 (julio a septiembre de 1930), 270-280.

[A collection of décimas which are thoroughly historical, though not very popular in tone. They are taken from Bachiller y Morales, Cuba: monografía histórica, entry no. 937.]

967. Córdova de Fernández, Sofía. "El folklore del niño cubano." RFLC, XXXIII:3-4 (julio-diciembre, 1923), 268-306; XXXIV:1-2 (enero-junio, 1924), 26-52; XXXV:1-2 (enero-junio, 1925), 109-156; 3-4 (julio-diciembre, 1925), 361-418; also, AFC, I:3 (1925), 248-270; 4 (24 de junio de 1925), 356-373 II:1 (enero de 1926), 72-82; 2 (mayo de 1926), 159-168; 3 (octubre de 1926), 247-264; 4 (junio de 1927), 369-386; III:1 (enero a marzo de 1928), 55-78; 3 (julio a septiembre de 1928), 257-274; 4 (octubre a diciembre de 1928), 59-76; IV:1 (enero a marzo de 1929), 72-89.

[In this general study of all phases of children's folklore, the author has occasion to comment upon the romance and its relative scarcity in Cuba as compared with the décima and other forms. There are texts of several romances, such as Las señas del esposo, Don Gato, and Alfonso XII (AFC, III:1, pp. 55-78); also, there is some attention to romances in the "Notas comparativas" (Vol. IV:1, pp. 72-89).]

968. Corona Raimundo, Manuel. Album de canciones cubanas; recopilación de canciones, boleros, guarachas, claves criollas, guajiras, puntos, habaneras y chistes originales del autor . . . y otros autores cubanos. Habana, 1915. 12 pp.

969. La coronación de Fernando VII. Habana: Imprenta del Gobierno y Capitanía General.

[Bachiller y Morales (ref. 936, Vol. III, p. 278) lists this publication in a section devoted to material publicado en 1809. He describes it as a "Poema que se refiere a la guerra con los franceses."]

970. Décimas sobre el asesinato cometido del 18 al 19 de enero de 1830.

[Bachiller y Morales (ref. 936, Vol. III, p. 394) lists the work in a section of publications for the year 1829 (!). He puts (¿Cuál?) in parentheses after the title.]

971. Declamación hecha en cuartetos contra la francesa perfidia. Habana: En la imprenta de don Esteban Boloña, agosto 8 de 1808.

972. Díaz, Manuel Armando. Cantares cubanos. 1898.

973. Don D. M. El dengue. Primera y segunda parte. Habana: Imprenta Fraternal.

[Bachiller y Morales (ref. 936, Vol. III, p. 389) puts this composition in a section of publications for the year 1828. He comments: "Don D. M. escribió sobre las circunstancias de esta enfermedad epidémica que llamó serendengue en su repetición. Concluía con unos boleros."]

974. Don J. M. [Don D. M. ?]. El globo con el dengue. Habana: Imprenta de Boloña.

[Bachiller y Morales (ref. 936, Vol. III, p. 389) puts this work in a section of publications for the year 1828. He comments: "También publicó otras dos colecciones de décimas el mismo M. sobre el dengue." See Don D. M., entry no. 973 above.]

975. Escoto, José A. "Albores de la poesía en Cuba." Revista de literatura cubana, 1916.

976. Espinosa, Aurelio M. "El tema de Roncesvalles y Bernardo del Carpio en la poesía popular de Cuba." AFC, V:3 (julio a septiembre de 1930), 193-198.

[Espinosa prints the text of a poem collected from Cuban oral tradition and given to him in 1928. Based upon the legend of Bernardo del Carpio, it is not itself a romance, though it contains lines lifted from romances (e.g., "¡Mala la hubisteis, franceses, en esa de Roncesvalles!"). The author offers it as "una elaboración erudita y moderna de un antiguo romance tradicional."]

977. Ferreiro, Pascual. Coplas. Habana: Imprenta Liberal.

978. _____. Coplas glosadas en décimas para cantar los aficionados. Habana. 16 pp.

979. _____. Décimas del parnaso cubano. Habana. 16 pp.

980. _____. El escándalo; décimas callejeras. 2 cuadernos. Habana. 32 pp.

981. _____. La guajira de Vuelta Abajo; décimas. 1.ª parte. 16 pp.

982. "El fuego grande del Cayo." AFC, V:1 (enero a marzo de 1930), 84-87.

[A description of a fire which occurred in 1819 in the village of Remedios along with two compositions in décimas which the event inspired. Both of them are very similar in style and tone to Mexican corridos.]

983. Fuentes y Matons, Laureano. Las artes en Santiago de Cuba. 1893.
[Henríquez Ureña (ref. 1079, p. 92) says it contains the tonada known as Má Teodora.]

984. Garrigó Roque, E. Historia documentada de la conspiración de los Soles y rayos de Bolívar. 2 vols. Habana: Imprenta "El Siglo XX," A. Muñiz y Hno., 1929. 28 cm.
[Chase (ref. 25, p. 136) says that it contains something about Má Teodora (Vol. I, p. 166).]

985. González, Isidro José. Extracto en verso de las más principales circunstancias del execrable bien sabido asesinato . . . [etc.]. Habana.
[Bachiller y Morales (ref. 936, Vol. III, p. 394) puts it in a section of publications which appeared in 1829. He notes that it is "Un pliego."]

986. González, Rafael. Canciones cubanas, guarachas, diálogos y boleros. Habana: Imp. La Prueba, 1909. 62 pp.

987. _____. Cantos campestres; colección de décimas glosadas (recopilación). 4 cuadernos. Habana: Imp. del Vapor, 1860.

988. _____. Cantos del trópico. 2.ª ed. Tercer cuaderno. Habana: Imp. Militar, 1865. 16 pp.

989. Gronlier, Enrique. El cancionero cubano, por un Guajiro de la Habana (décimas originales). Habana: R. Veloso, 1915. 12 pp.

990. _____. Cantos de mi patria; poesía y cantos populares. Habana, 1864.

991. _____. Lirios de la tarde; poesías y cantos populares. Habana, 1876.

992. Guerra, Armando (Francisco Martín Llorente). "Presencia negra en la poesía popular cubana del siglo XIX." EAfr, III:1, 2, 3, 4 (1939), 16-27.
[Salient facts about the life and works of Manuel Cabrera Paz (1824-1872) from the town of San Marcos, who, so the author believes, was the first poet to use Negro dialect in Cuban poetry. Most of his works are unpublished, but there appears in this article a considerable part of his composition in décimas, Exclamaciones de un negro en las fiestas efectuadas con motivo de la inauguración del patrono de este pueblo, San Marcos, el día 25 de abril de 1857; also the complete texts of Los esclavos en Cuba. Their tone is very popular. There is also mention of a romance by Cabrera Paz, El tulipán de Stambul.]

993. Guirnalda criolla, o el ruiseñor de las selvas; gran colección de décimas. Habana, n.d.

994. Hernández Crespo, Manuel. Cantos populares.
[Published "por 1880" according to Trelles (ref. 1062, p. 147).]

995. _____. Flora poética nacional (cantos populares). 1880.

996. Iglesia, Alvaro de la. Tradiciones cubanas; relatos y retratos históricos. Habana: Establecimiento Tipográfico Editorial de Maresma y Pérez, 1911. 181 pp. 19.5 cm.; Cuadros viejos; segunda serie de las tradiciones cubanas. Habana: Imprenta Moderna, 1915. 267 pp. 20.5 cm.; Cosas de antaño; tercera serie de las tradiciones cubanas. Habana: Imp. Maza y Ca., 1917. 300 pp. 20.5 cm.

[Sketches based on Cuban historical events, legends, and traditions and clearly written under the influence of Ricardo Palma. The only truly popular poetry I have found in the work are two guarachas which deal with the appearance of Halley's comet in 1910. One is in corrido form, the other is in décimas. These appear in Cosas de antaño (pp. 52-55). I have been unable to consult Cuadros viejos.]

997. La invasión de Cárdenas; romance histórico en que se refieren los sucesos acaecidos a consecuencia de la expedición de piratas que desembarcó en Cárdenas el 19 de mayo de 1850. Habana: Imp. del Tiempo, 1850. 47 pp.

998. Invasión de la Vuelta-Abajo; romance histórico por el autor del titulado "La invasión de Cárdenas." Habana: Imp. del Tiempo, 1851. viii, 55 pp.; 2.ª ed. corregida. Habana: Imp. del Tiempo, 1851.

[A long historical romance about the defeat of a group of North American filibusterers who attempted to invade Cuba in 1851. Though basically an artistic poem, it has considerable popular flavor.]

999. Iraizoz, Antonio. "La décima cubana en la poesía popular." AFC, IV:2 (abril a junio de 1929), 133-152.

[A very informative and well organized general discussion of the nature of the Cuban décima, something of the history of its development in Spain and in Cuba, the types of décimas which can be distinguished, and the manner in which they are composed and sung. Most of the emphasis is on semilearned or learned rather than popular compositions, though a few examples of topical patriotic décimas are given.]

1000. La isla. Cuaderno de décimas cubanas. Julio de 1876; Segunda parte por F. J. Zea. 1880.

1001. J. R. V. Décimas cubanas y canciones y guarachas modernas. 1.ª edición. Habana: Establecimiento Tipográfico de Canalejo y Xiqués, 1893. 143 pp. 19.5 cm.

[The collection contains ten décimas. One, Historia del célebre Manuel Vento, relates the death of an heroic bandit in a trap set by the police. Another, Contestación de un campesino á un aristócrata que le dijo guajiro, is a topical poem in which the rustic exalts his status as an honest and hard worker. A third, Décimas de la provincia de Pinar del Río, is a cry of distress of the province whose workers are unable to find work. A fourth, El tabaquero, comments upon the prosperity of the tobacco workers in Cuba. The other décimas in the collection are all lyrical poems. There are also fifty-two lyrical compositions in a section of "Canciones y guarachas."]

1002. El jardín cubano; nueva colección de cantos y glosas dedicados a los laboriosos y honrados campesinos de la Isla de Cuba. N. d.

1003. Lances del amor; canciones populares. Habana, n. d.

1004. León, Argeliers. "El patrimonio folklórico musical de Cuba." RBC, LXV:1-2-3 (enero-junio, 1950), 118-125.
[The author deals almost exclusively with techniques, styles, and influences in the music of Cuba. He refers in passing to the canto guajiro as being "asido en ciertos aspectos al romance hispánico" (p. 119). But this is his only mention of romances or other narrative songs.]

1005. La lira criolla; guarachas, canciones, décimas, recopiladas por El Vueltarribero. Habana: Librería é Imprenta "La Moderna Poesía," 1895. 132 pp.; also, 1897. 266 pp.
[A collection of popular songs. A few (in the 1895 edition, which I have examined) are narrative and historical, but they are not romances or corridos.]

1006. Llaverías, Joaquín. "Unas décimas políticas." AFC, I:1 (enero de 1924), 52-61.
[The texts of two poems preserved in the Archivo Nacional. One which deals with the quarrel between Napoleon and Fernando VII circulated in Cuba in 1808; the other is directed against the governor of Cienfuegos and appeared in 1832.]

Llorente, Francisco Martín. See Guerra, Armando, entry no. 992.

1007. López Prieto, Antonio. Parnaso cubano; colección de poesías selectas de autores cubanos, desde Zequeira a nuestros días. Habana: M. de Villa, 1881. lxxxi, 370 pp.
[Chacón y Calvo (ref. 957, p. 22) quotes in its entirety an Oda a la Purísima Concepción, which is an artistic romance by José Surí, a poet born in 1696. He took it from the introduction of this volume.]

1008. Macau, M. A. Cancionero folklórico. Habana, 1956. 111 pp.

1009. Mantecón, Enrique. Nuevos cantares arreglados por el habanero E. Mantecón. Habana, 1891.

1010. _____. Nuevos cantos cubanos arreglados por el poeta del pueblo E. Mantecón. Habana, n. d.

1011. Martínez, Domingo. Décimas cubanas y canciones y guarachas modernas. (Por J. R. V.) Habana, 1893.
[Trelles (ref. 1062, p. 148) lists this item. It surely must be the

volume which I have examined and which I have listed under J. R. V. (entry no. 1001). I apparently found no indication that Domingo Martínez was author or editor when I looked at the book several years ago.]

1012. Martínez y Cordero, Eliseo A. Cantos guajiros, por varios jóvenes cubanos. Santiago de Cuba, 1862.

1013. Martínez Moles, Manuel. Contribución al folklore; tradiciones, leyendas y anécdotas espirituanas. Tomos I, II, III and III, 2.ª parte. Habana: Imprenta de "El Fígaro", Cultural S. A., Imprenta "El Siglo XX," 1926, 1927, 1931, 1936. 20.5 cm. (Vol. I) and 21 cm.; Contribución al folklore; tipos populares de Sancti-Spiritus. Tomo IV. Habana: Cultural, S. A., 1929. 299 pp. 24.5 cm.; Contribución al folklore; vocabulario espirituano, refranes, frases proverbiales, dichos y dicharachos. Tomo VII. Habana: Cultural, S. A., 1928. 599 pp. 24.5 cm. [A note written by hand on the title page of Vol. I of the collection in the Indiana University library says that Vols. V and VI were never published.]

[Scattered through this vast work are many popular or semipopular compositions, mostly coplas and décimas. The two parts of Vol. III, in particular, contain a large number of décimas, many of which concern historical events of the latter part of the nineteenth century. For a study of this type of poetry the work represents a very important contribution. Also, in Vol. VII many coplas and décimas are used to document the speech and usage of the Sancti-Spiritus region of Cuba. As a whole, however, the work is not well organized and much that the author prints is not folklore, being in many instances purely learned literature. Such romances as there are belong to this latter category of literary production.]

1014. Martínez Torner, Eduardo. "La rítmica en la música tradicional española." Música (Barcelona), January, 1938, 33-34.

[Chase (ref. 25, p. 136) comments: "Discusses certain Spanish folk rhythms in relation to Cuban and Afro-American influences."]

Menéndez, Enrique, comp. See Pérez de Luarca, Manuel, entry no. 1029.

1015. Miraflores and El Camarioqueño. [A cuaderno of glosas]. Matanzas, 1841.

[Palma y Romay (ref. 1026, p. 322) says: "En el año de 1841 dos jóvenes de Matanzas, bajo los seudónimos de Miraflores y el Camarioqueño, han publicado un cuaderno de glosas, que son ciertamente las que hemos visto de colorido más local, como que sus autores han puesto especial cuidado en ello." He prints (pp. 322-323) a glosa taken from the cuaderno.]

1016. Nápoles Fajardo, Juan C. Cantos populares. Habana, 1863.

1017. Nápoles Fajardo, Juan C. Colección de poesías inéditas del popular vate cubano D. Juan C. Nápoles Fajardo (El Cucalambé). Gibara: Est. Tip. a cargo de M. Bim, 1886. 264 pp. 17.5 cm.

1018. _____. Voz del tiple; colección de décimas cubanas. Habana, 1861. also, Habana, 1881. 32 pp.

1019. Noda, Tranquilino S. de. Tradiciones cubanas. 1841.

1020. La nueva lira criolla; guarachas, canciones, décimas y cantares de la guerra por Un Vueltarribero. 4.ª ed. Habana: "La Moderna Poesía," 1900. 265 pp.; La nueva lira criolla; guarachas, canciones y décimas de la guerra por Un Vueltarribero. Habana, 1903. 283 pp.; La nueva lira criolla; nueva recopilación de guarachas, canciones, décimas y canciones de la guerra por Un Vueltarribero. Habana: Librería y Imprenta "La Moderna Poesía," 1918 [Cover says Primera parte, title page says Segunda parte]. (Trelles [ref. 1062, p. 106] says that the first edition was in 1897.)
[A large collection of Cuban songs of all descriptions. Some décimas criollas appear to be very significant. The subjects are similar to those of corridos; i.e., current politics, the deaths of famous men, etc. I have seen only the 1918 edition.]

1021. Ortiz, Fernando. La africanía de la música folklórica de Cuba. Habana: Ediciones Cárdenas y Cía., 1950. xvi, 477 pp. 24 cm.
[In the first chapter of this very fine study, there is considerable discussion of pre-conquest narrative poetry in the Antilles, particularly of the areito. Most of the data presented are taken from Las Casas, Fernández de Oviedo, and other chroniclers.]

1022. _____. "El 'aja' de las habaneras." AFC, III:4 (octubre a diciembre de 1928), 38-47.
[By way of treating this characteristic exclamation of the Cubans, Ortiz reprints a portion of the Obras escogidas of Arístides Rojas which contains two compositons in décimas. The first is a satirical poem written by Cubans and sent to Caracas in 1771 when a regiment was transferred there; the second is a reply by a Venezuelan poet wherein the typical "aja" of the Cubans is ridiculed. The poems are only semipopular.]

1023. _____. "La copla política en Cuba." AFC, II:4 (junio de 1927), 391-392.
[The author quotes commentary on and the texts of some satirical coplas políticas which circulated in Havana in the 1860's. They are taken from Antonio de las Barras y Prado (ref. 939).]

1024. _____. "La copla política en Cuba." AFC, III:2 (abril a junio de 1928), 177-179.
[Some texts of coplas políticas which circulated during the election of 1924.]

1025. _____. "La copla política en Cuba." AFC, III:4 (octubre a diciembre de 1928), 377.

[A single décima which was inspired by the execution of two Cuban patriots, Francisco Agüero y Velasco and Manuel Andrés Sánchez, in 1826.]

El Padre Capacho. See Rodríguez, José, entry no. 1048.

1026. Palma y Romay, Ramón de. "Cantares de Cuba." In Carbonell y Rivero, José Manuel. La poesía lírica en Cuba, Tomo I. Vol. I of Evolución de la cultura cubana. La Habana: Imprenta "El Siglo XX," 1928. Pp. 291-323.

[Written in 1854, this pioneer study seeks to exalt the popular poetry of the Cuban guajiro. Though Palma y Romay was mistaken in stating at the beginning of his work that the romance was unknown in rural Cuba, the chapter has much to recommend it, particularly a great many texts of glosas in décimas which the author says are of popular origin. Also, he calls attention to the poetry of Domingo del Monte, a poet who seeks inspiration in the guajiros and in popular forms, and he prints a romance by Del Monte entitled El desterrado del hato (pp. 311-314). But of the truly popular poets, he considers Francisco Pobeda the only one worthy of that name, and he prints some décimas of his. Finally, the author gives a number of Cuban coplas and describes (with some textual examples) poetic contests which resemble the contrapuntos of Chile and Argentina. The article is most informative and interesting, especially in view of its early date. It originally appeared in the Revista de la Habana, III(1854).]

1027. Pérez de Alejo, Miguel A. La bandurria; colección de décimas. (About 1886, according to Trelles [ref. 1062, p. 147].)

1028. _____. Canciones cubanas. Habana, 1881; also, Madrid, 1883.

1029. Pérez de Luarca, Manuel. Principales combates de la campaña de Cuba; décinas [sic] y romances . . . recopilados por Enrique Menéndez. Habana: Imprenta El Aerolito, 1897. 24 pp. 22 cm.

[A collection of popular poems intended for Spanish sympathizers opposed to Cuban revolutionists. Almost all are historical and a few are in corrido style. Most, however, are décimas.]

1030. Piedra-Bueno, Andrés de. "Glosa de la décima." Revista de la Biblioteca Nacional (Habana), Segunda serie, Tomo II:2 (abril-junio, 1951), 81-104.

[After tracing the history of the décima in Spain, the author turns his attention to poets who have used it in Cuba. He considers popular and learned poets from Padre Capacho, Pobeda, Nápoles Fajardo, et al. down to contemporary figures; and he prints a number of texts, some of them historical and semipopular in nature. This is the best brief survey of the décima in Cuba that I know of.]

1031. Poesía heroica al feliz éxito de la expedición del señor brigadier don I. Barradas, en las costas de Nueva España. Habana: Imp. de Boloña. 3 lvs.
[This is the first of several compositions, probably semiartistic or artistic in nature, which Bachiller y Morales (ref. 936, Vol. III, p. 395) groups in a section of publications for the year 1829. The other titles are: Canción al propio objeto, que concluye con una marcha patriótica. Habana, Imprenta Fraternal. 1 p.; Canto a la expedición del señor Barradas, con los retratos del rey Nuestro Señor y su amada esposa. Habana: Imp. de Boloña; and Pormenor de las operaciones ejecutadas en Nueva España por las fuerzas navales y terrestres al mando de los brigadieres don Angel Laborde y don Isidro Barradas. Habana: Imprenta de don José Boloña.]

1032. Poetas guajiros; colección de poesías recopiladas por Un Vueltabajero. Habana, 1904. 100 pp.

1033. Ponce, Manuel M. [Articles about Cuban popular music which appeared in Cuban newspapers.]

1034. Ponce de León, José E. (José G. Villa). Cancionero tropical; décimas populares. Matanzas, 1878.

1035. _____. Cantos del pueblo; colección de décimas. Habana, 1876. 8 pp.

1036. Poncet y Cárdenas, Carolina. "Cantares locales cubanos." AFC, I:2 (abril de 1924), 97-102.
[A brief discussion of coplas about geographical places. There are eleven copla texts and one décima.]

1037. _____. "El romance en Cuba." RFLC, XVIII:2 (marzo, 1914), 180-260; 3 (mayo, 1914), 278-321; also published in book form, Habana: "El Siglo XX," 1914. 131 pp.
[The author provides historical background of popular poetry in Cuba, particularly the décima, then treats the romance as an artistic genre and discusses the poets who, particularly during the last third of the nineteenth century, used romance meter to relate country customs, novelesque stories, and some historical or legendary events. Then she takes up the romances of Spain which have been preserved in Cuban popular tradition and studies then under three groupings: I. Romances que relatan escenas o tragedias de familias; II. Romances de asuntos religiosos; and III. Romances de personajes históricos. Many Cuban texts are provided of Las señas del esposo, Delgadina, Dónde vas, Alfonso XII, and others.]

1038. _____. "Romances de Navidad." Lyceum (Habana), V (1949):17, pp. 24-28.

1039. _____. "Romances de la pasión." AFC, V:1 (enero a marzo de 1930), 5-29.

[An excellent study of three categories of romances: Romances del presentimiento de la pasión, Romances de Jueves Santo, and Romances de Viernes Santo. Versions of romances from Cuba and New Mexico are related to Spanish and Gallegan-Portuguese ballads and, indeed, to medieval compositions from Italy, France, and other areas. This is one of the most scholarly comparative studies of American romances and their European sources.]

1040. Pormenor de las operaciones ejecutadas en Nueva España. [See entry no. 1031.]

1041. Portell Vilá, Herminio. "Catalina y el marinero." AFC, II:3 (octubre de 1926), 268-270.

[Reports a children's game and the text of the song which accompanies it. Very correctly the author observes: "tiene sabor de romance." It appears to be related to Delgadina.]

1042. _____. "Coplas políticas de antaño." AFC, III:4 (octubre a diciembre de 1928), 48-50.

[Texts of some political coplas about political figures of the last decade or so of the nineteenth century.]

1043. Rey Aguirre, Mariano del. Humanos sentimientos y sublime interés.

[Bachiller y Morales (ref. 936, Vol. III, p. 286) lists this work without further bibliographical data. He puts it, however, in a list of publications from the year 1812. He describes it: "Décimas al trágico suceso del actor Affaro. Don Mariano del Rey Aguirre, escribió 26 décimas a este asunto que excitaron una hilaridad general por sus absurdos, pero que tenían el mérito de la sonoridad. Al efecto usó de palabras de su invención, como Zeluta, aromatea, eterna anugia y apócrifos Lapones."]

1044. Rodríguez, Federico. Cantos populares recopilados por Un Aficionado. Santiago de Cuba, 1891.

1045. _____. Colección de décimas campesinas y glosas de amor. Guanabacoa. 16 pp.

1046. _____. Ecos de la sabana; cuadernos de décimas campestres propias para el guajiro cubano, por Hatuey. Matanzas, 1890. 84 pp.

1047. _____. Ultimas canciones cubanas. Habana, 1887.

1048. Rodríguez, José (El Padre Capacho). Poesías. La Habana: Impresora de Boloña, 1823.

[Rodríguez was a semipopular poet who wrote around the middle of the eighteenth century. Carbonell y Rivero (ref. 950, pp. 56-75) has a section about him wherein he prints the poet's most famous composition, El apasionado del número siete, a poem in décimas, along with some other poetry and some parts of a play, El príncipe jardinero.]

1049. Rodríguez García, J. A. "Sobre El romance en Cuba, estudio de C. Poncet." Cuba intelectual (La Habana), Núms. 34-35 (1914); also, in Esbozos críticos. Habana, 1915.

[Apparently a fairly extensive criticism of the book by Carolina Poncet y Cárdenas.]

Rojas, Arístides. See Ortiz, Fernando, entry no. 1022.

1050. Rosales y Moreira, Francisco. Musa popular. Sagua la Grande: Imprenta "La Patria," 1908. iv, 223 pp. 23 cm.

1051. Sánchez de Fuentes y Peláez, Eduardo. La canción cubana; conferencia, marzo 16 de 1930, sesión de la Academia Nacional de Artes y Letra [sic]. Habana: Molina y Campañía, 1930. 46 pp. 23 cm.

[An interesting lecture on the musical aspects of many types of Cuban songs and their historical backgrounds. There is nothing, however, on romances, décimas, or other types of truly popular songs.]

1052. _____. El folk-lor en la música cubana. Habana: Imprenta "El Siglo XX," 1923. 191 pp. 18.5 cm.

[Despite its title, the book deals almost exclusively with music which is not folklore. It is of no importance to the study of romances, corridos, décimas, and the like.]

1053. _____. Folklorismo; artículos, notas y críticas musicales. Habana: Imp. Molina y Compañía, 1928. 343 pp. 20.5 cm.

[The title is deceptive; much of the book is about learned artists (e. g., musicians like Heifitz). There are some essays about popular dances and music (such as the areito), but there seems to be nothing about romances, corridos, décimas, coplas, and the like.]

1054. _____. "Influencia de los ritmos africanos en nuestro cancionero." In Carbonell y Rivero, José Manuel. Las bellas artes en Cuba. Vol. XVIII of Evolución de la cultura cubana. Habana: Imprenta "El Siglo XX," 1928. Pp. 155-202.

[Chase (ref. 25, p. 139) comments: "Studies not only the African, but also the indigenous and Spanish elements in Cuban music. Includes 23 illustrations."]

1055. _____. "La música cubana y sus orígenes." BLAM, Año IV, IV(diciembre de 1938), 177-182.

[Consideration of some of the elements which have entered into Cuban music: the Indian, the Spanish, and the African. An interesting essay, but as in his other works the author makes no clear distinction between true folklore and things that are momentarily "popular." There is nothing about corridos, romances, coplas, décimas, and the like. The author is mainly concerned with dances such as the bolero and the danzón.]

1056. Santo de Regla.
[Palma y Romay (ref. 1026, p. 322) refers to ". . . Santo de Regla, famoso improvisador, de época más reciente (than Padre Capacho), cuyas décimas repetidas de boca en boca conserva, no sólo el pueblo, sino mucha gente de nota en la memoria."]

1057. Surí y Aguila, José.
[A poet born in 1696 who was famous as an improviser. Carbonell y Rivero (ref. 950, p. 77) and López Prieto (ref. 1007, p. 22) print some works of his which are in romance form.]

1058. Terwilliger, L. Ray. Novísima recopilación de canciones, guarachas y boleros de actualidad. Habana, 1903. 30 pp.

1059. El tiple cubano; colección de décimas cubanas. Habana, 1900.

1060. El tiple cubano; décimas criollas, cantos del pueblo de Cuba. Habana, 1902. 252 pp.

1061. Torre y Sola, Enrique de la. Cantos populares cubanos, por el Cantor del Tínima. Matanzas, 1894.

1062. Trelles, Carlos M. "Notas bibliográficas acerca del folklore cubano." AFC, I:2 (abril de 1924), 103-111; II:2 (mayo de 1926), 137-158.
[A very unsatisfactory bibliography because of the carelessness with which it has been compiled and the sketchy nature of most entries. It contains, however, some invaluable items not listed elsewhere. I am personally indebted to it for many of the incomplete entries listed in this section which remain incomplete because of my inability to locate the works themselves or any listing of them in any other place.]

1063. "El triunfo de la gloria." El papel periódico (Habana), 8 de abril, 1798.
[An anonymous poem in romance form with seven-syllable lines. Menéndez y Pelayo prints the whole text (ref. 82, Vol. I, pp. 216-218). It is about Achilles.]

1064. Valdés, Carlos Genaro. Tesoro popular; colección escogida de cantos cubanos, recopilados por C. G. V. Habana, 1879. 159 pp.; also, 4.ª ed. Habana, 1890.

1065. Valdés Rodríguez, Esperanza. "La copla política en Cuba." AFC, III:3 (julio a septiembre de 1928), 279-280.
[The texts of some décimas that circulated during the period of oppression following the Ten Tears' War, which ended in 1878.]

1034.
Villa, José G. See Ponce de León, José E., entry no.

Zea, F. J. See La isla, entry no. 1000.

DOMINICAN REPUBLIC

The quality of folklore studies in the Dominican Republic has been high. Though modern scholarly interest in the popular songs of the area dates from no earlier than some youthful observations of the great Dominican scholar, Pedro Henríquez Ureña, several folklorists and investigators of unusual competence have recently collected and studied the musical folklore of their small country. Most outstanding among these are Emilio Rodríguez Demorizi, Flérida de Nolasco, and Edna Garrido de Boggs, all of whom have contributed most in the field of the collection and interpretation of texts, and Julio Arzeno, who has produced a study of musical folklore that has evoked critical acclaim.

Though the décima seems to predominate in the Dominican Republic as in other areas of the Antilles, the presence of a strong romance tradition has been proved by the collection of many texts from oral tradition. It may well be that the Dominican scholars, who seem to have been particularly intrigued by the literary relationships between their own popular traditions and those of Spain, succeeded in uncovering more romances than investigators in other regions of the Caribbean area merely because of greater persistence on their part in seeking out songs of peninsular origin. But it is more likely that the vigorous romance tradition which the conquerors brought with them to the New World simply struck deeper roots in the island which was first settled by the Spanish and that there it has resisted with somewhat more success than elsewhere the encroachment of the décima.

To be noted among the genres, besides the décima, which lie on the fringes of the romance tradition in the Dominican Republic are the ubiquitous coplas and certain minor types such as the plena and the famous dance-song known as the merengue, the texts of which belong to the copla tradition.

For the bibliography of Dominican folk songs and ballads we must depend upon the works of scholars already mentioned; there are no separate bibliographical studies in the field.

DOMINICAN REPUBLIC

1066. Alix, Juan Antonio. <u>Décimas</u>. Santo Domingo, 1927.
[Henríquez Ureña (ref. 1079, p. 213) calls Alix "un coplero popular que alcanzó extenso renombre en todo el país como el que mejor supo reproducir en sus versos las actitudes, los hábitos, los sentimientos y el habla del campesino dominicano . . . ." His dates were 1833-1917.]

1067. _____. <u>Diálogo</u> <u>entre</u> <u>en</u> <u>guajiro</u> <u>dominicano</u> <u>y</u> <u>un</u> <u>Papá</u> <u>Bocó</u> <u>haitiano</u>. 24 pp.
[A composition in <u>décimas</u>. Henríquez Ureña, who cites it (ref. 1079, p. 211), can't remember the date of its publication.]

1068. _____. <u>Viaje</u> <u>de</u> <u>Gerardo</u> <u>Etanislao</u> [sic]. 1885.
[Mentioned by Henríquez Ureña (ref. 1079, p. 214). Apparently it is a composition in <u>décimas</u>.]

1069. Arzeno, Julio. <u>Del</u> <u>folk-lore</u> <u>musical</u> <u>dominicano</u>. Santo Domingo: Imp. "La Cuna de América," Roques Román Hnos., 1927. 25 cm.
[Chase (ref. 25, p. 139) comments: "Julio Arzeno's monograph . . . covers the field of folk music with exceptional thoroughness. Profusely illustrated with musical examples, Arzeno's treatise deals with every type of folk and popular music in the Dominican Republic, analyzing each form musically and also relating it to the social background of the people."]

1070. Boggs, Edna Garrido de. <u>Folklore</u> <u>infantil</u> <u>de</u> <u>Santo</u> <u>Domingo</u>. Madrid: Ediciones Cultura Hispánica, 1955. 661 pp. 21 cm.
[An extremely valuable collection of children's folklore, extensively annotated and well organized. Included are many poems and songs, among them <u>romances</u>, <u>décimas</u>, and the like. Besides the <u>romances</u> found in the section entitled "Romances y romancillos" (pp. 159-190), there are many others scattered through the book in sections on children's games.]

_____. See also Garrido, Edna, entry no. 1076.

1071. <u>Carta</u> <u>de</u> <u>un</u> <u>soldado</u> <u>a</u> <u>su</u> <u>madre</u> <u>después</u> <u>de</u> <u>la</u> <u>acción</u> <u>de</u> <u>Puerto-Caballo</u>. See González Tablas, R., entry no. 1078.

1072. Cerón, José D. <u>Canciones</u> <u>dominicanas</u>, <u>compiladas</u>, <u>transcriptas</u> <u>y</u> <u>arregladas</u> <u>para</u> <u>voz</u> <u>y</u> <u>piano</u>. Ciudad Trujillo: Editora Montalvo, 1947. 143 pp. 26 cm.
[A collection of songs which enjoyed popularity between about 1880 and 1915. Words and music for piano are given. All the compositions are learned or semilearned and are of no interest to the study of the <u>romance</u> or any other literary theme.]

1073. Estévanez, Nicolás. <u>Fragmentos</u> <u>de</u> <u>mis</u> <u>memorias</u>. Segunda edición. Madrid: Est. Tip. de los Hijos de R. Alvarez, a cargo de Arturo Menéndez, 1903. 547 pp. 18.5 cm.
[Rodríguez Demorizi (ref. 1104, p. 15) prints a <u>romance</u> taken from

the above (p. 169). It was written by a discontented Spanish soldier who was fighting in Santo Domingo in 1861-1865.]

1074. García, Juan Francisco. "Formando la música folklórica dominicana." Boletín del folklore dominicano (Ciudad Trujillo), Año I:1 (junio, 1946), 10-14.

[The author defends the thesis that, contrary to some opinions, the Dominican Republic may be said to have its own folklore, though it is admittedly derived from Spanish antecedents. As perhaps the best proof of his point of view, the author cites an old form, the mediatuna, which, as he describes it, must have been very similar to the contrapunto or pallada of Chile. It was in décimas. Other forms of popular song are mentioned in passing: chuines or cantos de vela, the merengue, and others.]

1075. García Rodríguez, José M. "Joyas cantarinas de la poesía popular." Boletín cultural (Ciudad Trujillo), Núm. 39.

1076. Garrido, Edna. Versiones dominicanas de romances españoles. Ciudad Trujillo: Pol Hermanos, 1946. 110 pp. 23 cm.

[Following a brief discussion of the development of the romance tradition in the Dominican Republic, the author offers texts with music of a number of romances gathered from oral tradition. Included are almost all the usual compositions of Spanish origin, such as Delgadina, Gerineldo, La esposa infiel, Las señas del esposo, and others. There are brief commentaries with most of them.]

_____. See also Boggs, Edna Garrido de, entry no. 1070.

1077. Golibart González, Porfirio. Nuestra música popular; apuntes para su historia. Ciudad Trujillo: Editorial Stella, 1947. 52 pp. 21.5 cm. (Title on the outer cover: Romanticismo tradicional.)

[A brief history of the music of the Dominican Republic. There are some coplas in the section devoted to the merengue (pp. 41-45).]

1078. González Tablas, R. Historia de la dominación y última guerra de España en Santo Domingo. Madrid: Impr. á cargo de F. Cao, 1870. 229 pp. 24 cm.

[Rodríguez Demorizi (ref. 1104, p. 14) says that this book contains a poem in romance meter, Carta de un soldado a su madre después de la acción de Puerto-Caballo (pp. 180-181). It was a poem which circulated among the Spanish troops fighting in Santo Domingo, 1861-1865.]

1079. Henríquez Ureña, Max. Panorama histórico de la literatura dominicana. Rio de Janeiro: Companhia Brasileira de Artes Gráficas, 1945. 337 pp. 24 cm.

[Chap. VIII, "Manifestaciones folklóricas" (pp. 91-100), is a good survey of the development of folklore from the colonial period to the present. Several poets and singers are mentioned (Má Teodora,

Meso Mónica, et al.), some texts of pasquines are provided, and there is consideration also of some romances. Chap. XIV, "Poesía popular y poesía criolla" (pp. 209-219), treats coplas and décimas inspired by the wars of the nineteenth century and also the works of learned poets who were influenced by such genuinely popular poetry. The whole work is an excellent basic source because it contains good bibliography for further investigation.]

1080. Henríquez Ureña, Pedro. "Reflorescencia." La cuna de América (Santo Domingo), No. 77 (18 de diciembre de 1904).
[Rodríguez Demorizi (ref. 1104, pp. 12-13) quotes some comments from the above work in which Henríquez Ureña considers the relative acceptance in the Dominican Republic of the romance, the décima, and the redondilla.]

———. "Romances en América." See entry no. 55.

1081. Hernández, Julio Alberto. Album musical.
[Henríquez Ureña (ref. 1079, p. 313) indicates that it contains several sections on popular music and an article by Rafael Vidal, "Música vernacular."]

1082. Las invasiones haitianas.
[An early romance first printed by Rodríguez Demorizi (ref. 1104).]

1083. Lopez de Gomara, Francisco. Historia general de las Indias. Vol. XXII of Biblioteca de Autores Espanoles. Madrid, 1852. xxi, 601 pp.
[Passages to be noted: in the discussion of areitos and religious ceremonies, the term romance is used to describe Indian compositions (pp. 173-174); an account of the incident when a malcontent in Pizarro's army sent a copla voicing complaints to Panama (p. 225); and two lines of popular poetry quoted by Carvajal by way of commentary upon an event (p. 268).]

1084. Marchena, Enrique de. Del areito de Anacaona al poema folklórico; brindis de Salas en Santo Domingo. Ciudad Trujillo: Montalvo, 1942. 95 pp. 22 cm.
[Chase (ref. 25, p. 141) comments: "The first part of this book is concerned chiefly with various aspects of Dominican folk music. The music of the so-called "areito de Anacaona," quoted from Bachiller y Morales, is given on p. 25."]

Mendoza, Vicente T. "La canción del novio desairado." See entry no. 1445.

1085. Morel, Tomás E. Del llano i de la loma; tradiciones, fantasías criollas, tonadas, coplas i cantares cibaeños. Santiago: Editorial "Corazón de Jesús," 1937. 120 pp. 21 cm.
[According to Henríquez Ureña's description of the work (ref. 1079,

p. 219), it has two aspects: ". . . el de la recopilación folklórica y el de la creación propia . . . ."]

1086. Nolasco, Flérida de. "Intimas relaciones del folklore universal." Cuadernos dominicanos de cultura (Ciudad Trujillo), Año IV, Vol. IV:47 (julio de 1947), 23-33.

[To develop the thesis implicit in her title, the author uses the romance line, "Abreme la puerta, Elena," and others very close to it. She finds examples from many countries, mostly versions of La amiga de Bernal Francés, but some, such as a merengue sung and danced on Christmas Eve, are quite far removed from the romance.]

1087. _____. La poesía folklórica en Santo Domingo. Santiago: Editorial El Diario, n.d. [1946?]. 4, 367 pp. 23 cm.

[An important study which includes a chapter on traditional romances. Texts are given for many compositions from Spanish tradition (mostly the same romances found throughout Spanish America).]

1088. _____. Santo Domingo en el folklore universal. Ciudad Trujillo: Impresora Dominicana, 1956. 449 pp. 23 cm.

[Boggs (ref. 13 [1956], p. 21) says: "Treats religious dances, cult of the Cross, poetic theme of lover who calls at the door, and other themes of classic Spanish poets and Dominican folk poetry. 90 p. of texts of Dominican décimas and 45 p. of coplas and plena verses . . . ."]

1089. _____. Vibraciones en el tiempo. Ciudad Trujillo: Editora Montalvo, 1948. 214 pp. 23 cm.

[Boggs (ref. 13 [1948], p. 66) says: "Historical survey of music in the Dominican Republic, including consideration of folkmusic in such forms as the plena, carabiné, mediatuna, yuca, chenche, zapateo, mangulina, and merengue, with some il. verses and music."]

1090. Nuevo y curioso romance en que se da cuenta de la victoria alcanzada por los españoles . . . guerra de Santo Domingo de América. Salamanca.

[Rodríguez Demorizi (ref. 1104, p. 14), in referring to the war with Spain from 1861-1865, says: "Algunos romances de los soldados españoles tenían gran popularidad y corrían impresos en España." He cites this one published in Salamanca as an example.]

1091. Peguero, Luis José. Romance en que se dice que los valientes dominicanos han sabido defender su Isla Española.

[An artistic romance about an incident in 1763 by a poet who died in 1792. Rodríguez Demorizi prints its text (ref. 1104, pp. 17-28).]

1092. Peña Morell, Esteban. La folkmúsica dominicana.
[Henríquez Ureña (ref. 1079, p. 313) cites the work.]

1093. Penson, César Nicolás. Cosas añejas. Ciudad Trujillo: Impresora Dominicana, 1951. xii, 332 pp. 21 cm. (Biblioteca dominicana, Série I, Vol. V.) (The first edition, according to the prologue, was published in 1891).

[There is a glosa in décimas (pp. 325-326) which the author collected from oral tradition from a centenarian, presumably in 1891. Also, a copla or two are to be found intercalated into the prose legends which make up the book.]

1094. _____. Reseña histórico-crítica de la poesía en Santo Domingo. 1892.
[Henríquez Ureña (ref. 1079, p. 100) indicates that the work contains coplas from the Dominican Republic along with others imported from Spain.]

1095. Prestol Castillo, Fredy. "Fabla, gesta y cantares del valle de Neiba." La Nación (Ciudad Trujillo), octubre, 1944.
[Henríquez Ureña (ref. 1079, p. 211) indicates that this article deals with popular poetry from the period of civil strife, 1868-1874.]

1096. Ramos B., Nicolás. A la masa obrera; décimas. Hato Mayor del Rey: La Romana, Imprenta Artibonito, 3 de noviembre, 1945. 6 pp.

1097. _____. El caso de Cibahuete; décimas por Nicolás Ramos B. Hato Mayor del Rey: Tip. El Heraldo, 1946. 2 lvs.

1098. _____. Décimas; el caso del llano y el de Mata de Palma en la velación. Hato Mayor del Rey: Tip. El Heraldo, 1946. 4 lvs.

1099. _____. Décimas; dos historias muy importantes. Hato Mayor del Rey: Tip. El Heraldo, 1946. 2 lvs.; also, Hato Mayor del Rey: Diario de Macorís, enero de 1946. 2 lvs.

1100. _____. Décimas; historia de doña Lola y la del billetero. Hato Mayor del Rey: Tip. Leonidas, 1945. No pagination.

1101. _____. Décimas; una historia por el caso de Venezuela. Hato Mayor del Rey: Diario de Macorís, enero de 1946. 3 lvs.

1102. _____. El día que llegó la harina; décimas. Hato Mayor del Rey: El Heraldo, 5 de diciembre, 1946. 2 lvs.

1103. _____. Por el cataclismo y el caso de Samaná. Hato Mayor del Rey: El Heraldo, 27 de noviembre, 1946. No pagination.

1104. Rodríguez Demorizi, Emilio. Del romancero dominicano. Santiago: Editorial El Diario, 1943. 115 pp. 22.5 cm.
[A collection of artistic romances on historical subjects preceded by an informative introduction which outlines the development of the romance, popular as well as artistic, from colonial times to the present. The author treats particularly the general supplanting of romances by décimas in Hispaniola. Included is a very useful bibliography of artistic romances (pp. 10-11).]

1105. Rodríguez Demorizi, Emilio. "Del romancero dominicano." In Miscelánea de estudios dedicados a Fernando Ortiz por sus discípulos, colegas y amigos con ocasión de cumplirse sesenta años de la publicación de su primer impreso en Menorca en 1895. Vol. II. Habana: Ucar García, 1956. Pp. 1267-1274.
[Boggs (ref. 13 [1956], p. 46) says: "Surveys early traces of balladry in Santo Domingo."]

1106. _____. Poesía popular dominicana. Vol. I. Ciudad Trujillo: Editorial La Nación, 1938. 300 pp. 19.5 cm.
[An important study of semilearned poetry grouped by authors' names. Most compositions are in décimas, but there are a few romances.]

1107. Saldaña Suazo, José A., comp. Album folklórico dominicano de las históricas canciones antiguas pro-centenario, 1844-1894. Ciudad Trujillo: n. p., 1944. No pagination.

1108. Serrano Poncela, Segundo. "Mujeres del romancero." Panorama (Santiago), II(1944):18, pp. 5-13.

1109. Tejada, Valentín. "Música popular dominicana." AmerH, VII:2 (agosto, 1940), 45-48.
[A discussion of the dance-song known as the merengue. Several coplas which are sung by merengueros are quoted. Some are comments on politics and important personages in the life of the Dominican Republic.]

1110. Valverde, Sebastián E. Aporte a la investigación del folklore en Santo Domingo. Santiago: Editorial Panorama, n.d. 16 pp.

Vidal, Rafael. "Música vernacular." See Hernández, Julio Alberto, entry no. 1081.

ECUADOR

The romance in Ecuador has been studied only in a most perfunctory manner and by no folklorist or scholar of real stature. Indeed, the whole of Ecuadorian folklore has been almost completely neglected, the only significant work in the field of popular song and poetry being Juan León Mera's nineteenth-century anthology of popular verse. This voluminous collection contains mostly coplas, along with some décimas and a few narrative poems of interest to students of the romance tradition. But it dates from a period when folklore was in its infancy, and the collection is of relatively limited value to modern scholars. The only truly scientific investigation of Ecuadorian folklore that we have is the work of Raoul and Marguerite Harcourt. This monumental study embraces the Andean region of both Ecuador and Peru, but it is concerned solely with Quechua, not mestizo or Spanish folklore, and its pertinence to my subject is limited to the possible influence that Indian genres such as the yaraví may have had upon romances of the area. Since this is a problem which has never been studied and cannot be dealt with until more romance texts are available, we can only speculate as to the possibility of fruitful investigation in this field.

ECUADOR

1111. A las siete palabras del Redentor en la cruz.
[A romance by a "Musa Quitense" said by Menéndez y Pelayo to be mentioned by Juan de Velasco in El ocioso de Faenza (ref. 1129).]

1112. Andrade, Mariano.
[Menéndez y Pelayo (ref. 82, Vol. II, pp. 20-21) quotes a romance by this poet. It is found in Juan de Velasco's El ocioso de Faenza (ref. 1129).]

Arróspide de la Flor, César. See Vargas Ugarte, Rubén, entry no. 1128.

Arroyo, César. "Romancero del pueblo ecuatoriano." See entry no. 4.

Basadre, Jorge. See entry no. 1746.

1113. Canto y baile; nueva colección de canciones. Guayaquil: Imp. Colón, 1910. 16 pp.

1114. El cantor; colección de canciones nuevas para todo el mundo. Series A, B, and C. Guayaquil: Tip. Miniatura, n.d. 16 pp. each.

1115. Cantor popular; colección de canciones nuevas. Guayaquil: Imp. El Universo, 1911. 12 pp.

1116. Carrión, Alejandro, ed. Los poetas quiteños de «El Ocioso en Faenza». Tomo I, Historia y crítica; Tomo II, Textos poéticos. Quito: Casa de la Cultura Ecuatoriana, 1957-1958. 21 cm.
[Vol. I deals with Juan de Velasco and his anthology of poetry known as El Ocioso de Faenza. Carrión describes the manuscript and its contents in detail and has chapters on the principal poets from Quito who contributed to the anthology. Lesser lights are treated in a more cursory manner. Vol. II contains texts of the poets from Quito only. All compositions are typical neo-classical poetry, but some of it is written in romance form, though more of it is in décimas.]

1117. Cornejo V., Justino. "Poesía popular ecuatoriana." Anales de la Universidad de Guayaquil (Guayaquil), Núm. 2 (1950), 193-218.
[The Zárates (ref. 1719, p. 22) quote some references to décimas which they took from this work.]

1118. Durán, Sixto M. "La musique aborigène et populaire de L'Equateur." In Art populaire, travaux artistiques et scientifiques du ler Congrès International des Arts Populaires, Prague, 1928, Vol. II. Paris: Editions Duchartre, 1931. Pp. 117-118.
[Chase (ref. 25, p. 144) says: "Brief comments on the principal folk music forms of Ecuador."]

1119. Evia, Jacinto de. Ramillete de varias flores poéticas, recogidas, y cvltivadas en los primeros abriles de sus años. Por el maestro Xacinto de Evia, natural de la ciudad de Guayaquil, en el Peru. Dedicale al licenciado d. Pedro de Arboleda Salazar, prouisor, vicario general y gouernador deste obispado de Popayàn, por ausencia del ilustrissimo señor doctor don Melchor Liñán de Cisneros, del consejo de Su Magestad, obispo dèl. Con licencia. En Madrid: En la imprenta de Nicolás de Xamares, mercader de libros. Año de 1676. 9, 406 (i. e., 408) pp.

[According to Menéndez y Pelayo (ref. 82, Vol. II, p. 11), the work contains poems of Evia, an Ecuadorean, and two other poets, one of whom is Domínguez Camargo of Bogotá. Some of the poems of the latter apparently are romances, and Menéndez y Pelayo (p. 15) mentions also a romance of Evia.]

1120. Guevara, Darío. "Breve ojeada sobre el desarrollo científico del folklore en el Ecuador." FACI, Año III:3 (noviembre, 1955), 52-70.

[Contains a comment (p. 62) about la necesidad de investigar y compilar "los romances anónimos, loas y dramas y otras expresiones de la poesía popular que resurgen en las fiestas tradicionales."]

1121. _____. "Introducción al estudio del folklore ecuatoriano, I-III." Museo histórico (Quito), VII(1955):21, pp. 111-137.

1122. _____. "Presencia del Ecuador en sus cantares." LetE, Año VI:55-60 (abril-agosto de 1950), 9-10.

[An informative survey of the history of popular poetry in Ecuador from the famous episode of the copla smuggled into Panama to criticize Pizarro down to recent times. There are texts of several popular or semipopular compositions, many of them pasquines, and a passage from Atahualpa Huañui (La muerte de Atahualpa) in romance form.]

Harcourt, Raoul and Marguerite. See entry no. 1812.

Holzmann, Rodolfo. See Vargas Ugarte, Rubén, entry no. 1128.

1123. Jiménez de la Espada, Marcos. "Colección de yaravíes quiteños." In Congreso Internacional de Americanistas, Actas de la Cuarta Reunión, Madrid, 1881, Vol. II. Madrid: Imprenta de Fortanet, 1883.

[According to Chase (ref. 25, p. 144), the work contains twenty yaravíes, four dances, and three tonadas.]

1124. León Mera, Juan. Antología ecuatoriana; cantares del pueblo ecuatoriano. Quito: Imprenta de la Universidad Central del Ecuador, 1892. xxvi, 504 pp. 25.5 cm.

[A very large collection of popular poetry, mostly coplas, though there are some décimas and other popular genres. Some of las composiciones in the section entitled "Versos militares y políticos" are topical, and a few are narratives (e.g., Versos sobre el combate de la Loma de los Molinos [pp. 298-299], a poem which is very similar to Mexican corridos in subject matter, strophic pattern, style, and other details). Two compositions in Quechua (pp. 352-363) are seminarrative in character, and some of the topical semipopular poetry in the appendix (pp. 367 ff.) is of interest.]

1125. Moreno, Segundo Luis. La música en la provincia de Imbabura. Quito: Tipografía Salesianas, 1923. 39 pp.

1126. Romance a la entrada y ejercicio de fuego que hizo la tropa que volvió de Quito, 1768.
[Menéndez y Pelayo (ref. 82, Vol. II, p. 144) mentions this composition.]

1127. Salgado, Luis H. "Música vernácula ecuatoriana." Casa de la cultura ecuatoriana (Quito), IV(1951):11, pp. 365-376.

1128. Vargas Ugarte, Rubén; Arróspide de la Flor, César; and Holzmann, Rodolfo. Folklore musical del siglo XVIII. Lima: Scheuch, 1946. 16 pp.
[Boggs (ref. 13 [1946], p. 66) says: "Reproduces music of 18 yaravíes from Quito reported by Marcos Jiménez de la Espada in 1881, with words, and comments on each."]

1129. Velasco, Juan de. El Ocioso de Faenza.
[Menéndez y Pelayo (ref. 82, Vol. II, p. 22) indicates that this was a miscellany of six volumes in manuscript form. It contained the poetic works of a number of Jesuit poets. Though he says that the last three volumes have been lost from the Biblioteca Nacional de Quito, where all six were deposited, he notes that the principal compositions were published by Juan León Mera. For a recent partial edition of the work, see Carrión, Alejandro, entry no. 1116.]

1130. Viescas, Ramón.
[Menéndez y Pelayo (ref. 82, Vol. II, p. 19) says of this Ecuadorean poet, without mentioning any titles: "Los romances y décimas de donaire, que componía con mucha facilidad, no carecen tampoco de gracia."]

GUATEMALA

Guatemala has produced no important investigations in the field of popular poetry and song. While it is clear that romances and coplas exist in Guatemalan tradition, only a few of them have been collected and studied.

GUATEMALA

1131. Batres Jáuregui, Antonio. Los indios, su historia y su civilización. Guatemala: Establecimiento Tipográfico La Unión, 1894. 5, xii, 216 pp. 25.5 cm.
[There is a section about the music and dances of the Indians (pp. 65-72). As far as poetry and songs are concerned, the author merely notes their existence; though he praises them, he actually says little about them. But he discusses dances in more detail.]

1132. _____. Vicios del lenguaje y provincialismos de Guatemala. Guatemala: Encuadernación y Tipografía Nacional, 1892. 560 pp. 25 cm.
[In illustrating linguistic phenomena, the author frequently cites poetry, usually the works of known authors but occasionally popular coplas.]

1133. Bergaño y Villegas, Simón. Proclama por D. Simón Bergaño y Villegas. En Guatemala, por Beteta, n.d. [1810?].
[Menéndez y Pelayo (ref. 82, Vol. I, p. 185) says that this is an hoja suelta in the Archivo de Indias and that it deals with Spain's war for independence. He does not say that it is a romance, but the four initial lines which he prints seem to indicate that it is.]

1134. Estrada, R. El romance. Guatemala, 1949. 28 pp.

1135. Navarrete, Carlos. "Notas para un estudio del corrido en Guatemala." Tlàtoani (México, D. F.), 2a. época, Núms. 8-9 (noviembre de 1954), 19-23.
[Texts of two Guatemalan versions of Delgadina with a comparative analysis of these vis-à-vis versions from Mexico and Nicaragua.]

1136. Recinos, Adrián. "Algunas observaciones sobre el folklore de Guatemala." JAF, XXIX(1916), 559-566.
[Some stories and songs from Guatemala. Included are some coplas.]

HONDURAS

As a cursory examination of this brief section will reveal, practically nothing is known about the romance tradition in Honduras. The fact is that there has been little study of any branch of Honduran folklore.

HONDURAS

1137. Cancionero tropical. Tegucigalpa: Imprenta Calderón, 1945.

1138. Cevallos, P. F. Folklore hondureño. 2.ª ed. Tegucigalpa: Tip. Nacional, 1948. 116 pp.
[Boggs (ref. 13 [1948], p. 26) indicates that the work contains material from the Comayagua region.]

1139. Mariñas Otero, Luis. "Panorama de la música hondureña." Cuadernos hispanoamericanos (Madrid), No. 103 (julio, 1958), supplement at the end of the issue numbered pp. 1-12.
[A brief account of the history of music, both popular and artistic, in Honduras. Though the author treats folklore, he does not mention romances, corridos, or coplas as genres cultivated in Honduras. However, a few dances are mentioned by name.]

Morelet, Arthur. See entry no. 1505.

1140. Ortega, Pompilio. Patrios lares. Tegucigalpa: Imprenta Calderón, 1946. 124, IV pp. 22 cm.
[A mélange of folklore materials, mostly tales and legends. There is some attention to popular verse and song, for the most part coplas. There is, however, one song (p. 52) which is close to the form and style of Mexican corridos; also, there is a romance by José Trinidad Reyes (p. 110) which has a touch of popular flavor.]

MEXICO

Mexican popular poetry and song have attracted the attention of several good investigators. Most important among those who worked prior to 1930 were Rubén M. Campos, whose interests encompassed the whole of Mexican folklore, and Higinio Vázquez Santa Ana, who confined himself more to music and song, with particular emphasis upon the romance-corrido tradition. Though uncritical procedures in collecting folklore materials and erratic scholarship characterize the work of both of these men, Vázquez Santa Ana helped arouse his countrymen's interest in the romance, corridos, coplas, and other songs of Mexico; and the voluminous works of Campos, despite their glaring deficiencies, represent the first serious attempt in Mexico to deal with the whole broad sweep of the country's rich and varied folklore. The early efforts of these two investigators were supplemented by a brief but very useful compilation of some romance texts which were published by Pedro Henríquez Ureña and Bertram D. Wolfe in 1925.

In part because the books of Campos were responsible for kindling widespread interest in Mexican folklore, and in part, no doubt, because his unsystematic scholarship surely led others to attempt to improve upon his work, the period since 1930 has seen the appearance in Mexico of a number of competent folklorists and literary scholars interested in their country's popular literature. Easily the most outstanding of these has been Vicente T. Mendoza, whose studies of romances, corridos, décimas, and innumerable other types of popular songs have won him wide acclaim. Particularly notable are his studies of the musical aspects of folk songs and dances. Specifically in the field of the romance-corrido and closely related genres, other figures such as Jesús Bal y Gay, Daniel Castañeda, Clementina Díaz y de Ovando, Armand Duvalier, Celestino Herrera Frimont, Héctor Pérez Martínez, Margarita Prieto, Jesús Romero Flores, Virginia Rodríguez Rivera, Celestino Serrano Martínez, and Frances Toor have made worthy contributions.

In the field of folklore bibliography Mexico is poor; few of her folklorists have been even moderately good bibliographers, and the only systematic work has been done by a North American, Ralph S. Boggs. Despite its merit, however, his bibliography of Mexican folklore appeared almost twenty years ago and is now out of date.

Mexican folklore is not delimited, of course, by the political boundaries of present-day Mexico, and, interestingly enough, the songs and poetry of Mexicans or descendants of Mexicans living in the United States were studied systematically many years before their counterparts in Mexico proper received comparable attention. Beginning with the works of Charles F. Lummis at the end of the nineteenth century, continuing through the scholarly investigations of Aurelio M. Espinosa over a period of more than half a century, and including during the past decade or two contributions by scholars such as Vicente S. Acosta, Arthur M. Campa, J. Frank Dobie, Frank Goodwyn, Aurora Lucero-White Lea, Brownie McNeil, Américo Paredes, and John Donald Robb, the romances, corridos, and other popular literature of the southwestern part of the United States have been the subject of some excellent investigations.

MEXICO

1141. "A caza de la música popular." <u>Boletín del Departamento de Música de la Secretaría de Educación Pública</u> (Mexico), No. 3 (septiembre, 1946), 91-92.

Abascal, Carlos. See García Bravo y Olivera, R., entry no. 1331.

1142. Acosta, Vicente S. "Some Surviving Elements of Spanish Folklore in Arizona." M. A. thesis, University of Arizona, 1951.
[An excellent work which contains much material about <u>romances</u> and <u>corridos</u> in Arizona and surrounding areas. There are many texts which are of great interest.]

Aguirre, Clemente. <u>Colección de jarabes, sones y cantos populares tal como se usan en el estado de Jalisco.</u> See Mendoza, Vicente T., entry no. 1455.

1143. Aguirre y Villar, José de. <u>Estatva de la Paz/ antiguamente colocada/ en el Monte Palatino,/ por Tito, y Vespasiano/ Consules./ Y aora nuevamente trasladada/ a los Reynos de España, y Francia por la Catholica Mages-/tad de Nuestro Rey, y Señor D. Phelipe V (que Dios/ guarde) en las felicissimas Nupcias del Serenissimo Señor D. Luis I. Principe de Asturias, con la Serenissima Señora/Hija del Señor Duque de Orleans, y las de la Señora Doña/ María Luisa Gabriela Infanta de España, con la Chris-tianissima Magestad del Señor Rey de Francia./ Cuya alegorica translacion/ celebraron los ingenios Zacatecanos, en el festivo Poetico/ Certamen, qué a expensas de la lealtad del Conde de San-/tiago de la Laguna, Coronel de Infanteria Española,/ D. Joseph de Vrquiola, se celebró en dicha Ciudad/ dia 27 de Septiembre del año de 1722. -/ Con la descripción del obelisco,/ que se le erigió a el Señor/ Don Lvis I./ que de Dios goza en su Real Coronacion/ el año de 1724./ Sacalo a luz, y consagra/ a la Catholica Magestad del Señor/ Don Phelipe V./ (que Dios guarde) el Coronel de Infanteria D. Joseph/ Rivera Bermudez, Conde de Santiago de la Laguna./ Con licencia de los Superiores./ En Mexico: Por Joseph Bernardo de Hogal. Impressor mayor/ de dicha Ciudad. En la Calle nueva.</u> 4.° 3 preliminary lvs., 128 pp.
[Núñez y Domínguez (ref. 1515, p. 251) indicates that the dedication of the volume is dated Zacatecas, 21 de julio de 1727. He discusses (pp. 187-190) the "festivo poético certamen" reported in this book as having taken place in Zacatecas on September 27, 1722, and he prints the texts of several poems which won prizes, including a very contrived artistic <u>romance</u>.]

1144. Alarcón, Pedro. "Romance."
[A <u>romance</u> which won first prize in a poetry contest held at the University of Mexico in 1724 in honor of the Marqués de Casa Fuerte, Viceroy of Mexico. Nuñez y Domínguez prints the text (ref. 1515, pp. 213-214).]

1145. Alcevedo López, Santos. Macehualcuicatl; cantos populares. México: Vargas Rea, 1954. 42 pp. 21 cm.

1146. Almeida Portugal, Maria de Glória Rangel de. Olhando o México. Rio de Janeiro, D. F.: Leuzinger, 1939. 120 pp.

1147. Altamirano, Ignacio M. "La navidad (En las montañas)." In Album de navidad. México: Imprenta de Ignacio Escalante y C.ª, 1871. Pp. 199-296. (There are many other editions with a change of the title to "La navidad en las montañas.")

[A version of En el portal de Belén (pp. 241-245) is in corrido form.]

1148. _____. "Prólogo" of Romancero nacional by Guillermo Prieto. México: Oficina Tip. de la Secretaría de Fomento, 1885. Pp. iii-xliv.; reprinted in La literatura nacional; revistas, ensayos, biografías y prólogos; edición y prólogo de José Luis Martínez, Vol. III. México: Editorial Porrúa, 1949. Pp. 161-218.

[One of the first essays about the popular songs of Mexico. Its historical importance is great, notwithstanding the fact that some of Altamirano's hypotheses have been disproved by subsequent investigations.]

Alva Ixtlilxóchitl, Fernando de. See Méndez Plancarte, Alfonso, entry no. 1433.

1149. Amador, Armando C. "The Poetry of Mexican Folk Songs." PAM, XLIII:5 (November, 1930), 361-363.

[An attempt to explain the great appeal of Mexican folk songs in general. The author's thesis is contained in the subtitle of his article: "Originality and Emotivity Found in Plaintive Melodies Inspired by Universal Impulses." Romances and corridos are not treated as such, but the article, though not of great importance, is of interest to students of any kind of popular song and verse.]

1150. Anaya Monroy, Fernando. "Algunas experiencias sobre recolección de folklore." ASFM, VIII(1954), 7-21.

[Corridos are discussed along with other types of folklore, and several fragmentary texts are given.]

1151. Anda, José Guadalupe de. Los bragados. México: Compañía General Editora, 1942. 190 pp. 18 cm.

[Contains a Corrido de Policarpo Bermúdez (p. 120). Though it is probably the work of the novelist himself, it is written in the style of truly popular corridos.]

1152. Aragón, Fernando de. Libro de oro de la canción; un siglo de canciones populares. Méxcio, 1951. 160 pp.

1153. Arguedas, José María. Review of Vicente T. Mendoza's "La música tradicional española en México" (NuM, Año VIII:29 [1er. trimestre, 1953], 5-34). FACI, Año II:2 (octubre, 1954), 185-190.

[A long and very informative review in which Arguedas contrasts

Mendoza's findings of overwhelming Spanish influence on the music of Mexico with the situation in Peru, where Indian influence on popular music was apparently much stronger.]

1154. Arlt, Gustave O. "Bibliography of California Folklore." CFQ, II(1943), 63-70, 169-175, 245-251, 347-352.
[Contains a few references to folk songs in Spanish.]

1155. Armistead, Samuel G., and Silverman, Joseph H. "Dos romances fronterizos en la tradición sefardí oriental." NRFH, XIII:1-2 (enero-junio, 1959), 88-97.
[Contains two fragmentary texts of romances fronterizos found in the oral tradition of some recent Sephardic immigrants to the West Coast of the United States.]

1156. _____. "Hispanic Balladry Among the Sephardic Jews of the West Coast." WF, XIX:4 (October, 1960), 229-244.
[Seven texts without music of romances collected from the oral tradition of Sephardic Jews in Los Angeles, California. The authors document and comment upon the texts and their relationship to general Hispanic tradition.]

Atl, Dr. See Murillo, Gerardo, entry no. 1508.

1157. Austin, Mary. "New Mexico Folk Poetry." Pal, VII:7-8 (Nov. 30, 1919), 146-150.
[Tully (ref. 1665, p. 13) says that it contains some coplas and other folk songs, but she does not mention romances or corridos.]

1158. _____. "Sources of Poetic Influence in the Southwest." Poetry (Chicago), XLIII:3 (December, 1933), 152-163.
[A discussion of the Indian, Spanish, and English elements which have entered into the folk poetry of the southwest. Among other things, the author treats the corrido, which, she believes, contributed much to the New Mexican type of cowboy ballad. There are translations of two coplas and of two strophes from a corrido about Pancho Villa.]

1159. _____, Otero-Warren, Adelina, and Lucero, Aurora. "New Mexico Folk Song." Pal, VII:7-8 (Nov. 30, 1919), 152-153, 156-159.
[Tully (ref. 1665, p. 14) says: "Words of several Spanish songs, including coplas, on entriega de novios, hymns and love songs."]

1160. Avila, Juan. "Notas Californias [sic]." Orange County Historical Series (Santa Ana, California), II(1939), 16.
[Swan (ref. 1640, p. 105) quotes an historical copla taken from the above.]

1161. Bal y Gay, Jesús. "Romance y corrido." BIMMF, Año I:1 (enero, 1940), 10-20.
[Part I of a study whose second part did not appear because the Boletín suspended publication. The author takes issue with Mendoza's

definition and classification of corridos as found in his recently published El romance español y el corrido mexicano.]

1162. Baqueiro Foster, Gerónino. "El alma de Andalucía en el folklore musical de Guerrero." Nacion, 30 de enero de 1949, suplemento dominical, p. 10; 6 de febrero de 1949, sup. dom., p. 10; 13 de febrero de 1949, sup. dom., p. 13; first appeared in the DdeG, 15 de enero de 1949, p. 2.

[Discusses the importance of the seguidillas of Andalusia as the source of almost all the present dances of Andalusia and also of many American dances and songs such as the jarabes, the chilenas (which are a form of the zamacueca), the malagueñas, etc. The verses which accompany these are often coplas with octosyllabic lines. Some examples are provided.]

1163. _____. "Aspectos de la música popular yucateca en tres siglos." RevMM, IV:1 (7 de enero de 1944), 3-7.

[In tracing the history of music in Yucatan from colonial times to the present, the author discusses the mixture of Spanish and Indian elements and treats several types of compositions, principally the son. But there is no mention of romances or corridos. The most interesting fact brought to light is the popularity of the Cuban bolero and the Colombian bambuco in Yucatan.]

1164. _____. "El canto popular en la Revolución." Nacion, 20 de noviembre de 1949, suplemento dominical, pp. 6-7.

[Considers the effect of the Revolution upon the propagation of truly popular Mexican music and the interplay between the latter and more artistic music of foreign origin or Mexican music which shows foreign influences. The article is quite superficial and corridos receive only slight attention.]

_____. See Santamaría, Francisco J., entry no. 1610.

1165. Barbosa, Manuel. Apuntes para la historia de Michoacán. Morelia: Talleres de la Escuela Industrial Militar Porfirio Díaz, 1905. 320 pp.

[Contains many fragments of popular songs, several of which appear to be from early corridos about military events which date from the second quarter of the nineteenth century.]

1166. Barker, George C. Pachuco; An American-Spanish Argot and Its Social Functions in Tucson, Arizona. Tucson, Arizona, 1950. 38 pp. 23 cm. (University of Arizona Bulletin, Social Science Bulletin, No. 18.)

[Contains a pachuco parody of El hijo desobediente.]

1167. Barker, Ruth Laughlin. Caballeros. New York: D. Appleton & Co., 1931. 380 pp. 22 cm.

[Contains a great deal of general description of life in New Mexico and considerable information about folklore. There is some attention to music and songs, but only passing mention of ballads, and nothing specific about romances, corridos, or other narrative poetry.]

1168. Barriga Rivas, Rogelio. Río humano. México: Ediciones Botas, 1949. 214 pp. 21 cm.
[A novel which contains a Corrido de la Hacienda de Jauja (pp. 67-75), a copla (p. 119), and some children's songs (pp. 200-203).]

1169. Benítez Valle, Manuel. [Article about the Corrido del caballo mojino.] Actualidades de Zacatecas (Zacatecas, Zac.), 19 de septiembre de 1952.
[Esparza S. (ref. 1291, p. 16) makes reference to the above article, which he declares is full of inaccurate information about the corrido.]

1170. Beristáin de Sousa, Joseph Mariano, ed. Cantos de las musas mexicanas con motivo de la colocación de la estatua equestre de bronce de nuestro augusto soberano Carlos IV. México: Don Mariano de Zúñiga y Ontiveros, calle del Espíritu Santo, 1804. 10 unnumbered pp., 138 pp.
[In an introduction the author describes the organization of a contest which he directed in 1803 whereby prizes were to be given for the best poems submitted in various categories on specified subjects related to the erection of the famous statue of Carlos IV in Mexico City. Among these was one award for the best romance about the plaza, the pedestal, and the statue itself. Three romances appear in this volume, the one which received the prize and two others. All are romances heroicos written in pompous neoclassical style. There is nothing popular about them.]

1171. Bernal, Rafael. "Las tres canciones de la tierra fría." RevMM, I:7 (7 de abril de 1942), 148-150.
[Includes seven coplas and a song entitled Amigo pulque from the area around the Nevado de Toluca. There is nothing about romances or corridos.]

1172. Boas, Frank. "Notes on Mexican Folk-lore." JAF, XXV (1912), 204-260.
[Includes two amorous décimas (pp. 233-235), some coplas (pp. 231-233), but no romances or corridos.]

1173. Boatright, Mody C., ed. Mexican Border Ballads and Other Lore. Austin, 1946. vii, 140 pp. 23 cm. (Publications of the Texas Folklore Society, Vol. XXI.)
[Contains a chapter entitled "Corridos of the Mexican Border" by Brownie McNeil. See entry no. 1417.]

_____. See Goodwyn, Frank, entry no. 1344.

1174. _____, Hudson, Wilson M., and Maxwell, Allen, eds. "And Horns on the Toads." Dallas: Southern Methodist University

Press, 1959. vii, 237 pp. 23.5 cm. (Publications of the Texas Folklore Society, No. XXIX.)
[Among other articles it contains "The Bury-Me-Not Theme in the Southwest" by Américo Paredes (pp. 88-92), "The Personification of Animals in the Relación of Mexico" by Donald M. Lance (pp. 108-121), and "Rails Below the Rio Grande" by John T. Smith (pp. 122-135).]

1175. Boatright, Mody C., Hudson, Wilson M., and Maxwell, Allen, eds. Folk Travelers, Ballads, Tales, and Talk. Dallas: Southern Methodist University Press, 1953. 261 pp. 23.5 cm. (Publications of the Texas Folklore Society, No. XXV.)
[Contains "The Love Tragedy in Texas-Mexican Ballads" by Américo Paredes (pp. 110-114) and "Signature in Ballad and Story" by Robert C. Stephenson (pp. 97-109).]

1176. _____, eds. Madstones and Twisters. Dallas: Southern Methodist University Press, 1958. 169 pp. 24 cm. (Publications of the Texas Folklore Society, No. XXVIII.)
[Includes "The Mexican Corrido: Its Rise and Fall" by Américo Paredes (pp. 91-105).]

1177. _____, eds. Mesquite and Willow. Dallas: Southern Methodist University Press, 1957. viii, 203 pp. 23 cm. (Publications of the Texas Folklore Society, No. XXVII.)
[Contains "The Legend of Gregorio Cortez" by Américo Paredes (pp. 3-22).]

1178. _____, eds. Texas Folk and Folklore. Dallas: Southern Methodist Press, 1954. xv, 356 pp. 23.5 cm. (Publications of the Texas Folklore Society, No. XXVI.)
[Contains "El contrabando del Paso" (pp. 152-155), "Corrido de Kansas" (pp. 150-152) by Brownie McNeil, "Corrido de Texas" (pp. 157-158) and "Deportados" (pp. 155-157) by Paul S. Taylor, "El toro moro" (pp. 147-150) by Frank Goodwyn, and "Versos de los bandidos" (pp. 143-147) by J. Frank Dobie.]

1179. Boca Angel, Manuel. El Cortesano y Discreto Político y Moral Príncipe de los Romances, Relox concertado para sabios dispertador de ignorantes, por D. Manuel Boca Angel. Impreso en México por los Herederos de la Viuda de Miguel Rivera Calderón. — Empedradillo. Año de 1724.; other editions: Imprenta de la Viuda de Bernardo Calderón, 1658; Impreso en México por Francisco de Rivera Calderón, en la calle de San Agustín, 1709; Herederos de doña María Rivera, 1755.
[All the above editions of the work are listed by Mendoza (ref. 1487, p. 783).]

1180. Boggs, Ralph Steele. "Una bibliografía completa, clasificada, y comentada, de los artículos de Mexican Folkways (MF), con índice." BBAA, VI(1942), 221-265.
[A very useful bibliography which facilitates use of Mexican Folkways.]

1181. _____. "Bibliografía del folklore mexicano." BBAA, III (1939), in appendix with special pagination, 1-122.
[Probably the most valuable bibliography of Mexican folklore that has been compiled. It contains many references to corridos and other popular songs.]

1182. _____. "El folklore mexicano." AFA, 1945, p. 109.
[A very brief discussion of folklore in general and of Mexican folklore in particular. There is a very brief bibliography. The article is of no interest to the student of the romance and corrido.]

1183. _____, and the members of his seminar at the Escuela Nacional de Antropología in 1945. "Mapa preliminar de las regiones folklóricas de México." FA, IX:1-2 (June and December, 1949), 1-4+map.
[A brief report on a seminar in which each student made a map showing the geographical distribution of versions of certain specific folklore themes (the romance of Delgadina was one of the subjects studied). Boggs made the tentative composite map offered here.]

Bork, William. See Seibold, Doris, entry no. 1616.

1184. Braddy, Haldeen. Cock of the Walk; Legend of Pancho Villa. Albuquerque, New Mexico: University of New Mexico Press, 1955. ix, 174 pp. 24 cm.
[In narrating the life and exploits of Villa, the author quotes many texts of folk songs, some of them corridos. Most are given only in English translation, though a few original Spanish texts are also provided.]

1185. _____, and McNeely, John H. "Francisco Villa in Folk-Songs." Arizona Quarterly (Tucson), X:1 (Spring, 1954), 5-16.
[A study of the character of Pancho Villa as it is revealed in corridos and in other popular songs.]

1186. Brenner, Anita. Idols Behind Altars. New York: Payson and Clarke, Ltd., 1929. 359 pp. 23 cm.
[There is treatment of the corridos and particularly of the illustrations which José Guadalupe Posada and other artists provided for corridos and other popular literature.]

1187. _____. "Mexican Ballads." MF, I:5 (February-March, 1926), 11-17.
[A discussion of the nature and the significance of Mexican corridos. The text of the Corrido de la muerte de Felipe Carrillo Puerto is included along with an English translation.]

1188. Breve Razón del Carro y Loa de Nicolás Rodríguez Juárez (pintor), que con motivo de la restauración de Orán por Felipe V. costeó el Gremio de Cereros, Confiteros y Tintoreros. México. Año de 1732. Impreso por Joseph Bernardo de Hogal.
[Listed by Mendoza (ref. 1487, p. 785).]

1189. Breve Relación del descubrimiento de la Isla de Jauja. Contiene además: Curiosa glosa que embía un amante a una señora, con la respuesta de la Dama. En la Imprenta de los Herederos del Lic. D. José Jáuregui. Calle de San Bernardo. Año de 1779.
[Listed as a romance by Mendoza (ref. 1487, p. 785).]

1190. Buchanan, Annabel Morris. American Folk Music. Ithaca, N. Y.: National Federation of Music Clubs, 1939. 57 pp. reproduced from typewritten copy.
[Chase (ref. 25, p. 223) says: "Bibliography and list of music, including Mexican and Spanish-American songs, p. 56."]

1191. Bustamante, Carlos María de. Cuadro histórico de la revolución de la América Mexicana, comenzada en quince de septiembre de mil ochocientos diez, por el ciudadano Miguel Hidalgo y Costilla . . . dedicada al ciudadano general José María Morelos. 5 vols. México: Imprenta de La Aguila [sic], 1823, 1823, 1825, 1826, 1827. 20 cm.; also, Cuadro histórico de la revolución mexicana, comenzada en 15 de septiembre de 1810 por el ciudadano Miguel Hidalgo y Costilla, cura del pueblo de los Dolores, en el obispado de Michoacán. Dedícalo al Exmo. Sr. D. Ignacio Trigueros, Secretario del Despacho y de Hacienda, Carlos María de Bustamente. Segunda edición corregida y muy aumentada por el mismo autor. 5 vols. México: Imprenta de J. Mariano Lara, 1843, 1844, [1844?], 1844, 1846. 22.5 cm.; also, 3.ª ed. 3 vols. Méjico: Impr. de J. R. Navarro, 1854-1855. 21 cm. [Library of Congress Catalogue says: "The 3d edition contains only the first 29 letters of those published in the 1st and 2d editions." There were 151 letters in all.]; also, a re-editing of the 2. ed. corregida y muy aumentada por el mismo autor. 5 vols. México: Talleres Linotipográficos "Soria," 1926. 29.5 cm.; also, Resumen histórico de la revolución de los Estados unidos mejicanos: sacado del "Cuadro histórico", que en forma de cartas escribió el lic. d. Carlos María Bustamante, i ordenado en cuatro libros por d. Pablo de Mendibil. Londres: R. Ackermann, 1828. xxv, 423 pp. 21 cm.; also, Resumen histórico de la revolución de los Estados Unidos Mejicanos, sacado del "Cuadro histórico" que en forma de cartas escribió el Lic. D. Carlos María Bustamante y ordenado en cuatro libros por D. Pablo de Mendibil. Segunda edición. México: Editorial Jus, 1955. xxix, 406 pp.; also, Continuación del cuadro histórico de la revolución mexicana, por el autor del mismo Lic. D. Carlos María de Bustamante; dedícala al supremo gobierno general de la federación mexicana; época de la independencia. Tomo VI. México: Imprenta de Alejandro Valdés, 1832. 187 pp. 20 cm.; also, 2 vols. México, 1953. 25 cm. (Publicaciones de la Biblioteca Nacional de México, Nos. 2-3.)
[Bustamante makes many references to popular songs and poetry and he frequently quotes the texts of popular and semipopular composiciones. Some are décimas, some are coplas or pasquines, some are

merely called canción. Several, however, seem to be close to the corrido tradition, though none is printed under that title. For detailed treatment of Bustamante's work as a source of information about popular poetry, see entry no. 1627.]

1192. Cabrera, Ana S. "Canciones populares mejicanas." Nac, 2 de febrero, 1936.

1193. _____. "Corridos o baladas." In Folklore de las Américas; primera antología, ed. by Félix Coluccio. B. A.: Ateneo, 1949. Pp. 272-275.
[A very superficial attempt to describe the corrido of Mexico. A few isolated strophes of corridos are included by way of illustration.]

_____. Rutas de América. See entry no. 20.

1194. Calaveras mexicanas de Chicago; edición anual dedicada a la H. Colonia Mexicana. Chicago, noviembre de 1955. 22 pp. 27.5 cm.
[Contains calaveras about more than one hundred figures prominent in the Mexican colony in Chicago, Illinois, and Indiana Harbor and Gary, Indiana. There is a short discussion of "La celebración de el (sic) día de muertos y el origen de las 'calaberas'" with some engravings of José Guadalupe Posada (p. 11).]

1195. Calaveras resurrectas; 16 años de calaveras políticas del Taller de Gráfica Popular. México: Taller de Gráfica Popular, 1954. 17 unnumbered leaves printed on both sides. 22.5 cm.
[Reproductions of a great many calaveras and other popular literature printed by the Taller. Included is a Corrido de Stalingrado. All of the compositions show militant left wing bias.]

1196. Campa, Arturo L. "Bernal Francés y La esposa infiel." FICU, II trimestre de 1941:4, pp. 35-36.
[The author points out the differences between two romances which have often been confused, and he offers a New Mexican version of each.]

1197. _____. A Bibliography of Spanish Folklore in New Mexico. Vol. II:3 of The University of New Mexico Bulletin, Language Series. Albuquerque, September, 1930. 28 pp. 23 cm.
[Not really a bibliography, this work is a catalogue of folklore materials collected by Campa in New Mexico. They are listed merely by title under headings such as décimas, indita, cuando, romance, corrido, etc. There are eighteen romances and eight corridos listed.]

1198. _____. "Spanish American Folksongs from the Collection of Leonora Curtin." [Albuquerque, 194?] 66 pp. typewritten.
[A carbon copy is in the Library of Congress. There is no music.]

1199. Campa, Arturo L. Spanish Folk-Poetry in New Mexico. Albuquerque, New Mexico: University of New Mexico Press, 1946. 224 pp. 23 cm.
[A fundamental study of the popular poetry and songs of New Mexico. There is a chapter on the romance and another on the corrido. Many valuable texts are included.]

1200. _____. The Spanish Folksong in the Southwest. Vol. IV:1 of The University of New Mexico Bulletin, Modern Language Series. Albuquerque, New Mexico, Nov. 15, 1933. 67 pp. 23 cm.
[A study of several kinds of popular songs. There are texts of romances, décimas, and other genres.]

1201. _____. "Spanish Folksongs in Metropolitan Denver." SFQ, XXIV:3 (September, 1960), 179-192.
[Contains texts and study of some folk songs collected among persons of Mexican and Spanish descent living in the Denver area. Some corridos, traditional Spanish romances, and inditas are included.]

1202. _____. "Spanish Folksongs in New Mexico." Ph. D. diss., Columbia University, 1940.
[This work is the preliminary form of Spanish Folk-Poetry in New Mexico. See entry no. 1199.]

1203. _____. "Today's Troubadours." New Mexico (Santa Fe), XIV:9 (September, 1936), 16-17, 49-50.
[Tully (ref. 1665, p. 25) says: "Discussion of the changing, yet vital, tradition of the trovador in the Southwest."]

1204. Campos, Rubén M. El folklore literario de México; investigación acerca de la producción literaria popular (1525-1925). México: Talleres Gráficos de la Nación, 1929. 690 pp. 23.5 cm. (Publicaciones de la Secretaría de Educación Pública.)
[An extensive, though somewhat careless, study of Mexican folklore. There is a section on the corrido; also there are examples of practically every genre of popular poetry and song to be found in Mexico: e.g., coplas, décimas, etc. Notwithstanding its shortcomings, the volume is a fundamental work for the study of almost any aspect of Mexican folklore.]

1205. _____. El folklore literario y musical de México de Rubén M. Campos; selección y notas preliminares por Alfonso Ramos Espinosa. México: Secretaría de Educación Pública, 1946. 95 pp. 20 cm. (Biblioteca enciclopédica popular, Vol. 126.)
[Extracts from several of Campos' books. A section on the corrido is included and some texts are given.]

1206. _____. El folklore musical de las ciudades; investigación acerca de la música mexicana para bailar y cantar. México: Talleres Linotipográficos "El Modelo," 1930. 457 pp. 23.5 cm. (Publicaciones

de la Secretaría de Educación Pública.)
[The volume is misnamed because it deals almost exclusively with artistic music (songs, zarzuelas, operettas, and operas) and has only very indidental attention to true folklore. There are, to be sure, a few coplas that might be called semipopular.]

1207. _____. "El folklore musical de México." BLAM, III(abril de 1937), 137-142.
[A brief survey of certain aspects of the history of Mexican songs from colonial times to the present. There is mention of canciones, sones, seguidillas, tonadillas, etc., but there is no consideration of romances or corridos.]

1208. _____. El folklore y la música mexicana; investigación acerca de la cultura musical en México (1525-1925). México: Talleres Gráficos de la Nación, 1928. 351 pp. 24 cm. (Publicaciones de la Secretaría de Educación Pública.)
[A fairly extensive but badly organized study of Mexican music and the contribution of Mexican folklore to its development. Though there is only incidental reference to the corrido, there is a long section on coplas with many texts (pp. 130-149). Also, a few texts of popular or semipopular songs are of interest because they are topical in nature. Most of the book, however, is concerned with Mexican composers, orchestra leaders, and singers.]

1209. _____. "Las fuentes del folklore mexicano." RMM, I:1 (15 de mayo de 1919), 18-23.
[A defense of the thesis that the spirit of the Mexican race, which the author traces back to pre-Hispanic times, remains alive in popular verse and song. A number of cantares populares (i.e., coplas) are cited. The article is of minor importance.]

1210. _____. "La música popular de México." REM, Año I:1 (agosto de 1949), 81-91.
[A brief discussion of the background of Mexican music, particularly during the pre-Hispanic period. Some of the material presented, notably some passages taken from Torquemada, deal with Indian poetry and songs about persons and events; hence, it might be of value in tracing the development of the corrido tradition in Mexico.]

1211. _____. "Los orígenes del arte popular mexicano." AnMN, Quinta época, I(1934).
[A discussion of various popular arts, including music, with particular attention to the relationship between Aztec and modern Mexican practices. Corridos are not treated, but there is some attention to coplas.]

1212. _____. La producción literaria de los aztecas. México: Talleres Gráficos del Museo Nacional de Arqueología, Historia y

Etnografía, 1936. 464 pp. 26 cm.

[After an introductory section of ten chapters about the Aztecs and their literature, including two chapters specifically about poetry, Campos publishes a number of texts taken from Sahagún's Cantares mexicanos, the cantos of Nezahualcóyotl, and other sources. Also cited are pertinent fragments of chronicles such as those of Torquemada, Durán, Sahagún, and many others. Much that is included hardly seems to be literary or to deal with genuine literature, but its historical interest is not to be denied. The volume is of value in seeking origins of Mexican literature, learned or popular.]

1213. Canciones y corridos sinarquistas. México, 1940. 48 pp.

1214. Casa, Enrique C. de la. "La influencia franciscana en el folklore nuevomexicano." RHM, XIII(1947), 159-163.

[The author believes that the Franciscans were responsible for introducing into New Mexico religious romances which are still being sung. He bases his arguments mainly upon texts provided by Arturo L. Campa and Roberto L. Vialpando, both of whom had recently finished dissertations on New Mexican folklore.]

Casas, Bartolomé de las. See Fabié, Antonio, entry no. 1311.

1215. Cassidy, Ina Sizer. "Folklore in New Mexico." NMFR, II(1947-1948), 3-6.

[A brief and superficial general survey of New Mexican folklore with mention of Indian, Spanish, and Anglo-American elements. There is very incidental and unimportant reference to the corrido.]

1216. Castañeda, Daniel. El corrido mexicano, su técnica literaria y musical. México: Editorial "Surco," 1943. 122 pp. 21.5 cm.

[An excellent study of the prosody, versification, and music of the corrido with numerous texts and musical transcriptions.]

1217. _____. "La música y la Revolución Mexicana." BLAM, Año V, Tomo V(octubre de 1941), 437-448.

[An excellent essay about the impulse which was given to popular music of all kinds by the Revolution. The author is particularly interested in the social and political conditions which brought sones, corridos, huapangos, and other types of popular songs out of the small villages and into the cities, where they often supplanted the European music which had predominated in urban Mexico until the Revolution.]

1218. _____. "La música y la Revolución Mexicana." Eurindia (México), marzo de 1936, 13-15; marzo-abril de 1937, 28-29.

[This apparently is not the article which appeared with the same title in BLAM (entry no. 1217). The latter is dated México, D. F., 1939.]

1219. _____. "Sinopsis de la investigación en el corrido mexicano." LetrasM, Año VII, Vol. I:7 (15 de julio, 1943), 4-5.
[The first chapter of Castañeda's book, El corrido mexicano (entry no. 1216). It was in press at the time this extract appeared.]

1220. Castillo Nájera, Francisco. Corridos y canciones del siglo XIX; glosa al programa de Concha Michel (Palacio de Bellas Artes). México: Secretaría de Relaciones Exteriores, Departamento de Información para el Extranjero, 1946. 22 pp. 22.5 cm.
[A short but informative discussion of several important aspects of the Mexican corrido.]

1221. _____. El Gavilán, corrido grande. París: Ediciones Estrella, Imprenta Española de J. Solsona y Coll, 1934. 92 pp. 29 cm.; also, 2.ª edición. [México]: Editorial México Nuevo, 1939. xi, 153 pp. 24 cm.
[A long artistic corrido which imitates the style of popular corridos. The author includes a valuable essay about the popular songs of his native state of Durango.]

1222. _____. "Profundidad y dimensión del corrido." Nacion, 9 de octubre de 1949, suplemento dominical, pp. 8-9.
[A very fine summary of general facts about the corrido, its nature, its history, its subject matter, and the like. Several texts without music are given. Those with titles are: En mil novecientos once, diremos año primero; Reyes Ruiz; A la probe de Belén; Guadalupe Rayos; Pos sí Rosita, Rosa Morada; and Corrido de Joaquín Murrieta.]

1223. Castro Leal, Antonio. "Dos romances tradicionales." CuC, VI:3 (noviembre de 1914), 237-244.
[A brief discussion of the status of the study of romances in Mexico with emphasis upon the fact that until 1914 only Dr. Max Leopold Wagner had studied them seriously. Then Castro Leal provides two romance texts which he collected in Mexico City, one of Gerineldo, the other of Conde Sol, though there is confusion between the two since the informant sang them as one song. Also, the text of a Canción de la viuda, a Mexican version of Las señas del marido, is provided as part of a discussion of the use of consonantal rhyme and the division of Mexican romances into strophes.]

1224. El Catalán Serralonga. Relación famosa, más otro romance burlesco de Los Amantes de Teruel.
[Mendoza (ref. 1487, p. 783) lists the work among romances which appeared in Mexico during the colonial period.]

1225. Cavo, Andrés. Los tres siglos de México . . . con notas y suplemento por el licenciado Carlos María de Bustamante. 4 vols. México: L. Abadiano y Valdés, 1836-1838. 21.5 cm.; also, México: Imprenta de J. R. Navarro, 1852. 417 pp. 27.5 cm.
[Contains some references to historical songs of the eighteenth century (pp. 123 and 157 of the 1852 ed.).]

1226. Ceballos Novelo, Roque J. "Folklore." Chap. IX of Vol. II of La población de Teotihuacán, ed. by Manuel Gamio. México: Talleres Gráficos, 1922. Pp. 283-417.

[Includes brief mention of corridos (pp. 295-297) and the texts of three so-called corridos, along with other songs (p. 400). The music of these compositions appears in plates 77, 78, and 79. Only Benito Canales seems really to qualify as a true corrido.]

1227. Chacón, Rafael. "Memorias."

[From these unpublished memoirs of Captain Chacón, Espinosa (ref. 1302, p. 274) quotes these lines: "En el año 1840 ó 1841 salió el General Armijo a encontrar una expedición armada de tejanos que venían por todo el Río Colorado (Canadian). En la Laguna Colorada, cerca de Tecumcari, los encontró y los tomó prisioneros. Venían bajo el mando de un Capitán Cook y un Narváez. Los mandó para Chihuahua, bajo el mando del Capitán Damacio Salazar . . . Había un poeta, D. Jorge Ramírez, que compuso un cuando, del cual me acuerdo sólo los siguientes versos: . . . ." (Espinosa quotes the fifteen lines which Chacón remembers.) From this same source comes a composition which Espinosa heads "Sobre la revolución de 1837" (p. 272), five cuartetas in corrido form.]

1228. Charlot, Jean. "José Guadalupe Posada, His Technique and Style." Artes de México (Edition in English) (México), IV:21 (January and February of 1958), 45-47.

[Routine appreciation of Posada's merits as a popular artist.]

1229. Chávez, Angélico. "The Mad Poet of Santa Cruz." NMFR, III(1948-1949), 10-17.

[An absorbing study of such facts as are known about Miguel de Quintana, who was born in Mexico City about 1670 and died in Santa Cruz de la Cañada, New Mexico, in 1748. A poet who wrote occasional verses for weddings, wakes, and other functions, Quintana suffered a change of personality about 1732 which caused two priests to bring his case to the attention of the Inquisition. From its files comes the information here presented, including some compositions which show that Quintana was at least slightly deranged from a guilt complex, albeit not really insane and not an evil man. Though not popular or topical, the mere four quatrains which are offered here are in octosyllabic lines rhymed in the abcb pattern with both assonance and consonance, a circumstance of possible importance in studying the development of the corrido, which so frequently follows this pattern.]

1230. Chávez, Carlos. "Mexican Music." In Renascent Mexico, ed. by Hubert Herring and Herbert Weinstock. New York: Covici, Friede Publishers, 1935. Pp. 199-218.

[Chávez comments (p. 214) upon the corrido as a mestizo musical and literary form which should make a contribution to Mexican music.]

1231. _____. "La música propia de México." MusRM, II:1 (15 de octubre de 1930), 3-7.

[The author avers that because of social, political, and other divisions in the past, Mexico does not yet posses a true national consciousness. He feels, however, that the elements exist for the creation of truly Mexican music. In dividing Mexico's musical history into three periods (I. La cultura aborigen; II. El mestizaje; III. El nacionalismo de la Revolución), he places the corridos in the second period.]

1232. _____. "Nacionalismo musical: I. El arte popular y el no popular. II. El fin extra-artístico en el arte popular. III. Paralelo entre el arte popular. IV. La creación nacionalista." MusRM, I:3 (15 de junio de 1930), 28-32; 4 (15 de julio de 1930), 18-22; 6 (15 de septiembre de 1930), 3-11.

[A superb essay on the fundamental differences between popular and non-popular art in general. The relationship between the two types, particularly the attempts to create "nationalistic" art by fusing them, constitutes the core of the article. Although the corrido is mentioned only very briefly, the penetrating ideas expressed are applicable to the corrido as well as to any other type of popular art.]

1233. Chávez Orozco, Luis. "El romance en México." Contemporáneos, revista mexicana de cultura (México), VII:25 (junio de 1930), 253-267.

[A good brief treatment of the history of the romance in Mexico. Includes a text of the Cerco de Zamora which appears in an eighteenth-century manuscript of the Cantares de Nezahualcoyotzin. There are some absorbing speculative comments on the psychological reasons for the decline of the romance in America.]

1234. Cincuenta grabados de José Guadalupe Posada, edición homenaje en el primer centenario de su nacimiento. México: Museo Nacional de Artes Plásticas, Instituto Nacional de Bellas Artes, 1952. In a cloth box there are fifty loose engravings and an introductory study by Fernando Gamboa, "José Guadalupe Posada; sus tiempos, el hombre, su arte." 10 unnumbered pp.

[Several of the engravings are from hojas sueltas of corridos.]

1235. Cisneros, María Guadalupe. De la literatura jalisciense: El folklore literario musical. México: Universidad Nacional Autónoma, 1933. 133 pp. 23.5 cm.

[Contains several corridos and other types of popular poetry along with much valuable information about Jalisco and its popular literature and music.]

1236. Cobos, Rubén. "El folklore nuevomexicano." El Nuevo Mexicano (Santa Fe), 13 de octubre, 1949 ("El verso o copla popular y los valses chiqueados"); 15, 22, 29 de diciembre, 1949, 5, 12, 19 de enero, 1950 ("Poesía narrativa"); 26 de enero, 2, 9, 16 de febrero, 1950 ("Algunos corridos de procedencia dudosa"); 30 de marzo, 6 de abril, 1950 ("Indita").

[A very informative brief treatment of the subjects indicated with several very valuable texts gathered from New Mexican oral tradition. There are romances of Spanish origin (Las señas del esposo, Romance de Francisquita, Por el rastro de la sangre, and others).]

1237. Cobos, Rubén. "The New Mexican Memoria, or In Memoriam Poem." WF, XVIII:1 (January, 1959), 25-30.

[A useful description of the New Mexican memoria, a poem written in memoriam of a deceased person for publication in a newspaper. Usually the work of a relative or a close friend, it was not intended to be sung. The author gives three representative texts and notes that in form and in content the memoria closely resembles the corrido and the indita.]

1238. Colín, Mario, comp. Corridos de Texcatitlán. Toluca, 1948. 42 pp.

1239. _____, comp. Corridos de Tlatlaya y Amatepec. Toluca, 1949.

1240. _____, comp. Corridos populares del Estado de México, con notas de Celedonio Serrano Martínez. México, 1952. 85 pp. 21.5 cm.

[A very valuable collection of texts together with some brief studies, mostly by Serrano Martínez, about various aspects of the corrido in Mexico. Particularly notable is the discussion of the bola suriana, which to my knowledge has not been so well treated elsewhere.]

Coluccio, Félix. See entry no. 31.

1241. Corbin, Alice. "New Mexico Folk-Songs." Poetry (Chicago), XVI(April-September, 1920), 254-263, notes on pp. 290-292.

[Translations into English of several New Mexican folk songs, including the Corrido de Macario Romero (pp. 254-256) and some coplas (pp. 260-261). There are two artistic poems by the author which are designed to interpret the folk spirit of New Mexico.]

1242. "Corrido de la enamorada." Nacion, 20 de noviembre de 1949, suplemento dominical.

[A corrido, semipopular in tone, about an event which took place in Cholula in 1917 during the Revolution.]

1243. "Corrido del terremoto." Todo (México), No. 1218 (8 de agosto de 1957), 56.

[A photographic reproduction of a broadside which appeared after the earthquake of July 28, 1957.]

1244. Corridos and other songs in the Archivo de Bellas Artes, Sección de Música, México, D. F.

[This is a large body of folklore materials which school teachers have gathered from oral tradition and sent to the Archivo de Bellas Artes, where it is collected together in large notebooks, one for each state and territory of the Republic. The material is very uneven; much of it has been collected without knowledge of proper methods of folklore research, and quite a lot of it has been lost or misplaced from the volumes where it was originally gathered together. Nevertheless, there remains much that is of value, including versions of romances, corridos, coplas, etc., some with music]

1245. Corridos and other types of popular literature which are in the Benjamin Franklin Library, México, D. F.

[There is a large collection of several hundred broadsides of corridos and other popular verse in the Benjamin Franklin Library. Most are from the presses of Antonio Vanegas Arroyo and Eduardo Guerrero, the two most prominent publishers of popular literature during the past three-quarters of a century. The compositions date from the last years of the nineteenth century and contain many corridos of the Mexican Revolution. It is an invaluable collection.]

1246. Corridos, romances, décimas, and other popular verse in the Biblioteca del Museo Nacional, México, D. F.

[Catalogued merely as Folklore, there is in the Biblioteca del Museo Nacional a volume which contains some invaluable broadsides and cancioneros of the nineteenth century. The earliest compositions date from the first half of the century.]

1247. Corridos and romances in the Biblioteca Nacional de México, México, D. F.

[In a large collection of popular literature, mostly from the presses of Antonio Vanegas Arroyo and Eduardo Guerrero, there are many corridos, a few romances, and a large number of compositions of other types.]

1248. Corridos and romances in the library of the University of New Mexico, Albuquerque, N. M.

[There are several volumes of typewritten texts of romances, corridos, and other genres of popular verse collected from oral tradition in New Mexico.]

1249. "Corridos de la Revolución." Nacion, 19 de noviembre, 1939.

[The texts of four corridos without commentary or music. They are: Triste despedida de Emiliano Zapata, El fusilamiento de Cirilo Arenas, Corrido de Benito Canales, and El cuartelazo felicista.]

1250. Corridos mexicanos. México: Editorial Albatros, 1950. 96 pp. 17 cm. (Colección Adelita, No. 6.)

[Texts and music of thirty-five corridos of popular origin.]

1251. Cowell, Sidney Robertson. "The Recording of Folk Music in California." CFQ, I(1942), 7-23.

[After summarizing sources of information about folk music in California, the author describes a large collection of recordings which he and some thirty-five assistants made between 1938 and 1940. Some of these are in Spanish, though as he describes them they seem to be mostly of lyrical character or children's songs, not narrative ballads. Obviously, however, he cannot mention in this article all the material collected. The recordings are now deposited with the Department of Music at the University of California (Berkeley) and in duplicate in the Archivo of American Folk Song at the Library of Congress in Washington.]

_____. See Lomax, Alan, entry no. 1399.

1252. Cue Cánovas, Agustín. "La música en Guerrero." El Popular (México), 24 de enero de 1949, pp. 7, 10.

[A report on the ninth session of El Congreso Mexicano de Historia which was being held in Guerrero. The program consisted of a study by Vicente T. Mendoza, "La música tradicional en Guerrero" (see entry no. 1478), a paper on artistic music by Jesús C. Romero, and one on musical folklore by Gerónimo Baqueiro Foster. The reporter summarizes in some detail the contents of the studies presented. Only that of Mendoza seems to have touched on romances or corridos.]

1253. Cuéllar, Alfredo B. Charrerías. México: Imprenta Azteca, 1928.

[A collection of poems, articles, essays, and the like about charros and their traditions. Some are by Cuéllar, but much of the book is by other persons. Manuel Musquiz Blanco contributes an article, "La canción mexicana," which is superficial but not uninteresting. Jacobo Dalevuelta is represented by his artistic Corrido del jaripeo, which concerns a festival at the Rancho del Charro in 1927.]

1254. Curioso romance en que se refieren y declaran unas amorosas quejas, que un galán da á su dama, por experimentar poca correspondencia en ella. Puebla: Imp. de D. Pedro de la Rosa, 1817. 2 lvs.

1255. Curtis, F. S. "Spanish Folk-Poetry in the Southwest." SWR, X:2 (January, 1925), 68-71.

[A brief discussion on a non-technical level of the background of Spanish-language popular songs, proverbs, drama, and the like in New Mexico and the southwest. Though there is nothing specific about romances or corridos, some of the description of popular street singers in Santa Fe is interesting and pertinent to the study of ballad literature.]

1256. _____. "Spanish Songs of New Mexico." PTFS, IV(1925), 18-20.

[Treats popular songs and gives some texts with music. None is a genuine corrido or romance, but there are versions of some revolutionary songs (La cucaracha and La Adelita), and Las coplas de Don Simón are mentioned.]

1257. Dalevuelta, Jacobo (Fernando Ramírez de Aguilar). Cariño a Oaxaca. México: Ediciones Botas, 1938. 172 pp. 21 cm.

[Contains an artistic corrido by the author, Cariño a Oaxaca (pp. 169-172). Written very much in the popular manner, it evokes the places, sounds, foods, etc. of Oaxaca.]

1258. _____. Estampas de México. México: n.p., 1930. xi, 320 pp. 23.5 cm.

[A collection of articles about Mexican folklore, drama, popular poetry, and the like. Treatment of the corridos is superficial, but the texts of several interesting compositions are provided. Most of these, however, can be found in other standard works.]

_____. See Cuéllar, Alfredo B., entry no. 1253.

1259. Dávila Garibi, José Ignacio. "La toponomía mexicana en boca de nuestros pregones, copleros, cancioneros y otros ingenios populares." AFSM, VI(1945), 47-81; also in book form, México: Ed. San Ignacio de Loyola, 1946. 121 pp.

[The author refers in passing to corridos which are related to his subject. There is more attention to coplas and other types of popular literature.]

1260. Delgado, Antonio I. "La chilena en Guerrero." Cuauh, No. 1 (febrero de 1950), 34-35.

[Discusses the importance in the state of Guerrero of the chilena, a song-dance derived from the Chilean cueca. It is clear that the texts of the chilena are usually lyrical coplas, but some, including a few examples given here, deal with political events and other nonlyrical subjects.]

1261. Delmotte, J. Romance en elogio de los alumnos del Colegio premios a los alumnos del importante Seminario de Minería, verificada el día 29 de octubre de 1830. México: Galván, [1830?].

1262. _____. Romances en elogio de los alumnos del Colegio Nacional de Minería. México: Galván, 1828. 15 pp.

1263. Demarest, Donald, and Taylor, Coley, eds. The Dark Virgin; The Book of Our Lady of Guadalupe; A Documentary Anthology. Porter's Landing, Freeport, Maine, and New York: Coley Taylor, Inc., 1956. xvi, 256 pp. 24 cm.

[Contains an English translation of a corrido entitled De las apariciones de la Virgen de Guadalupe (pp. 208-212). It was circulating in Coyoacán in 1954 on hojas sueltas and its author is Silvino C. N. Martínez. The translation is rhymed and not too good; nor was the Spanish original apparently very distinguished.]

1264. Descripcion poetica/ de las/ fiestas/ con que la nobilissima/ ciudad de Mexico/ celebró/ el buen sucesso/ de la empressa/ contra los otomanos/ en la restauracion/ de la plaza de Oran/ con licencia de los superiores. / En Mexico por Joseph Bernardo de Hogal, / Ministro e Impressor del Real, y Apostolico Tribunal/ de la Santa Cruzada en todo este Reyno. Año de 1734. (Reproduced photographically in AnMN, Epoca 4a., IV:2 (marzo y abril, 1926), plates between pp. 182-183.)
[An artistic romance in the usual rhetorical style of the period.]

1265. Díaz del Castillo, Bernal. Historia verdadera de la conquista de la Nueva España. 3 vols. México: Editorial Pedro Robredo, 1944. 24.5 cm. (There are innumerable editions of this work.)
[Contains some fragments of romances and pasquines which circulated among the soldiers of the army of Cortés (Vol. I, p. 155; Vol. II, pp. 213, 214, 310-311).]

1266. Díaz y de Ovando, Clementina. "El corrido de la Revolución." Revista de la Universidad Veracruzana (Xalapa, Ver.), No. 6 (abril-junio, 1958), pp. 161-181.
[A good study of the characteristics of the Mexican corrido as it developed during the Revolution. Such matters as style, tone, the personality of corrido heroes, etc. are treated and a great many corrido texts are given by way of illustration.]

1267. ———. "Literatura popular contemporánea." AIIE, No. 21 (1953), 31-53.
[The author examines the nature of the Mexican corridos and documents her discussion with strophes taken from corridos of recent times, mostly compositions written since the outbreak of the Revolution. This is a very informative study both as to the character of the poems and the Mexican psychology which is revealed in them.]

1268. ———. "El romancero y la conquista de México." UnivMex, III:31 (julio de 1949), 7-8; 32 (agosto de 1949), 25-26.
[A well conceived article which, besides citing all the well known references to romances in Bernal Díaz' chronicle, cites other allusions to romances in Díaz' work and seeks out the ballads which inspired them.]

1269. ———. "El valor histórico de los corridos de la Revolución en Zacatecas." Nacion, suplemento dominical, 19 de diciembre, 1948.

1270. Diccionario de la lengua castellana . . . [de] la Real Academia Española [known as the Diccionario de Autoridades]. Vol. II. Madrid: Imprenta de Francisco del Hierro, 1729. 10, 714 pp. 34 cm.
[Contains the first definition of the term corrido that has so far come to light (p. 617): "Corrido. Usado como substantivo es cierto tañido, que se toca en la guitarra u otro instrumento, a cuyo son se cantan las que llaman Xácaras. Diósele este nombre por la ligereza y velocidad con que se tañe."]

1271. Disselhoff, Hans Dietrich. "Zwei mexicanische Corridos aus Colima." IAA, XI(1937), 98-106.
[Contains the texts of two corridos gathered from oral tradition in Colima in 1931: Antonio Salazar and Marcos Torres. Both concern the Cristero uprising. In offering the texts, the author comments upon them and discusses the role of the corrido in Mexican tradition, with references also to its relationship to the romances of Spain.]

1272. Dobie, J. Frank. "El [sic] canción del Rancho de los Olmos." JAF, XXXVI(1923), 192-195.
[A corrido about the difficulties encountered by some cowboys who were trying to cross the Nueces River with a herd of cattle.]

1273. _____, ed. Texas and Southwestern Lore. Austin, Texas, 1927. 259 pp. 24 cm. (Publications of the Texas Folk-Lore Society, No. VI.)
[Contains (pp. 7-22) "Folklore of the Texas-Mexican Vaquero" by Jovita González (see entry no. 1337).]

1274. _____. "Texas-Mexican Border Broadsides." JAF, XXXVI(1923), 185-191.
[Photographic reproductions of some broadsides from Brownsville, Texas: Poesía pronunciada por Ismael de la Cerna momentos antes de ser fusilado en Guatemala, Asesinato de Francisco Villa, Trágica muerte del niño Epifanio Salazar, Tragedia Falcón-Cuellar, Tierna despedida de los hermanos Higinio y Manuel Mercado.]

1275. _____. "Versos de los bandidos." In Texas Folk and Folklore, ed. by Mody C. Boatright, Wilson M. Hudson, and Allen Maxwell. Dallas: Southern Methodist University Press, 1954. Pp. 143-147. (Publications of the Texas Folklore Society, No. XXVI.)
[The text of a corrido preceded by an introduction. There is an English translation of the text.]

1276. _____. "Versos of the Texas Vaqueros." PTFS, No. IV (1925), 30-43.
[Offers the texts of four songs, the first three of which belong to the corrido tradition, though they are not called corridos. Their titles: Versos de los bandidos, Versos de Montalgo, La cancion del Rancho de los Olmos, and El abandonado.]

1277. Domínguez, Francisco. Album musical de Michoacán. México: Talleres Gráficos de la Nación, 1941. 30 pp. 31.5 cm.
[Contains words and music of some popular songs, a few of which are called corridos.]

1278. _____. Sones, canciones y corridos michoacanos. 3 cuadernos. México: Talleres Gráficos de la Nación, n.d.
[A collection of songs with music, some of which are called corridos and some canciones charaperas, which, according to the author, is

another name for corridos in Michoacán. Only one, however, the Corrido de la gotera, in Cuaderno III, is a narrative.]

1279. Dorantes de Carranza, Baltasar. Sumaria relación de las cosas de la Nueva España. México: Imprenta de Museo Nacional, 1902. viii, 491 pp. 23.5 cm.

[Contains a romance by Mateo Rosas de Oquendo in which the poet satirizes the low quality of the immigrants who were coming to América (pp. 150-154).]

1280. Dromundo, Baltasar. "Las canciones revolucionarias." LyP, XII:9 (septiembre, 1934), 419-430.

[This is Chap. X of the author's book, Emiliano Zapata.]

1281. _____. "Los cantos de la Revolución Mexicana." In Homenaje a Enrique José Varona en el cincuentenario de su primer curso de filosofía (1880-1930). La Habana: Publicaciones de la Secretaría de Educación, Dirección de Cultura, 1935. Pp. 429-438; also, UnivMex, II(1931), 213-222.

[An analysis of the songs, particularly the corridos, which grew out of the Revolution. The author tries to show the spirit of the times which produced them.]

1282. _____. Emiliano Zapata, biografía. México: Imprenta Mundial, 1934. 285 pp. 24 cm.

[Chap. X, "Las canciones revolucionarias," treats various types of Revolutionary songs, particularly the corridos, and the singers, such as Marciano Silva, who composed and sang them. In the appendix of his work, the author gives the texts of several corridos.]

1283. _____. Francisco Villa y la "Adelita." Victoria de Durango: n.p., 1936. 45 pp. 23.5 cm.

[A highly romanticized account of Villa's relationship to the supposed heroine of the famous song, La Adelita. In the course of his narrative the author quotes many strophes of the song and also of other popular compositions, including corridos. Also, the paper cover of the volume contains an artistic poem by Dromundo, Romance de la ciudad de Durango.]

1284. Durán, Diego. Historia de las Indias de Nueva-España y islas de Tierra Firme; la publica con un atlas de estampas, notas e ilustraciones José F. Ramírez. 3 vols. Mexico: Editora Nacional, S. A., 1951. 23 cm.

[There is a description of public ceremonies in honor of Indians killed in battle where there apparently were professional singers who related the deeds of the deceased in song (Vol. I, pp. 293 ff.). Also, there is mention of professional singers attached to the houses of noblemen to sing the glories of their ancestors (Vol. II, p. 233).]

1285. Durán, Gustavo. Fourteen Traditional Spanish Songs from Texas. Washington, D. C.: Music Division, Panamerican Union, 1942.

vi, 20 pp. 30.5 cm.
[Included in this collection of texts with music are four corridos:
La pérdida de Puebla, José Mosquera, Leandro Rivera, and La corrida de Kansas. The other songs are of various types.]

1286. _____. "Romance, corrido y plena." BUPan, LXXVI:11 (noviembre de 1942), 630-639.
[A fine study of the relationship between the Spanish romance, the Mexican corrido, and the Puerto Rican plena. The first two, according to Durán, are closely related, while the plena, a satirical and jocose type of song, is quite different from the corrido with which it is contrasted here. Many important aspects of the music of these genres are stressed, such as the unimportance of melodies in the preservation of the romance and the corrido, the fact that corrido melodies are of recent origin, etc.]

1287. Duvalier, Armand. "Romance y corrido." Cri, Año IX, Tomo XV:87 (septiembre de 1937), 8-16; 88 (noviembre de 1937), 135-141.
[An important analysis of the literary aspects of the corrido, particularly with reference to its relationship to the Spanish romance.]

1288. Earle, Henry Edmond. "An Old-Time Collector; Reminiscences of Charles F. Lummis." CFQ, I(1942):2, pp. 179-183.
[Reminiscences of the author about his work with Charles F. Lummis in transcribing songs on wax disks. He mentions "romances," but he admits that, at least upon beginning his work, he knew no Spanish. Also, he speaks of Bécquer's Las golondrinas as being a romance; so his comments are of doubtful value.]

1289. Ellis, Florence Hawley. "Tomé and Father J. B. R." NMHR, XXX:2 (April, 1955), 89-114; 3 (July, 1955), 195-220.
[Contains the text of the Indita del '84 (pp. 206-207), a narrative poem which reports a terrible flood in 1884 at Tomé, a small town about twenty-five miles south of Albuquerque. It is a corrido except in name.]

1290. Escarpit, Robert. Contracorrientes mexicanas. México: Antigua Librería Robredo, 1957.
[A collection of essays about Mexican life, one of which deals with the corrido in laudatory terms.]

1291. Esparza S., Cuauhtémoc. "El caballo mojino." UnivMex, VIII:10 (junio de 1954), 14-16.
[A detailed historical account of the horse race which inspired the corrido along with many details pertaining to the composition of the song and its subsequent vicissitudes. Several texts and a musical transcription are provided.]

1292. Espinosa, Aurelio M. "An Extraordinary Example of Spanish Ballad Tradition in New Mexico." In Stanford Studies in

Language and Literature, 1941. Stanford University, California: Published by the University, 1941. Pp. 28-34.

[The author adds some versions to an earlier study of a romance from New Mexico which relates the Virgin's intercession with Christ to save the soul of one of her devotees. Here he publishes four examples from New Mexico, three from Argentina, and some strophes of a long Spanish poem of the sixteenth or seventeenth century which, though learned in nature, seems to have been inspired by the now lost peninsular version of the popular romance.]

1293. Espinosa, Aurelio M. "Folklore de California." In Miscelánea filológica dedicada a D. Antonio M.ª Alcover. Palma de Mallorca: Imprenta Vda. de S. Piza, 1932. Pp. 111-131.

[Additions to the author's collection of California folklore in the Homenaje a Menéndez Pidal (see ref. 1305). There are sections entitled "Romances vulgares y otros poemitas romancescos" (ten compositions), "Coplas de cuna y rimas infantiles" (twenty compositions), "Coplas populares" (fifty-two amorosas and twenty-eight sentenciosas y burlescas). Bibliographical data and commentary are provided for some compositions.]

1294. _____. "Folklore español de Nuevo México. Traducido de The Journal of American Folk-Lore, vol. XXIII, Octubre-Diciembre de 1910, núm. XC, por el Prof. Carlos E. Porter." RChHG, Año II, Tomo II:5 (primer trimestre de 1912), 189-229.

[The article translated deals with various types of folklore, but not with romances, corridos, or other narrative poetry. There are a few coplas, however. In addition to translating Espinosa's article, Porter adds a few notes of his own.]

1295. _____. "Folklore infantil de Nuevo Méjico." RDTP, X(1954), Cuaderno 4.°, 499-547.

[A collection of ninety-two children's games, songs, etc. A few are coplas, but none of the compostions seems to be a genuine romance. Wherever possible the author gives for each poem a bibliography of Spanish and American variants which would be very useful for comparative purposes. There is also an excellent bibliography at the end.]

1296. _____. "Miscellaneous Materials from the Pueblo Indians of New Mexico." PhilQ, XXI:1 (January, 1942), 121-127.

[A collection of Indian folklore of various types. Included are some songs and verses with Indian texts and English translations. These are called by the author Ballad-Like Refrain from San Juan, I; Ballad-Like Refrain from San Juan, II; Ballad-Like Refrain from San Juan, III. They are fragments of only two or three lines each, but they have some romance-corrido characteristics (most notably despedidas).]

1297. ———. "New Mexican Spanish 'coplas populares.'" Hisp, XVIII:2 (May, 1935), 135-150.
 [The author discusses the vigor of the Spanish copla tradition in New Mexico and offers a number of New Mexican coplas as examples. He divides them into groups according to subject matter.]

1298. ———. "New-Mexican Spanish Folk-Lore." JAF, XXVI (1913), 97-122.
 [This section of Espinosa's continuing study treats proverbs and coplas which incorporate proverbs.]

1299. ———. "New-Mexican Spanish Folk-Lore." JAF, XXIX (1916), 505-535.
 [In this section of Espinosa's continuing study there is a section entitled "Nursery Rhymes and Children's Songs" (pp. 519-535) which contains some popular poetry in the ballad tradition, such as El piojo y la liendre.]

1300. ———. "New Mexican Spanish Folklore (Abstract)." Transactions and Proceedings of the American Philological Association (Hartford, Conn.), XLII(1911), lxiii-lxv.
 [A report on the folklore materials collected in New Mexico and southern Colorado by the author during the years 1902-1910. There are discussions of twenty-four categories including Nos. I, Traditional Spanish Ballads; II, Modern Ballads; III, Vulgar Ballads; IV, Décimas; XI. Satirical Ballads Against Americans and the Church; XIII, Popular Songs; and XIV, Cancionero popular mexicano, which deals with coplas.]

1301. ———. "Otro romance español tradicional." Universidad de los Andes (Mérida Venezuela), I(1938):3, pp. 121-127.
 [A study of a religious romance found in New Mexico, Un angel triste lloraba de ver la cuenta que dió.]

1302. ———. Romancero de Nuevo Méjico. Madrid: C. Bermejo, impresor, 1953. xxiv, 302 pp. 24.5 cm.
 [This is a fundamental work on the subject. After an introduction (pp. 1-16) the author offers his collection of romance texts: Parte I, Romances novelescos tradicionales (sixteen romances, eighty versions of these); Parte II, Romances novelescos varios (twenty-seven romances, fifty-seven versions of these); Parte III, Romances religiosos tradicionales (twelve romances, thirty-eight versions); Parte IV, Romances religiosos varios (nineteen romances, thirty-two versions); Parte V, Corridos, cuandos, inditas (eleven composiciones, seventeen versions); and Parte VI, Fragmentos de romances sobre la historia de España y algunas narraciones poéticas sobre la historia de Nuevo Méjico (five compositions, five versions). The remaining sections of the book are: Lista de los recitadores de nuestros romances y otras narraciones, con su edad y lugar de residencia, y de las fuentes de los materiales encontrados en manuscritos (pp. 277-287); Las melodías

de nuestros romances (twenty-eight melodies) (pp. 289-302). At the beginning of the volume there is a general bibliography of 113 entries (pp. vii-xi) and there are also specialized bibliographies for many of the romances.]

1303. Espinosa, Aurelio M. "Romancero nuevomejicano." RH, XXXIII(1915), 446-560; "Addenda." XL(1917), 215-227; "Nota adicional al Romancero nuevomejicano." XLI(1917), 678-680.

[The initial collection contains 138 compositions or variants. Among these are many traditional Spanish romances and also some corridos, décimas, and other types of popular poetry. The addenda contain versions of two more romances, Camino del Calvario and La Virgen presiente la pasión.]

1304. _____. "Romances españoles tradicionales que cantan y recitan los indios de los pueblos de Nuevo Méjico." BBMP, IX(1932), 97-109.

[After summarizing the history of the Spanish period in New Mexico and adjacent territory, the author studies the romances which have survived among the Indians who speak Spanish. Included are five versions of Camino del Calvario, two of La Virgen sueña la pasión, one of El niño perdido, and one of Delgadina.]

1305. _____. "Los romances tradicionales en California." In Homenaje ofrecido a Menéndez Pidal, Vol. I. Madrid: Librería y Casa Editorial Hernando, 1925. Pp. 299-313.

[A fundamental study with romance texts collected from oral tradition in California.]

1306. _____. "Spanish Folklore in New Mexico." NMHR, I (1926), 135-155.

[Essentially an appeal for more investigation in the field of New Mexican folklore. Among other things, the author stresses the importance of romances and gives complete texts of La aparición and Camino del Calvario.]

1307. _____. "Spanish Tradition Among the Pueblo Indians." In Estudios hispánicos; homenaje a Archer M. Huntington. Wellesley, Mass.: Wellesley College, 1952. Pp. 131-141.

[Among many evidences of Spanish influences is cited the fact that the Pueblo Indians still sing traditional Spanish ballads. The text of one, Por el rastro de la Cruz, is given (p. 139).]

1308. _____. "Traditional Ballads from Andalucía." In Flügel Memorial Volume. Stanford University, California: Published by the University, 1916. Pp. 93-107.

[Thirteen romance texts collected in California among recent immigrants from Andalusia. There is an introduction which discusses the romance tradition in California, and each text is accompanied by notes.]

1309. _____. "Traditional Spanish Ballads in New Mexico." Hisp, XV:2 (March, 1932), 89-102.
[A discussion of the truly traditional ballads thus far discovered in New Mexico. Some texts contained herein have appeared elsewhere, others are new.]

1310. Esteva, Guillermo A. La música oaxaqueña. Oaxaca: Talleres Tipográficos del Gobierno, 1931.
[Boggs (ref. 1181, p. 55) cites this work.]

1311. Fabié, Antonio María. Vida y escritos de fray Bartolomé de las Casas. 2 vols. Madrid: Imprenta de Miguel Ginesta, 1879. 22.5 cm.
[In one passage (Vol. II, p. 240) Las Casas refers to the singing of a romance ("Mira Nero a Tarpeya/á Roma como se ardía").]

1312. La Falange (México), 1922.
[A magazine which, according to Henríquez Ureña (ref. 1367, p. 382), contains a Mexican version of El caballero que busca mujer.]

1313. Farwell, Arthur. Folk-Songs of the West and South: Negro, Cowboy, and Spanish-American. Newton Center, Mass.: The Wa-Wan Press, 1905. 4, 11 pp.
[Mattfeld (ref. 78, p. 35) says that it contains (pp. 6-10) two Spanish American folk songs recorded by Charles F. Lummis and arranged for voice and piano.]

_____. See Lummis, Charles F., entry no. 1409.

1314. Ferrer, J. "Cantares mexicanos." RABA, LXXXVII (1940): 195-196, pp. 3-11.

1315. Fogelquist, Donald F. "The Figure of Pancho Villa in the Corridos of the Mexican Revolution." University of Miami Hispanic-American Studies (Coral Gables, Fla.), No. 3 (March, 1942), 11-22; also translated with the title: "La figura de Pancho Villa en los 'corridos' de la Revolución Mexicana." AmerH, XVII:3 (marzo, 1943), 59-66.
[A study of the figure of Pancho Villa as revealed in representative corridos, fragments of which are quoted textually.]

1316. _____. "The Figure of Pancho Villa in the Literature of the Mexican Revolution." Ph. D. diss., University of Wisconsin, 1941. vii, 507 pp.
[In treating various aspects of Villa's life and character, the author frequently cites corridos, although they are all compositions the texts of which are available elsewhere.]

1317. _____. "Pancho Villa in the Mexican Ballad." Revista interamericana, revista dedicada al estudio de la cultura interamericana, publicada por el Instituto de Asuntos Interamericanos en colaboración con los Pícaros de Quevedo, fraternidad honorífica de la Universidad de la Florida. I(1940):2, pp. 15-17.

[Boggs (ref. 13 [1942], p. 48) indicates that this article contains the text of a corrido sung in Chihuahua, Mexico.]

1318. Folklore. There exists in the Biblioteca del Museo Nacional in Mexico City a volume catalogued thus which contains many nineteenth-century broadsides of romances, décimas, corridos, etc. See entry no. 1246.

1319. "El folklore de la muerte." PyS, XIV(1950), 431-432, 437, 444.

[Boggs (ref. 13 [1950], p. 26) says: "Indicates theme of death in folk dance, poetry, and prayer, in Mexico."]

1320. Folletos de divulgación científica y literaria. México: Universidad Nacional de México, 1922.

[Henríquez Ureña (ref. 1367, p. 378) says that one of these contains texts of Delgadina, Venga a nos el tu reino, and Cántico de sol.]

1321. Freire-Marreco, Barbara. "New-Mexican Spanish Folk-Lore." JAF, XXIX:CXIV (October-December, 1916), 536-546.

[A sketchy though important contribution of some songs sung in velorios among the Indians of the pueblo of Santa Clara. Included is a long cántico about the miracles of San Antonio which is essentially a corrido in form. There are also some oraciones which belong to the romance tradition.]

1322. Frías, Heriberto. El amor de las sirenas <Los destripados>. Mazatlán: Casa Editorial de Valadés y Cía., Sucs., 1908. 477 pp. 19.5 cm.

[A character in the novel sings La Valentina and an accompanist says that he learned the song some time before in Durango and Sinaloa (pp. 227-229). Also, there is an episode wherein some coplas and other songs are sung (pp. 239-245).]

1323. Galindo, Miguel. "El alma de la raza; afinidades hispanoamericanas." BGE, Quinta época, XII (Tomo XXXVIII de la colección completa) (1928), 321-347.

[An attempt to explain the character of language, religion, art, music, and the like by a pseudo-scientific examination of racial factors. In a section on music (pp. 334-347) in which the author tries to seek out what is uniquely Mexican, he clearly tends to depreciate what is truly popular and considers genres like the waltz to be the highest form of popular expression! With the exception of La Adelita, La Valentina, and a few other songs, the compostions he mentions as representative of the best products of the Mexican genius are mostly sentimental love songs in the European tradition of urban Mexicans. He mentions corridos in very unflattering terms and he usually touches on other truly popular genres with equal disapproval.]

1324. _____. Historia de la música mexicana. Colima: Tipografía de "El Dragón," 1933. 636 pp. 24 cm.
[On several occasions the corridos and their music are mentioned in passing in this rather chaotic, though not entirely unrewarding, book.]

1325. _____. La música popular y el sentimiento de la patria. Colima: El Dragón, 1923. 27 pp. 18.5 cm.
[The author believes his country should develop its own popular music from the Spanish and Indian elements in its culture rather than from foreign elements. But his conception of what is popular is revealed when he mentions waltzes, mazurkas, schottisches, etc. as examples of the genres he wishes to cultivate. The article may be ignored.]

1326. Gallardo, Aurelio Luis. Leyendas y romances; ensayos políticos. San Francisco: Enrique Payot y Cía., 1868. 299, ix pp. 23 cm.

1327. Gallop, Rodney. Mexican Mosaic. London: Faber and Faber, Ltd., 1939. 299 pp. 22.5 cm.
[Though there is a great deal about musical folklore in this book of travel impressions, the only item related to my subject is an alabado (p. 129) which is in romance form.]

1328. Gama, Pedro Manuel. "Romance."
[A romance which won third prize in the contest described in my notes to ref. 1143. Nuñez y Domínguez prints its text (ref. 1515, pp. 215-216).]

1329. Gamboa, Fernando. "José Guadalupe Posada; sus tiempos, el hombre, su arte." See entry no. 1234, Cincuenta grabados; reprinted also in Life and Work of the Engraver José Guadalupe Posada, entry no. 1396.
[An excellent study of the artist, his life, his times, the printers who published his work, and his contribution to Mexican art. There is much interesting information about Antonio Vanegas Arroyo, the printer of romances, corridos, and other types of popular literature, for whom Posada worked.]

1330. Gamio, Manuel. Mexican Immigration to the United States. Chicago: University of Chicago Press, 1930. xviii, 262 pp. 21 cm.
[Chap. VII studies the songs of Mexican immigrants. Several corrido texts with English translations are provided.]

_____. See Ceballos Novelo, Roque J., entry no. 1226.

1331. García Bravo y Olivera, R. "Corrido grande de Pancho Villa." Novedades, 22 de enero de 1956, suplemento dominical Núm. 357, p. [6].
[The author writes this full page article in the form of a letter to

Don Manuel Zorrilla Rivera in order to communicate to him information about a Corrido grande de Pancho Villa written by Carlos Abascal, a fellow oaxaqueño. The latter, a corridero (to use the term which the author employs) wrote this long semiartistic poem of about 500 cuartetas to narrate the life and deeds of Villa. Except for its length, the poem is very close to the style and form of the popular corridos, a fact which is not surprising since Abascal is said to be a true poet of the people. About ninety-five strophes of the composition are quoted textually.]

1332. García Cubas, Antonio. El libro de mis recuerdos. México: Imprenta de Arturo García Cubas, Hermanos Sucesores, 1904. 635 pp. 28.5 cm.; 2nda edición. México: Manuel León Sánchez, 1934. 639 pp. 30.5 cm.

[A veritable mine of information about Mexican history, customs, folklore, and the like. There is considerable material about folk songs, including the texts and music of a few (e.g., Las margaritas [p. 439], El payo [p. 547]). But though some of these are historical, they are not narrative and there are no true romances or corridos. Perhaps the most interesting of the historical poems are some décimas about the statue of Carlos IV (pp. 444-445).]

1333. García Gutiérrez, Jesús. "Dos canciones populares." DH, III:11 (15 de septiembre de 1942), 574-577.

[A short article devoted to criticizing the lack of orderly and disciplined work among Mexico's folklorists, many of whom are mentioned by name, and to presenting the background of two very well known songs, La paloma and Adiós, Mamá Carlota. The latter is topical and historical in nature, though learned in origin and unrelated to the romance-corrido tradition.]

1334. García Icazbalceta, Joaquín. "Provincialismos mexicanos." MAM, Tomo III. México: Imprenta de Francisco Díaz de León, 1886; reprinted in the author's Vocabulario de mexicanismos, comprobado con ejemplos y comparado con los de otros países hispano-americanos. México: Tip. y Lit. "La Europea," de J. Aguilar Vera y C.ª, 1899. Pp. [v]-xviii.

[In considering the problem of studying the spoken Spanish of the New World, the author stresses the documentory value of popular literature, especially of "coplas o cantarcillos anónimos" (p. 189).]

_____. See Pomar, Juan Bautista, entry no. 1547.

1335. Garibay K., Angel María. Historia de la literatura náhuatl. Primera parte (Etapa autónoma: de c. 1430 a 1521). México: Editorial Porrúa, S. A., 1953. 501 pp. 24 cm.; Segunda parte (El trauma de la conquista (1521-1750). México: Editorial Porrúa, S. A., 1954. 426 pp. 24 cm.

[In the Primera parte there are data about Indian singers and their compositions, some of which were historical in that they dealt with past events and heroic deeds (pp. 161 ff.). The author describes the historical songs of the Aztecs and compares them with modern corridos (pp. 218 ff.), and there is mention of a romance written by Fernando Ixtlilxóchitl (p. 255). Later he quotes a passage from Durán regarding the singers attached to the homes of nobles to sing of the heroic deeds of their ancestors (p. 339), and he prints a passage from Pomar concerning the custom of singing songs about illustrious people (p. 342). In the Parte segunda there are some lines taken from a narrative poem about the conquest of Mexico and found in the Cantares mexicanos. Garibay suggests the hypothesis that it was collected from oral tradition no later than 1524 and declares that it might be considered "el más antiguo de los 'corridos' mexicanos que celebran los hechos nacionales (p. 90)." He also offers a partial text of another poem about the fall of Tenochtitlán which he thinks was in oral tradition around 1523 (p. 91).]

1336. Gómez Leal, Efraín. "Divagaciones sobre el folklore." RFCC, Núm. 5 (abril de 1949), 145-151.
[Though there are no romances or other narrative poems, the author describes the singing of coplas and prints the texts of several of them.]

1337. González, Jovita. "Folk-Lore of the Texas-Mexican Vaquero." In Texas and Southwestern Lore, ed. by Frank Dobie. Austin, 1927. Pp. 7-22. (Publications of the Texas Folk-Lore Society, No. VI.)
[After discussing the background of the vaquero, the author offers some of his stories and songs. The songs are not corridos or other narratives, but there is mention of one form of corrido, the tragedia, of which the author says: "There is only one type of song that is typically of the vaquero, and that is the tragedia." Unfortunately, she provides no texts.]

1338. ———. "Tales and Songs of the Texas-Mexicans." In Man, Bird, and Beast, ed. by J. Frank Dobie. Austin, 1930. Pp. 86-116. (Publications of the Texas Folk-Lore Society, No. VIII.)
[Among the popular songs offered here is a narrative in décimas about one Remigio Treviño, who was captured and executed in 1863 for a raid on Río Grande City. Of it the author says: "This is the earliest Mexican ballad composed on Texas soil that I have found." Also, there is a version of El payo ("Estaba un payo sentado/ en las trancas de un corral").]

1339. González Bravo, Antonio. "La canción popular mexicana." México, revista trimestral (México), Año I:1 (julio de 1937), 9-12.
[A superficial study of popular songs, including corridos, which is based mostly on the work of Rubén S. Campos and Los niños y la poesía en América by the Argentine scholar Ernesto Morales.]

1340. González Casanova, Pablo. "Un corrido 'macarrónico' hispano-azteca." IL, II(1934), 20-23; reprinted from AnMN, Epoca IV, Vol. VIII(1933), 93-96.

[Two texts of a "corrido" about two Indians making love. It is written in burlesqued language, a mixture of Spanish and Indian elements, and should really nor be classified as a corrido.]

1341. _____. Sátira anónima del siglo XVIII. México, D. F.: Fondo de Cultura Económica, 1953. 234 pp. 17.5 cm.

[This volume contains a number of interesting texts, mostly semi-popular in character. Most of them are décimas, but there are a few romances and some coplas.]

1342. González Hurtado, Rodolfo. Leyendas del Bajío. México: Editorial "Cultura," 1931. 230 pp. 19 cm.

[There is some attention to popular songs, though without specific mention of corridos or romances.]

1343. González Obregón, Luis. México viejo; noticias históricas, tradiciones, leyendas y costumbres. México, D. F.: Editorial Patria, S. A., 1945. xv, 742 pp. 23 cm. (There are other editions.)

[Contains a fragment of a satirical copla sung by the soldiers of Iturbide (p. 666).]

1344. Goodwyn, Frank. "Ballad of Manuel Rodríguez." In Mustangs and Cow Horses, ed. by J. Frank Dobie, Mody C. Boatright, and Harry H. Ransom. Austin, 1940. Pp. 304-306. (Publications of the Texas Folk-Lore Society, No. 16.)

[A fragmentary text with music of a corrido which the author heard sung by a Mexican vaquero on the King Ranch. It concerns a cowboy who, after having been thrown from his horse, decides to take up cotton picking.]

1345. _____. "Folk-Lore of the King Ranch Mexicans." In Southwestern Lore, ed. by J. Frank Dobie. Austin, 1931. Pp. 48-62. (Publications of the Texas Folk-Lore Society, No. IX.)

[Among other things, the author prints the text and music of a corrido entitled El toro moro.]

1346. _____. "A North Mexican Ballad: José Lizorio." WF, VI(1947), 240-248.

[The author seeks the origins of the Corrido de José Lizorio in ancient literature. He treats such themes as the mother's curse on her son, the significance of José falling with his arms crossed, and the like. The text of the corrido which he prints is taken from Mendoza's El romance español y el corrido mexicano.]

1347. _____. "Ramón Miranda and His Songs." WF, VIII(1949), 219-234.

[An article about a wandering Mexican singer from Michoacán who was singing in taverns around Chicago. The compositions which are given as examples of his work are not corridos or other types of narratives. Some, however, like Aquí en los Estados Unidos, are commentaries which are very close to satirical corridos.]

1348. _____. "El toro moro." In Texas Folk and Folklore, ed. by Mody C. Boatright, Wilson M. Hudson, and Allen Maxwell. Dallas: Southern Methodist University Press, 1954. Pp. 147-150. (Publications of the Texas Folklore Society, No. XXVI.)
[The text of a corrido preceded by a short introduction. An English translation is provided.]

1349. _____. "Versos populares de los tejanos de habla española." ASFM, V(1944), 415-433.
[A very useful collection of popular poetry in Spanish which the author gathered in Texas. Included are some décimas and several corridos which are published with the name of versos.]

Gorostiza, Manuel Eduardo de. See entry no. 1588.

1350. Gould, Cassius W. "An Analysis of the Folk Music in the Oaxaca and Chiapas Area of Mexico." Ph. D. diss., Northwestern University, 1954. 327 pp.
[According to the summary in Dissertation Abstracts, No. 11 (November, 1954), pp. 2085-2086, this study deals in passing with corridos, though it is apparent that its main emphasis is on Indian music.]

1351. Gras, José, ed. Canciones del terruño; libro de canciones modernas. Primera edición. Contiene canciones españolas, mexicanas, colombianas, de zarzuelas, operetas, jotas, canciones populares, aires típicos mexicanos, corridos y todas las canciones más escogidas y en boga en la actualidad. Los Angeles, California: Librería Española, 1925. 118 pp.

1352. Grijalva de León, Ricardo. Pancho Datos, cantor popular de la Revolución Mexicana y el más genial improvisador. 2ª ed. México, 1957. 49 pp. 33 cm.
[An artistic poem in sextillas but written in a popular style somewhat in the manner of Martín Fierro. The hero of the composition is Francisco Datos Cabrera, apparently a popular singer who took part in the Madero revolution in the neighborhood of the La Laguna region.]

1353. Gruening, Ernest. Mexico and Its Heritage. New York: D. Appleton-Century Co., 1928. xix, 728 pp. 23 cm.
[The last chapter, entitled "Cultural Products of the Revolution" (pp. 635-653) includes treatment of the corrido. Some texts with English translations are given.]

1354. Guerrero, Eduardo, ed. Canciones y corridos populares, Tomo I. México, 1924. 230 broadsides stapled together for circulation in book form.

[These are corridos which Guerrero published originally as hojas sueltas for sale to popular corridistas who depended upon his print shop as a source of such broadsides.]

1355. Guerrero, Eduardo, ed. Corridos históricos de la Revolución desde 1910 a 1930 y otros notables de varias épocas. México, 1931. 110 broadsides stapled together.

[A very important collection of hojas sueltas.]

1356. _____, ed. La musa popular; corridos de amor y cantos sentimentales del pueblo mexicano. México, 1931.

[Another collection similar to those listed in the two previous entries. This collection, however, contains relatively few corridos.]

1357. _____, ed. Versos jocosos para reír y pasar el rato. México, n.d. 103 broadsides stapled together.

[This collection of broadsides contains very few corridos.]

1358. Guitar Method with Guitar Arrangements of Spanish-American Folk Songs of New Mexico. New Mexico: Works Project Administration, Music Project (New Mexico), 1939. Mimeographed.

[Chase (ref. 25, p. 226) says: "Includes 9 Spanish songs collected in New Mexico (Spanish words only)."]

1359. Hansen, Terrence L. "Corridos in Southern California." WF, XVIII:3 (July, 1959), 203-232; 4 (October, 1959), 295-315.

[A collection of thirty-three corrido texts with music and English translations. Gathered in southern California, some of them are variants of well known Mexican corridos; others have not appeared elsewhere.]

1360. Hare, Maud Cuney. "Folk Music of the Creoles." Musical Observer (New York), XIX:9 (September-October, 1920), 16-18; 10 (November, 1920), 12-14.

[Chase (ref. 25, p. 26) comments: "Includes a section on Spanish-Creole music."]

1361. Hechos del Cap. D. Miguel Velázquez Lorea. Alguacil del Santo Tribunal de la Inquisición. Alcalde de la Santa Hermandad y Juez de la Acordada. Año de 1732. Imprenta de Joseph Bernardo de Hogal.

[Mendoza lists the work (ref. 1487, p. 785).]

1362. Hediger, Ernest S. "Mexico's Corrido Goes to War." IAmM, I:6 (October, 1942), 28-32.

[An article which includes several texts of corridos inspired by Mexico's entry into World War II.]

1363. Helfritz, Hans. "Volksmusik in Mexiko." NMus, XVII:39 (Dezember, 1938), 9.

[A brief article about Mexican popular songs. The author first describes mariachi orchestras and their music and then devotes a few lines to singers of corridos. His main contribution is the music only of La tragedia del Chojo Ladislao. There is no indication where he discovered this corrido.]

1364. Hendrix, William S. "The Source of 'Oh, Bury Me Out on the Prairie.'" Hisp, XXVII(1944), 29-33.

[The author suggests that the American cowboy song may be related to the Spanish romance theme which contains the line, "No me entierren en sagrado."]

1365. Henestrosa, Andrés. "Las canciones del Istmo de Tehuantepec." UnivM, I:6 (julio de 1936), 6-7.

[The author states that there is practically no truly autochthonous music in Tehuantepec; such production as there has been is merely adaptation of models from outside, mostly Spanish. Also, he notes that the music of such adaptations is usually better than the words. There is no mention of romances or corridos. However, in speaking of one Lázaro Pineda of Ixhuatán, Henestrosa says: ". . . Lázaro, a su vez, mejor poeta que músico, canta en las ferias de su pueblo una descripción de la tierra donde no falta el elogio de las calles, de los frutos y del río donde no se estanca el cielo." Such a song must be related to certain regional corridos of similar nature.]

1366. _____. "Música mestiza de Tehuantepec." RevMM, I(1942): 5, pp. 107-109; 7, pp. 151-154.

[The author believes that the music of Tehuantepec is a synthesis of Spanish and Indian elements: "Estas canciones son, por fuera, indias, por dentro, europeas, es decir, españolas." He refers particularly to La llorona, La petenera, and La sandunga, that is, to semipopular songs, usually by known composers. There is no mention of romances, corridos, or other narrative types. He includes, however, some snatches of copla texts, though he apparently believes that they are only dichos.]

1367. Henríquez Ureña, Pedro, and Wolfe, Bertram D. "Romances tradicionales en México." In Homenaje ofrecido a Menéndez Pidal, tomo II. Madrid: Librería y Casa Editorial Hernando, 1925. Pp. 375-390.

[One of the earliest systematic collections of romances from Mexico. There are versions of many traditional Spanish compositions along with interesting Mexican adaptations of some of these to corrido form.]

1368. Herrera Frimont, Celestino. Corridos de la Revolución. Pachuca, Hidalgo: Ediciones del Instituto Científico y Literario, 1934. 169 pp. 23 cm.

[Thirty-five corrido texts, some with music. There is also a brief introductory study of the corrido.]

1369. Herrera Frimont, Celestino. "Los corridos de la Revolución." LyP, XII:7 (julio, 1934), 326-335.

[The text of this article is the same as that which appeared earlier in El Universal Ilustrado (see the next entry). However, the author adds here the texts of two corridos, Los combates de Celaya and La persecución de Villa, along with some bibliographical notes.]

1370. _____. "Los 'Corridos' y la Revolución." El Universal Ilustrado (México), 23 de enero, 1930, 30-31, 39.

[An introduction to the corrido with passages from several texts to illustrate the nature of the genre. The article is preceded by a note: "De la selección de 'Corridos' de la Revolución, que se editará próximamente en esta ciudad" (see entry no. 1368).]

1371. _____. "La máquina loca." El Universal Ilustrado (México), 15 de mayo, 1930, p. 23.

[The incident of the "máquina loca" during Carranza's flight from Mexico City in 1920 inspired a famous corrido which is probably treated in this article by an investigator who, at the time he wrote this, was actively interested in the corridos of the Revolution.]

1372. Herring, Hubert. See Chávez, Carlos, entry no. 1230.

1373. Hill, Gertrude. "Folklore in Southwestern Literature, with Special Reference to New Mexico." Pal, LXIV:9-10 (October, 1957), 265-271.

[A useful listing of bibliographical sources of information about the folklore of the Southwest. Among the subjects treated are corridos and other popular songs of the area.]

Hodge, F. W. See Watkins, Frances E., entry no. 1680.

1374. Horta, Manuel. Ponciano Díaz, silueta de un torero de ayer. México: Imprenta Aldina, 1943. 195 pp. 20 cm.

[A biography of the famous matador with mention of some of his predecessors. Included are several texts of corridos: Lino Zamora (pp. 47-51), a song about Ponciano Díaz (pp. 77-78), a corrido about the death of Bernardo Gaviño (pp. 88-92), and one on the death of Ponciano Díaz (pp. 188-192). There are a few other isolated fragments of corridos scattered through the book.]

Hudson, Wilson M. See Boatright, Mody C., entries nos. 1174-1178.

1375. Hurtado, G. Nabor, comp. Sones, canciones y corridos de Nayarit. Secretaría de Educación Pública, 1935. 25 pp. mimeographed.

1376. Inclán, Luis G. El libro de las charrerías. Edición y prólogo de Manuel Toussaint. México: Librería de Porrúa Hnos. y Cía., 1940. xiv, 313 pp. 17.5 cm.

[An edition of several of Inclán's works. Three are in décimas

(Recuerdos del Chamberín, El capadero de la Hacienda de Ayala, and Don Pascasio Romero) and they are written in semipopular style. There are bibliographical data about the various editions of these works.]

1377. International Institute of Intellectual Cooperation. Musique et chansons populaires. Paris: Societé des Nations, Institut International de Coopération Intellectuelle, 1934. 256 pp. 22.5 cm.
[The Library of Congress card indicates that there is a section on Mexico contributed by the Ministry of National Education. Mexico seems to be the only Hispanic country represented.]

1378. "Isabel Villaseñor: homenaje." Humanismo (México), Nos. 9-10 (marzo-abril, 1953), 45-52.
[Contains a brief eulogy of Isabel Villaseñor followed by the texts of three of her corridos. Though they are semilearned compositions, they deal with current events and were written to circulate on a semipopular level as left-wing propaganda.]

1379. Kennedy, Stetson. "Cantantes callejeros y La cucaracha." SFQ, VI(1942), 149-151.
[The author reports that street singers in Key West and Tampa sing La cucaracha with improvised verses. He provides the texts of some representative strophes.]

Kinscella, Hazel. See Spizzy, Mable Seeds, entry no. 1636.

1380. Kittle, J. L. "Folk Music of the Upper Rio Grande." SWR, XXX:2 (Winter, 1945), 192-195.
[The author discusses alabados, dances, and entregas de novios and gives some melodies without literary texts. There is no mention of romances, corridos, or coplas, but there is some discussion of the art of puetas and their style of singing.]

1381. Komadina, Tonia Ann. "The Spanish Folksong in New Mexico." M. A. thesis, University of New Mexico, 1934. 93 pp.
[Perfunctory treatment of folk songs in general with an appendix containing mostly lyrical love songs. No romances or corridos are mentioned.]

1382. Kress, Dorothy M. "El folklore mexicano de la época colonial." ND, XIX:1 (enero de 1938), 14-15.
[An unimportant description of the whole of Mexican folklore for the general reader. The comments on corridos, coplas, El Negrito Peota, and other similar subjects are very elementary.]

1383. Lance, Donald M. "The Personification of Animals in the Relación of Mexico." In "And Horns on the Toads," ed. by Mody C. Boatright, Wilson M. Hudson, and Allen Maxwell. Dallas: Southern

Methodist University Press, 1959. Pp. 108-121.

[Studies the origin of the relación in Spain and then offers texts and commentary on several Mexican compositions. Among them is El casamiento de Huitlacoche.]

1384. Larreba, A. "El cantar popular; esbozo crítico literario, escrito con motivo de los «Cantares» de Carlos Ciaño." El diario del hogar (México), 6 de enero de 1884, 4-5; reprinted in RevM, I:9 (7 de mayo de 1942), 200-204.

[In discussing the simple, unpretentious poetry of the Asturian poet, Carlos García Ciaño, the author calls upon other poets to attempt the difficult task of writing compositions that will appeal to the common people. He quotes some strophes, mostly in copla form, from the type of poems which he has in mind. Although all, with perhaps one exception, appear to be nonpopular in tone, they are close to traditional coplas, and the author's comments show that he is moving toward a literary appreciation of genuine popular poetry.]

1385. Lea, Aurora Lucero-White. Literary Folklore of the Hispanic Southwest. San Antonio: The Naylor Company, 1953. xv, 247 pp. 22 cm.

[Part II (pp. 113-149) is entitled "The Romances (Ballads)-Corridos." It contains sections on the romance, corridos, and corrido style. Many texts are provided and there is a brief bibliography (pp. 241-243).]

1386. _____. "Our Treasury of Spanish Folklore." NMFR, IX(1954-1955), 15-19.

[The author reminisces on her life as a collector of folklore materials, and she prints the text of one version of Delgadina.]

_____. See also Lucero-White, Aurora, entry no. 1405.

1387. Leal, Luis. "Un corrido cervantino." UnivMex, IX:12 (agosto de 1955), 21, 32.

[The author calls attention to a romance jácaro of Andalusian origin which Cervantes incorporates textually into his play, El rufián dichoso. A romance about the death of a bullfighter, it is compared to Mexican corridos about similar themes. In style the Spanish poem is, indeed, strikingly similar to corridos.]

1388. _____. "La cucaracha." UnivMex, VIII:5 (enero de 1954), 15-17.

[The author show that the famous song of the Villistas was known in Mexico during the nineteenth century and that its origins are undoubtedly in the Spanish peninsula. Vicente T. Mendoza adds some documents at the end of Leal's article in support of its thesis.]

1389. _____. "El 'ejemplo', género literario popular." UnivMex, VIII:9 (mayo de 1954), 14-17.

[The author traces the origins of ejemplos (popular poems which narrate situations where a moral transgressor is punished for his sins) back to chronicles of the colonial period. From modern times he gives some compositions in verse, including some corridos. Vicente T. Mendoza provides some "Apostillas al tema" in support of Leal's thesis and includes additional verses that supplement the original article.]

1390. León, Nicolás. El Negrito Poeta mexicano y sus populares versos; contribución para el folk-lore nacional. México: Imprenta del Museo Nacional, 1912. 234 pp. 16.5 cm.

[The author summarizes what little is known about José Vasconcelos, El Negrito Poeta, who apparently died about 1760. Then, after giving a bibliography of the calendars which from about 1856 were responsible for publicizing and popularizing episodes and verses associated with the famous singer, the author, in six sections or chapters, relates incidents and verses contained in the calendars. The outstanding merits of El Negrito Poeta were his quick wit and his skill as a repentista poet. His poems were usually four-line coplas, though there is one instance of a cuarteta glossed by décimas.]

1391. Leredo, Pablo. "La Revolución en estrofas de corridos." Revista de revistas (México), 20 de noviembre, 1932.

[A brief study of the Mexican Revolution as reflected in certain strophes of corridos. There are brief quoted passages from La Adelita, La batalla de Celaya, La persecución de Villa, La triste despedida de Emiliano Zapata, and La muerte de Pancho Villa (though the author himself does not provide these titles). Interesting as an early attempt to view the Revolution through its songs, the article is quite sketchy because Leredo is obviously not familiar with very many corridos.]

1392. Lerín, Manuel. "La poesía y la Revolución Mexicana." La República (México), No. 45 (1 de enero de 1951), 25.

[A brief treatment of the relationship between Mexican poetry and the Revolution. The author suggests that a study of the corrido for its historical value would be fruitful.]

1393. Leslie, John Kenneth. "Un romance español en México y dos canciones de los vaqueros norteamericanos: la influencia del tema 'no me entierren en sagrado.'" RDTP, XIII(1957), Cuaderno 3.°, 286-298.

[The author cites additional evidence which supports the thesis of William S. Hendrix (see entry no. 1364) that the American cowboy songs, Oh, Bury Me Out on the Prairie and Bury Me Not on the Lone Prairie, are probably derived from the "No me entierren en sagrado" theme of Spanish-Mexican romance tradition.]

1394. Lesser, Alexander. "Bibliography of American Folklore, 1915-1928." JAF, XLI(1928), 1-60.

[A bibliography which contains some entries about Mexican popular songs and poetry.]

1395. El libro de oro de la poesía mexicana. Romancero de la independencia, poesías folklóricas y patrióticas. 2 vols. México, 1958.

1396. Life and Work of the Engraver José Guadalupe Posada. Vol. IV, No. 21 (January and February of 1958) of Artes de México (Edition in English). Forty-seven numbered pages and many unnumbered pages of illustrations. There is also an edition in Spanish.

[A complete number of the publication devoted exclusively to Posada, the famous illustrator of corridos and other forms of popular literature. There are three articles: "José Guadalupe Posada, the Popular Artist" by Diego Rivera, "José Guadalupe Posada, His Times, the Man, His Art" by Fernando Gamboa, and "José Guadalupe Posada, His Technique and Style" by Jean Charlot. In addition there is a fine collection of engravings by Posada.]

1397. Lira, Miguel N. Héroes de corridos. México: En la imprenta de Miguel N. Lira, Fábula, 1946. 87 pp. 15 cm.

[In an introductory essay replete with illustrative corrido texts, the author (who is Mexico's most outstanding cultivator of artistic corridos) seeks to characterize the salient qualities of corrido heroes, not only in Mexico but all over America. Then he offers the texts of seventeen corridos. The first thirteen are of popular origin, most of them being old favorites; the last four are artistic corridos by Lira himself and by other cultivators of the genre.]

1398. "List of Works in the New York Public Library Relating to Mexico (Language, Art and Folklore)." BNYPL, XIII:12 (December, 1909), 809-810.

[A useful early bibliography of materials about Mexico, though it has been superseded, of course, by more recent works.]

Lomax, Alan. See Lomax, John A., entry no. 1401.

1399. _____, and Cowell, Sydney Robertson. American Folk Song and Folk Lore; A Regional Bibliography. New York: Progressive Educational Association, 1942. 59 pp. 21.5 cm.

[Chase (ref. 25, p. 223) says: "Section 10, Spanish-American, p. 49-52."]

1400. Lomax, John. "Two Songs of Mexican Cowboys from the Rio Grande Border." JAF, XXVIII(1915), 376-378.

[Two texts without music of songs which are, in reality, corridos, though neither bears the name. Both treat incidents of purely local interest to cowboys working on a certain ranch. Their titles: La corrida de los toros and Los vaqueros de Las Catarinas.]

1401. _____, and Lomax, Alan. American Ballads and Folk Songs. New York: Macmillan, 1934. xxxix, 625 pp. 26.5 cm.

[Contains some songs in Spanish which were collected along the

Texas border (pp. 361-368). Included is a version of the Tragedia de Heraclio Bernal with music, text, and English translation.]

1402. López, Patricio Antonio. Breve, claro, llano, simple, narrativo y verdadero Romance a la violenta muerte que proditoriamente ejecutó D. José de Estrada Tuñón el día 13 de julio del año de 1720 en el coronel D. Gonzalo Gámez Mexía, Gentilhombre de la Cámara de Su Majestad y Gobernador que fue de la Nueva Veracruz. Que entonces escribió D. Patricio Antonio López, Cacique zapoteca de uno de los Valles de Antequera y dedicó al Corregidor y Juez que fue de esta causa, a cuyo celo se debió el desagravio de la Justicia, con la punición del homicida y degüello que en él se ejecutó en la plaza de esta Corte. . . . Con licencia de los Superiores, en la Imprenta de la Vda. de Miguel de Ortega y Bonilla, Año de 1724.
[The title as given above comes from Mendoza (ref. 1487, p. 784). Torres-Ríoseco and Warner (ref. 1658, p. 53) provide a more accurate, though imcomplete, transcription of the original with antiquated spelling and punctuation.]

1403. _____. Triumphos aclamados contra vandoleros por la real justicia que . . . a conseguido el capitan D. Miguel Velazques Lorea . . . le ha honrado. Obsequioso escribe . . . D. . . . Puebla: M. de Ortega, 1723. (20) pp.
[Cited by Torres-Ríoseco and Warner (ref. 1658, p. 54).]

1404. _____. Triumphos, que la real justicia ha conseguido de otros 40. vandoleros con los hechos en la vida; y estremos en la muerte, de Manuel Calderas, uno de sus principales caudillos, condenado con todos sus compañeros por famosos grazatores, en la pena de el ultimo suplicio: por el cap. Don Miguel Velasquez Lorea . . . con la sucesión de ella en D. Joseph Velasquez Lorea, su hijo y sucesor. Lleva estampado el horroroso, y ferreo instrumento con que se haze justicia de los delinquentes. Lo escribe . . . D. . . . México: Rivera, 1726. (12) pp.
[Cited by Torres-Ríoseco and Warner (ref. 1658, p. 54).]

1405. Lucero-White, Aurora. "The Corrido and Other Poetic Compilations of New Mexico." Unpublished MS in the files of the New Mexico Writers' Project, Santa Fe, New Mexico.

1406. _____. The Folklore of New Mexico. Vol. I. Santa Fe: Seton Village Press, 1941. 49 pp. 23.5 cm.
[A collection of folksongs and stories including several corridos and romances, some from general Hispanic traidtion, some from New Mexico.]

_____. See Austin, Mary, entry no. 1159.

1407. Luján, Joseph. Nueva Relación Famosa, intitulada: El Theatro de Morpheo. Discurrióla en México Joseph Luján. Con las licencias necesarias. En la Imprenta de la Biblioteca Mexicana, enfrente de San Agustín. Año de 1861 [sic].

[Listed by Mendoza (ref. 1487, p. 784). His entry is exactly as copied above, but the date must be wrong; it undoubtedly was 1761.]

1408. Lummis, Charles F. The Land of Poco Tiempo. New York: Charles Scribner's Sons, 1893. xii, 310 pp. 23 cm.; also 1906; also 1925.

[Chap. IX, "New Mexican Folk Songs," contains a description of the manner of singing folk songs in New Mexico. Though there are no texts of romances or corridos as such, those of some other types of narrative or topical songs are given with music. Also, there are some coplas printed under the heading of dichos.]

1409. _____. Spanish Songs of Old California; Pianoforte Accompaniments by Arthur Farwell. Los Angeles: privately printed, 1923. 35 pp.; also, New York: G. Schirmer, 1929 [?]. 3 unnumbered pp., 31 pp. (Schirmer's American Folk-Song Series, No. 11).

[A collection of fourteen traditional songs, none of them corridos. One, however, El charro ("Estaba un charro sentado/en las trancas de un corral"), is the narrative song of Hispanic tradition usually known as El payo.]

_____. See Watkins, Frances E., entries nos. 1680 and 1681. See also Earle, Henry Edmond, entry no. 1288.

1410. M. B., Dr. "Cantares infantiles." El mundo ilustrado (México), II:14 (31 de julio de 1910).

[Mendoza (ref. 1463, p. 101) gives some verses derived from Mambrú which he found in this article.]

1411. McCoy, William J. Folk Songs of the Spanish Californians. San Francisco: Sherman, Clay and Co., 1926. 31 pp.

1412. MacCurdy, Raymond R. "Un romance tradicional recogido en Luisiana: Las señas del marido." RHM, XIII(1947), 164-166.

[A version of Las señas del marido which the author found in Delacroix, Louisiana. Text and music are provided.]

1413. _____, and Stanley, Daniel D. "Judaeo-Spanish Ballads from Atlanta, Georgia." SFQ, XV(1951), 221-238.

[Texts and music of eight ballads sung by a Jewish woman who learned them in Rhodes. They include Amadí, La doncella guerrera, A la orilla de una fuente, La dama y el pastor, La malcasada del pastor, La traición, Trubador (sic), and Don Bueso.]

McNeely, John H. See Braddy, Haldeen, entry no. 1185.

1414. McNeil, Norman Laird ("Brownie"). The Brownie McNeil Collection of Mexican corridos in the University of Texas Fine Arts School Library.

1415. _____. "El contrabando del Paso" and "Corrido de Kansas." In Texas Folk and Folklore, ed. by Mody C. Boatright, Wilson M. Hudson, and Allen Maxwell. Dallas: Southern Methodist University Press, 1954. Pp. 150-152. (Publications of the Texas Folklore Society, No. XXVI.)

[Texts of two corridos with brief introductions. English translations of the texts are provided.]

1416. _____. "Corridos de asuntos vulgares Corresponding to the Romances vulgares of the Spanish." M. A. thesis, University of Texas, 1944. xxxv, 329 pp.

[After a brief introduction which outlines the history of the romance in Spain and the corrido in Mexico and Chile, the author provides texts with explanatory notes of a large number of corridos grouped according to subject matter (e.g., outlaw ballads, historical ballads, "place" ballads, etc.). The texts and notes are very useful. The main deficiency of the work is the author's failure to cite the sources of the texts which he prints.]

1417. _____. "Corridos of the Mexican Border." In Mexican Border Ballads and Other Lore, ed. by Mody C. Boatright. Austin, Texas, 1946. Pp. 1-34. (Publications of the Texas Folk-Lore Society, No. XXI.)

[A very interesting study of some corridos from Texas. Texts, music, and very helpful historical data about the songs are provided.]

1418. Major, Mabel; Smith, Rebecca W.; and Pearce, T. M. Southwest Heritage; A Literary History with Bibliography. Albuquerque: University of New Mexico Press, 1938. 165 pp. 23.5 cm.

[Chap. III, "Spanish Folk Dramas and Songs," discusses corridos briefly and superficially along with autos, alabados, and other types of popular literature.]

1419. María y Campos, Armando de. Imagen del mexicano en los toros. México: Editorial Al Sonar el Clarín, 1953. 268 pp. 19 cm.

[Contains the texts of two corridos about a contest between the rival bullfighters, Francisco Jiménez and Juan León, in 1887 (pp. 143-147). Also, there is a copla that might be a fragment of a corrido (p. 239).]

1420. _____. Los payasos, poetas del pueblo (El circo en México). México: Botas, 1939. 262 pp. 19.5 cm.

[A study of the popular poetry associated with circuses in Mexico from the eighteenth century to the present. Many of the songs composed and sung by clowns are similar in form to corridos.]

1421. _____. Ponciano, el torero con bigotes. México: Ediciones Xochitl, 1943. 218 pp. 18.5 cm.

[A biography of the famous torero based in large part upon popular poems and corridos. Many texts are given.]

1422. María y Campos, Armando de. Los toros en México en el siglo XIX, 1810-1863; reportazgo retrospectivo de exploración y aventura. México: "Acción Moderna Mercantil," 1938. 112 pp. 23 cm.

[The text of a well known corrido about the death of Bernardo Gaviño is reprinted (pp. 97-99).]

1423. Marino Flores, Anselmo. "Bibliografía antropológica del estado de Guerrero." BBAA, XV-XVI(1952-1953), Parte I, 233-289.

[A very useful bibliography which contains several references to corridos which were new to me. Most are items which appeared in the Diario de Guerrero on the occasion of the IX Reunión del Congreso Mexicano de Historia held in Chilpancingo in January, 1949. Many of the items are annotated. Unfortunately, there are many typographical errors in the work.]

1424. Martínez, José de J. Canciones mexicanas. 2 vols. México: E. Munguia, 1916.

[Chase (ref. 25, p. 187) comments: "Includes Valentina, La cucaracha, Bonitas las tapatías." The early date of the volume would make its texts of some of these famous Revolutionary songs very interesting.]

1425. Martínez, José Luis. Literatura mexicana, siglo XX, 1910-1949. Segunda parte: guías bibliográficas. México: Antigua Librería Robredo, 1950. 202 pp. 21 cm.

[A very useful bibliography of Mexican literature listed by authors. It incorporates works of all kinds, including a great many volumes dealing with popular literature and music. It lists only books, however; no articles are included. Its most serious deficiency is its failure to give complete bibliographical data (e.g., publishers, number of pages, and the like).]

Mattfeld, Julius. See entry no. 78.

Maxwell, Allen. See Boatright, Mody C., entries nos. 1174-1178.

1426. Mayer-Serra, Otto. "Mexican Musical Folklore." The Etude (Philadelphia), LXI:1 (January, 1943), 17, 58, 72.

[A brief consideration of the corrido and the mariachi takes up this first installment in a proposed series of articles. The author treats the history of the corrido and its literary and musical characteristics. The discussion is, of course, quite elementary in keeping with the character of the publication in which it appears.]

1427. _____. Panorama de la música mexicana desde la independencia hasta la actualidad. México: El Colegio de México, 1941. 193 pp. 23.5 cm.

[A very complete history of Mexican music. The only direct mention of the corrido, however, seems to be in a passage where the author comments on the European and indigenous elements to be found in the corrido's music (pp. 149-150).]

1428. Mechling, William Hubbs. "Stories and Songs from the Southern Atlantic Coastal Region of Mexico." JAF, XXIX(1916), 547-558.

[Among other folklore materials from the area around Veracruz and southern Mexico, the author prints a version of the Corrido de Macario Romero, a décima, and some other versos.]

1429. Los mejores corridos mexicanos. México: n.p., n.d. 96 pp. 16.5 cm.

[A collection of thirty-five texts of corridos and songs without music. Most, though not all, are well known compositions.]

1430. Melgarejo Vivanco, José Luis. "La décima en Veracruz." ASFM, IV(1943), 61-72.

[A study of the décima as it is known in Veracruz. There are eleven textual examples, but all are lyrical or sententious, not narrative.]

1431. Mena Brito, Bernardino. "La verdad sobre 'La Valentina', himno de la Revolución Mexicana." UniversalMex, 4 de enero de 1946, p. 4 of the first section.

[The author quotes from a novel of Heriberto Frías, El amor de las sirenas, which was published in 1908 and which contains (pp. 227-230) the episode here quoted wherein a character sings La Valentina, several strophes of which are given.]

1432. Méndez de Cuenca, Laura. El espejo de Amarilis. México, 1901.

[Henríquez Ureña (ref. 1367, p. 382) describes this work as a "libro que se publicó en Méjico como folletín del diario El Mundo . . . ." From it he publishes a Mexican version of El caballero que busca mujer.]

1433. Méndez Plancarte, Alfonso. Poetas novohispanos, primer siglo (1521-1621). México: Ediciones de la Universidad Nacional Autónoma, 1942. lii, 168 pp. 19.5 cm. (Biblioteca del estudiante universitario, Vol. 33.)

[Includes the texts of several artistic romances and romancillos by Juan Díaz, Mateo Rosas de Oquendo, Francisco Bramón, Fernando de Alva Ixtlilxóchitl, and Juan Ruiz de Alarcón. There is also a good introduction and a great number of bibliographical data.]

1434. _____. Poetas novohispanos, segundo siglo (1621-1721); parte primera. México: Ediciones de la Universidad Nacional Autónoma, 1944. lxxvii, 191 pp. 19.5 cm. (Biblioteca del estudiante universitario, Vol. 43.); Poetas novohispanos, segundo siglo (1621-1721); parte segunda. México: Ediciones de la Universidad Nacional Autónoma, 1945. lxxiii, 229 pp. 19.5 cm. (Biblioteca del estudiante universitario, Vol. 54.)

[A collection which contains, among many other types of poetry, a few romances and décimas. All are, of course, artistic, though several are narrative in nature or at least inspired by current events.]

1435. Mendizábal, Miguel O. de. "La poesía indígena y las canciones populares." BolMN, Epoca 4a., II:4 (octubre a diciembre de 1923), 79-84; reprinted in Obras completas, Tomo II. México: Talleres Gráficos de la Nación, 1946. Pp. 421-430.

[An excellent treatment of the role of music and poetry during pre-Hispanic times, the interest of early missionaries in the Indians' aptitude for music, and the subsequent decline of this interest. The article concludes with brief attention to the corrido. Without giving any text or citing any source, the author declares that one of the first songs composed by Indians in Spanish was a song (tocotín) which was sung at a church fiesta and which was in the nature of a corrido.]

1436. Mendoza, Eufemio. Colección de documentos para la historia de México. Tomo I: Fragmentos de la crónica de la provincia de Franciscanos de Santiago de Xalixco. México: Imprenta de V. G. Torres, 1871. 505 pp. 19 cm.

[Contains repeated references to the importance Franciscans placed upon teaching the Indians to sing and to play musical instruments. Occasionally there is mention of music and musical instruments played in the streets and at gatherings of the common people outside of churches.]

1437. Mendoza, Vicente T. "El álbum de 24 canciones y jarabes mexicanos." BLAM, V(1941), 515-541.

[A study of some Mexican popular songs published in a collection printed in Hamburg in the nineteenth century. Though it does not deal with narrative corridos, it brings in popular poetry related to Cielito lindo and similar songs.]

1438. _____. "El apólogo español en la producción folklórica de México." UnivM, V:27 (abril de 1938), 11-19.

[After showing how animals play an important role in Spanish folklore, the author turns his attention to their importance in the folklore of Mexico. From both countries he offers texts as evidence. Most are coplas, though a few are romances.]

1439. _____. "La auténtica música de México." La República (México), II:2 (1 de marzo de 1950), 49.

1440. _____. "La cachucha." In Homenaje a don Luis de Hoyos Sainz. Madrid: Gráficas Valera, 1949. Pp. 223-233.

[A very interesting study of the song and dance which originated in Cádiz around 1810-1812 as a patriotic expression of Spanish resistance to Napoleon and then spread over Europe and, as Mendoza shows here, to Cuba, Puerto Rico, Peru, Chile, and Mexico. He prints a composition of twelve cuartetas in corrido meter taken from a broadside published in Mexico in 1840. Its political theme places it very close to the corrido tradition, though it is obviously a more sophisticated type of poetry than the truly popular corrido.]

1441. _____. "La calandria." FPL, No. 30 (junio y julio de 1953), 970-971, 976.

[The author describes twelve versions of a popular song, La calandria, and gives complete texts of several from New Mexico and Mexico. Most are seven-syllable romances, though one version is octosyllabic. There is music for eight versions of the composition, which is perhaps most characteristically a children's romance.]

1442. _____. "La canción chilena en México." RMC, Año IV: 28 (abril-mayo, 1948), 7-21.

[Mendoza gives texts and music of some Chilean songs gathered by him and others in Guerrero, Oaxaca, and other areas of Mexico. He believes that they came into Mexico through Acapulco, particularly during the days of the gold rush. A few of the texts might qualify as coplas, but none is a romance or corrido. The article may be significant, however, in establishing relationships between the popular verse and music of the two countries. Chile, like Mexico, has a strong romance-corrido tradition.]

1443. _____. "La canción de 'La zagala' en México." TI, No. 71 (1950), 20-21.

[Boggs (ref. 13 [1950], p. 61) says: "Gives texts of this romantic ballad from Cataluña, Soria, Puerto Rico, New Mexico, and Mexico, and notes it is mentioned among Sephardic Jews in Smyrna."]

1444. _____. "La canción de mayo en México." BLAM, V(1941), 491-514.

[A penetrating study of the spring song in question and its relation to romances and corridos in Mexico.]

1445. _____. "La canción del novio desairado." AIIE, No. 22 (1954), 55-88.

[A comparison of texts of many versions of a wedding song of Spanish origin which has spread throughout the Spanish-speaking world. There are versions from Spain, Santo Domingo, Puerto Rico, Argentina, New Mexico, and Mexico, a few of them with music. The songs deal with the theme of the abandoned lover who watches as his sweetheart marries another. One Mexican version is called a corrido, and almost all the versions, including those from Spain, are in octosyllabic cuartetas with changing rhyme in each strophe.]

1446. _____. "Una canción extremeña." RHM, Año X:1-2 (enero y abril, 1944), 174-179.

[A Mexican song from Jalisco El Kirie-Leisón is compared with one from Extremadura, Ya no va el cura a la ilesia. Their texts are very closely related, though there is no similarity in the music which accompanies them. Though not romances, they are of interest in determining geographical relationships between the popular songs of Spain and America.]

1447. Mendoza, Vicente T. "La canción hispano-mexicana en Nuevo México." NuM, Año II:5 (enero, 1947), 25-32.

[A brief survey of New Mexican popular songs with special reference to their relationship to their Spanish counterparts. There are brief sections on romances, corridos, inditas, coplas, décimas, etc. Though there is nothing particularly new in the material presented, the article is a good synthesis of what is known about the general subject of New Mexican popular music.]

1448. _____. "Una canción isabelina en México." DH, IV:4, pp. 214-220.

[A discussion of a song about Isabel II which has been adapted to Mexican history and widely circulated. Though not a genuine romance or corrido, it falls into the category of political verse.]

1449. _____. La canción mexicana; ensayo de clasificación y antología. México: Instituto de Investigaciones Estéticas, 1961. 672 pp. 23 cm.

[The latest of the author's outstanding studies of Mexican music. The introduction is an "Ensayo de clasificación" in which lyrical songs are classified in a variety of ways (e.g., by chronological order, by the meter of their versification, by musical form, by the character of their texts, etc.). The anthology, which makes up the bulk of the volume (pp. 127-631), contains the texts and music of over 300 composiciones. There are a number of plates and extensive indices. While this work is concerned only with lyrical songs, not ballads, there are a number of compositions which are historical in character.]

1450. _____. "Una canción provenzal en México." AIIE, No. 5 (1940), 57-76; also, Nacion, 5 de enero, 12 de enero, 1941.

[The author traces back to its origins in Provence a song-dance, known as Oh, blanca virgen o Al pie de tu ventana, which is widely known in the central area of Mexico from coast to coast. The song is popular or semipopular all along the line, and though it has nothing to do with the romance-corrido tradition, like any of Mendoza's efforts to trace Mexican songs back to their peninsular origins, it may be valuable in the future in determining the geographical relationship between the popular songs of Mexico and Spain.]

1451. _____, ed. Canciones mexicanas (Mexican Folk Songs). New York: Hispanic Institute in the United States, 1948. xv, 126 pp. 26 cm.

[Words and music of a selection of Mexican songs of various types. There is a section of corridos (pp. 25-49); also, there are coplas, décimas, and canciones históricas scattered through the volume.]

1452. _____. "El casamiento del piojo y la pulga." AIIE, No. 6 (1940), 65-85; also, Nacion, 30 de marzo, 6 de abril de 1941.

[The author traces the Casamiento del piojo y la pulga from Spain to

America and offers texts, usually with music, of fourteen versions of the song, mostly from Mexico.]

1453. _____, ed. Cincuenta corridos mexicanos. México: Ediciones de la Secretaría de Educación Pública, 1944. 117 pp. 32 cm.
[Texts and piano accompaniment for fifty corridos of various types.]

1454. _____, ed. Cincuenta romances. México: E. D. I. A. P. S. A., 1944. 117 pp. 32.5 cm.
[Texts and music of fifty romances from Spain, Mexico, and other regions of America.]

1455. _____. "Una colección de cantos jaliscienses." AIIE, No. 21 (1953), 59-73.
[Mendoza reports on the contents of a very valuable collection of songs from Jalisco which is in the Biblioteca Nacional de México, Colección de jarabes, sones y cantos populares tal como se usan en el Estado de Jalisco, by Clemente Aguirre, an eminent musician of the nineteenth century. It is apparent from the description of the sixty-six compositions that most are sones, jarabes, and the like, and that few, if any, have anything to do with the romance-corrido tradition. But the collection might bear looking into. It is almost certain that a student of the copla in Mexico would find data here.]

1456. _____. "La copla musical en México." ASFM, V(1944), 189-217.
[A study of the copla with several texts.]

1457. _____. El corrido de la Revolución Mexicana. México, 1956. 151 pp. 23 cm. (Biblioteca del Instituto Nacional de Estudios Históricos de la Revolución Mexicana.)
[A series of six "lessons" (i.e., lectures) given at the National University by Mendoza. He traces the history of the Revolution through its corridos by citing pertinent strophes which reflect popular attitudes and reactions to what happened on the Mexican scene.]

1458. _____. "El corrido en México." UnivM, III:15 (abril, 1937), 28-33.
[Mendoza's first published article about the corrido. Included here is treatment of the Spanish origins of the corrido, a discussion of the terminology used in speaking of different types of compositions, consideration of the antiquity of the romance-corrido tradition in America, and analyses of the literary and musical form of the genre. Of great importance at the time it appeared, this article has been incorporated almost verbatim into Mendoza's El romance español y el corrido mexicano and may be ignored by anyone who has consulted this latter work.]

1459. _____. El corrido mexicano; antología. México: Fondo de Cultura Económica, 1954. xliv, 467 pp. 17.5 cm. (Letras mexicanas, No. 15.)

[Besides giving the texts of 172 corridos of many different kinds, some with music, the author offers an introduction which, in its general lines, is a synthesis of the ideas already stated in El romance español y el corrido mexicano. There are, however, some divergences from earlier hypotheses which make the work interesting.]

1460. Mendoza, Vicente T. "El cuando." NuM, Año III:11 (julio, 1948), 188-205.

[Texts and music of all the cuandos from Mexico and New Mexico that Mendoza has been able to gather. He studies the nineteenth-century background of the cuando and considers, without venturing any conclusions, its possible relationship with the songs of the same name which are sung and danced in Argentina, Chile, and possibly Cuba. Though this genre of song is not, in reality, a part of the romance-corrido tradition, it apparently exists on about the same popular level, and at some periods in history it may well have been very close to narrative or satirical ballads.]

1461. _____. "La décima en la literatura popular de México." UnivMex, II:22 (octubre, 1948), 12-14.

[The author sums up briefly the contents of his work La décima en México (see entry no. 1462). He reproduces here two hojas sueltas and prints the text of another décima.]

1462. _____. La décima en México. B. A.: Instituto Nacional de la Tradición, 1947. 683 pp. 24 cm.

[The fundamental and indispensable work upon the décima in Mexico. An exhaustive study, it is replete with hundreds of texts, including many which were inspired by historical events. These tend, however, to be more satirical than narrative.]

1463. _____. "Derivaciones de la canción de Mambrú en México." ASFM, I(1938-1940), 91-101; also, El Heraldo (Barranquilla, Colombia), 29 de marzo de 1941; also, Nacion, 29 de junio de 1941.

[A discussion of the many forms which the song Mambrú has assumed in Mexico. The author provides several texts and some bibliographical data also.]

1464. _____. Ensayo sobre el folklore musical mejicano: canciones y danzas; estudio de sus características melódicas y cadenciales; instrumentos populares. Premio de la Raza, 1951, otorgado por la Real Academia de Bellas Artes de San Fernando.

1465. _____. "El espíritu imitativo del pueblo de México en sus canciones." PyS, 1944. Pp. 595, 597-600.

[After pointing out that from the time of the conquest observers have noted a Mexican genius for imitation, the author offers a very interesting collection of parodies dating from the first years of the nineteenth century to the present. None seems to be in romance meter and none is a corrido. A good many, however, are historical in nature.]

1466. _____. "Estudio y clasificación de la música tradicional hispánica de Nuevo México." Unpublished MS in the library of the University of New Mexico.
[A study based on the J. D. Robb collection of folk music recordings. Robb (ref. 1579, p. 15) mentions Mendoza's treatment of the Corrido de doña Elena in this monograph.]

1467. _____. "El folklore en San Luis Potosí y en los estados circundantes." Letras potosinas (San Luis Potosí, México), XII(1954): 111, pp. 10-16.
[Boggs (ref. 13 [1954], p. 22) says: "Date and texts in brief synthesis of folk lit., songs, dances, customs, festivals, food and drink, beliefs, speech, and proverbs, from San Luis Potosí and neighboring Mexican states."]

1468. _____. "Folklore musical de México." FACI, Año I:1 (noviembre de 1953), 36-40.
[A brief summary of the history of Mexican popular music. Beginning with consideration of the Indian and Spanish elements which merged at the time of the conquest of America, Mendoza shows how a truly mestizo music emerged in Mexico during the nineteenth century. There is mention of Spanish romances and considerable attention to the rise of the corrido during the latter part of the nineteenth century. Nothing here is new, but the article is a good synthesis of what is known about the subject.]

1469. _____. "Folklore y música tradicional de Baja California y Sonora." ASFM, X(1955), 53-69.
[Romances and corridos are mentioned along with other types of songs. There are few texts, however, that can be related to either of these genres.]

1470. _____. "The Frontiers Between 'Popular' and 'Folk.'" JIFMC, VII(1955), 24-27.
[In pointing out the differences between what is "popular" (i. e., fashionable or in vogue) and what is "folk," the author sketches briefly the whole history of Mexican music and its relationship to society. He mentions the romance of colonial times but does not treat the corrido.]

1471. _____. Glosas y décimas de México. México: Fondo de Cultura Económica, 1957. 371 pp. 17.5 cm.
[An admirable collection of décima texts (184 in all) along with an introductory study which treats such matters as the history of the décima, the subjects which inspired it, the style and the language of the genre, etc.]

1472. Mendoza, Vicente T. "El grupo musical mexicano llamado 'mariachi,'" Revista universitaria (Guadalajara, México), I:2 (mayo-julio de 1943), 87-89.

[A good article which describes the composition of the mariachis, the regions where they flourish, and the character of the music which they play and sing. Corridos, romances, and relaciones are mentioned along with other genres as being played by mariachis.]

1473. _____. Lírica infantil de México. México: El Colegio de México, 1951. 177 pp. 24 cm.

[A good collection of children's verses, including a few romances.]

1474. _____. "Mensajes y mensajeros en la poesía tradicional de México." FACI, Año III:3 (noviembre, 1955), 71-84.

[After sketching the role of various types of messengers in Spanish romances and other popular poetry, the author considers Mexican popular poems, mostly romances and corridos but including some lyrical compositions. Most deal with birds which carry letters of love to a sweetheart.]

1475. _____. "Mexican and Central American Oral Literature." In Encyclopedia of Literature. Vol. II. New York: Philosophical Library, 1946. Pp. 688-691.

[Contains brief mention of traditional romances and of corridos.]

1476. _____. "La música en la época de la Reforma, la Intervención y el Imperio." Duoro litoral (Porto, Portugal), Oitava Série, I-II(1957), 25-59.

[Contains a mine of hitherto unkown information about the popular and semipopular songs inspired by the events of the 1850's and early 1860's. Though the author also treats artistic music, most of his work deals with songs of various types about historical events: valonas, corridos, décimas, and the like.]

1477. _____. "Música popular del Bajío." México en el arte (México, D. F.), No. 7 (primavera de 1949), 87-99.

[A survey of the popular music of the Bajío region. There are texts and music of a wide variety of songs ranging from the religious to the sentimental. Included are some romances, coplas, and one corrido, the Corrido de los agraristas y cristeros del Cerro del Piloncillo.]

1478. _____. "Música tradicional de Guerrero." NuM, Año IV:15 (julio, 1949), 198-214; also, "La música tradicional en Guerrero." DdeG, 15 de enero de 1949, p. 2; 20 de enero, p. 4.

[In his general treatment the author touches briefly upon the romances and relaciones of the region. Also, there is a short discussion of the bola suriana, the most characteristic type of corrido in the Guerrero area.]

1479. _____. "La música tradicional española en México." NuM, Año VIII:29 (1er. trimestre, 1953), 5-34.

[The author traces the history of Spanish influence upon the popular music of Mexico. Among other genres he deals with romances, coplas, décimas, and corridos. There are fourteen musical examples, including one version of Las señas del marido which comes from Puebla. Though the article contains little that is new, it is an excellent summary of the subject.]

1480. _____. "Origen de la canción mexicana." PyS, 1945. Pp. 75-78.

[The author points out that Indian and Spanish influences have contributed to the formation of the songs of Mexico. As evidence of the former, he cites only some popular songs about animals. To illustrate Spanish influences, however, he gives some strophes from many different types of songs: romance, corrido, relación, villancico, seguidilla, petenera, copla, alabado, etc. The article, however, is written only for the general reader and is not intended to be of much substance.]

1481. _____. "Panorama de cincuenta años de música popular mexicana." RHM, Año XX:3 (julio, 1954), 267-272.

[An excellent short summary of the rise of nationalism in Mexican music over the past half century. Among other things, the author mentions in passing both pre-Revolutionary and Revolutionary corridos.]

1482. _____. Panorama de la música tradicional de México. México: Imprenta Universitaria, 1956. 258 pp. 23 cm.

[A comprehensive survey of traditional music in Mexico from pre-Hispanic times to the present. After an introduction, the main text of the book is divided into three sections: I. La música indígena; II. La música española de los siglos XVII y XVIII; III. La música mexicana. Then there follows a section of 231 musical examples and a section of literary texts to accompany the musical examples. Finally, there is a section of very interesting illustrations. Included in all this are short chapters on the romance, the copla, the corrido, the valona, etc. There are musical and literary examples of each genre.]

1483. _____. "Un romance castellano que vive en México." ASFM, I(1938-1940), 69-78.

[A romance by Juan del Encina has found its way into Spanish folklore and thence into Mexican tradition. Known in Spain as El enamorado y la muerte, it is called Versos de la parca in Mexico. The author gives a complete text from Chapantongo, Hidalgo, and a fragment from Chontalpa, Tabasco.]

1484. Mendoza, Vicente T. "El romance de Las señas del esposo." BAFA, Año III:1 y 2 (noviembre y diciembre de 1940), 10-14; also, ASFM, I(1938-1940), 79-89.

[The author speculates about the Spanish origins of the romance and offers five Mexican versions of it. Three are from Mexico City, two are from Michoacán.]

1485. _____. "Un romance de relación en México: El casamiento del Huitlacoche." AIIE, No. 1 (1937).

1486. _____. "El romance en tierras michoacanas." Universidad Michoacana (Morelia, Michoacán), IV:19 (marzo, abril de 1942), 83-93.

[The author discusses the strong romance tradition of Michoacán and gives some texts collected there. Included are versions of Delgadina, Las señas del esposo, Alfonso XII, El casamiento del Huitlacoche, and El caballero que busca esposa.]

1487. _____. El romance español y el corrido mexicano; estudio comparativo. México: Universidad Nacional Autónoma de México, 1939. xviii, 835 pp. 23 cm.

[The most complete study that has been made of the romance-corrido in Mexico and the inevitable point of departure for any investigation related to the subject. The first part of the volume is a literary-musical study of the romance in Spain and the corrido in Mexico (pp. 13-231). The second part of the work is a collection of texts of romances and corridos, almost all with music. In all there are 496 texts (pp. 233-782). There are bibliographical data in all sections. While the book is a study of all phases of the romance-corrido tradition, its most valuable contribution undoubtedly lies in its exhaustive study of the music of these genres.]

1488. _____. "Testamentos." RINT, Año I, entrega 1a. (enero-junio de 1948), 39-50.

[A study of the testamento, a type of folk composition found both in Spain and in America. After tracing it back to peninsular religious romances like La muerte de Cristo and to animal romances like La loba parda, Mendoza gives as American examples of the genre some décimas from Panama; the text of a nineteenth-century broadside from Mexico, Testamento y muerte del perro Munito, which belongs to the romance-corrido tradition; and several testamentos in dialogue form from Guadalajara, Guanajuato, Querétaro, and Mexico City.]

1489. _____. "La toponimia en las coplas de México." PyS, 1954, pp. 205-212, 214-216, 218, 220.

_____. See Leal, Luis, entry no. 1388.

1490. _____, and R. R. de Mendoza, Virginia. Folklore de San Pedro Piedra Gorda, Zacatecas. México: Talleres Gráficos de

la Nación, 1952. 498 pp. 30 cm.
[A thorough study of the folklore of the village indicated. Included are the texts and music of some romances and corridos collected from oral tradition (pp. 63-67, 69-76, 77-87). There are also some coplas (pp. 95-117).]

  Mendoza, Virginia R. R. de. See Rodríguez Rivera, Virginia, entry no. 1583.

  1491. Menéndez Peña, Hilario. Cantares huastecos o versos de huapango. México: Fototipia de Hauser y Menet, 1922. 12 pp.

  1492. _____. Monografías y cantares huastecos. México: Compañía General Editora, 1944. 140 pp.

  1493. Menéndez Pidal, Ramón. "El romancero en la colonización de México." ABC (Madrid), 12 de octubre, 1948, [p. 1].
[An unimportant restatement of some of the evidence that the romance went to América with the conquerors.]

  1494. Mérida, Carlos, ed. Frescoes in Ministry of Education by Diego Rivera. México: Frances Toor Studies, 1937. (Mexican Art Series, No. 2.)
[Contains English translations of two corridos. One is entitled The Proletarian Revolution; the other, which is nameless, begins: "In Cuautla, Morelos, there lived an unusual man . . . ."]

  Mexican Folk Music. See Secretaría de Educación Pública, Sección de Música, entry no. 1614.

  Michel, Concepción (Concha). See Castillo Nájera, Francisco, entry no. 1220.

  1495. Millán Maldonado, Amalia. Folklore; tesis que presenta la alumna . . . para obtener el título de profesora de folklore. México: Universidad Nacional Autónoma de México, Escuela Nacional de Música, 1942. 79 pp.
[Boggs (ref. 13 [1944], p. 37) notes that there is treatment of the folklore of Oaxaca, including folk music.]

  1496. Miranda, José, and González Casanova, Pablo. Sátira anónima del siglo XVIII. México: Fondo de Cultura Económica, 1953. 234 pp. 17.5 cm. (Letras mexicanas, No. 9.)
[A very important collection of eighteenth-century popular and semi-popular literature. Included are texts of romances, décimas, pasquines, etc.]

  1497. Moncada G., Francisco. "Recopilación folklórica." ASFM, VII (1951), 73-86.
[Among many other folklore materials gathered by the author, there are some romances, coplas, and other types of popular songs.]

  1498. Monguió, Luis. "El corrido mejicano como canto de libertad." Atenea, LXXVI:228-229 (junio-julio de 1944), 248-261; also,

"El corrido mexicano, canto de libertad." RAmer, IV (noviembre de 1945), 257-266; reprinted in the author's Estudios sobre literatura hispanoamericana y española. México: Ediciones de Andrea, 1958. Pp. 85-96.
[A very important study of the historical development of the corrido and of certain thematic aspects of the genre as a form of popular expression. The version of the article printed in the Revista de América is slightly modified, though there are no fundamental changes.]

1499. Monguió, Luis. "Voice of Mexico: The Corrido." The Pacific Spectator (Stanford, California), II:1 (Winter, 1948), 98-106.
[A brief treatment of the corrido's background and its character. There are several partial texts. This is, in reality, a reworking in English of the author's earlier article listed in ref. 1498.]

1500. Montero, Marco Arturo. "La música popular mexicana." Claridad (B. A.), XIX:342 (abril, 1940), 81-95.
[The author traces the development of popular music in Mexico from about the beginning of the nineteenth century to 1940. The work is interesting, though superficial. Along with a few fragments of political songs of the last century, there are texts of the Corrido de Carlos IV and Los trenes eléctricos.]

1501. Montes de Oca, José G. "En tierra de conejos." MRANC, XLVI:3-6 (marzo-junio, 1926), 155-165.
[A consideration of some folklore from Tuxpan, Jalisco. Some coplas, but no corridos, are quoted textually.]

1502. _____. Estampas de Durango. Méjico-Tenochtitlán: Fidel Guerrero, 1938. 94 pp. 18.5 cm.
[A collection of short sketches about life in Durango, some of considerable interest to folklorists. One entitled "Francisco Villa en el alma popular" sketches the salient facts about Villa's life as treated in legend and tradition. The only song mentioned, however, is Adelita.]

1503. _____. Manchas de color. México-Tenochtitlán: Imp. M. León Sánchez, 1939. 156 pp. 19 cm.
[A collection of essays on folklore, customs, and the like. Corridos, coplas, sones, and other types of popular songs are mentioned, and the text of one corrido, Los lagartijos, is given (pp. 15-16).]

1504. _____. Mirador. Méjico-Tenochtitlán: Imprenta Moderna, 1936.
[Some essays about Mexican folklore and customs. Along with chapters entitled "El jarabe tapatío" and "Las mañanitas," there is one called "Doce de diciembre en la Villa," which includes the text of a song which in form is very similar to the corridos. It is sung by the cantadores of the Villa de Guadalupe.]

1505. Morelet, Arthur. Voyage dans l'Amérique Centrale, l'isle de Cuba et le Yucatan. 2 vols. Paris: Gide et J. Baudry, 1857. 24 cm.

[Contains the text of a copla (Vol. I, p. 295) which the author heard a girl sing in Campeche. Though this text is unimportant, the same might not be true of a collection of ten melodies which Morelet transcribes without words on some unnumbered pages at the end of Vol. II. There are melodies from Tabasco, Yucatan, Peten, and Honduras. Some of them might be significant, though there is no indication of the words which were sung to them.]

1506. Moreno, Daniel. Figuras de la Revolución Mexicana. México: Ediciones Andrea, 1960. 112 pp. (Biblioteca mínima mexicana, No. 33.)

[Section VIII of this work, "La literatura," contains a passage on the corrido.]

1507. Moreno, Delfino C. "El bandido Agustín Lorenzo." MF, V:2 (April-June, 1929), 86-88.

[A sketch of the career of this Mexican hero who was active during the period of the war against Maximilian. Two strophes of a corrido about him are quoted.]

1508. Murillo, Gerardo (Dr. Atl). Las artes populares de México. 2 vols. México: Librería Cultura, 1921; also, 2 vols. México: Editorial "Cultura," 1922. 30.5 cm.

[A fundamental early work about all kinds of popular art (literature, ceramics, feather mosaics, toys, music, etc.). Chap. III, "Literatura-Poesía-Estampería," deals with corridos, sucesos, and other types of popular literature. Many corrido texts are given which have not appeared elsewhere, and there are photographic reproductions of some typical broadsides. In the second edition there is some rearrangement of sections. The chapter referred to above is in Vol. II, Chap. XXIII.]

1509. Music of the Gold Rush Era; History of Music Project. Prepared with the assistance of the Works Progress Administration of California; sponsored by the city and county San Francisco, 1939. 212 pp. mimeographed. (History of Music in San Francisco Series, Vol. I.)

[Chase (ref. 25, p. 225) comments: "Ch. 1, Music at Mission Dolores, p. 1-9, deals with Indian singers and primitive orchestras. Ch. 2, Fandangos and fiestas p. 10-20, deals with the music and dances of the Spanish Californians."]

1510. "Música, danza y cantos del antiguo México." PrBA, 15 de diciembre, 1935.

Musique et chansons populaires. See International Institute of Intellectual Cooperation, entry no. 1377.

Musquiz Blanco, Manuel. See Cuéllar, Alfredo B., entry no. 1253.

1511. Novo, Salvador. "Literatura del pueblo." MF, July-September, 1929, 132-145; also, in En defensa de lo usado y otros ensayos. México: Editorial Polis, 1938. Pp. 103-110.
[The author stresses the value of the corrido as a manifestation of the character of the Mexican pueblo and also its literary importance as an offspring of the Spanish romance. Some bibliography on the corrido is given, and there are texts of La amiga de Bernal Francés and the Corrido de doña Elena.]

1512. Nueva Relación y Curioso Romance de Diego de Frías y Antonio Montero. Impreso en México por Joseph Bernardo de Hogal. En la calle de Capuchinas. Año de 1734.
[Listed by Mendoza (ref. 1487, p. 784).]

1513. Núñez y Domínguez, José de Jesús. "Una curiosidad literaria de la guerra con los Estados Unidos en 1847: El Padre Nuestro de los Yankees." Memorias de la Academia de Historia Mexicana (México), XVIII(1959), 106-109.
[Paredes (ref. 91, p. 57) says: "Concerns text collected by Chilean in Mexico in 1853 of satirical 'Lord's Prayer of the Yankees'; folk poetry of U. S.-Mexican war."]

1514. _____. Historia y tauromaquia mexicanas. México: Ediciones Botas, 1944. 277 pp. 19.5 cm.
[Contains the texts of some corridos about bullfighters.]

1515. _____. "Un virrey limeño en México." AnMN, Epoca 4a., IV:1 (enero y febrero de 1926), 1-132; 2 (marzo y abril de 1926), 133-272.
[The work deals with Juan de Acuña y Bejarano, Marqués de Casa Fuerte, Viceroy of New Spain from 1722-1734. It is replete with references to artistic poetry of the time, much of which the author prints. In addition, there is some material about an episode between the Negrito Poeta and the Viceroy in which the famous repentista poet made fun of the royal official (pp. 68-70). Most of this comes from the work of Nicolás León about the Negrito Poeta. Also, there is a fragment of a romance (p. 203) which was sung on a festive occasion in 1724 in honor of the Viceroy.]

1516. Obras de eloqüencia y poesía premiadas por la Real Universidad de México en el certamen literario que celebró, el día 28 de diciembre de 1790. Con motivo de la exaltación al trono de nuestro católico monarca el Sr. D. Carlos IIII. México: Por Don Felipe de Zúñiga y Ontiveros, 1791. 20 cm.
[In ref. 1658 the contents of this volume are listed. Several of the compositions are romances endecasílabos.]

1517. "Ocho corridos mexicanos." Bellas artes (México), Año 1:3 (abril de 1956), 29-32.
[Words and music of Lucio Vázquez, El caballo criollo, Valente Quintero, Bonito San Juan del Río, Zenaida ingrata, Eres alta y delgadita, El novillo despuntado, and Cananea.]

O'Higgins, Paul. See Toor, Frances, entry no. 1652.

1518. Once cantos de México. México: Sección de Investigaciones Musicales del Departamento de Música del Instituto Nacional de las Bellas Artes de la Secretaría de Educación Pública, 1951.
[Said (in BBAA, Vol. XIV [1951], part II, p. 195) to contain words and music of the Corrido de Reyes Ruiz and also a copla.]

1519. Orcillo, Rubén S. "La canción mexicana." RdE, Año V:44 (abril, 1930), 185-192; 45 (mayo, 1930), 247-251.
[The author traces the history of Mexican music from pre-Hispanic times. There is perfunctory treatment of the corrido which may be ignored.]

1520. Orea, Basilio. "Romance tradicional de Bernal Francés en México." ASFM, IX(1954), 81-115.
[A study of thirty-one Mexican and New Mexican versions of the romance-corrido indicated. They were collected from oral tradition. The author demonstrates statistically their relationship to their Spanish counterparts and analyzes the Mexican adaptation of the Spanish romance.]

1521. Ortiz de Montellano, Bernardo. La poesía indígena de México. México, 1935. 93 pp. 20.5 cm.

1522. Otero, Nina. Old Spain in Our Southwest. New York: Harcourt, Doran and Co., 1936. ix, 192 pp. 21 cm.

Otero-Warren, Adelina. See Austin, Mary, entry no. 1159.

1523. P. G. C. "Nanas o coplas de cuna." Ethnos (México), Epoca I, Vol. I(1920-1922), 88-93.
[Chase (ref. 25, p. 189) comments: "Texts of cradle songs."]

1524. Palacios, Emanuel. "Relato folklórico del folklore de Jalisco." Tiras de colores (México), I:24 (16 de mayo, 1944), 2-4.

1525. Palant, _____. Historia de la música en México. 1866.
[Boggs (ref. 1181, p. 64) says: "Contiene aires y canciones populares de México desde lo más antiguo hasta 1866."]

1526. Paredes, Américo. "Ballads of the Lower Border." M.A. thesis, University of Texas, 1953. v, 228 pp. typewritten.
[After an introduction devoted to describing the nature of the lower border area and the importance of the ballads of that region, the author offers the texts of twenty-eight ballads collected from oral tradition

and provides excellent commentaries on each of them. Such matters as historical background, literary relationships, and the like are treated.]

1527. Paredes, Américo. "The Bury-Me-Not Theme in the Southwest." In "And Horns on the Toads," ed. by Mody C. Boatright, Wilson M. Hudson, and Allen Maxwell. Dallas: Southern Methodist University Press, 1959. Pp. 88-92. (Publication of the Texas Folklore Society, No. XXIX.)
[A consideration of the "No me entierren" theme with a few texts.]

1528. _____. "El corrido de Gregorio Cortez, A Ballad of Border Conflict." Ph. D. dissertation, University of Texas, 1956. x, 454 pp. typewritten.
[An exhaustive study of Gregorio Cortez as a prototype of the ballads of the Mexican border. Based on eleven versions of the corrido, the study relates the historical facts which gave rise to the ballad, the legend and traditions developed in the song, the stylistic and literary characteristics of the composition, its importance in showing how songs of this type evolve, etc. There is an extensive bibliography.]

1529. _____. "El corrido de José Mosqueda." WF, XVII:3 (July, 1958), 154-162.
[The author gives the text of the corrido as collected by John and Alan Lomax in Brownsville, Texas, in 1939. He then shows how the ballad is cast in the mold of corridos about border heroes, not in the pattern of songs about criminals, as might have been expected in view of the fact that Mosqueda was only a minor train robber. Paredes considers the corrido "a good example of the triumph of form over narrative intent in the ballad."]

1530. _____. "The Legend of Gregorio Cortez." In Mesquite and Willow, ed. by Mody C. Boatright, Wilson M. Hudson, and Allen Maxwell. Dallas: Southern Methodist University Press, 1957. Pp. 3-22. (Publication of the Texas Folklore Society, No. XXVI.)
[Relates in prose the legend of Gregorio Cortez as a story-teller might narrate it. There is reference to the corridos about the hero, but no texts are given.]

1531. _____. "The Love Tragedy in Texas-Mexican Balladry." In Folk Travelers, Ballads, Tales, and Talk, ed. by Mody C. Boatright, Wilson M. Hudson, and Allen Maxwell. Dallas: Southern Methodist University Press, 1953. Pp. 110-114. (Publication of the Texas Folklore Society, No. XXV.)
[Treats the importance of community dances, fandangos, as a form of border entertainment before the Mexican Revolution and discusses briefly two corridos about girls who were killed at such dances by jealous suitors. There is background material and a few strophes of Rosita Alvírez and Juanita Alvarado.]

1532. ———. "Luis Inclán, First of the Cowboy Writers." American Quarterly (Philadelphia), XII:1 (Spring, 1960), 55-70.
[An interesting treatment of Inclán based mostly upon the work of Núñez y Domínguez. Paredes mentions Inclán's importance as a writer and publisher of popular verse, mainly décimas.]

1533. ———. "The Mexican Corrido: Its Rise and Fall." In Madstones and Twisters, ed. by Mody C. Boatright, Wilson M. Hudson, and Allen Maxwell. Dallas: Southern Methodist University Press, 1958. Pp. 91-105. (Publication of the Texas Folklore Society, No. XXVIII.)
[A good discussion of the history of the corrido in Mexico with particular emphasis on the chronology of its development and the possibility that the Texas-Mexico border area was the region in which it assumed its unique form and characteristics.]

1534. ———. Recordings of over 350 ballads and other songs made on the lower Río Grande border. They now form part of the University of Texas Folklore Collection.

1535. ———. "With His Pistol in His Hand"; A Border Ballad and Its Hero. Austin: University of Texas Press, 1958. 262 pp. 23.5 cm.
[An excellent study in depth of the Corrido de Gregorio Cortez and of the ballad hero himself. This work is a revision of the doctoral dissertation listed in entry no. 1528. Besides offering the texts of many versions of the corrido and presenting an excellent factual account of the hero's life for purposes of comparing it with the story of his feats as narrated in the corrido, the author provides an extensive bibliography.]

———. See also entry no. 1646.

1536. Paz y Melia, A. "Cartapacio de diferentes versos a diversos asuntos compuestos o recogidos por Mateo Rosas de Oquendo." Bulletin Hispanique (Bordeaux), VIII:2 (Avril-Juin, 1906), 154-162; 3 (Juillet-Septembre, 1906), 257-278; IX:2 (Avril-Juin, 1907), 154-185.
[A study of the life and works of Mateo Rosas de Oquendo with numerous textual examples of his poetry. Several of these are romances about Mexican and Peruvian subjects.]

1537. Pearce, T. M. "The Bad Son (El Mal Hijo) in Southwestern Spanish Folklore." WF, IX(1950), 295-301.
[Mentions the Corrido de José Lizorio and El hijo desobediente along with several legends which treat the theme indicated.]

1538. ———. "Corrido del presidente Roosevelt." NMFR, I (1946-1947), 7-8.
[After a brief background report on the appearance of this corrido in Aguascalientes the day after Roosevelt died, the author gives its text along with an English translation.]

1539. Pearce, T. M. "What is a Folk Poet?" WF, XII(1953), 242-248.
[The biography and a study of the art of Próspero S. Baca, a popular singer of Bernalillo, New Mexico. There is discussion of the various types of songs which he writes and sings, including corridos.]

———. See Major, Mabel, entry no. 1418.

1540. Pedrero, Alfonso, "El romance de Joaquín González Balboa." ASFM, V(1945), 41-48.
[A poem, apparently nonpopular in origin, which is published with the notation: "Coleccionado por el Lic. Alfonso Pedrero," though without saying where or in what form.]

Pérez, Rebeca, Vda. de Nava. See Pinedo, Manuel D., entry no. 1544.

1541. Pérez Martínez, Héctor. Diez corridos mexicanos. Segunda edición. México: Publicaciones del Departamento de Bibliotecas de la Secretaría de Educación Pública, 1935. 64 pp. 16 cm. (Biblioteca del obrero y campesino, No. 9.)
[Ten texts of revolutionary corridos which are of little value because they have been altered to suppress all references to God or religion. There is a brief introduction entitled "Breves notas sobre el corrido" (pp. 5-8).]

1542. ———. Trayectoria del corrido. México: n.p., 1935. 99 pp. 23.5 cm.
[An important early study of the corrido, its history, its characteristics, etc. There are several valuable corrido texts.]

1543. Pérez Vizcaíno, Alfonso. Romances de Jalisco. Guadalajara, 1951. 19 pp.

1544. Pinedo, Manuel D., and Pérez, Rebeca, Vda. de Nava. "Recolección folklórica en Valparaíso, Zacatecas." ASFM, VI(1950), 503-538.
[Includes some romances (Delgadina and others), a number of coplas, a Canto de la época de la independencia, and several canciones.]

1545. Plenn, Abel. "Mexico's Folk Music." Mexican Life (México), X(1934):7, pp. 15-16, 43-44.

1546. Poemas folklóricos y patrióticos; corridos de la Revolución. México: Libro Mex Editores, 1957. 166 pp. 18.5 cm.
[A collection of poems without introduction or commentary of any kind. Along with artistic poetry by various Mexican poets of greater or lesser merit, ten texts of corridos are included.]

1547. Pomar, Juan Bautista. "Relación de Tezcoco." In Nueva colección de documentos para la historia de México, Vol. III: Pomar y Zurita, ed. by Joaquín García Icazbalceta. México: Imprenta de

Francisco Díaz de León, 1891. Pp. 1-69.

[Pomar, in listing his sources (p. 1), mentions that he sought out "cantares antiquísimos de donde se coligió y tomó lo más que se ha hecho y escrito . . . ." Also, in another place (pp. 39-40) he discusses the writing of historical songs by noblemen and commoners, though it seems clear that he is thinking mainly of nonpopular compositions.]

1548. Ponce, Manuel M. "Apuntes sobre música mexicana." BLAM, Año III, Tomo III(abril de 1937), 37-42.

[The author outlines the little that is known about pre-conquest Indian music in Mexico and then observes that modern Mexican popular music is essentially Spanish, though somewhat altered by the Mexican milieu. Very incidental mention of corridos as an example of mestizaje in Mexican music may be ignored.]

1549. _____. "El folk-lore musical mexicano; lo que se ha hecho, lo que puede hacerse." RevMM, I:5 (15 de septiembre, 1919), 5-9.

[Romero (ref. 1590, p. 724) indicates that Ponce complains of the "poco ordenada labor de los folkloristas."]

Poncet y Cárdenas, Carolina. See entry no. 1039.

Porter, Carlos E. See Espinosa, Aurelio M., entry no. 1294.

1550. Porter, Katherine Anne. "Corridos." The Survey (New York), LII:3 (May 1, 1924), 157-159.

[An early attempt to describe Mexican corridos for the North American reading public. Though elementary in character, it is well done.]

1551. Posada, José Guadalupe. Las calaveras y otros grabados. B. A.: Editorial Nova, 1943.

_____. For works about Posada see entries nos. 1194, 1234, 1329, 1396, 1551, 1582, 1648, 1652, 1666, and 1692.

1552. Pozzi, Leo. "Folklore messicano." Le vie d'Italia e dell'America Latina (Milan), V(1928), 1228.

1553. Prieto, Margarita. Del rabel a la guitarra; el corrido mexicano como un derivado del romance español. México: Imprenta Universitaria, 1944. [viii], 132 pp. 17.5 cm.

[A very good summary of what is known about the corrido and its relationship to the Spanish romance. There are numerous texts and a bibliography.]

1554. Primera Parte de los Romances del Valiente Francisco Esteban, más otro del Castigo que Dios obró en un mal hombre por haberle quitado la vida a otro para robarlo. Imprenta de Francisco de Rivera Calderón. Año de 1717.

[Mendoza (ref. 1487, p. 783) lists this work. The second part of the composition is listed in entry no. 1615.]

1555. Prometheo/alegorico/que la insigne iglesia/metropolitana/ de/Mexico,/dispuso en su entrada,/al Exmo. señor,/don Jvan Antonio/Vasquez de Acuña,/Marques de Cassa Fverte,/del Orden de Santiago; Commendador de Adelpha/en la de Alcantara, de el Consejo de su Magestad/en el de Guerra, General de los Reales Exercitos:/Governador de Mescina, en el Reyno de Sicilia;/Commandante General de Mallorca, VI-REY/Governador, y Capitan General, de esta Nueva/ España, y presidente de su Real Audencia/de Mexico./ Con Licencia en Mexico:/ Por JOSEPH BERNARDO DE HOGAL,/en la Calle de la Acequia. Año 1722. (Reproduced photographically in AnMN, Epoca 4a., IV:1 [enero a febrero, 1926], plates between pp. 30-31.)

[An anonymous artistic poem written in romance and romance real meters. See also entry no. 1663.]

1556. "Quadretti di folclore messicano." Le vie d'Italia e dell'America Latina (Milan), VI(1929), 714.

1557. Quetzacóatl, órgano de la Sociedad de Antropología de México. Five numbers published from May, 1929, to July, 1931.

[There is a text of Macario Romero collected at Huejotzingo (Vol. I, No. 1 [mayo de 1929], p. 24). Mendoza (ref. 1487, p. 798) lists the title of this publication merely as a bibliographical item. This one corrido text, however, is the only reference to the romance-corrido which I could find in the five numbers of the review that were published.]

1558. Quevedo, Francisco. Lírica popular tabasqueña; cantares yucatecos; estudios folklóricos. Tabasco: Imprenta del Gobierno Constitucionalista, 1916. 107 pp.

[A collection of articles about the folk songs of Tabasco and Yucatan. The work is impressionistic and completely romantic in its approach, but respectable in view of its early date. Little in it is of enduring interest, however. Although there is much discussion of popular trovadores, no mention is made of corridos. The author is concerned almost exclusively with lyrical songs and coplas.]

1559. _____. La poesía popular tabasqueña y los poetas que la imitan. Villahermosa, Tabasco: Imprenta "La Económica," 1933. 26 pp.

[Treats poets of Tabasco who seem to have been influenced by popular poetry. There is, however, nothing about narrative poetry; all the texts given are lyric in character.]

1560. Rael, Juan B. "Un cantar hallado en Tucumán." RevIb, IX:17 (febrero de 1945), 73-77.

[The author notes that a composition in Carrizo's Cancionero popular del Tucumán is closely related to La muerte, a song collected in New Mexico. Though philosophical and not narrative in content, because of its poetic form the song seems to lie on the fringes of the corrido tradition.]

1561. _____. The New Mexican Alabado. Stanford, California: Stanford University Press, 1951. 154 pp. 25 cm.

[An excellent compilation of alabados (hymns sung by the penitentes of New Mexico) along with much valuable information and commentary. Most of the texts are written in octosyllabic lines and many are genuine romances, some of which can be traced back to Spanish origins.]

1562. _____. "New Mexico Folklore Bibliography." NMFR, III (1948-1949), 38-39; IV(1949-1950), 34-35; V(1950-1951), 37-38; VI(1951-1952), 30-31.

[Each bibliography contains from nineteen to twenty-eight titles, some of which concern corridos and other popular songs.]

1563. Ralliere, J. B. Cánticos espirituales con música. Las Vegas, New Mexico: La Revista Católica, 1916.

[See Ralliere, J. B., Colección de cánticos espirituales, entry no. 1565.]

1564. _____. Cánticos espirituales, dispuestos en nuevo orden sin añadiduras por un Padre D. L. C. D. J. El Paso, Texas: Editorial Revista Católica, 1933.

[See Ralliere, J. B., Colección de cánticos espirituales, entry no. 1565.]

1565. _____. Colección de cánticos espirituales. Las Vegas, New Mexico: Imprenta de la Revista Católica, 1892.

[A collection of 217 alabados (religious hymns), according to Rael's description (ref. 1561, p. 9). He indicates that eight printings were made before the compositions were rearranged in what amounts to a new edition in 1933 (see entry no. 1564). The music for these hymns appeared in another volume (see Ralliere, J. B., Cánticos espirituales con música, entry no. 1563).]

Ramírez, José F. See Durán, Diego, entry no. 1284.

Ramírez de Aguilar, Fernando. See Dalevuelta, Jacobo, entry no. 1257.

1566. Ramírez Plancarte, Francisco. La ciudad de México durante la revolución constitucionalista. Segunda edición. México: Ediciones Botas, 1941. 598 pp. 23.5 cm.

[In several chapters the author interrupts his narrative to print the texts of popular songs of the time. Among these are some corridos. Also, there are some interesting pasquines, a few of them in verse.]

Ramos Espinosa, Alfonso, ed. See Campos, Rubén M., entry no. 1205.

1567. Rangel, Nicolás. "Cuatro diálogos insurgentes." BAGN, III:3 (tercer trimestre de 1932).

[Saldivar (ref. 1606) says that Rangel publishes here a great deal of information about songs concerning Mexican independence which are in the Archivo General de la Nación. Since Rangel neglects to list his sources, Saldívar's monograph is an attempt to locate these in the Archivo.]

1568. Rangel, Nicolás. Historia del toreo en México, época colonial (1529-1821). México: Imp. Manuel León Sánchez, 1924. 374 pp. 24.5 cm.

[Contains two pasquines from the eighteenth century, one a cuarteta (p. 183), one a décima (p. 191).]

Ransom, Harry H., ed. See Goodwyn, Frank, entry no. 1344.

1569. Redfield, Robert. Tepoztlán, A Mexican Village. Chicago: University of Chicago Press, 1930. xi, 247 pp. 21 cm.

[The author devotes considerable attention to the corridos and other popular literature of Tepoztlán. He provides several texts of Zapatista corridos which, though poorly transcribed, are of interest.]

_____. See Handbook of Latin American Studies, entry no. 51.

1570. Reed, John. Insurgent Mexico. New York: D. Appleton and Co., 1914. viii, 325 pp. 19.5 cm.

[While associated with Mexican armies during the early days of the Revolution, the author became familiar with a number of corridos about Madero, Huerta, Villa, and others. He prints English translations of some of these very valuable ballads in this work. Unfortunately he does not provide the original texts in Spanish.]

1571. Reindorp, Reginald C. La décima de Nuevo México. San Salvador [?], 1946. 108 pp.

[A study of the décima which incorporates numerous texts. Though most of them are amorous or sacred compositions, two are political in character. The work is a revision of an unpublished M.A. thesis which is in the library of the University of New Mexico, "The New Mexican Décima."]

1572. Relación de Doña Blanca. Impresa en México por los Herederos de Doña María de Rivera. En la calle de San Bernardo. Año de 1764; also, México: En la Oficina de don Alexandro Valdés, 1819. 4 lvs.

[The first entry is taken from Mendoza (ref. 1487, p. 784); the 1819 edition is listed in Torres-Ríoseco and Warner (ref. 1658, p. 72).]

1573. Relación del Ciego Toluqueño, con motivo de haber oído publicar el superior bando de indulto general, que concede a los insurgentes, en los términos que en el se expresan, la notoria humanidad de nuestro Exmo. Sr. Virrey D. Francisco Xavier Venegas. México: Imp. de Don Mariano de Zúñiga y Ontiveros, 1811. 14 pp.

[Torres-Ríoseco and Warner (ref. 1658, p. 72) list the work.]

1574. Renk, Eldred Joseph. "The Mexican Corrido and the Revolution; A People's-Eye View of Events in War, Religion, and Politics." Ph. D. diss., University of Washington, 1951.

[Part I, "General Aspects of the Corrido," includes sections on subject matter, metrics and form, literary formulas, and musical structure. Part II, "The Corrido and the Revolution," is the body of the thesis and contains eight chapters which deal with the history of Mexico from the time of Díaz through about 1940 as it is reflected in corridos. The appendix contains two sample hojas sueltas and a short bibliography.]

1575. Rey, Agapito. Cultura y costumbres del siglo XVI en la península ibérica y en la Nueva España. México: Ediciones Mensaje, 1944. 150 pp. 20.5 cm.

[One portion of the book, "Romances y canciones populares" (pp. 65-91), is a study of the popular songs of Spain and Mexico with particular attention to points of comparison which reveal a continuing Spanish tradition in Mexico. Many genres are mentioned, but there is special reference to romances and corridos, and some partial texts are given by way of illustration.]

1576. Ricard, Robert. "Contribution à l'étude des fêtes de 'Moros y cristianos' au Mexique." JSAP, XXIV of the nouvelle série (1932), 51-84.

[A very fine study of the subject from colonial times to the present. The work is extensively documented and the bibliographical notes make this contribution the inevitable point of departure for any further study of the theme. Much of the text of the dance-drama as performed in Teotihuacán is in romance meter.]

1577. Ríos Franco, Buenaventura. Un yucateco en Zacatecas. México: Ediciones Botas, 1940.

[Esparza S. (ref. 1291, p. 16) indicates that Ríos Franco gives some incorrect information about the Corrido del caballo mojino (pp. 184-187).]

1578. Rivera, Diego. "José Guadalupe Posada, the Popular Artist." Artes de México (Edition in English) (México), IV:21 (January and February of 1958), [3-4].

[These two pages of fairly routine praise serve as an introduction to an entire number of the publication which is devoted to Posada.]

1579. Robb, John Donald. Hispanic Folk Songs of New Mexico. Albuquerque: University of New Mexico Press, 1954. viii, 83 pp. (University of New Mexico Publications in the Fine Arts, No. 1.)

[A discussion of various types of New Mexican folk songs with treatment of their literary and musical characteristics; also discussion of religious folk plays. There are texts, rhymed translations, and music of fifteen songs, including two corridos (Corrido de Elena and Corrido de la muerte de Antonio Mestas), an indita (Indita de

Amarante Martínez), and a so-called relación (Mi carro Ford), though the author himself states that the term relación is not used in New Mexico.]

1580. Robb, John Donald. "The J. D. Robb Collection of Folk Music Recordings." NMFR, VII(1952-1953), 6-20.
[A list of 1,096 recordings of folk music, mostly from New Mexico but with some made in Mexico. Many are corridos and romances.]

1581. _____. "The Sources of a New Mexico Folksong." NMFR, V(1950-1951), 9-16.
[A report on the author's successful efforts to seek out information about the circumstances surrounding the death of Antonio Maestas as reported in the Corrido de Antonio Maestas. The text and music of one version of the corrido are given.]

1582. Rodríguez, Antonio. "El grabado; su función pública y su carácter estético." Espacios, revista integral de arquitectura y artes plásticas (México), enero de 1950, no pagination.
[In this article on engraving there is reference to José Guadalupe Posada, and several of his works are reproduced photographically. Included are some broadsides of corridos: La persecución de Pancho Villa, El "Buen Vecino," and El eclipse del peso. Though reduced in size, the texts of these reproductions are still legible.]

1583. Rodríguez Rivera, Virginia. "La copla en México." RHM, Año X:1-2 (enero y abril, 1944), 161-174.
[A collection of texts grouped according to subject matter. There is music for some of them. No data are given as to where they were collected.]

1584. _____. "La copla mexicana; estudio preliminar." ASFM, I(1938-1940), 103-121.
[A brief treatment of the Mexican copla with a short bibliography.]

_____. See Mendoza, Vicente T., entry no. 1490.

1585. Rojas, Arnold R. Lore of the California Vaquero. Fresno, California: Academy Library Guild, 1958. 162 pp. 22 cm.

1586. Rojas Garcidueñas, José, ed. "Versos dedicados a la inundación de Salamanca." ASFM, XI(1957), 73-75.
[The text of a corrido taken from a broadside which the editor reprints with a few notes to clarify certain passages. The subject of the composition is a flood which occurred in 1912.]

1587. "Romance."
[An anonymous romance heroico which closed the poetry contest described in my notes to ref. 1143. Núñez y Domínguez prints its text (ref. 1515, pp. 216-217).]

1588. [Romance]. Crónica científica y literaria [México ?], No. 235, 29 de junio de 1819.
[Menéndez y Pelayo (ref. 82, Vol. XXVII, p. 113) prints two lines of the poem, which is very artistic in tone, and suggests that it should probably be attributed to Manuel Eduardo de Gorostiza.]

1589. Romance y corta esplicación de la historia de la estatua de Carlos IV, primera parte. México: Imp. de los Rebeldes, 1852. 2 pp.
[Torres-Ríoseco and Warner (ref. 1658, p. 75) list it.]

1590. Romero, Jesús C. "El folklore en México." BGE, LXIII (1947), 657-798.
[A long and rambling history of folklore investigations in Mexico. In making a distinction between folklore and arte popular, the author discusses the corrido.]

1591. ———. "La música en Guerrero." DdeG, 14 de enero de 1949, p. 2.

1592. Romero Flores, Jesús. Anales históricos de la Revolución Mexicana; sus corridos. México: El Nacional, 1941. 332 pp. 19 cm.
[A large collection of corrido texts taken from broadsides and covering the period from the latter part of the nineteenth century through the administration of Lázaro Cárdenas.]

1593. Romero de Terreros, Manuel. "Corrido de la Hacienda de Xalpa, estado de México." ASFM, IV(1943), 145-149.
[A semipopular corrido designed to be sung on the hacienda mentioned.]

Rosas de Oquendo, Mateo. See Paz y Melia, A., entry no. 1536; also, entry no. 21.

1594. Ross, Patricia Fent. "The Mejicanos of Cuetzalan." Mesoamerican Notes (México), II(1950), 94-101.

1595. Rossi, Giuseppe Carlo. "Poesia popolare spagnola nel Nordamerica." Idea (Roma), VI(1954):25.
[Said to be a review of Aurelio M. Espinosa's Romancero de Nuevo Méjico.]

1596. Rubio, Darío. Refranes, proverbios y dichos y dicharachos mexicanos. México, 1937. xxx, 469 pp. 24 cm.; also, 2. ed., corr. y aumentada considerablemente. 2 vols. México: Editorial A. P. Márquez, 1940. 23 cm.
[Occasionally the author quotes coplas or other popular poems by way of illustrating proverbial expressions.]

1597. El ruiseñor mexicano; colección de canciones populares. San Antonio, Texas: Lozano, 1921; 3.ª edición. San Antonio, Texas: Lozano, 1924. 172 pp.
[A collection of popular songs of many types. Some are corridos,

parodies of corridos, or songs on the fringes of the corrido tradition: El presidiario, Corrido del descarrilamiento, El venadito, Adelita, Mamá Carlota, Nuevos versos de Don Simón, and others.]

1598. Ruiseñor yucateco. Primera y segunda partes. Mérida: Editores Galo Fernández; also, México: El Parnaso Mexicano, n. d.
[Mendoza (ref. 1482, p. 54) cites the work as a source of coplas and (p. 50) as a source of romances.]

1599. Ruiz, Eduardo. Historia de la guerra de intervención en Michoacán. México: Ofic. Tip. de la Secretaría de Fomento, 1896. x, 698 pp. 22 cm.
[There are coplas scattered throughout the book (pp. 232, 386, 432, 625, 629, 632, 646, and 650). Also, there is an account of the circumstances surrounding the writing of Adiós a Mamá Carlota (pp. 647-648), and the text of the song is given.]

1600. _____. Un idilio a través de la guerra. México: Librería de la Vda. de Ch. Bouret, 1923. xiii, 392 pp. 19 cm.
[A historical novel about the war against the French, the work contains several coplas and other popular songs (pp. 27-33, 56, 107, 259, 263-266, 286 [a strophe from Adiós a Mamá Carlota), 359, and 360).]

1601. Saavedra, Alfredo M. "La expresión folklórica militar." ASFM, II(1941), 207-223.
[A study of military slang. It includes a corrido from Zirándaro, Guerrero, called Despedimiento de un militar ascendido.]

1602. Sahagún, Bernardino de. Historia general de las cosas de Nueva España. 5 vols. México: Editorial Pedro Robredo, 1938. 24.5 cm.
[Although there are many references to songs, dances, areitos, etc. throughout this work, particularly in the Libro segundo (Vol. I, pp. 77-253), none seems to be related directly to ballads or to popular poetry or song of a narrative character.]

1603. Salado Alvarez, Victoriano. "Sobre la poesía popular americana." La Unión Hispanoamericana (Madrid), enero de 1920, 13-14.
[After citing passages from Bernal Díaz which attest to the popularity of romances among the men of Cortés, the author expresses a belief that investigation into Mexican oral tradition should uncover many Spanish romances.]

1604. Saldívar, Gabriel. Historia de la música en México. México: Secretaría de Educación Pública. Impreso en los talleres de la Editorial Cultura, 1934. vii, 324 pp. 24 cm.
[In this general history of music in Mexico, Saldívar touches briefly on certain aspects of popular music, including corridos.]

1605. _____. "El jarabe, baile popular mexicano." AnMN, 5a. época, II:1, 2, 3 y 4 (1937), 305-326 and 35 pp. of plates. (Vol. XXVII of the complete collection of the Anales.)

[An excellent study of the jarabe in Mexico with many musical examples. There are a few copla texts which accompany jarabes.]

1606. _____. "Mariano Elízaga y las canciones de la independencia." BGE, LXIII:3 (mayo-junio de 1947), 641-656.

[A valuable study of some insurgent songs from the period of Mexican independence. Though none is called a corrido, several are obviously related to the corrido tradition. Saldívar seeks to show that Elízaga could not have written one of the songs, a march, which has been attributed to him.]

1607. Sánchez Escobar, Rafael. Narraciones revolucionarias mexicanas, histórico-anecdóticas. Tlalpan, D. F.: Talleres Tipográficos de la Casa de Orientación para Varones, 1934. 221 pp. 19.5 cm.

[Leal (ref. 1388, pp. 15-16) indicates that Sánchez Escobar has some comments about the origins of the famous Villista song, La cucaracha, which reveal that it was known in Campeche before the Revolution.]

1608. Sánchez García, Julio. "Notas sobre el folklore de Zacatecas." ASFM, VIII(1954), 81-104.

[In treating various types of folklore from Zacatecas, the author mentions romances and corridos and gives some texts.]

1609. Sandburg, Carl. The American Songbag. New York: Harcourt, Brace and Co., 1927. xxiii, 495 pp. 26.5 cm.

[In a section called "Mexican Border Songs" (pp. 289-304) are found words and music of La cucaracha, Mañanitas, Lo que digo, El abandonado, Cielito Lindo, Adelita, and Versos de Montalgo. English translations are provided. The Versos de Montalgo is a true corrido collected in Texas.]

1610. Santamaría, Francisco J. Antología folklórica y musical de Tabasco; arreglo y estudio musical de Gerónimo Baqueiro Foster. Villahermosa, Tabasco: Imprenta Ayuntamiento, México, 1952. xlviii, 462 pp. 31 cm.

[Baqueiro Foster's excellent introduction traces the history of music in Tabasco from colonial times to the present. He mentions the failure of the romance to develop there into the corrido. He has much to say, however, about coplas and the music and dances associated with them (the son, etc.). In the collection of 171 musical compositions there is one corrido about the death of two aviators. Entitled Sidar y Rovirosa, it is the work of the Tabascan composer, Lauro Aguilar y Palma.]

1611. Santos, Carlos, comp. El cancionero mexicano. Los Angeles: Imprenta Española, n.d.

1612. Schinhan, Jan Philip. "Spanish Folklore from Tampa, Florida: (No. VI) Folksongs." SFQ, III:2 (September, 1939), 129-153.

[A very complete technical analysis of the music of thirty-one recordings of Spanish and Cuban songs made by R. S. Boggs in Tampa, Florida. There are no texts and the titles which are mentioned do not belong to the romance tradition.]

1613. Schmeckebier, Laurence E. Modern Mexican Art. Minneapolis: The University of Minnesota Press, 1939. xvii, 198 pp. 27 cm.

[In dealing with Diego Rivera's frescoes in the Ministry of Education, the author gives English translations of the two corridos which the artist illustrated: The Proletarian Revolution and The Mexican Revolution. They are the same translations which appear in Frescoes in Ministry of Education, edited by Carlos Mérida.]

1614. Secretaría de Educación Pública, Sección de Música. Mexican Folk Music. México, D. F. Mimeographed.

[Chase (ref. 25, p. 188) comments: "37 songs (corridos, etc.) for voice and piano."]

1615. Segunda Parte de los Romances del Valiente Francisco Esteban, más otro romance del Miserable estado en que pone al alma la culpa mortal, más una canción (zéjel) acerca de la Confesión. Impreso en México por Francisco Rivera Calderón. Año de 1717.

[Mendoza (ref. 1487, p. 784) lists this work. The first part of the composition is listed in entry no. 1554.]

1616. Seibold, Doris, and Bork, William. Versos del sombrero blanco. Tucson: University of Arizona, 1949. 20 pp. (University of Arizona Bulletin, General Bulletin 14, Vol. XX, No. 2.)

[Boggs (ref. 13 [1950], p. 56) says: "Collected by Seibold and her high school pupils in Patagonia, Santa Cruz county, and edited with introduction by Bork. Texts of 87 versos or coplas (usually 4 verses of 8 syllables with rime or assonance in second and fourth, on some variation of love theme), in Spanish. Recited by men and women to partner during 'White Hat' dance."]

1617. Serrano Martínez, Celedonio. "Convivencia del romance español y el corrido mexicano en Guerrero." Cuauh, Núm. 3 (septiembre de 1950), 40-46.

[Following a discussion of the popular poetry of the state of Guerrero, the author gives the texts of a number of corridos which are derivados from Spanish counterparts. He collected them from popular singers. Their titles: Casamiento del piojo y la pulga, El piojo y la chinche, El piojo y la pulga, Casamiento del conejo y la liebre, Casamiento de la primavera y el pájaro Jacobo, Casamiento del rábano y la lechuga, and Estribillo del ratón casado. They are written in varying meters.]

1618. ———. "El corrido popular en Guerrero." DdeG, 20 de enero de 1949, p. 4.

1619. _____. El Coyote, corrido de la Revolución. México, 1951. 333 pp.

[An artistic poem modeled on popular corridos. There are some comments in the author's notes upon corridos in general and upon his own composition.]

1620. _____. "Cuatro corridos anónimos dedicados a don Benito Juárez." Cuauh, Núm. 1 (febrero de 1950), 26-33.

[The author offers the texts of four compositions which he collected in Guerrero from two "juglares." To two of these he gives the title Corrido histórico a Maximiliano de Austria; the other two he calls Corrido patriótico dedicado a Juárez. All are written in the long lines of thirteen and fourteen syllables which the author says are characteristic of the corridos of Guerrero. They are probably of fairly recent origin and, with the possible exception of the first Corrido histórico, they all seem to show strong learned influences.]

1621. _____. "Definición del corrido." El maestro mexicano (México), 3a. época, Año VI, Tomo VI:24 (septiembre de 1956), 38-39; 25 (octubre de 1956), 34-36.

[In the first installment the author seeks to describe the corrido and its role in Mexican life. He gives a personal definition which is excellent; certainly it is as good as or better than any other attempt to define the genre. The second installment, which bears a subtitle, "Origen y antigüedad del corrido," is a very important challenge to the almost universally accepted theory that the corrido derives from the Spanish romance. The author holds that the extreme metrical variety of the corrido proves that many other poetic genres besides the romance contributed to its development. Though some of his conclusions call for careful study before they can be accepted, this article is one of the freshest studies of the corrido to appear in many years.]

1622. _____. "Diferencias entre el corrido mexicano y el romance español." Cuauh, Núm. 2 (abril de 1950), 44-47.

[The author points out such differences as the following: (1) the corrido is not confined exclusively to the epic narrative tone; (2) corridos are complete compositions; they are not fragments of longer poems; (3) the corrido contains fewer superstitious elements (signs, omens, etc.); (4) the corrido treats heroic figures more realistically; they usually have no more than human proportions; etc. The article is of interest, though some of its conclusions may be open to question.]

1623. _____. "Romances tradicionales en Guerrero." ASFM, VII(1951), 7-72.

[A valuable study which contains a great many texts.]

_____. See Colín, Mario, entry no. 1240.

1624. Sifuentes, R. Fernando. "Comparative Study of the New Mexican and Mexican Popular Songs." M.A. thesis, University of

New Mexico, 1939. 102 pp. typewritten.

[A study of songs, including many folk songs, though there is no mention of romances or corridos.]

1625. Silva y Aceves, Mariano. "La colección folklórica de la Biblioteca del Museo Nacional." AnMN, Epoca 4a., Tomo I:3 (julio y agosto de 1925), 269-320.

[The author points out the need for study of Mexico's folklore and describes the rich collection of hojas which are in the Museo Nacional. He divides them into six groups and proposes to treat each category separately. In this article he covers only the first of these, Hojas de asuntos religiosos. He describes these in considerable detail and provides excellent photographic reproductions of some in handsome plates. In an appendix to the article he numbers the hojas and reproduces the texts of all of them (twenty-nine in number). They are of diverse types: mañanitas, décimas, alabanzas, despedimentos, alabados, cuandos, etc. A few are narrative décimas in the style of corridos, though they are not so named.]

Silverman, Joseph H. See Armistead, Samuel G., entry no. 1155.

1626. Simmons, Merle E. "Attitudes Toward the United States Revealed in Mexican Corridos." Hisp, XXXVI:1 (February, 1953), 34-42.

[A study of Mexican attitudes toward the United States as revealed in the strophes of corridos published over the past half century or more.]

1627. _____. "Unas canciones y poesías históricas de la época de la independencia mexicana." RHM, XXIV:4 (octubre de 1958), 369-379.

[A study of the texts of some popular songs from the period around 1810-1820 which appeared in the Cuadro histórico de la revolución de la América Mexicana by Carlos María de Bustamente (see entry no. 1191). The texts of a number of these are given as are some of Bustamante's comments about the popular songs of his day.]

1628. _____. "Francisco I. Madero en los corridos mexicanos." Boletín bibliográfico de la Secretaría de Hacienda y Crédito Público (México), No. 76 (25 de noviembre de 1956), pp. 1, 4; No. 77 (26 de noviembre de 1956), pp. 4; No. 78 (27 de noviembre de 1956), p. 4; No. 79 (28 de noviembre de 1956), p. 4.

[A study of the figure of Francisco I. Madero as revealed in the texts of a number of corridos. Photographic reproductions of some broadsides are included with the article.]

1629. _____. The Mexican Corrido as a Source for Interpretive Study of Modern Mexico (1870-1950). Bloomington, Indiana: Indiana University Press, 1957. xviii, 619 pp. 23.5 cm. (Indiana University

Publications, Humanities Series, No. 38.)

[An introductory chapter treats the nature of the corrido and traces the history of its development up to 1870. Chap. II discusses the types of corridos which were current before the Revolution of 1910. In the remainder of the book wherein the period from 1910 to 1950 is treated, there are chapters on each of the important presidents of Mexico and on the caudillos, Pancho Villa and Emiliano Zapata; chapters on political, agrarian, labor, and religious reform; and a final chapter on Mexico's relations with the United States and North Americans. There is an extensive bibliography of corridos and of works consulted.]

1630. _____. "The Mexican Corrido as a Source for Interpretive Study of Modern Mexico (1870-1950); With a Consideration of the Origins and Development of the Corrido Tradition." Ph. D. diss., University of Michigan, 1951. v, 546 pp. typewritten.

[This work has been published in greatly expanded and revised book form (see entry no 1629).]

1631. _____. "Porfirio Díaz in Mexico's Historical Ballads." NMHR, XXXI:1 (January, 1956), 1-23.

[A study of Porfirio Díaz as he appears in Mexican corridos from the latter part of the nineteenth century until recent times. This study is reprinted as Chap. III of The Mexican Corrido as a Source for Interpretive Study of Modern Mexico (1870-1950), entry no. 1629.]

1632. Simpson, Eylar N. The Ejido, Mexico's Way Out. Chapel Hill, North Carolina: The University of North Carolina Press, 1937. xxi, 849 pp. 24 cm.

[Contains texts with English translations of two corridos, Centro ejidal de Rancho Nuevo (pp. 129-130) and Las esperanzas de la patria por la rendición de Villa (pp. 437-438); also, the English translation only of a corrido without title about the completion of a federal rural school in Octlán (pp. 313-314); also, a corrido fragment with an English translation (p. 229).]

1633. Smith, John T. "Rails Below the Rio Grande." In "And Horns on the Toads," ed. by Mody C. Boatright, Wilson M. Hudson, and Allen Maxwell. Dallas: Southern Methodist University Press, 1959. Pp. 122-135. (Publication of the Texas Folklore Society, No. XXIX.)

[A study of the Mexican attitudes toward railroads as revealed in four corridos.]

Smith, Rebecca. See Major, Mabel, entry no. 1418.

1634. Spell, Lota M. "Las canciones populares hispano-americanas en los Estados Unidos." BLAM, V(1941), 201-205.

[A discussion of the reasons why Spanish American songs have been popular in the southwestern part of the United States along with a short résumé of the work of such collectors as Lummis, Hague, Espinosa, et al. There is brief mention of romances, décimas, corridos, inditas, and other genres.]

1635. Spell, Lota M. Music in Texas. Austin, Texas, 1936. 157 pp. 23 cm.
[Chase (ref. 25, p. 223) comments: " 'Spanish-American folk music,' p. 14-22, includes 6 songs with Spanish words and English translation."]

Sperotti Piñero, Emma Susana. See entry no. 401.

1636. Spizzy, Mable Seeds, and Kinscella, Hazel Gertrude. La Fiesta; A Unit of Early California Songs and Dances. Lincoln, Nebraska: The University Publishing Co., 1939. 45 pp. 21.5 cm.

Stanley, Daniel D. See MacCurdy, Raymond R., entry no. 1413.

1637. Stelzmann, A. " 'Calaveras' in Lateinamerika; Zum mexikanischen Totenfest, Día de los muertos." IAR, III(1937), 114-116.

1638. Stephenson, Robert C. "Signature in Ballad and Story." In Folk Travelers, Ballads, Tales, and Talk, ed. by Mody C. Boatright, Wilson M. Hudson, and Allen Maxwell. Dallas: Southern Methodist University Press, 1953. Pp. 97-109. (Publication of the Texas Folklore Society, No. XXV.)
[In dealing with the art of the professional story-teller, the author has occasion to make passing references to ballad literature in Spain and England and to the corridos of Mexico. These latter references are very minor and have to do with the popular poet's claims to authorship of his composition.]

1639. Stevenson, Robert. Music in Mexico; A Historical Survey. New York: Thomas Y. Crowell Co., 1952. 300 pp. 24 cm.
[The author comments in several places on the corrido. Especially interesting is some information about its music.]

1640. Swan, Howard. Music in the Southwest, 1825-1950. San Marino, California: The Huntington Library, 1952. x, 316 pp. 24 cm.
[In Chap. VI, "The Music of Mission, Rancho, and Pueblo," the author deals with some Spanish-language songs and gives three texts, one of which is a historical copla about a general, one Manuel Michetorena. It apparently dates from about 1820-1825.]

Taylor, Coley. See Demarest, Donald, entry no. 1263.

1641. Taylor, Paul S. "Corrido de Texas" and "Deportados." In Texas Folk and Folklore, ed. by Mody C. Boatright, Wilson M. Hudson, and Allen Maxwell. Dallas: Southern Methodist University Press, 1954. PP. 155-158. (Publication of the Texas Folklore Society, No. XXVI.)
[Two corrido texts preceded by brief introductions. English translations are provided.]

1642. _____. "Songs of the Mexican Migration." In Puro Mexicano, ed. by J. Frank Dobie. Austin, Texas, 1935. Pp. 221-245. (Texas Folklore Society Publications, No. XII.)
[Among the songs whose texts are published here are several very interesting corridos which have not appeared elsewhere.]

1643. Téllez Girón, Roberto. "Investigaciones folklóricas: La sierra norte de Puebla." BIMMF, Año I:1 (enero, 1940), 35-65.
[A report on folklore investigations into the traditional music of Puebla and Veracruz. Twenty-nine folk tunes with commentaries are included. None, however, is narrative in so far as can be detected from their titles, and no texts are given except for some lyrical décimas.]

1644. Tiempo, semanario de la vida y la verdad. (México), 1942-.
[In reporting on current events, this excellent weekly news magazine occasionally prints the strophes of popular corridos.]

1645. Tinker, Edward Larocque. "Campaigning with Villa." SWR, XXX:2 (Winter, 1945), 148-154.
[The author relates (pp. 153-154) that at the Battle of Celaya he heard Villa's soldiers singing corridos about events which had happened only twenty-four hours earlier.]

1646. _____. Corridos & Calaveras. Austin: The University of Texas, 1961. 60 pp. 31 cm.
[Contains a discussion of the history of two closely related genres of popular literature, the corrido and the calavera. The author defines their nature and provides several photographic reproductions of some typical hojas sueltas. Translations of the texts of these are provided by Américo Paredes (pp. 41-58).]

1647. Toor, Frances, ed. Cancionero mexicano. México: Mexican Folkways, 1931. 36 pp.
[A collection of popular songs of various types. Some are corridos.]

1648. _____. "Guadalupe Posada." MF, IV:3 (July-September, 1928), 140-189.
[A study of the artistic and political importance of José Guadalupe Posada. There is a large collection of engravings by the famous illustrator of corridos and other popular literature.]

1649. _____. "Noticias de los pueblos." MF, IV:4 (October-December, 1928), 232-241.
[Discusses some of the calaveras which were circulating in 1928 and gives the texts of two of them, both in the nature of corridos: Calaveras de la última rebelión (pp. 236-237) and Calaveras de las próximas elecciones (pp. 238-240).]

1650. _____. "Our Song Number." MF, III:2 (1927), 78-84.
[The author outlines here the nature of several types of Mexican

popular songs, including the corrido, which she characterizes as "the most important." The article is an introduction to a group of songs.]

1651. Toor, Frances, ed. A Treasury of Mexican Folkways. New York: Crown Publishers, 1947. xxxii, 566 pp. 23.5 cm.
[A survey of Mexican folklore intended primarily for the general reader. It contains, however, a great deal of material in accessible form, including some discussion of the corrido and other popular songs.]

1652. _____, O'Higgins, Paul, and Vanegas Arroyo, Blas, eds. Las obras de José Guadalupe Posada. México: Publicada por Mexican Folkways, Talleres Gráficos de la Nación, 1930. 215 pp. 35.5 cm.
[A collection of 406 engravings, many of which illustrated corridos. However, no corrido texts are given.]

1653. Torquemada, Juan de. Monarquía indiana. Tercera edición. 3 vols. México: Editorial Salvador Chávez Hayhoe, 1943, 1943, and 1944. 29.5 cm.
[A photographic reproduction of the Spanish edition "En Madrid en la Oficina a costa de Nicolas Rodríguez Franco/Año de 1723." On several occasions Torquemada treats historical songs of the Aztecs and the existence of more or less professional cantores (see Vol. I, Bk. II, Chap. XLI, p. 147, and Chap. LXXXVIII, p. 230; Vol. II, Bk. X, Chap. XXXIV, p. 296, and Bk. XIV, Chap. XI, pp. 550-552; and Vol. III, Bk. XVII, Chap. III, p. 214).]

1654. Torre, Manuel. "Genealogía y valor poético de la copla." Nacion, 11 de noviembre, 1951.

1655. Torre, M. de la. "Del folklore religioso: Notas sobre el villancico y los romances de Reyes." RMM, I(1942):3, pp. 57-60.

1656. Torres Quintero, Gregorio. México hacia el fin del virreinato español. Paris-Mexico: Librería de la Vda. de Ch. Bouret, 1921. 157 pp. 24.5 cm.
[Contains (pp. 60-61, 150-152) a few strophes of popular songs copied from Luis González Obregón's México viejo.]

1657. _____. Versos, cuentos y leyendas. Colima: Imp. del Gobierno del Estado a cargo de F. Munguía Torres, 1893. 190 pp. 17.5 cm. (On the cover: Colima: Imp. de Ignacio F. Fuentes, a cargo de F. Munguía Torres, 1894.)

1658. Torres-Ríoseco, Arturo, and Warner, Ralph E. Bibliografía de la poesía mexicana. Cambridge, Mass.: Harvard University Press, 1934. xxxix, 86 pp. 23.5 cm.
[An excellent bibliography which contains indispensable information for the study of popular as well as artistic poetry.]

1659. Torri, Julio, ed. Romances viejos. México: Editorial Cultura, Tipografía Murguía, 1918.
[A collection of Spanish romances. The editor's introduction merely

summarizes the accepted theories about the origin and development of the various types of romances. The possibility that any of the compositions printed might be alive in Mexican tradition is not considered.]

1660. Toscano, Salvador. "Los romances viejos en México en el siglo XVI y un romance anónimo a Cortés." FyL, No. 27 (julio-septiembre, 1947), 127-132.

[Summarizes evidence of the romance's popularity in America during the sixteenth century. There follows the text of a romance about Cortés which was printed in Spain but which Toscano, for reasons which he explains, believes was written in America.]

1661. Toussaint, Manuel. "Estudios folklóricos." RMM, I:3 (15 de julio, 1919), 23-25.

[Chase comments (ref. 25, p. 183): "First of a series of articles on Hispanic-Mexican folk music. Quotes text of La canción de Mambrú."]

1662. _____. "Folklore histórico: La canción de Mambrú." Revista mexicana de estudios históricos (México), I (enero-febrero, 1927), 101-104.

[A study of Mambrú in France, Spain, and Mexico. One Mexican version is given.]

_____, ed. See Inclán, Luis G., entry no. 1376.

1663. Triumphal/pompa/en qve la nobilissima/ciudad de Mexico/dispvso a la entrada,/del Exmo. Señor,/Don Jvan Antonio/Vasquez de Acuña,/Marques de Cassa Fverte/del Orden de Santiago, Commendador de Adelpha/en la de Alcantara, de el Consejo de su Magestad/en el de Guerra, General de los Reales Exercitos:/Governador de Mescina, en el Reyno de Sicilia;/Commandante General de Mallorca, VI-REY/Governador, y Capitan General, de esta Nueva/España, y presidente de la Real Audiencia/de Mexico./Con Licencia en Mexico: Por JOSEPH BERNARDO DE HOGAL,/en la Calle de la Acequia. Año 1722. 8 lvs. (Reproduced photographically in AnMN, Epoca 4a., IV:1 (enero a febrero, 1926), plates between pp. 30-31.)

[Of this work one page of double columns is written in romance meter. See also entry no. 1555.]

1664. El trovador mexicano; la colección más completa de canciones populares. Cuarta edición. San Antonio, Texas: Librería de Quiroga, n.d.

[A collection of texts of all kinds of popular songs. It includes Mamá Carlota (a version which is quite different from the traditional one), El corrido del descarrilamiento (a parody), El venadito, and many other composiciones.]

1665. Tully, Marjorie F. An Annotated Bibliography of Spanish Folklore in New Mexico and Southern Colorado. Albuquerque, New Mexico: The University of New Mexico Press, 1950. 124 pp. 23 cm. University of New Mexico Publications in Language and Literature,

No. 3.)
[A good bibliography that includes a few items which have to do with the corrido.]

1666. Twenty-Five Prints of José Guadalupe Posada. México: La Estampa Mexicana, 1942. 27 cm. (The outer tied cardboard covers, which are cloth covered, bear the title: José Guadalupe Posada, 1851-1913.)
[A folder which contains engravings which illustrated cancioneros and other forms of popular literature, though no corridos. On the back side of the title page there is introductory comment in Spanish and English about Posada and his work.]

1667. Van Der Voort, Antoni, comp. Old Spanish Songs as Sung by Sra. Da. María Antonia Jimeno de Arata. Santa Barbara, California: Santa Barbara Music Shoppe, 1928.
[Chase (ref. 25, p. 225) says: "19 songs of the early Californians, for voice with piano accompaniment (Spanish texts only)."]

1668. Van Stone, M. R. Spanish Folk Songs of New Mexico. Chicago: Seymour, 1928. 41 pp. 31.5 cm.
[Words and music of twenty-three songs with English translations. There are no genuine corridos, but there are versions of Adelita, La cucaracha, and Don Simón (printed here with the title Don Simón de mi vida).]

1669. Vanegas Arroyo, Arsacio. José Guadalupe Posada: 36 grabados. México, 1943. 31 pp. 35 cm.
[Engravings of the famous artist, some of which illustrated corridos and other types of popular literature. There is a brief introduction concerning Posada and his art.]

Vanegas Arroyo, Blas. See Toor, Frances, entry no. 1652.

1670. Vásquez, Genaro V. Música popular y costumbres regionales del estado de Oaxaca. México, 1924. 44 pp.

1671. Vázquez Santa Ana, Higinio. Canciones, cantares y corridos mexicanos. México: Ediciones León Sánchez, n. d. 280 pp. 18.5 cm.; Vol. II. México: n. p., 1925. 328 pp. 20 cm.
[Two extensive collections of texts including many corridos. There is music for a few compositions.]

1672. ———. Fiestas y costumbres mexicanas. 2 vols. México: Ediciones Botas, 1940, 1953. 19.5 cm.
[Vol. I, the only one I have been able to examine, contains a few popular songs and corridos.]

1673. ———. Historia de la canción mexicana. México: Talleres Gráficos de la Nación, 1931. 255 pp. 23 cm.
[The author comments on the art of popular singers and poets and gives the texts of a few corridos.]

1674. _____. Sones, corridos y canciones para canto y piano. México, n. d.
[Chase (ref. 25, p. 188) comments: "10 anonymous songs, arranged for voice and piano (Spanish text only)."]

1675. Verdadero romance de Lucinda y Velardo. Puebla: Imp. de Don Padre de la Rosa, 1817. 2 lvs.

1676. Verdadero romance en que se refiere un lastimoso caso que le sucedió a una dama, natural de la ciudad de Truxillo, nombrada, Rosaura, a la cual su amante la sacó de su casa engañada con palabra de casamiento; y despues de haverla gozado, la dejó amarrada a un tronco en sierramorena: y el egenplar castigo que en él y en un primo suyo que fue cónplice, se egecutó. Reimp. en México en la Oficina de Don Alexandro Valdés, 1819. 2 lvs.

1677. Vialpando, Roberto L. "Estudio comparativo de algunos romances religiosos de los Hermanos Penitentes en Nuevo México." Diss., University of Utah, 1947.

1678. Villarreal, Concha de. Guitarras mexicanas. San Pedro, Coahuila: Talleres Gráficos de "El Látigo," 1937. 160 pp. 18.5 cm.

Villaseñor, Isabel. See entry no. 1378.

1679. Wagner, Max L. "Algunas apuntaciones sobre el folklore mexicano." JAF, XL(1927), 105-143.
[Folklore collected in 1914, mostly in Veracruz. Besides some tales, aguinaldos, and poetry of different kinds, there are some romances and a version of Mambrú.]

Warner, Ralph E. See Torres-Ríoseco, Arturo, entry no. 1658.

1680. Watkins, Frances E. (for F. W. Hodge). "Collectors and Collections: The Charles F. Lummis Collection of Spanish California and Indian Songs in the Southwest Museum, Los Angeles." CFQ, I(1942): 1, pp. 99-101.
[A description of the collection of 350 Spanish and 131 Indian songs which Lummis made on wax cylinders between 1901 and 1912. There is also mention of some manuscript books of popular singers which Lummis collected and which are now in the Southwest Museum Library in Los Angeles.]

1681. _____. " 'He Said It With Music; Spanish-California Folk Songs Recorded by Charles F. Lummis." CFQ, I(1942):4, pp. 359-367.
[This is, in reality, an expanded version of entry no. 1680. The author outlines Lummis' work in western folklore and describes somewhat more completely the collection made by Lummis which is in the Southwest Museum. Also, she provides more bibliographical data about the songs of the collection which have been published.]

Weinstock, Herbert. See Chávez, Carlos, entry no. 1230.

1682. Whatley, W. A. "A Mexican Popular Ballad." PTFS, IV(1925), 10-17.
[A discussion of the ballads of northern Mexico known usually as tragedias. There is a text of Heraclio Bernal with music.]

1683. Wolfe, Bertram D. "El corrido mexicano." M.A. thesis, Columbia University, 1931. 174 pp.

_____. See Henríquez Ureña, Pedro, entry no. 1367.

1684. Wood, Ben D. "A Mexican Border Ballad." PTFS, No. I (1916), 55-57.
[Reports on a broadside of La Adelita which was circulating in Nuevo Laredo, Tamaulipas.]

1685. Woods, Betty. "Easter Customs on the Río Grande." New Mexico (Santa Fe), XXVIII:4 (April, 1950), 45-47.
[Rael (ref. 1562 [1950-1951], p. 38) says: "Description of a party where New Mexico Spanish folk dances and coplas were used."]

1686. Woolsey, A. W. "A Contemporary Texas Tragedy Related in Two Mexican 'Corridos'." Hisp, XXVIII:4 (November, 1945), 505-507.
[Texts of two corridos which relate a traffic accident in which almost thirty people died.]

1687. Works Project Administration, Federal Music Project, Unit No. 1. Spanish American Folk Songs. New Mexico, 1936-1937. Mimeographed.
[Among its fifteen folk songs with music and texts (with English translations) is the Corrido de Victorio, a song about an Apache uprising in 1878.]

1688. _____, Unit No. 2. Spanish American Folk Songs. New Mexico, 1936-1937. Mimeographed.
[Among its eighteen folk songs with texts and music are Paso del norte (classified as a corrido) and the Corrido de José Elizoido.]

1689. _____, Unit No. 3. Spanish American Singing Games. Revised, 1940. 27 unnumbered lvs. Mimeographed. 28 cm.
[Thirteen singing games with music and texts with English translations. There is no mention of corridos or other narratives.]

1690. El xarabe loco de Hidalgo y Allende. [México, 1810.] 8 pp.
[Listed by Torres-Ríoseco and Warner (ref. 1658, p. 85).]

1691. Zorrilla, José. México y los mexicanos (1855-1857). México: Ediciones de Andrea, 1955. xxi, 158 pp. (Colección Studium, 9.)
[Zorrilla has a few comments about Mexican popular music (pp. 31-33) and popular poetry (pp. 78-81). Though there is nothing of great

moment, because of their early date and because of their source, they are of interest.]

1692. Zuno, José Guadalupe. "José Guadalupe Posada." UnivMex, VIII(abril de 1954), 21-22.
[Criticism of the work of Posada with special attention to the ironic elements contained therein.]

1693. _____. Posada y la ironía plástica. Guadalajara: Biblioteca de Autores Jaliscienses Modernos, 1958. 64 pp. plus 50 lvs. of photographs, engravings, and lithographs. 23.5 cm.
[A collection of good plates which are representative of Posada's work preceded by a commentary which is lively and informative but subjective rather than scholarly in tone. There is not much in it that is new as the author discusses Posada's life and art.]

NICARAGUA

Nicaragua is unique among Central American countries for the presence of a folklorist of recognized ability whose interest in the romance-corrido tradition of his country has resulted in his publishing a valuable volume about the poetry and songs of his native region. From the work of Ernesto Mejía Sánchez, it is clear that both romances and corridos in the Mexican pattern are widely cultivated in Nicaragua. But much work remains to be done. Mejía Sánchez' work is not exhaustive; indeed, his investigations do not attempt to do more than indicate the possibility of fruitful research into musical folklore. Unfortunately, capable scholars are lacking. Mejía Sánchez is the only Nicaraguan of stature who has studied the romance-corrido tradition of his country.

NICARAGUA

1694. Acuña Escobar, F. De la música popular nicaragüense. San Sebastián, Elite (Managua), febrero, 1946, págs. 27-31.
[The above entry, which is unclear, is copied exactly as it appears in RDTP, III(1947), 631.]

1695. Cuaderno del Taller de San Lucas (Managua). No. 1 (1942), No. 2 (1943), No. 4 (1944), No. 5 (1951).
[Lidia Rosalía de Jijena Sánchez (ref. 60) quotes some popular poetry taken from this series. Though none of it is truly popular, the cuadernos might bear looking into. She fails to list No. 3.]

1696. Cuadra, Pablo Antonio. "Canta el pueblo." Camino, Boletín del Instituto de Folklore Nicaragüense (Granada), No. 1 (19 de mayo, 1944), p. 3.
[Boggs (ref. 13 [1944], p. 59) indicates that the article deals with three ballads.]

1697. _____. "Horizonte patriótico del folklore." FICU, No. 2 (diciembre, 1940), p. 23.
[Gives texts of Nicaraguan versions of Las señas del esposo and the Corrido de la casada infiel. There is brief commentary by the author.]

1698. _____. [Nicaraguan Folklore.] La Prensa (Managua), 21 de octubre, 1940, p. 3; 4 de noviembre, 1940, pp. 2-3; 18 de noviembre, 1940, p. 5; 25 de noviembre, 1940, p. 5; 13 de enero, 1941, p. 3.

1699. Delgadillo, Luis A. "Del folklore musical en Nicaragua." Gaceta musical (Paris), I:9 (septiembre, 1928), 24-26; reprinted in Música (Bogotá), I:3 (junio, 1941), 57-58.
[A rambling discussion with most attention to Indian elements in Nicaraguan musical folklore. The author laments his countrymen's lack of interest in their folklore and in the efforts of composers like Delgadillo himself who have tried to use it in symphonic compositions. Though the article is inherently insignificant, a few details may be of some interest.]

1700. _____. "La música indígena y colonial en Nicaragua." REM, Año I:3 (abril de 1950), 43-57.
[A survey in which the author, in considering some popular dances, has occasion to quote the texts of a few coplas with music. But neither romances nor corridos are mentioned.]

1701. Fletes Bolaños, Anselmo. Regionales. Managua: Tipografía y Encuadernación Nacionales, 1922. 105 pp. 20.5 cm.
[The volume is made up principally of poetry written by the author in imitation of popular style. But besides his own compositions, which succeed extremely well in their purpose, he presents some genuinely popular jalalelas (i.e., coplas) by way of showing the kind of poetry that he is seeking to imitate. The poems and some introductory passages about them by Fletes Bolaños are of considerable interest. At the end there is also a list of nicaraguanismos.]

1702. Froebel, Julius. Seven Years' Travel in Central America, Northern Mexico, and the Far West of the United States. London: Richard Bentley, Publisher in Ordinary to Her Majesty, 1859. xiv, 587 pp. 23 cm.

[The author relates (p. 66) that while he was spending a night in the town of Tipitapa, Nicaragua, he heard a woman singing a song called the Versos de la viuda.]

1703. García, Secundino. Cancionero folklórico nicaragüense, Tomo I: Cantos al Niño Dios. Managua: Talleres Nacionales, 1945. 79 pp. 23 cm.

[A valuable collection of texts and music gathered from oral tradition. There are two sections: "Cantos al Niño Dios antes de su nacimiento" (twenty-four compositions) and "Cantos al Niño Dios después de su nacimiento" (sixty-one compositions). Only two or three are in romance or redondilla form, but there are some compositions with seven-syllable lines that have the romance rhyme pattern.]

1704. Mejía Sánchez, Ernesto. "Panorama del folklore nicaragüense." PyS, XII(1948), 305-306, 308-310.

[Boggs (ref. 13 [1948], p. 31) says: "Brief survey of Nicaraguan folklore: tales, beliefs, dances, music, arts, etc., giving some ideas of the nature of these materials."]

1705. _____. Romances y corridos nicaragüenses. México: Imprenta Universitaria, 1946. 122 pp. 23.5 cm.; first appeared in ASFM, V(1945), 69-181.

[The best study of the subject that has been made. Besides giving many texts of both romances and corridos, the author provides much background material about the romance-corrido tradition which is of significance to the history of narrative poetry in all areas of America.]

1706. _____. "La Virgen María en el romancero nicaragüense." Juventud, Congregación Mariana de Jóvenes Varones de Jalteva, Granada, Nicaragua, I(1943):12, pp. 15-16, 18-20.

1707. Música nicaragüense. Publicaciones del Ministerio de Relaciones Exteriores, República de Nicaragua: Talleres Tipográficos Hnos. Márquez, S. de R. L., n.d. 86 unnumbered pp. 31 cm.

[A collection of songs arranged for piano. Included are two compositions called corridos: Managua and Nicaragua mía, by Tino López. An introductory note says that López is the most popular cultivator of the corrido in Nicaragua, though Gilberto Vega also has written them. As examples of Vega's work, the volume includes only Tacho en Montelimar, a tango, and ¡Oh! Nicaragua, printed under the heading of canción. It appears that for the anonymous editor of this volume anything which sings the praises of a locality is a corrido.]

1708. Rosales G., F. J. Algo sobre música vernácula; la influencia española y mexicana sobre nuestra música regional y consideraciones personales del autor. Managua, 1944. 50 pp. (Publicaciones del Ministerio de Instrucción Pública de Nicaragua, Año I, No. 4.)

1709. Stout, Peter F. Nicaragua: Past, Present and Future. Philadelphia: J. E. Potter, 1859. 372 pp. 18.5 cm.
[Mejía Sánchez (ref. 1705, p. 11) cites a passage in this work wherein Stout, who had been Vice-Consul of the United States in Nicaragua in 1850, relates that he once heard a Nicaraguan girl singing a romance about the Cid.]

1710. "Teatro callejero nicaragüense: El Güegüence o macho ratón." Cuaderno del Taller San Lucas (Granada), Año I(1942):1.
[Mejía Sánchez (ref. 1705, p. 11) describes El Güegüence as a "comedia bailete anónima de la época colonial" and says that in an eighteenth-century manuscript of the play there are four references to corridos. These appear on pp. 102 and 104 of the above article.]

1711. Valle, Rafael Heliodoro. "Un romance en Nicaragua y en la inquisición." Revista del Archivo y Biblioteca Nacionales (Tegucigalpa, Honduras), XXVII:9-10 (marzo y abril, 1949), 454-469.
[The text of a romance dated 1808 and presented here as the earliest piece of poetry so far discovered in Nicaragua. Entitled Cartilla moderna para entrar a la moda, the poem, which is a picaresque testamento of a dying father who tells his son how to get along in the world, was the cause of inconclusive proceedings of the Inquisition against the supposed author of the romance, one Gregorio Marenco of Taustepe, Nicaragua. The documents of the Inquisition and the text of the romance are in the Archivo General de México. However, González Casanova, in Sátira anónima del siglo XVIII (ref. 1423), shows that the poem in question was circulating in Mexico around 1770.]

1712. Vega Miranda, Gilberto. La canción nicaragüense. Managua, 1945. 54 pp.

PANAMA

The <u>romance</u> tradition apparently is weak in Panama; at least it is hardly represented at all in the few studies which have been made of the popular poetry and song of the Isthmus area. In these works the <u>décimas</u> and <u>coplas</u>, known sometimes by local names, predominate. Though the investigators who have studied the musical and poetic folklore of Panama are few in number, the studies of Narciso Garay, Myron Schaeffer, and Dora and Manuel Zárate are of fairly high calibre.

PANAMA

1713. Garay, Narciso. <u>Tradiciones y cantares de Panamá; ensayo folklórico</u>. N.p.: Imp. L'Expansion Belge, 1930. 208 pp. 27 cm.
[A very rewarding article about many different aspects of the musical folklore of Panama. It includes a large number of texts with music. There appear to be no true narratives in <u>romance</u> or other meters, but among the <u>tamboritos</u> and <u>mejoranas</u> are some political songs, or <u>coplas</u>, and there is a popular drama, or <u>farsa</u>, as the author calls it, which is written in <u>romance</u> meter. Also worthy of mention are some <u>décimas</u>, though they are subjective and satirical rather than narrative.]

1714. Schaeffer, Myron, and others. "Catorce tamboritos panameños." <u>BIFP</u>, I:1 (julio, 1944), i-vi (preface and introduction entitled "El tamborito"), 1-29 (texts and music of the collection proper).
[Some of the <u>copla</u> texts which accompany the Panamanian dance known as the <u>tamborito</u> are related to Spanish <u>coplas</u>; others comment on local political events.]

1715. _____ and others. "La mejorana, canción típica panameña." <u>BIFP</u>, I:2 (noviembre, 1944), 1-50.
[A study in Spanish and English of the <u>mejorana</u> of Panama (a <u>redondilla</u> glossed by four <u>décimas</u>). Several texts and some representative musical transcriptions are given. The <u>mejorana</u> is sung exclusively by men and seems to deal with practically any subject, including historical events. One example given here relates the life of Simón Bolívar, and Schaeffer says that he knows of two which "recount the life and ambitions of Cristóbal Colón."]

1716. _____. "Panama Songfest." <u>IAm</u>, III:7 (July, 1944), pp. 29-30, 45.
[The author relates his experiences in recording some Panamanian songs. He gives the text of one of these, which is in <u>décimas</u> and deals with the catastrophic effects of World War II.]

1717. Zárate, Dora Pérez de. <u>Nanas, rimas y juegos infantiles que se practican en Panamá</u>. Panamá: Ediciones del Ministerio de Educación, Departamento de Bellas Artes y Publicaciones, 1957. 201 pp.

_____. See Zárate, Manuel F., entry no. 1719.

1718. Zárate, Manuel F. "Substancia y carácter de la décima popular panameña." <u>Universidad, órgano de la Universidad de Panamá</u> (Panamá), 2. semestre (1952-1953):32, pp. 158-187.
[Boggs (ref. 13 [1953], p. 49) says: "Comments and gives examples of <u>décimas a lo divino, de argumento, de amores, chistosas</u>, and <u>líricas</u>, from Panama."]

1719. _____, and Zárate, Dora Pérez de. <u>La décima y la copla en Panamá</u>. Panamá: Talleres de "La Estrella de Panamá," 1953. 548 pp. 23 cm.
[The first section of the volume contains critical studies of the

décima (pp. 8-81) and the copla (pp. 83-98). The treatment of the décima is particularly thorough (its history, its importance as a popular form, its literary and artistic form, its psychological content, and the like). The discussion of the copla follows a similar pattern, although it is less exhaustive. The body of the work is a large collection of décimas arranged in sections according to the nature of their subjects (pp. 111-507). A collection of copla texts (pp. 509-538) contains 280 examples. There is also a section of "Voces y locuciones" (pp. 99-107) and a sketchy bibliography (pp. 108-109).]

PARAGUAY

Almost nothing is known about the popular poetry and song of Paraguay. No other country of America has been so neglected in the field of folklore studies. A laudable attempt to provide a guide for future investigators of Paraguay's folklore has been undertaken by Paulo de Carvalho Neto in two bibliographies published in the <u>Boletín bibliográfico de antropología americana</u>. Though extremely tentative in character, as the bibliographer himself points out, they represent the only serious effort that has been made in the field. It is worthy of note that very few of Carvalho Neto's entries appear to deal with ballads or other popular songs written in Spanish. Compositions in Indian languages seem to be better represented.

PARAGUAY

Azara, Félix de. See entry no. 156.

1720. Baez, Jorge. La canción de la epopeya y las leyendas (poesías y prosas). Asunción: Imp. M. Brossa, 1928. Pagination chaotic. 18.5 cm.

Campo, Luzán del. See entry no. 182.

1721. Carvalho Neto, Paulo de. "Bases bibliográficas para el estudio sistemático de la antropología paraguaya." BBAA, XIII (enero-diciembre, 1950), Parte I, 179-210.
[Following an introductory essay, the author provides a bibliography divided into five sections: "Las culturas indígenas," "Las culturas negras," "Las culturas europeas y europeizadas," "Los contactos raciales y culturales," and "El folklore paraguayo." Entries are in chronological order within each section. The section on folklore consists of only eleven entries, none of which seems to be concerned directly with ballad literature.]

1722. _____. "Nuevos aportes a la bibliografía del folklore paraguayo (primera serie)." BBAA, XIX-XX(1956-1957), Parte I, 175-191.
[A bibliography dedicated exclusively to folklore. Although it is only tentative in character and Carvalho Neto has been able to consult only a part of the books and articles which he lists, his work represents a valuable tool for future investigators. There are about three hundred entries.]

1723. Centurión, Carlos R. Historia de las letras paraguayas. 3 vols. B. A.: Editorial Ayacucho, 1947. 20 cm.
[In Vol. I the chapter entitled "Los días iniciales de la conquista y de la colonia" (pp. 13-36) contains some information about and texts of popular and semipopular poetry. Most, though not all, of this material is taken from Ciro Bayo's Romancerillo del Plata (entry no. 163 in the section for Argentina). Besides a few other scattered texts that are in the nature of coplas or pasquines, there are a few compositions which are of interest in "La musa popular. — Mitos. — Tradiciones. — Leyendas" (pp. 299-307). One in Spanish and Guaraní is a most interesting historical poem which seems to be related to the romance-corrido tradition.]

1724. González, J. Natalicio. Proceso y formación de la cultura paraguaya. Asunción-B. A.: Editorial Guarania, 1938. 22.5 cm.
[Centurión (ref. 1723, Vol. I, p. 309) indicates that this work contains the text of the romance from the colonial period entitled Santo Tomás en el Paraguay. Centurión himself prints the text (p. 23), and apparently both he and González took it from Ciro Bayo's Romancerillo del Plata (entry no. 163).]

1725. Moreno González, Juan Carlos. Datos para la historia de la música en el Paraguay. Asunción, 1953. 32 pp.
[Listed by Carvalho Neto (ref. 1722, p. 184) without indication of the kind of folklore which it treats.]

1726. Rodríguez Alcalá, Teresa Lamas Carísima de. Tradiciones del hogar. Asunción: Imp. La Mundial.
[In a bibliography on Paraguay (BBAA, XIII(1950), Parte I, p. 210) there is a section on folklore. This is the only title which even remotely sounds as though it might contain something about popular poetry or song.]

1727. Rojalaga D., Máximo A. Contribución para la formación de la bibliografía del folklore paraguayo. Centro de Estudios Antropológicos de la Facultad Nacional de Filosofía del Paraguay, 18 de septiembre, 1950. 1 p. mimeographed. (III série de publicaciones; Comunicaciones sobre el folklore paraguayo, Documento 3.)
[Boggs (ref. 13 [1950], p. 30) says: "Cites 21 pubs. between 1906-1945 on Paraguayan folklore."]

Schallehn, Hellmut. See entry no. 485.

PERU

In numerous chronicles about the conquest of Peru are to be found passages of importance in the study of popular poetry and song. Some of these attest to the vigor of the romance and copla tradition among the conquering soldiers of the Spanish armies; others reveal that the Incas and other tribes of the Andean region possessed narrative songs about historical events and heroic figures which may have made the Spanish ballads seem to the conquered natives almost akin to indigenous traditions.

It must be admitted at once that in the literary studies of Peru's romances which have been made up to the present time (and in varying degree the same situation prevails in the case of other genres of popular poetry and song in Spanish), there is not much evidence of significant indigenous influence upon the spirit, the style, or the vocabulary of the texts so far collected; they seem to possess the same general characteristics as romance texts gathered in areas of Spanish America where Indian cultures are weak or nonexistent. Nor do some excellent studies of Indian folklore, like those of Raoul and Marguerite Harcourt, reveal as much Hispanic influence as might have been expected after four centuries of Spanish domination. In short, the interaction between the two cultures in the field of popular song and poetry seems to be relatively small, though it would perhaps not be amiss to investigate the subject further. Unhappily there has been a rather deep schism among Peruvian scholars, though the best of them usually were not involved, between indigenistas, who have idealized the pre-conquest cultures of Peru and sought blindly to attribute all that is good in Peruvian tradition to indigenous influences, and hispanicistas, who with equal vehemence have depreciated Peru's Indian heritage and interpreted their country's culture almost exclusively within the framework of Hispanic civilization. It is possible that literary scholars, folklorists, and other researchers trained to study dispassionately the true character of Peruvian culture might in the future detect more Indian elements in popular literature in Spanish than presently seem to be evident; and, likewise, there may be more Spanish influence on the Indian folklore of the Andean region than our present knowledge would lead us to believe.

Though a frightening amount of work remains to be done in Peruvian folklore studies, to state this truism detracts in no way from the accomplishments of several notable scholars who have made outstanding contributions in the field of popular poetry and song. Guillermo Lohmann Villena has done some very scholarly work in extracting from chronicles of the conquest references to both Indian and Spanish poems and songs of a popular or semipopular character; Raoul and Marguerite

Harcourt have studied in masterful fashion the contemporary Indian cultures of the Andean area, with considerable attention to folklore in Quechua; and Emilia Romero has provided a literary study of the Peruvian romance which ranks among the best of its kind in all of Spanish America. Other scholars too have made useful contributions, among them César Angeles Caballero whose work on the bibliography of Peruvian folklore was the first serious effort in that branch of study, Dionicio Rodolfo Bernal, Jesús Lara, Augusto D. León Barandiarán, Raúl Porras Barrenechea, Horacio H. Urteaga, Rubén Vargas Ugarte, and Leopoldo Vidal Martínez. It goes without saying that few of these investigators have been primarily interested in romances, though their studies of décimas, coplas, and typically Peruvian genres like yaravíes, mulizas, marineras, and the like are sometimes related to the tradition of narrative poetry and song. Without doubt the most significant contribution in recent years to the study of Peruvian foklore is the excellent Bibliografía del folklore peruano compiled by Mildred Merino de Zela in collaboration with José María Arguedas and others. Published in 1960, it gives future investigators an indispensable tool for systematic research.

Until a short time ago, the only serious attempt to study the musical characteristics of Peruvian popular songs had been the Harcourts' fine treatment of purely indigenous music. Thus the recent appearance of Robert Stevenson's excellent book, The Music of Peru; Aboriginal and Viceroyal Epochs, fills a glaring gap, at least in part, as it brings systematic study of the whole field of Peruvian music much closer to the present.

I should like to state, finally, that I have not attempted to incorporate here the extensive bibliography of and about Juan del Valle y Caviedes. This famous cultivator of artistic romances, who wrote around the end of the seventeenth century, has been studied by numerous scholars, and I refer interested readers to Guillermo Lohmann Villena's fine study (entry no. 1833) for information about him.

PERU

1728. Acosta, José de. Historia natural y moral de las Indias, Vol. II. Madrid: R. Angeles, Impr., 1894. 19 cm. The first edition appeared in Sevilla in 1590.
[Acosta (Bk. VI, Chap. XXVIII, pp. 225-226) comments on singing and dancing among Peruvian Indians. Referring to their compositions, he declares: "Algunos de estos romances eran muy artificiosos, y contenian historia . . . ."; also that the Peruvians "también han puesto en su lengua composiciones y tonadas nuestras, como de octavas y canciones, de romances, de redondillas . . . ."]

1729. Alviña, Leandro. "La música incaica. Tesis para el bachillerato, 1919." RUCuzco, Año XIII, Vol. II, segundo semestre, 1929.
[Raygada (ref. 1869, p. 179) calls this thesis the "primer trabajo serio publicado sobre la música peruana."]

1730. Angeles Caballero, César. "El amor en el canto popular ancashino." FPL, II:22 (diciembre de 1949), 648.
[Boggs (ref. 13 [1950], p. 58) says: "Gives verses only in Spanish (2 in Quechua), of 23 folksongs on the theme of love, mostly quatrains, from Ancash, Peru."]

1731. _____. "Anotaciones a una obra de A. Malaret." Letras peruanas, revista de humanidades, Año I:3 (octubre, 1951), 77-78.
[Ref. 1758 (p. 5) says: "Consigna coplas."]

1732. _____. "Cuatro versiones sobre una copla." CroL, 27 de abril, 1952.
[Ref. 1758 (p. 5) says: "Copla atribuida a Raymondi y muy difundida en el Dpto de Ancash, al cual se refiere."]

1733. _____. Bibliografía del folklore peruano (primera contribución). Lima: Empresa Editorial Rimac, 1952. 23 pp. 22 cm.
[A brief but useful list. It is not, however, an annotated bibliography.]

1734. _____. "Bibliografía sobre temas folklóricos." Lima, 1953. 3 pp. mimeographed. 35 cm.

1735. _____. "Los estudios folklóricos peruanos en el último decenio (1942-1952)." TradP, Año IV, Vol. VI:15 (enero, 1954), 13-28.
[A valuable survey. As part of the article, Angeles Caballero offers a "Bibliografía folklórica de las revistas: Folklore, Tradición, Mar del Sur y Letras peruanas." This is very useful, though it is only a list of articles and, unfortunately, is not an annotated bibliography.]

1736. _____. Peruanismo, lenguaje popular, y folklore en un libro de Aurelio Miró Quesada. Lima, 1955. 20 pp.
[Boggs (ref. 13 [1955], p. 25) says: "Repr. of Letras, 1954. Vocabulary of words of food and drink, folklore motives, and names of dances, songs, and musical instruments, regional expressions, and coplas, taken from Miró's Costa, sierra y montaña, 2. ed., Lima, 1947."]

1737. Arguedas, José María. "La canción popular mestiza en el Perú; su valor documental y poético." PrBA, 18 y 25 de agosto, 1940, 23 de febrero, 1941.

[The author is concerned with the problem of "mestizaje" in popular song and poetry, but with primary emphasis on artistic poetry written by known poets. He deals mostly with waynos, but there is treatment also of the yaraví and the muliza. Nowhere does he mention romances or corridos.]

1738. _____. Review of Vicente T. Mendoza's "La música tradicional española en México." FA, Año II:2 (octubre, 1954), 185-190.

[A long and very interesting review of Mendoza's article (entry no. 1565) in which Arguedas contrasts Mendoza's discovery of overwhelming Spanish influence on the music of Mexico with his own investigations in Peru, where Indian influence on popular music was much stronger.]

_____. See Bibliografía del folklore peruano, entry no. 1758.

1739. Arias Larreta, A. "Amautas y haravicus; arribo y trayectoria de la copla española." Sayarí (Lima), enero de 1946, 11-16.

1740. Arona, Juan de (Pedro Paz Soldán y Unanué). Diccionario de peruanismos. Lima: Imprenta de J. F. Solís, 1883. lxv, 529 pp. 22 cm.; also, Paris: Desclée de Brouwer, 1938. (Biblioteca de cultura peruana, Vol. X.)

[Arona mentions corrido as a term used in Chile and many other places, but says: "Sólo por acá no hemos tenido la dicha de conocer corridos . . ." (p. 131 of the Lima edition). The volume is of interest also because the lexicographer often quotes strophes from coplas, romances, and other popular poetry.]

1741. Arroyo Ponce, Gamaliel. "Literatura oral de Tarma." APF, I(1955), 70-85.

1742. Ayanque, Simón (Esteban Terralla y Landa). Lima por dentro y fuera. En consejos económicos, saludables, políticos y morales que da un amigo a otro con motivo de querer dexar la Ciudad de México, por pasar a la de Lima. Obra jocasa y divertida. En que con salados conceptos se describen, además de otras cosas, las costumbres, usos y mañas de las madamitas de allí, de acá y de otras partes. La da a luz Simón Ayanque. Madrid: Villalpando, 1798. xii, 192 pp.; reprinted in Lima, 1829, 1838, 1842 and 1854; also in Madrid, 1836; and in Paris, 1842 and 1854.

[Written by a poet who was an Andalusian and a kind of court poet under Viceroy Teodoro de la Croix, this poem, which dates from about 1792, is, according to Menéndez y Pelayo (ref. 82, Vol. II, pp. 145-146), ". . . una sátira contra la sociedad limeña en diez y siete romances de lo más pedestre, chabacano y grosero que puede leerse . . . ." See also Literatura peruana by Sánchez (ref. 1879, Vol. IV, pp. 128-134) for a treatment of this poet.]

1743. Azar, L. "La epopeya del yaraví." FPL, II:18 (abril de 1948), 546-547.

[A very pompous essay on the yaraví and the poet Melgar. Its value to investigations concerning the yaraví is doubtful and it is of no importance to the study of any other forms of popular poetry.]

1744. Barbacci, Rodolfo. "Bases para el estudio del folklore musical peruano." Cultura peruana (Lima), Año V:22 (agosto de 1945), no pagination.

1745. Barriga, Víctor M. "Poesías populares con temas históricos." FenL, No. 9 (1953), 413-423.

[Some poetry inspired by Peru's struggle for independence. Some are romances, some are décimas, and some are in other verse forms. They deal with San Martín's entry into Peru in 1820 and with other figures of the period. None of the poems is truly popular, but some coplas and other poems of similar tone are close to the style of semipopular pasquines and are of real interest.]

1746. Basadre, Jorge, ed. Literatura incaica. Paris: Desclée de Brouwer, 1938. 18 cm. (Biblioteca de cultura peruana, Vol. I.)

[One poem from Ecuador, El adiós del indio (pp. 100-101), sounds in Spanish translation much like some corridos. Not exactly narrative, it is a sentimental commentary on the necessity of having to go far away to live. The Quechua original is in romance form with assonance in a-a.]

1747. Baudouin, Julio. Folklore de Lima, visión y síntesis. Lima: Ediciones Biblioteca Peruanología, [1947]. 73 pp. 18 cm.

Béclard d'Harcourt, Marguerite. See entry no 1812.

1748. Beltrán Avila, Marcos. Capítulos de la historia colonial de Oruro. La Paz: n.p., 1925. ii, 323 pp. 21 cm.

[Contains texts of some Peruvian political pasquines: one in quintillas about the rebellion of Tupac Amaru in 1780-1781 (p. 128); a single cuarteta about unrest in Oruro in 1783 (p. 198); and some verses written by one Patricio Gabriel Menéndez, who was arrested for fomenting unrest in Oruro in 1784 (pp. 200-201).]

1749. Beltroy, Manuel. "La literatura peruana precolombina." Proceedings of the Eighth American Scientific Congress, Held in Washington, May 10-18, 1940, Vol. II (Anthropological Sciences). Washington: Department of State, 1942. Pp. 253-264.

[Dispassionate consideration of pre-conquest Indian literature in Peru, neither "Hispanicist" nor "Indianist" in tone. With reference to popular songs, Beltroy finds that, notwithstanding abundant examples of compositions about love, agricultural tasks, domestic rites, etc. which folklore investigations have uncovered, it is generally necessary to seek epic or semi-epic types in written sources, mainly the chronicles.]

1750. Bermejo, Sergio. "Lambayeque y su folklore." FPL, III (1954):34, p. 1925.

1751. Bermúdez de la Torre y Solier, Pedro José de. Romance heroico, aclamación afectuosa aplaudiendo la muerte que el Príncipe de Asturias dió a un toro. 1730.
[Sánchez (ref. 1879, Vol. III, p. 183) cites this work without providing complete bibliographical data about it.]

1752. _____. A romance which appeared in the Fúnebre pompa of Pedro de Peralta y Barnuevo.
[Sánchez mentions this poem (ref. 1879, Vol. III, p. 183).]

1753. Bernal, Dionicio Rodolfo. "El huaino." Comer L, 1 de enero, 1944, p. 13.
[The author finds that the huaino is a combination of several Spanish elements such as "seguidillas, coplas, polos, boleros, tiranas soleás y cantares cultos de España." Taking issue with rabid indigenistas, he compares the texts of some Peruvian huainos with songs from Spain and other parts of America to show that several huainos long considered to be Indian songs are related to compositions from Hispanic tradition. Literarily speaking, many of the texts cited are coplas.]

1754. _____. "Lo español en el folklore peruano." Comer L, 1 de enero, 1948, p. 6 of the first section.
[Severe though courteous criticism of Jesús Lara and other indigenistas. Bernal cites evidence to show that Spanish romances influenced songs generally considered to be of purely Quechua origin. He quotes some passages from Herrera's Historia general de las Indias about the role of the romance, particularly with regard to the efforts of religious orders to proselytize among Peruvian Indians.]

1755. _____. La muliza cerreña; teorías e investigaciones, origen y realidad folklórica, su técnica literaria y musical; folklore peruano; con un estudio sobre el origen del cantar popular en el Perú. Lima: Compañía de Impresiones y Publicidad, 1947. 239 pp. 18 cm.
[A study of the muliza cerreña, which thrives in the area of Pasco, and an anthology of mulizas which comprises more than half the book. There is also a fairly extensive bibliography. Despite a rather detailed study, the true nature of the muliza never becomes very clear, and the anthology helps little since the examples given are of the most diverse types. Furthermore, most are only semipopular and not truly traditional songs. A few are in romance meter, but most are not; and a short chapter entitled "Romance y muliza" (pp. 65-71) proves little about any possible relationship between the two genres, inasmuch as Bernal bases his comparisons upon thematic similarities only and his

Spanish examples are not even romances. Furthermore, they are from learned sources (Gómez Manrique et al.). The book does contain, however, some interesting data about the background of Spanish poetry in Peru (the chronicles, Indian sources, etc.), and one muliza about the Chilean war, dated 1881 by Bernal (pp. 24-25), is a historical narrative. Though learned in flavor, it is close to the style of Mexican corridos.]

1756. _____. "Panorama del cantar popular de los departamentos de Junín y Pasco." Automovilismo y turismo (Lima), Año II:33 (setiembre de 1945), no pagination.

1757. Betanzos, Juan de. Suma y narración de los incas. In Segunda parte de la crónica del Perú . . . escrita por Pedro Cieza de León, ed. by Marcos Jiménez de la Espada. Madrid: Imprenta de Manuel Ginés Hernández, 1880. 140 pp. 22 cm. (Biblioteca hispano-ultramarina, Vol. V.). Though this is the first edition of the chronicle written in 1551, there have been subsequent editions.
[There are descriptions (pp. 83-84, 128) of the singing of narratives to recall historical events and the deeds of deceased rulers.]

1758. Bibliografía del folklore peruano, ed. by José María Arguedas, Mildred Merino de Zela and others. México-Lima: Daniel Boldó, Impresor, México, D. F. (Instituto Panamericano de Geografía e Historia), 1960. xv, 186 pp. 24 cm.
[One of the best bibliographies of folklore that exist in Spanish America. Divided into fifteen sections and containing over 1800 entries, the work has one section entitled "Literatura oral" (pp. 5-45). There are also useful indices at the end of the volume.]

1759. Bonilla del Valle, Ernesto. "Del folklore peruano; Los responseros." ComerL, 3 de noviembre, 1948, edición de la tarde, p. 8.
[In the nonscholarly manner of a literary costumbrista, the author describes the customs of an unidentified mountain village on the Day of the Dead. He deals in particular with blind singers of responsos who appear on this day, apparently from nowhere, to sing in honor of the dead. Unfortunately, he does not describe the nature of their songs, nor does he give any texts.]

1760. Borregán, Alonso. Crónica de la conquista del Perú. Sevilla: Imprenta de la Escuela de Estudios Hispano-Americanos, 1948. 118 pp. 25 cm.
[Contains (p. 55) the text (a cuarteta) of a song which some buffoons sang on Corpus Christi Day, 1541, to mock the enemies of Pizarro.]

1761. Breña Pacheco, Leonor. "La poesía popular huancavelicana." ComerL, 30 de abril, 1939.

1762. Bulnes, Gonzalo. Historia de la expedición libertadora del Perú. Tomo I. Santiago, 1887.

[Sánchez (ref. 1879, Vol. V, p. 35) prints some lines of an anonymous romance from the period of the wars of independence. Entitled Las limeñas a las santiaguinas, it is taken from this work (p. 392).]

1763. Burga, Napoleón. "Tradiciones épicas de los antiguos peruanos." Sphinx, Nos. 6-7 (julio-octubre, 1939), 81-86.

[Boggs (ref. 13 [1940], p. 54) says: "Chroniclers of old Peru indicate the aborigenes preserved their legendary material in epic poems."]

1764. Bustamante, Manuel E. Apuntes para el folklore peruano. Ayacucho: Imp. La Miniatura, 1943. ii, 178, iv pp. 21.5 cm.

[A collection of articles about many types of folklore from Ayacucho. There is a section on "Música vernacular" in which there are a few coplas and yaravíes, some in Spanish, some in Quechua. There is no mention of romances or corridos.]

1765. Cabrejo, Miguel E. Añoranzas cruceñas. Lima: Imprenta del Colegio Militar, 1951. 85 pp. 22 cm.

[Costumbristic sketches about Santa Cruz, department of Catamarca, Peru. There is much folklore material with a little about popular music, particularly in the chapter entitled "La música cruceña" (pp. 77-80), where there is mention of yaravíes, marineras, and other genres. A few texts are given, but the whole is very sketchy, and nothing treated here seems to be related to romances, corridos, or coplas.]

1766. Cadenas, Pedro de. "Las hazañas del capitán Diego de Zerpa."

[Ricardo Palma (ref. 1854, p. v) refers to this work as an unpublished poem.]

1767. Calancha, Antonio de la. Corónica moralizada del Orden de San Agustín en el Perú, Vol. I. Barcelona: Pedro Lacavallería, 1638. 922 pp. of text plus an introduction and a long appendix.

[Calancha relates (p. 128) the episode in which Francisco de Carvajal ordered a confesor to recite the Romance de Gaiferos. See Gutiérrez de Santa Clara and others.]

1768. Calvete de Estrella, Juan Cristóbal. Rebelión de Pizarro en el Perú y vida de don Pedro Gasca, ed. by A. Paz y Melia. 2 vols. Madrid: Imprenta y Fundición de M. Tello, 1889. 16.5 cm. (Colección de escritores castellanos, Vols. LXX and LXXVI.) This is the first edition of the sixteenth-century MS.

[Of interest are these passages: a version of the episode in which Francisco de Carvajal ordered a confesor to recite the Romance de Gaiferos (Vol. I, p. 387); two lines of a romance which the same Carvajal sang at a time when Gonzalo Pizarro's fortunes were at low ebb (Vol. II, p. 22); and the texts of some coplas sung in 1548 in a procession which celebrated the victory of Pedro de Gasca over Gonzalo Pizarro (Vol. II, pp. 199-202). See Gutiérrez de Santa Clara for his versions of all these incidents.]

1769. Camino Calderón, Carlos. Diccionario folklórico del Perú. Primera parte. Lima: Compañía de Impresiones y Publicidad, 1945. xii, 227 pp. 21.5 cm.

1770. _____. "Diccionario folklórico del Perú." CroL, 12-19 de octubre, 1947; 16 de noviembre, 1947; 14 de marzo, 1948.

1771. _____. Tradiciones de Piura. Trujillo: Imprenta Moderna, n.d.
[There are texts of a few coplas in these sketches written under the influence of Ricardo Palma.]

1772. _____. Tradiciones de Trujillo. Trujillo: Imprenta Moderna, 1944. 37.5 cm.

1773. Cancionero aprista. [Lima]: Editorial Apra, [194?]. 32 pp. 20 cm.

1774. El cancionero arequipeño. Arequipa: Tipografía Muñiz, 1905.
[A collection of popular songs and poetry, a very few of which vaguely resemble the narrative poems of romance-corrido tradition.]

1775. Canciones del Ande. Recopilación de yaravíes, mulizas, huaynitos, cachuas. See Martínez G., Narciso, entry no. 1837.

1776. Candela, Julio. "Folklore y música." Pauta (Lima), noviembre de 1945, pp. 8, 16.

1777. Cárdenas, Fortunato E. La huerta de Tarma. Tarma: Imprenta La Voz de Tarma, 1946. 201 pp.
[Ref. 1758 (p. 7) says: "Recopilación de textos de mulizas, huaynos, tristes, yaravíes; valses anónimos y de autor conocido."]

1778. Castañeda, C. A. Armonías peruanas. Cuaderno 2.° Iquique, 1910.
[Carrizo (ref. 200, p. L) refers to similarities between some songs found here and the popular songs of Salta.]

1779. Castilla, J. Antonio. "En defensa de nuestra música vernácula." Xauxa (Jauja), Año VII:16 (octubre de 1949), 28-29.

Castillo y Tamayo, Francisco del (El ciego de la Merced). See Vargas Ugarte, Rubén, entry no. 1903.

1780. Castro Pozo, Hildebrando. Nuestra comunidad indígena. Lima: Tipografía "El Lucero," 1924. xxiv, 498 pp. 19 cm.
[There are coplas and other forms of popular poetry scattered through this volume. In addition, Chap. IX, "Emotividad estética comunal" (pp. 309-431), is devoted primarily to popular music, dances, and poetry. There are discussions of many genres, including several which are unique and often ill-defined. Usually the author contributes little to clarifying terminology, but by correlating his comments with other sources, some significant conclusions might ultimately be reached about such types as cantarcillos, serranos, cumananas, décimas,

yaravíes, marineras, and the like. One composition, Décimas a Jorge Chávez (pp. 372-373), is a narrative about the death of a Peruvian aviator and has much of the flavor of Mexican corridos. While the author's procedures are not always scholarly, the volume is one of the best available sources of information about popular music and literature in Peru.]

1781. Cavero, José Salvador. Sollozos de una quena. Huamanga, 1946.

[Angeles Caballero (ref. 1735, p. 19) indicates that the work contains folklore from Ayacucho.]

1782. Chávez Aliaga, Nazario. "El folklore cajamarquino." ComerL, 20 de marzo, 1955, p. 2.

[Ref. 1758 (p. 8) says: "Consigna coplas."]

1783. Cieza de León, Pedro de. La crónica del Perú. B. A.: Espasa-Calpe, 1945. 294 pp. 18 cm.; also, Lima: Gil, 1924. The first edition was published in Sevilla, 1553.

[There is a reference to narrative songs (p. 168 of the 1945 edition) which, according to Cieza de León, "recitan (los Incas) en sus lenguas como a manera de endechas." Vidal Martínez (ref. 1910, p. 186) quotes from the 1924 edition (p. 138) a line in which Cieza de León relates that in Quito Indian men and women joined hands to dance and sing "recontando en sus cantares y endechas las cosas pasadas."]

1784. _____. Guerras civiles del Perú; Guerra de las Salinas. Madrid: Imprenta de Miguel Ginesta, 1877. vi, 534 pp. 22.5 cm. (Colección de documentos inéditos para la historia de España, Vol. LXVIII.)

[Contains a cuarteta about the war between Almagro and the Pizarros (p. 266). It is apparently a pasquín. There is also a fragment of a romance which was sung to Almagro in order to warn him of danger to his life (p. 199).]

1785. _____. Segunda parte de la crónica del Perú, que trata del señorío de los incas Yupanquis y de sus grandes hechos y gobernación, ed. by Marcos Jiménez de la Espada. Madrid: Imprenta de Manuel Ginés Hernández, 1880. 12 unnumbered lvs., 279 pp. 22 cm. (Biblioteca Hispano-Ultramarina, Vol. V.)

[There is a long and important passage (Chap. XI, pp. 34-37) about the singing of narrative songs among the Incas. Cieza de León compares their songs about battles and the deeds of their rulers with romances and villancicos.]

1786. Cisneros Córdova, E. "Del folklore peruano de la Hoya del Mantaro." Altura (Huancayo), Año I(1936):1, pp. 44-47.

1787. Cobo, Bernabé. Historia del Nuevo Mundo. 4 vols. Sevilla: Imp. de E. Rasco, 1890-1893. 22 cm. This is the first edition, though the MS. dates from 1653.

[Contains a paragraph (Chap. XVII of Vol. IV, p. 232) about the <u>arabis</u> of the Incas ("en ellos referían sus hazañas y cosas pasadas"). Also, there is mention (Chap. XII of Vol. III, p. 157) of the singing of songs in memory of one of the great Inca rulers, Pachacútic-Inca-Yupanqui.]

1788. <u>Colección de mulizas del año 1889 a 1936</u>. Cerro de Pasco: Imp. de la Librería "Los Andes, n.d. 120 pp. 15.5 cm.

[Texts of <u>mulizas</u> with a few <u>huaynitos</u>. All are lyrical and subjective, even when slightly topical, and most are not even semipopular. All bear an author's name or initial.]

Concolorcorvo. See entry no. 231.

<u>The Conquest of Peru as Recorded by a Member of the Pizarro Expedition</u>. See Sinclair, Joseph H., trans., entry no. 1888.

<u>La conquista del Perú, llamada la nueva Castilla</u>. See Sinclair, Joseph H., trans., entry no. 1888.

1789. Delgado, Luis Humberto. "Arte vernáculo." <u>ComerL</u>, 1° de septiembre, 1935.

1790. Delgado Vivanco, Edmundo. "El caballo en los cantares populares." <u>TradP</u>, VIII:16-18 (enero, 1954-junio, 1956), 22-35.

1791. _____. "El 'mal de ausencia' y las despedidas en el folklore." El <u>Aillu</u> (Cuzco), I(1945):1-2, pp. 59-116; also in book form, Cuzco, 1948. 57 pp. 24 cm.

[Boggs (ref. 13 [1951], p. 44) says: "Words only of 326 folksongs of absence and leave taking, with comments, usually Quechua text with free Spanish translation, from Andean Peru."]

1792. _____. <u>El río en el folklore</u>. Cuzco, 1948. 60 pp.; reprinted from <u>Letras, órgano de la Facultad de Letras de la Universidad del Cuzco</u>.

[Boggs (ref. 13 [1951], p. 43) says: "Words only of 145 folksongs and wainus of love, absence, death, bandits, orphans . . . from Cuzco and and Apurímac basin of Andean Peru, with notes and comments. Some in Spanish text only, but many in Quechua with free Spanish translation. Usually themes have something about a river."]

1793. Donaire Vizarreta, Juan. <u>Campiña igueña; aspectos folklóricos</u>. Lima: Imp. La Moderna, 1941. 134 pp. 17 cm.

[The last chapter, "Los cantores" (pp. 97-134), is a fine description of the singers of the Valle de Ica on the Peruvian coast. The author mentions only <u>décimas</u>, but several that he quotes are narratives about battles, the deaths of bandit heroes, and similar subjects. In substance and in general style, if not in form, they belong to the same tradition as Mexico's <u>corridos</u>. Also, throughout the book the author frequently quotes <u>coplas</u> and other types of popular songs.]

1794. Enríquez de Guzmán, Alonso. Libro de la vida y costumbres de D. Alonso Enríquez. Madrid: Imprenta de Miguel Ginesta, 1886. vi, 542 pp. 22.5 cm. (Vol. LXXXV of Colección de documentos inéditos para la historia de España, ed. by the Marqués de la Fuensanta del Valle, José Sancho Rayón and Francisco de Zabalburu.) This is the first edition in Spanish of the sixteenth-century MS.

[Contains (pp. 369 ff.) two compositions about the death of Almagro. The second of these is an artistic romance which Medina prints (ref. 623). There is also mention in a letter written in 1530 of the singing of a romance, Allá ensarta la olla (p. 177); and Enríquez quotes in its entirety a décima which begins: "Si muero en tierras ajenas . . ." (pp. 176-177).]

1795. Escandón, Ignacio de. Epoca Gali-cana egira Gali-lea. Lima, 1762. 4 lvs.

[According to Menéndez y Pelayo (ref. 82, Vol. II, p. 147), this work is a romance written to celebrate the opening of the first public cockpit in Lima.]

1796. Estete, Miguel de. El descubrimiento y la conquista del Perú. . . . La publica con una introducción y notas Carlos M. Larrea. Quito: Imprenta de la Universidad Central, 1918. 51 pp. plus photographic reproductions of the 12 lvs. of the manuscript. 27.5 cm. This is the first edition in Spanish of the sixteenth-century MS.

[Estete speaks (p. 32) of the importance of songs in preserving the memory of past battles and events among the Incas; also, he describes (p. 35) the singing of songs about the deeds of the Inca rulers in public ceremonies celebrated in the presence of their mummified corpses.]

1797. Farfán, J. M. B. "Poesía folklórica quichua." RevIA, II (1942):12, pp. 525-625.

[A collection of 117 poems in Quechua with translations into Spanish. They are grouped into three sections for Peru, Bolivia, and Ecuador, but there are no commentaries nor any other classification; hence, old poems are mixed indiscriminately with the works of modern poets. The only truly narrative poem is No. CXV, Elegía a la muerte de Atawallpa, the translation of which sounds much like a corrido.]

1798. Fernández, Diego. Primera y segunda parte de la historia del Perú. Sevilla: Hernando Díaz, 1571. 5 lvs., 130 lvs. 28.5 cm. There are also modern editions.

[Contains numerous important references to the singing of romances and other types of popular poetry during the conquest of Peru: Part I, Bk. II, Chap. XXXII, the singing of romances and coplas to celebrate the triumphs of Gonzalo Pizarro; Chap. XLIX, Carvajal's demand that a confessor recite the romances of Gayferos and the Marqués de Mantua; Chap. LIV, Carvajal's reciting of two lines of popular poetry by way of commenting on an event; Chap. LXV, another instance of Carvajal's reciting popular poetry; Chap. XCIII, a report on the singing of coplas when Gasca entered Lima in 1548: Part II, Bk. II, Chap. XXXV, report of a verse about political events; Chap. XLV, mention of a time when Hernández Girón commented on a battle by reciting two lines of popular poetry.]

1799. Fernández, Justo. Antología de la tradición y la leyenda ancashinas. Huaraz, 1946.

1800. Fernández de Oviedo y Valdés, Gonzalo. Historia general y natural de las Indias. 4 vols. Madrid: Imprenta de la Real Academia de la Historia, 1851-1855. 32 cm. There are also other editions. The first was in 20 vols., Sevilla and Salamanca, 1535-1537.

[The author comments on the murder of Pizarro by quoting two lines of popular poetry (Vol. IV, p. 352); Francisco Carvajal reacts to the desertion of some soldiers from the army of Gonzalo Pizarro by reciting two lines of popular poetry (Vol. IV, p. 443); and a conquistador replies to a question by recalling two lines from a romance (Vol. IV, p. 507).]

1801. Flores Chinarro, Francisco. ¡Cuidado con las jaranas! Lima: Taller de Linotipía Guadalupe 1032, 1949. 71 pp. 17 cm.

1802. Folklore musical del siglo XVIII. Lima: Empresa Gráfica Scheuch, S. A., 1946. No pagination. 28 cm.

1803. Fuente, Nicanor de la. La feria de los romances.

[Selections from this work appear in "Breve antología poética," MP, Año XVI:167 (febrero, 1941), 87-92. A brief note in the introduction of this anthology describes La feria de los romances as "una serie de romances inspirados en las bellas tradiciones y motivos regionales." Three poems from the work, all artistic in style, are printed in the "Breve antología poética."]

1804. _____. "Lo que canta el pueblo del norte." FPL, Núm. 30 (junio y julio de 1953), p. 953.

[Contains two humorous coplas which are popular in tone.]

1805. Gálvez, José. Una Lima que se va. Ciudad de los Reyes del Perú: Editorial Euforion, 1921. iii, 262 pp. 16 cm.; also, 2.ª ed. corr. Lima: Editorial P. T. C. M., 1947. viii, 199 pp. 22 cm.

[There is reference (p. 106 of the 1921 ed.) to a bandit, one Luis Pardo, whose exploits inspired a "romance criollo," one line of which the author prints. Also, he refers (p. 247) to a woman, María la cantinera, who "daba tema a la inspiración anónima del romancero."]

1806. _____. "La muliza." FPL, Núm. 30 (junio y julio de 1953), 938-940.

[In describing the nature of the muliza, the author has occasion to point out that only a few are political in character. Nevertheless, he quotes one strophe of an octosyllabic cuarteta which dates from 1856 and is a political commentary. On several occasions he also mentions that the muliza sometimes deals with historical subjects.]

1807. Garcilaso de la Vega, Inca. Comentarios reales de los incas, edición al cuidado de Angel Rosenblat del Instituto de Filología de la Universidad de Buenos Aires. 2 vols. B. A.: Emecé Editores, S. A., 1943. 24 cm. There are many editions, the first of which was published in Lisbon in 1609.

[In Bk. II, Chap. XXVII (Vol. I, p. 121, of this edition), the author describes songs about the deeds of Inca heroes and compares them to Spanish redondillas in their tone, though not in their meter and rhyme. There is also brief mention of the verses known as haráuec.]

1808. _____. Historia general del Perú (Segunda parte de los Comentarios reales de los incas), edición al cuidado de Angel Rosenblat del Instituto de Filología de la Universidad de Buenos Aires. 3 vols. B. A.: Emecé Editores, S. A., 1944. 23.5 cm. The first edition was in Córdoba, 1617.

[In Bk. I, Chap. VIII (Vol. I, p. 36, of this edition), there is a version of the episode in which a malcontent in Pizarro's army sent a complaint to Panama in the form of a cuarteta hidden in a ball of thread; and in Bk. VI, Chap. VI (Vol. III, pp. 24-26), the author quotes from Diego Fernández about the songs sung to welcome Gasca to Lima in 1548.]

Gonzáles de la Rosa, Manuel. See Morúa, Martín, entry no. 1849.

1809. González, Pedro. "El amigo espiritual." In Los místicos. París: Desclée de Brouwer, 1938. Pp. 210-216. (Vol. VII of Biblioteca de cultura peruana.)

[Some portions of this poem are in romance form. They are, of course, completely artistic in character. The work was first printed in Lima in 1779.]

1810. González Holguín, Diego. Vocabulario de la lengua general de todo el Perú llamada lengua Quichua, o del Inca. 2 vols. Cuidad de los Reyes: Francisco del Canto, 1608. 20.5 cm.

[Contains the following definition (Vol. I, p. 145): "Haraui o yuyaycucuna o huaynaricunattaqui. Cãtares de hechos de otros o memoria de los amados ausentes y de amor y aficion y agora se ha recibido por cantares deuotos y espirituales."]

1811. Gutiérrez de Santa Clara, Pedro. Historia de las guerras civiles del Perú (1544-1548). 6 vols. Madrid: Librería General de Victoriano Suárez, 1904-1929. 20 cm. (Colección de libros y documentos referentes a la historia de América, Vols. II, III, IV, X, XX, and XXI.) This is the first edition of the work which dates from the middle of the sixteenth century.

[In Vol. I (Vol. II of the Colección) there are two lines of a popular poem which were used to mock the captive viceroy, Vela Núñez (p. 377). In Vol. II (Vol. III of the Colección) there is mention of the fact that the deeds of Hernando Bachicao "estan escriptas en mano y en metro por un criado suyo llamado Jaun Baptista de Escobar" (p. 103). In Vol. III (Vol. IV of the Colección) are found some coplas in cuartetas which were composed to voice opposition to Francisco Carvajal when the latter entered the town of Paria in 1546 (pp. 57-58). In Vol. IV (Vol. X of the Colección) Carvajal on two occasions quotes fragments of popular poetry by way of commenting on a situation (pp. 266, 413), and Gutiérrez de Santa Clara himself uses two lines from a romance to describe the town of Guarco (p. 435). Furthermore, it is recorded that "Pedro Bejarano, el poeta," fled with the enemies of Gonzalo Pizarro (p. 465), and the chronicler also relates (pp. 254-255) the famous episode in which Francisco de Carvajal demanded that a confessor learn the romance of Gayferos and the coplas of the Marqués de Mantua so that he could recite them to him every day. In Vol. VI (Vol. XXI of the Colección) are found several texts of interest: two quintillas which are in reality political pasquines (pp. 125-127); another quintilla, also a pasquín, which was placed on a sign near the severed head of Carvajal after his execution (p. 130); one line from a copla which was to be sung at a dance (p. 186); and the texts of the poems (not romances, however) which representatives of the Inca empire recited to welcome Gasca to Lima in 1548 (pp. 217-224).]

1812. d'Harcourt, Marguerite. See Harcourt, Raoul, entry no. 1812.

1812. Harcourt, Raoul and Marguerite. "La musique dans la sierra andine de La Paz a Quito." JSAP, Nouvelle série, XII(1920), 21-53.
[A report on research begun in 1912 and still in progress on the music of the Quechua Indians. There seems to be nothing that is directly related to the romance. There is, however, some interesting material about the development of the yaraví (pp. 33-34, 45-46), and musical transcriptions of two yaravíes (pp. 49-50) are given. All texts, of course, are in Quechua.]

1813. _____. La musique des Incas et ses survivances. 2 vols. Paris: Librarie Orientaliste Paul Geuthner, 1925. 26 cm.
[The first volume of this monumental work is a fine collection of 204 songs and dances gathered by many collectors from Andean folklore, together with a long critical study of the entire field of Peruvian music and song. Most of the texts presented are in Quechua, but some are combinations of Quechua and Spanish, and some are entirely in Spanish. None seems to be related to the romance-corrido tradition, but a very few of them are coplas in the Spanish sense of the term. An excellent bibliography of 230 items is also included. The second volume is a collection of plates which are photographs of musical instruments used in many regions of America from Mexico to Bolivia.]

1814. Harcourt, Raoul and Marguerite. "La musique indienne chez les anciens civilisés d'Amérique." In Encyclopédie de la musique et dictionnaire du conservatoire, Partie I. Paris: Librarie Delagrave, 1922. Pp. 3337-3371.

[A fine synthesis of what is known about Indian music in the Americas. It is of no importance to the study of Indian literature, since it is concerned exclusively with music, but it would be of value to any study of popular songs which might be concerned with Indian influences on their music.]

1815. Hernández, José A. "Notas sobre la poesía popular peruana." Cultura peruana (Lima), Año II(1942), Vol. II:7; also in the author's Miscelánea antigua. Lima: Ed. Lumen, 1947; also, in CroL, 25 de abril, 1948.

[Ref. 1758 (p. 10) says: "Artículo sobre la poesía popular actual en relación con el acervo literario de la antigüedad. Intercala trozos de poesía y coplas."]

1816. Herrera, Antonio de. Historia general de los hechos de los castellanos en las islas y tierrafirme del Mar Océano, Vols. X and XII. Madrid: Imprenta y Editorial Maestre, 1952 and 1953. 25 cm. There are other editions, the first having appeared in Madrid in 1601.

[In Década V, Bk. IV, Chap. I (Vol. X of this edition, pp. 269-270), Herrera, following Cieza de León, reports on the practice among the Incas of composing "romances y cantares" to preserve the memory of the deeds of rulers; also, the custom of singing songs in the presence of the mummies of ancient rulers. In Década VI, Bk. III (Vol. XII of this edition), there are two instances where Herrera, again following Cieza de León, provides passages of interest: in Chap. IV (p. 192) an account of the episode in which Almagro's life is saved by a warning of treachery converyed through a well known romance sung by a loyal follower, and in Chap. IX (p. 223) a cuarteta about the war between Almagro and the Pizarros.]

1817. Herrera, Carlos Aquiles. El criollismo limeño. Lima: Imprenta La Moderna, 1944. 43 pp. 22 cm.

Herrera, Martín G. See León Barandarián, Augusto D., entry no. 1826.

1818. Hidalgo, A. J. Mulizas tarmeñas. Tarma: n.p., 1938. No pagination.

[Said to contain "canciones populares peruanas, antiguas y modernas."]

1819. "Idea general de los monumentos del antiguo Perú, é introducción á su estudio." MP, 17 de marzo de 1791.

[Raygada (ref. 1869, p. 178) quotes a few lines from the above about yaravíes and the term harawicuc, the Quechua word for poet. See also entries nos. 1886 and 1891.]

1820. Izquierdo Ríos, Francisco. "Aspectos del folklore de Chachapoyas." ComerL, 20 de julio, 1949, edición de la tarde, p. 8.
[A descriptive, though not scientific, treatment of various aspects of the folklore of Chachapoyas, a province and city on the eastern side of the Peruvian Andes. The author describes various dances, legends, processions, etc. There is no treatment of narrative poetry, but one cuarteta called a marinera might be classified as a copla.]

1821. _____. "Aspectos del folklore de Santiago de Chuco." FPL, II(1946):17, pp. 477-478.

1822. _____. "Música y bailes folklóricos de la selva." Trocha, revista peruana de cultura (Lima), Año I:1 (abril, 1951), pp. 3-4, 13-14.

1823. _____. Vallejo y su tierra. Lima: Empresa Editorial Rimac, n.d. 78 pp. 21.5 cm.
[The second part of the volume, "Aspectos del folklore de Santiago de Chuco" (pp. 40-78), includes songs, dances, riddles, and the like. Most interesting are some brief sections on several popular poet-singers. Though none of the compositions printed here is called a romance or a corrido, a few are topical and are very close to corridos in form and style. One compostion (p. 47) is as close to the corrido as any song which I have discovered in Peruvian popular literature.]

Jiménez Borja, Arturo. See Ministerio de Educación Pública del Perú, entry no. 1845.

1824. Lara, Jesús. La poesía quechua. México: Fondo de Cultura Económica, 1947. 190 pp. 21.5 cm.
[An impassioned statement of the belief of the Indigenistas that preconquest literature in Quechua was well developed and of great merit. Some comments on popular poetry such as the arawis, the jaillis (a narrative type which related heroic deeds), and other genres are most interesting.]

1825. León Barandarián, Augusto D. "Del folk-lore poético lambayecano." ComerL, 1° de junio, 1941, p. 17; 15 de junio, p. 17.
[These articles deal with verses which, though semipopular, are not really folklore. A few cuartetas in the first article, which contain satirical comments on certain individuals' physical traits and appearance, are close to coplas in style and tone. The second article contains nothing that is even remotely associated with truly popular poetry.]

1826. _____. "Del folklore poético lambayecano." ComerL, 28 de julio, 1944, p. 19.
[The text with critical commentary of a glosa (cuarteta and four décimas) about an imaginery army led by Christ and staffed by saints and archangels. The work of Manuel María López Tovar, an improvising popular poet of Tucumán, it has some measure of popular flavor. Also, the author deals briefly with another vernacular poet of

Chiclayo, Martín G. Herrera, who wrote a poem in cuartetas the text of which is given. The composition is neither popular in tone nor narrative.]

1827. León Barandarián, Augusto D. "Del folk-lore poético lambayecano." Automovilismo y turismo (Lima), Año II:34 (octubre de 1945), no pagination.

1828. _____, and Paredes, Rómulo. A golpe de arpa; folk-lore lambayecano de humorismo y costumbres. Lima: n.p., 1934. 397, iv pp. 24 cm.

[Scattered through this potpourri of Peruvian folklore are a number of coplas and décimas of more or less popular origin. There are no true romances or corridos, but some of the coplas are inspired by events and public figures. Some cuartetas, indeed, could conceivably be fragments of longer compositions related to the corrido tradition.]

_____ La lira andina. Cancionero folklórico peruano. See Martínez G., Narciso, entry no. 1838.

1829. Lira popular; ramillete de zarzuelas, canciones, yaravíes, habaneras y serenatas antiguas y modernas. 3ª edición corregida y aumentada. Cuzco, 1902.

1830. Lohmann Villena, Guillermo. "Apuntaciones sobre el arte dramático en Lima durante el virreinato." 3, Núm. 7 (diciembre, 1940), pp. 28-57.

[Contains (pp. 30-31) some comments about the singing of romances in colonial Peru, particularly with reference to their influence on the drama. The ideas expressed here are repeated with almost identical wording in refs. 1831 and 1832.]

1831. _____. El arte dramático en Lima durante el virreinato. Madrid: Talleres de Estades, Artes Gráficas, 1945. xviii, 647 pp. 22 cm.

[There are some comments (p. 5) on the role of the romances during the conquest of Peru; a passage (p. 6) from Relación de todo lo sucedido en la provincia del Perú regarding the romances and coplas which were sung when Gonzalo Pizarro entered Lima in triumph in 1546 and the musicians and poets who probably participated in the festivities; and data (p. 16) about the musicians who formed an orchestra of one of the viceroys.]

1832. _____. Historia del arte dramático en Lima durante el virreinato, I, siglos XVI y XVII. Lima: Imprenta Americana, 1941. xiii, 271 pp. 22 cm. (Biblioteca histórica peruana, Vol. III.)

[An earlier editing of ref. 1831. It contains exactly the same material with only slight differences in wording (pp. 4-5, 14.]

1833. _____. "Un poeta virreinal del Perú." RevIndM, Año VIII [sic, should be IX]:33-34 (julio-diciembre, 1948), 771-794.

[A fine study of Juan del Valle Caviedes and his works. It contains extensive bibliography and a listing of known codices (pp. 793-794). These items have not been included in the present bibliography and I refer any investigator interested in the romances of Caviedes to this article.]

1834. _____. "Romances, coplas y cantares en la conquista del Perú." In Estudios dedicados a Menéndez Pidal, Tomo I. Madrid: Consejo Superior de Investigaciones Científicas, Patronato Marcelino Menéndez y Pelayo, 1950. Pp. 289-315; also, MdS, Año II, Vol. III:9 (enero-febrero, 1950), 18-40.

[A very scholarly study of the popular poetry written in America about the conquest of Peru. All texts which the author has been able to uncover are given and their sources cited. This is by far the most thorough treatment of the subject which has been made up to the present time. It has contributed much to the present bibliography.]

López de Gomara, Francisco. See entry no. 1083.

López Tovar, Manuel María. See León Barandiarán, Augusto D., entry no. 1826.

1835. Macedo Arguedas, Alfredo. Escritos de esencia americana. Puno: Tipografía L. Camacho A., 1950. 29 pp. 22 cm.

[Angeles Caballero (ref. 1735, p. 18) indicates that the article deals with "La queja en el canto popular peruano." (pp. 5-8).]

1836. Macedo C., María Rosa. Paisaje y hombre de mi tierra. Lima: Imp. "Gmo. Lenta," 1945. 30 pp. 21.5 cm.

[Two costumbristic sketches about the region of La Quebrada de Humay near the Peruvian coast. A few isolated strophes of folk songs are quoted, including a relación which is a version of En el portal de Belén. It is in octosyllabic cuartetas with consonance and rhymed abcb. Also, there are some coplas.]

1837. Martínez G. Narciso, ed. Canciones del Ande. Recopilación de yaravíes, mulizas, huaynitos, cachuas. Lima: Narciso Martínez G., 1947. 64 pp. 16.5 cm.

1838. _____. La lira andina. Cancionero folkórico peruano. Lima: N. Martínez G., 1953. 64 pp.

[Ref. 1758 (p. 11) says: "Textos de huaynos, yaravíes y mulizas."]

1839. _____. Recopilación de los mejores yaravíes y huaynos del Perú. Con colaboración de folkloristas y compositores más destacados. Lima: N. Martínez G., 1953. 95 pp.

1840. Medina, José Toribio, ed. Colección de documentos inéditos para la historia de Chile, Vol. V. Santiago de Chile: Imprenta Ercilla, 1889. vi, 494 pp. 27.5 cm.

[There is a brief reference (pp. 174-175) to the romance protagonist Bernal Francés in a document relative to an incident which occurred in Peru in the sixteenth century. It appears in testimony given in a legal case by Alonso Enríquez de Guzmán (see ref. 1794 where this same document also appears).]

1841. Medina, José Toribio, ed. Colección de documentos inéditos para la historia de Chile desde el viaje de Magallanes hasta la batalla de Maipo, 1518-1818, Vols. VI and VII (Almagro y sus compañeros, III and IV). Santiago de Chile: Imprenta y Encuadernación Barcelona, 1895. 27.5 cm.

[A "Muñoz, el cantor" is listed (Vol. VI, p. 284) as being among the followers of Almagro. There is also mention (Vol. VII, p. 172) of one Licenciado León who is described as an "hombre demasiado bullicioso y tiene por costumbre, según su liviandad, de hablar siempre en copla . . . ."]

1842. Medina Díaz, L. "En torno a nuestra literatura infantil y folklore." CronL, 1 de noviembre de 1953.

1843. Mejía Baca, José. Aspectos criollos; contribución al folklore costeño. Lima: Imp. Lux de E. L. Castro, 1937. 123 pp. 18 cm.
[Costumbristic sketches about the cholos of the Peruvian coast. There is considerable attention to popular songs and dances, and the texts of some coplas in cuartetas are given. There seems to be, however, no attention to romances or other narrative genres.]

1844. _____. "En nacimiento de 'El triste'." 3, Núm. 2 (1939), 63-68.

Merino de Zela, Mildred. See Bibliografía del folklore peruano, entry no. 1758.

1845. Ministerio de Educación Pública del Perú. 10 charlas sobre folklore. Lima: Dirección de Educación Artística y Extensión Cultural, Sección Folklore, 1946. 51 pp. mimeographed. 33 cm.
[Said to contain the following: "Conferencias sostenidas en un ciclo de charlas organizado por la Sección Folklore y Artes Populares para los maestros. Hablaron sobre los siguientes temas: Federico Schwab, El Folklore como Ciencia; Arturo Jiménez Borja, Panorama del Folklore; Emilia Romero, Juegos Infantiles; Miguel Angel Ugarte, Muestra de Folklore Arequipeño; Carlos Sánchez Málaga, Folklore Musical; Jorge Muelle, Cultura y Folklore."]

1846. Miró Quesada S., Aurelio. Costa, sierra y montaña. Segunda edición aumentada. Lima: Editorial Cultura Antártica, S. A., 1947. 433 pp. 24 cm.
[Basically a kind of travelogue of various regions of Peru with costumbristic descriptions and narrations of all kinds. Occasionally the author includes folk poetry or songs, such as coplas, which he says he took from a book on Lambayeque which León Barandiarán had in preparation. There are also some décimas and huaynos scattered through the book.]

1847. Monge, Pedro S. "Aspectos de nuestra poesía popular." Xauxa (Jauja), No. 13 (octubre, 1947).

1848. Montesinos, Fernando. Memorias antiguas, historiales y políticas del Perú. Madrid: Imprenta de Miguel Ginesta, 1882. xxxii, 259 pp. 17 cm.
[After relating some historical events, the seventeenth-century chronicler says (p. 4): ". . . esto se colije de las poesías y cantares antiguos de los indios . . . ."]

1849. Morúa, Martín de. Origen e historia de los incas, obra escrita en el Cuzco (1575-90) por fray Martín Morúa, de la orden de la Merced. Publicada y anotada por Manuel Gonzáles de la Rosa. Lima, 1911; also, Historia de los incas, reyes del Perú. 2 vols. Lima: Imprenta y Librería Sanmarti y Ca., 1922, 1925. 21.5 cm. (Colección de libros y documentos referentes a la historia del Perú, Vols. IV and V of the 2a. serie.) The sixteenth century manuscript was not published until these editions were made in the twentieth century.
[My references are to the 1922-25 edition, which is the only one I have been able to consult. In Bk. I there is a passage (p. 143) in which Morúa speaks of yaravíes, "que son romances que ellos (the Indians) cantaban en su lengua . . . ."; also mention (p. 24) of the singing of "historias, sucesos y hazañas." In Bk. II there is an excellent description (p. 130) of the group singing and dancing of compositions (arabice) which "memoraban y recontaban las cosas pasadas."]

1850. Mostajo, Francisco. "Canciones del folklore peruano." CronL, 3 de diciembre de 1950.

Muelle, Jorge. See Ministerio de Educación Pública del Perú, entry no. 1845.

1851. Navarro del Aguila, Víctor. "Contribución a la bibliografía del folklore peruano." Revista del Instituto Americano de Arte (Cuzco), I:4 (diciembre de 1945), 33-52.

1852. Oviedo Herrera y Rueda, Luis Antonio. Poema sacro de la Passion de N. S. Jesu-Christo, que en vu romance castellano, dividido en siete Estaciones, Escrivia Don Lvis Antonio de Oviedo Herrera y Rueda. Lima: Francisco Sobrino, 1717. 62 unnumbered pp., followed by pp. 25-128; also, México, 1787. 94 pp.
[Menéndez y Pelayo (ref. 93, Vol. II, p. 132) describes this work as a "larguísimo romance, quizá el más largo que existe en castellano, a excepción de la Vida de la Virgen, de D. Antonio de Mendoza . . . ." Though born in Madrid, the poet, according to Menéndez y Pelayo, "por afecto y larga residencia pertenece al Perú."]

1853. Palma, Clemente. Don Alonso Henríquez de Guzmán y el primer poema sobre la conquista de América. Lima: n.p., 1935. 77 pp. 18.5 cm.
[A very fine critical study of Alonso Henríquez (or Enríquez) de

Guzmán and his work. Palma attributes to Enríquez de Guzmán personally two "anonymous" poems about the death of Almagro which appeared in the Libro de la vida y costumbres de don Alonso Enríquez (ref. 1794). After summarizing what is known of the poet-chronicler's life, Palma studies differences to be detected in published and manuscript versions of one of the poems, a work in octavas de arte mayor. Then, in an appendix, he prints the second poem, a romance. Also of interest is a listing (pp. 8-13) of all the early poems about the conquest of America that Palma is acquainted with.]

1854. Palma, Ricardo. Flor de academias y Diente del Parnaso. Lima: Oficina Tipográfica de El Tiempo, por L. H. Jiménez, 1899. xx, 478 pp.

[The prologue contains a discussion of the popular poetry current at the time of the conquest of America and later. There are examples of early romances. The two works here published, Flor de academias from the eighteenth century, and Diente del Parnaso written by Juan del Valle y Caviedes in the last years of the seventeenth century, contain romances, but they are not popular.]

1855. _____. Tradiciones peruanas. 6 vols. Madrid: Calpe, n. d. [1923-1925]. 24 cm. There are many editions.

[There are many coplas and a few romances and other popular poems scattered through this extensive work.]

Paz y Melia, A. See entry no. 1536.

Paz Soldán y Unanué, Pedro. See Arona, Juan de, entry no. 1740.

1856. Peralta y Barnuevo, Pedro de. Fúnebre pompa. Lima, 1728.

[Sánchez (ref. 1879, Vol. III, p. 183) indicates that there is a romance by Pedro José de Bermúdez de la Torre in this volume.]

1857. _____. "Romance de D. Pedro de Peralta Barnuevo, delante de una imagen de Cristo crucificado, siendo de edad de 18 años, cuando el temblor de 20 de octubre del año de 1687." In Los místicos. Vol. VII de Biblioteca de cultura peruana. Paris: Desclée de Brouwer, 1938. Pp. 194-195.

[An artistic romance taken from a manuscript in the Biblioteca Nacional in Madrid.]

1858. Pereda Valdés, Ildefonso. Valor folklórico y estilístico de las Tradiciones peruanas de Ricardo Palma. Los Angeles, California, 1940. (Reprint from Memoria del Segundo Congreso Internacional de Catedráticos de Literatura Iberoamericana.)

1859. Pérez Aragón, Alejandro. Folklore arequipeño. Arequipa: Editorial "De Todas Partes," 1943. 100 pp. 22 cm.

1860. Pino, J. J. del. "¿Cuál es el sentido psicológico de la música folklórica ayacuchana?" Huamanga (Ayacucho), Año XIV:71 (agosto de 1950), 10-13.

1861. ———. "¿Cuál es el sentido sicológico de la música folklórica ayacuchana?" Huamanga (Ayacucho), Año XI:64 (julio de 1946), 23-28.

1862. Pizarro, Pedro. Descubrimiento y conquista del Perú. Lima: Imprenta y Librería Sanmarti y Ca., 1917. xvi, 213 pp. 20 cm. (Colección de libros y documentos referentes a la historia del Perú, Vol. VI.) Though finished in 1571, this is the first edition of the work.
[Relates the incident (p. 7) wherein a malcontent among Francisco Pizarro's men sent to authorities in Panama a versified complaint which was concealed in a ball of cotton.]

1863. Pogo, Alexander. "The Anonymous La Conquista del Peru (Seville, April, 1534) and the Libro Vltimo del Svmmario delle Indie Occidentali (Venice, October, 1534)." Proceedings of the American Academy of Arts and Sciences (Boston), LXIV (May, 1928-May, 1930), pp. 177-286.
[Contains the same passage about the desire to emulate Roland which appears in Porras Barrenechea (ref. 1865).]

1864. Poma de Ayala, Phelipe Guamán. Primer nueva corónica y buen gobierno, publicada y anotada por Arthur Posnansky, F. R. A. I. La Paz, Bolivia: Editorial del Instituto "Tihuanacu" de Antropología, Etnografía y Prehistoria, 1944. v, viii, pp., no pagination of the text (references are given to the fojas of the original manuscript), but in the latter part of the volume there is some chaotic pagination. 21 cm.; an earlier edition in facsimile, Poma de Ayala, Felipe Huaman. Nueva corónica y buen gobierno (codex péruvien illustré). Paris: Institut d'Ethnologie, 1936. xxviii, 1168 pp. (incorrectly paginated). 27 cm. (Travaux et Mémories de l'Institut d'Ethnologie [of the Université de Paris], Vol. XXIII.) This is the first edition of the MS. which dates from about 1613.
[A poorly written chronicle which contains a vast amount of information about the Inca civilization. There are several references to Inca music, both songs and dances, though most are not precise enough to be of much value, except perhaps as corroboration of evidence gathered from other sources. Of this type are passages on Fojas 288, 290, 292, and 300 (in the La Paz edition, which is the only one I have seen). Beginning with Foja 317 there is a series of sections on music and fiestas with several texts of poetry and song, though none of it is narrative. On Foja 388, however, there is a seminarrative lament about the imprisonment of Atahualpa which is of interest. Also, there are some Indian compositions referred to as coplas (pp. 844, 847).]

1865. Porras Barrenechea, Raúl. "Notas para una biografía del yaraví." ComerL, 28 de julio, 1946, primera sección, p. II.

[A very fine study of the historical evolution of the yaraví from the aravi of pre-conquest times, which might be either sad or joyous, to the yaraví (a Hispanicized name), which came to be considered suitable only to express sadness and despair, and still later to the artistic compositions of learned poets who applied the latter name to melancholy poems which were entirely in the European, not the Indian tradition. Romances are mentioned only very incidentally, as when in passages from chronicles certain Indian songs are called "romances."]

1866. _____. "La primera copla de la conquista." MP, Año XVI, Vol. XXIII:169 (abril, 1941), 183-189.

[An extremely interesting attempt to unravel the mystery of the copla which a malcontent among Pizarro's army sent to Panama in a bundle of cotton. Originally said to have been sent from Isla del Gallo in 1527, it was actually written in San Miguel de Piura in 1532, according to the documentary proof which Porras Barrenechea offers here. He also provides evidence that Juan de la Torre, who was punished for composing the copla, was not the real author.]

1867. _____. Las relaciones primitivas de la conquista del Perú. Paris: Imprimeries Les Presses Modernes, 1937. 106 pp. 29.5 cm. (Cuadernos de la historia del Perú, No. 2; Serie: Los cronistas de la conquista, I.)

[In an appendix that contains a passage from La conquista del Perú, llamada la nueva Castilla, which Porras Barrenechea believes is the work of Cristóbal de Mena, there is a paragraph (p. 83) in which the men of Hernando Pizarro, appalled by the strength of an approaching enemy force, reassure each other by saying that each individual "haria mas que Roldan."]

1868. "Quando volvió vencedor Antequera."

[An eighteenth-century semipopular romance cited by Sánchez (ref. 1879, Vol. IV, p. 90) which is in a manuscript in the Biblioteca Nacional de Lima.]

1869. Raygada, Carlos. "Panorama musical del Perú." BLAM, Año II, Tomo II (abril de 1936), 169-214.

[Though primarily concerned with nonpopular music, the author devotes considerable attention to the problem of incorporating Indian folkloric themes into music on a higher level. There is nothing about romances or corridos, but Raygada reprints at length the most significant portions of some extensive polemics about the nature of the yaraví which appeared in Mercurio peruano in 1791 and 1792 (see refs. 1819, 1886, and 1891).]

Recopilación de los mejores yaravíes y huaynos del Perú. See Martínez G., Narciso, entry no. 1839.

1870. Recopilación de yaravíes. Cerro de Pasco: Imp. de la Liberería "Los Andes."

Relación de lo acaecido en Perú desde que Francisco Hernández Girón se alzó hasta el día que murió. See Varias relaciones del Perú y Chile, entry no. 1905.

1871. Relación de todo lo sucedido en la provincia del Piru desde que Blasco Nuñez Vela fue enviado por S. M. a ser visorey della, que se embarco a primero de noviembre del año de M. D. X. L. III. Lima: Imprenta del Estado, 1870. 203 pp. 27.5 cm.

[Contains a passage (p. 104) which refers to the singing of songs in praise of Gonzalo Pizarro and his deeds on the occasion of his triumphal entry into Lima in 1546.]

1872. Relación y verdadero romance que declara la in/considerada y atrevida sublevación que intentaban hazer los Indios mal/acordados y algunos mestizos en la ciudad de Lima. Se da razón de las promp-/tissimas y bien ordenadas providencias que se dieron para embarazo de tan/ossada execución, y del justo castigo que se dio a los culpados. / Con licencia: En la imprenta que está en la Plazuela de San Cristoval. Se hallarán en el primer Cajón de la Ribera, 1750.

[Sánchez cites this semipopular romance about an uprising in Peru in 1750 (ref. 1879, Vol. IV, pp. 97ff.). He describes the publication as "un folleto impreso a dos columnas" and declares that the romance, of which he prints a few lines, is "por demás prosaico en cuanto a estilo y muy meticuloso en cuanto a información histórica."]

1873. Rodríguez Moñino, Antonio. "Cancionerillo peruano del siglo XVII." MdS, Año IV, Vol. VII:20 (marzo-abril, 1932), 38-43.

1874. Romance en la fiesta con que los Batallones de Lima celebraron la imagen de Ntra. Sra. de Monserrat, 1766.

1875. [A romance which deals with the expulsion of los Jesuits in 1767]. El correo del Perú (Lima), II(1873):XXXVI, p. 289.

[Sánchez (ref. 1879, Vol. IV, p. 148) quotes a few lines from this anonymous semipopular romance which was first published over a century after the events which inspired it had taken place.]

1876. Romero, Carlos A. "Rebeliones indígenas en el Perú durante la colonia." Revista histórica (Lima), Tomo IX, Entrega IX (1935), 317-337.

[Sánchez (ref. 1879, Vol. IV, p. 99) indicates that this work contains the complete text of the Relación y verdadero romance (entry no. 1872 in this section) about a rebellion in Peru in 1750.]

1877. Romero, Emilia. El romance tradicional en el Perú. México: El Colegio de México, 1952. 136 pp. 23 cm.

[A very fine study of the romance in America and especially in Peru. Besides providing a good general study of the background of the romance, the author gives many texts gathered in Peru. Each section on a given composition is accompanied by bibliography to facilitate comparison of Peruvian texts with those from other parts of the Spanish world.]

Romero, Emilia. See Ministerio de Educación Pública del Perú, entry no. 1845.

1878. Romero, F. "La evolución de 'La marinera'." Ipna (Lima), Año III(1946):6, pp. 29-33; Núm. 7, pp. 11-21; Año IV(1947):8, pp. 12, 20.

1879. Sánchez, Luis Alberto. La litertura peruana; derrotero para una historia espiritual del Perú. 6 vols. Asunción del Paraguay: Editorial Guarania, 1951. 23.5 cm.

[In Vol. I, "La literatura aborigen: los incas y el folklore" (pp. 133-198) contains a vast amount of information about many important aspects of Peruvian Indian literature, popular and nonpopular, and a few texts are given. In Vol. II, "Romances y poemas de la conquista" (pp. 28-50) summarizes what is known about the subject indicated, though the discussion is far from exhaustive. Vols. III and IV contain some material about several artistic poets who wrote learned romances (Caviedes, Terralla y Landa, et al.), and in "La calle: los rebeldes" (Vol. IV, pp. 85-107) there is some interesting material about pasquines and other popular verse of the eighteenth century. Some texts are given along with important bibliographical data about poems and pasquines that are popular or semipopular in tone, many of which deal with Indian uprisings of the latter part of the eighteenth century. Vol. V contains some discussion with texts of the work of Melgar; also, a few texts of romances and pasquines from the period of independence.]

1880. _____. Los poetas de la colonia y de la revolución. Edición corregida [i.e., 2nd ed.]. Lima: Editorial P. T. C. M., 1947. 317 pp. 20.5 cm.

[A useful history of Peruvian poetry from the conquest through the period of the wars of independence. Occasionally the author cites poets who wrote artistic romances (Oquendo, Caviedes, et al.).]

Sánchez Málaga, Carlos. See Ministerio de Educación Pública del Perú, entry no. 1845.

1881. Santa María, F. Apuntes biográficos de don Fernando Márquez de la Plata y Orosco y de don Fernando Márquez de la Plata y Encalada.

[Without providing proper bibliographical data, Paredes (ref. 480, p. 115) cites a passage from the above work wherein, upon referring to the rebellion of Tupac Amaru, Santa María declares: "El pasquín, repugnante como es, llega a ser el eco de la condecencia (sic) de los oprimidos en los pueblos en que la libertad de hablar y de quejarse se ha colocado en el catálogo de los delitos."]

1882. Santillán, Fernando de. "Relación del origen, descendencia, política y gobierno de los incas por el licenciado Fernando de Santillán." In Tres relaciones de las antigüedades peruanas. Asunción del Paraguay: Talleres de J. Pellegrini, Buenos Aires, 1950. 353 pp. 23.5 cm. (This is a new edition of the work with the same title published by the Ministerio de Fomento de España in 1879.)

[On the first page of Santillán's Relación (p. 43 of this edition), the chronicler, in discussing the devices used by the Incas to preserve accounts of the past, says: "Lo que tienen memoria de las cosas antiguas es por algunos cantares en que se relatan los hechos pasados, y han venido aprendiéndoles de unos en otros . . . ."]

1883. Sas, André. "La formación del folklore peruano." BLAM, Año II, Tomo II (abril de 1936), 97-103.

[A study of the Indian, Spanish, and Negro elements which have entered into the formation of Perú's musical culture. Some of the author's ideas about the interaction among the different factors are most interesting, but there is nothing about romances or corridos and only very incidental mention of any specific genres.]

1884. _____. "La música popular en el Perú." MusRM, I:2 (15 de mayo de 1930), 11-23. (This is a translation with added commentary by Daniel Castañeda of an article by Sas which appeared first in Le courrier musical et théatral [Paris], enero de 1930.)

[Of considerable general interest, this article deals with technical aspects of Inca music during the pre-Hispanic period and with the influence of Spanish music, particularly religious music, after the conquest.]

1885. Schuller, Rudolf. "Contribution to the Narrative Poetry of Peru." Anthropos (St. Gabriel-Modling, Austria), XII-XIII(1917-1918):1-2.

Schwab, Federico. See Ministerio de Educación Pública del Perú, entry no. 1845.

1886. Sicramio [pseudonym]. "Rasgo remitido por la Sociedad Poética sobre la música en general, y particularmente de los yaravíes." MP, Núm. 101 (1791).

[Raygada (ref. 1869, pp. 179-180) quotes at length considerable material about a yaraví which appeared in this early article. See also entries nos. 1819 and 1891.]

1887. Sierra, Florencio de la. "La minga." FPL, Núm. 30 (junio y julio de 1953), 943-945.
[Includes some coplas.]

1888. Sinclair, Joseph H., trans. The Conquest of Peru as Recorded by a Member of the Pizarro Expedition. New York: The New York Public Library, 1929. 3 pp. facsimile, 47 pp. 31.5 cm.

[According to Pogo (ref. 1863), this is a facsimile reproduction of the anonymous La conquista del Perú, llamada de nueva Castilla, which is owned by the New York Public Library. This is the work which Porras Barrenechea (ref. 1867) attributes to Cristóbal de Mena.]

1889. Sivirichi, Atilio. "Hacia el nacionalismo musical." La Sierra (Lima), Nos. 16-17 (abril-mayo, 1928), 19-38.

1890. Stevenson, Robert. The Music of Peru; Aboriginal and Viceroyal Epochs. Washington: Pan American Union, 1959. xii, 331 pp. 17.5 cm.
[The best study of Peruvian music that is available. Along with extensive treatment of various kinds of folkmusic, there is some attention to the romance.]

1891. T. J. C. y P. "Carta sobre la música; en la que se hace ver el estado de sus conocimientos en Lima, y se critica el rasgo sobre los yaravíes impreso en el Mercurio, núm. 101." MP, IV:117, p. 108; "Conclusión del papel antecedente." MP, IX:118 (19 de febrero de 1792), 116.
[Raygada (ref. 1869, pp. 181-187) quotes apparently all the most important portions of this article, which deals in large measure with the yaravíes. It treats in particular the comments which Sicramio had made about them in an earlier article (see entries nos. 1819 and 1886).]

1892. Tamayo Vargas, Augusto. "Escritos, proclamas, coplas y cantares de la emancipación." ComerL, 3 de enero, 1954.

1893. _____. Literatura peruana. 2 vols. Lima: n.p., 1953-1954. 26 cm.
[Several sections of this history of literature deal with topics related to popular poetry and song. In Vol. I, see "Literatura quechua" (pp. 31-139) for a great deal of information about Indian poetry and song, poets, etc.; see also, "Coplas, cantares y romances" (pp. 152-170), a good survey of popular and semipopular literature in Spanish at the time of conquest. In subsequent chapters there is treatment of artistic poets, like Rosas de Oquendo and Caviedes, who cultivated the romance form. In Vol. II, the first two sections, "La crisis del coloniaje" and "Literatura de la emancipación" (pp. 7-98) contain discussion and texts of a great many poems, semipopular or artistic in character, from the eighteenth century and early years of the nineteenth century. Many are romances, coplas, or pasquines. This entire manual is of value as a point of departure for further study because of the vast amount of information which it contains and because of the bibliographical aids which are to be found in it.]

Terralla y Landa, Esteban. See Ayanque, Simón, entry no. 1742.

1894. Ugarte, Juan A. "La chicha, canción popular cantada en las fiestas que se dieron a la llegada del general San Martín." ComerL, 28 de julio de 1935, p. 7.

1895. Ugarte y Ch., Miguel Angel. Juegos, canciones, dichos y otros entretenimientos de los niños recogidos en la ciudad de Arequipa. Arequipa: Editorial Portugal, 1947. 96 pp. 21 cm.

_____. See Ministerio de Educación Pública del Perú, entry no. 1845.

1896. Unanue, Hipólito. "Rasgos inéditos de los escritores peruanos." MP, I:34 (28 de abril de 1791), 312-313.

1897. Urbina, Silverio. Recopilación de versos populares. Cerro de Pasco: Tip. Los Andes, 1921. 147 pp.
[Ref. 1758 (p. 15) says: "Contiene yaravíes, mulizas, huaynos."]

1898. Uriel García, José. Pueblos y paisajes sudperuanos. Lima, 1949.

1899. Urteaga, Horacio H. "Los copleros de la conquista; apostillas al libro de Luis Alberto Sánchez 'Historia de la literatura peruana'." MP, Año IV, Vol. VI:32 (febrero, 1921), 120-142.
[While praising Sánchez' brilliant work, Urteaga chides him for ignoring the work of the copleros of the sixteenth century. To remedy this deficiency, Urteaga offers a pioneer study of the subject which is highly meritorious, though it suffers from the fact that the author does not document his material. There is no attempt to hide his sources, since he mentions at one time or another almost all of them, both primary (Gutiérrez de Santa Clara, Alonso de Enríquez, Torres de Mendoza, et al.) and secondary (mostly Toribio Medina); but in giving the texts of many important romances and coplas he neglects to state where he found them. While most of this study has been superseded by Lohmann Villena's work, which is based in part upon this pioneer effort, some of its historical background still has value as a useful summary.]

1900. Valdez, Rodrigo de. Poema heroyco/hispano-latino/panegírico/de la Fundación y gran-/dezas de la muy noble y Leal/ciudad de Lima./ Obra póstuma/del M. R. P. M. Rodrigo de Valdez,/de la Compañía de Jesús, Cathedrático de/Prima jubilado y Prefecto Regente de/ Estudios en el Colegio Maximo de San Pablo./Sácala a luz/el Doct. don Francisco Garabito de León y Messia, Cura Rector/de la Iglesia Metropolitana de Lima, Visitador y Examinador/General de su Arzobispado, Exsobrino y primo/hermano del autor./Dedicale/al Rey nuestro Señor don Carlos Segundo, /Rey de las Españas/Emperador de las Indias, etc. . . En Madrid, en la imprenta de Antonio Román, año 1687.
[Valdez, a Peruvian born in Lima in 1609, wrote under the influence of Góngora. Sánchez (ref. 1879, Vol. III, p. 134) indicates that this poem in romance form consists of 572 quatrains. He prints a few lines from the poem and gives some bibliography about the work.]

1901. Valladares Quintana, María Lourdes. "Del folklore huanca." La Tribuna (Lima), 19 de setiembre de 1948.

1902. Varallanos, José. "El genio español en nuestro cantar popular." ComerL, 1° de enero, 1944, p. 14.
[A good article which stresses the Spanish elements in Peruvian

folklore and considers (the Indian contribution) relatively minor. There is some attention to popular poetry, mostly coplas, though with occasional reference to romances. The author discounts the originality of all Peruvian artistic poetry, even the work of such darlings of nationalist critics as Melgar. Everything in Peru, both artistic and folkloric, he considers basically Spanish.]

1903. Vargas Ugarte, Rubén. Fr. Francisco del Castillo y Tamayo. Lima, 1948. (Clásicos peruanos, Vol. II.)

[Tamayo Vargas (ref. 1893, Vol. II, pp. 33-38) prints a group of romances by Castillo y Tamayo, a repentista and costumbristic poet of the eighteenth century. Topical and semipopular, they are taken from this work by Vargas about the poet and his work.]

1904. _____, ed. Nuestro romancero. Lima: Tipografía Peruana, 1951. xi, 234 pp. 21.5 cm. (Clásicos peruanos, Vol. IV.); (Segunda serie). Lima: Tipografía Peruana, 1958. viii, 149 pp. 22 cm. (Clásicos peruanos, Vol. VI.)

[A very useful collection of historical poetry which encompasses Peruvian history from the conquest down to the end of the nineteenth century. A great many poems are romances, but very few are truly popular, though some might be considered semipopular. This does not lessen their interest as examples of the use of romance meter in Peruvian literary history, but, unfortunately, many compositions appear without identification of their sources and with insufficient bibliographical data.]

1905. Varias relaciones del Perú y Chile. Madrid: Imprenta de M. Ginesta, 1879. viii, 359 pp. 17.5 cm. (Colección de libros españoles raros o curiosos, Vol. XIII.)

[In one of the anonymous manuscripts printed here, Relación de lo acaecido en Perú desde que Francisco Hernández Girón se alzó hasta el día que murió, there are two romances concerning Hernández Girón and his rebellion in 1553. Both romances have been reprinted by Medina (ref. 623 pp. xlii-li).]

1906. Vásquez, Emilio. "Santo Domingo de Sicaya." Revista del Museo Nacional (Lima), XVII(1949), 57-106.

[Boggs (ref. 13 [1951], p. 26) says: "Describes various aspects of its folklore: speech, festival, dress, song . . . ."]

1907. Vega, Carlos. La música de un códice colonial del siglo XVII. B. A.: Instituto de Literatura Argentina, Sección Folklore, 1931.

[A study of a manuscript by Gregorio Dezuola, a monk who lived in Lima. It contains some poems in romance meter, including one about Pedro el cruel. All the poetry, however, is from Spain. Vega studies primarily the music which accompanied the texts, though the latter are, of course, provided.]

1908. Vellard, Jen Albert. "Folklore de los pescadores del Lago Titicaca." AFA, volume number lacking (1945), 81-88.

1909. Vergara Alba, J. Eduardo. "Cantares de mi tierra." <u>FPL</u>, III:35 (junio-julio, 1955), 1978 and 1996.
[Ref. 1758 (p. 15) says: "Coplas de la Prov. de Yungay."]

1910. Vidal Martínez, Leopoldo. <u>Poesía de los incas</u>. Lima: Empresa Editora Amauta, 1947. 208 pp. 21 cm.
[An excellent and well documented study of the subject. Divided into three main sections, the second of these, "La épica," has some discussions of various types of poetry (the <u>yaraví</u>, etc.) which are of interest as background for post-conquest popular poetry. Also, in the third section, which deals with dramatic poetry, there are some references to the relationship between narrative songs, the dance, and the drama. Most of the material presented is taken, of course, from chronicles.]

1911. _____. "Revaloración del yaraví." <u>MP</u>, Año XXII, Vol. XXVIII:241 (abril, 1947), 208-212.
[An attempt to show by careful documentation that, contrary to romantic tradition, the <u>yaraví</u> was not necessarily a sad song. Nor does Vidal Martínez believe that it was only lyric in nature, and he cites numerous passages from Morúa, Cobo, Garcilaso, and others which seem to indicate that <u>yaraví</u> was a generic term that embraced many types of compositions, including narratives of deeds and events.]

1912. Vienrich, Adolfo. <u>Azucenas quechuas por unos parias</u> (bilingüe). Tarma, 1905.
[Harcourt (ref. 1813, Vol. I, p. 556) refers to a poem on the death of Atahualpa which appears in the above work (p. 30).]

1913. Vivanco, Moisés. <u>Melodías peruanas</u>. <u>Peruvian Folk Songs</u>. <u>Album de siete composiciones para piano del folklore peruano</u>. B. A.: Ediciones Internacionales Fermata, [1944]. 11 pp. 31.5 cm.

1914. Vizcarra Rozas, Abraham. <u>Bosquejo del proceso de la música en el Perú</u>. Cuzco: Tip. "La Económica," 1940. 65 pp. 21 cm.
[Federics Schwab describes it as follows: "Estudia e interpreta las manifestaciones musicales a través de la historia peruana, limitándose a la música popular. El presente trabajo es una tesis presentada en la Universidad Nacional del Cuzco, para optar el título de doctor en la Facultad de Filosofía, Historia y Letras."]

1915. _____. "Folklore musical peruano." <u>RUCuzco</u>, Año XXIX: 78 (primer semestre de 1940), 163-198.
[A good general survey of the popular music of Peru. The author considers the mixing of Spanish and Indian elements and deals with modern songs and dances such as the <u>huayno</u>, the <u>marinera</u>, and <u>pregones</u>. Some of the <u>huayno</u> texts are <u>coplas</u>. There is also passing mention of <u>yaravíes</u> and <u>tristes</u>.]

1916. "Yaraví, versos de la tradición oral." <u>TradP</u>, Año III:12-14 (enero de 1953), p. 51.

1917. Yépez Miranda, Alfredo. "El folklore peruano." AmerH, V:1 (enero, 1940), 31-35; also, RUCuzco, Año XXIX:78 (primer semestre de 1940), 65-73.

[A broad discussion of the nature of Peruvian folklore with particular reference to the division of the country geographically and psychologically between the coast (city) and the mountains (the rural area). The texts of popular songs cited are not from romance or copla tradition, but the nature of the article is such that it is of significance to the study of any phase of Peruvian folklore.]

1918. Zárate, Fidel A. Los lares iluminados. Lima: Empresa Editora Peruana, 1941. 366 pp.

[Boggs (ref. 13 [1941], p. 35) mentions a section on Pablo, a Peruvian minstrel.]

1919. Zevallos Quiñones, Jorge. "Un romance español del siglo XVIII en el Perú." 3, Núm. 7 (diciembre de 1940), 63-70.

[Contains text and music of a Peruvian version of Las señas del esposo which Zevallos Quiñones collected from oral tradition. For comparative purposes, he gives two Spanish versions. His commentary is of little value since he obviously is not aware of the existence of this romance in other areas of America, nor is he aware of such phenomena as contamination of texts.]

PUERTO RICO

Serious study of Puerto Rico's popular poetry and song dates only from the second decade of the present century when J. Alden Mason collected and published some texts of romances, décimas, and other types of popular poetry. This modest beginning was followed in 1933 by an excellent literary study of La poesía popular en Puerto Rico by María Cadilla de Martínez, an extremely competent scholar who has dominated folklore studies in Puerto Rico during the past quarter of a century. Her several books and monographs have been supplemented, however, by an occasional meritorious contribution by other investigators, such as the Renadío del cantar folklórico de Puerto Rico of Monserrate Deliz.

PUERTO RICO

1920. Cadilla de Martínez, María. Costumbres y tradicionalismos de mi tierra. San Juan: Imprenta Venezuela, 1938. 196 pp. 18 cm.
[A collection of brief studies of many diverse aspects of Puerto Rican customs and traditions. Dances, villancicos, food, dress, sports, and the like are subjects of chapters. Scattered through the book are a number of coplas of various kinds. Of interest is Chap. XII, "Nuestra poesía popular del ciclo de pasión" (pp. 135-146), which contains some narrative poetry about Christ's crucifixion, though not in romance form. In this chapter, and also on pp. 188-193, there are some décimas glossing cuartetas.]

1921. _____. Juegos y canciones infantiles de Puerto Rico. San Juan: Casa Baldrich, 1940. 259, iv, iv pp. 23 cm.
[Among the songs and poetry treated are a number of traditional Spanish romances and coplas.]

1922. _____. La poesía popular en Puerto Rico. Universidad de Madrid, 1933. 366 pp. 25 cm.; also, San Juan: Imp. Venezuela, 1953. 366 pp.
[The best study that has been made of the popular poetry of Puerto Rico. Besides chapters on romances, coplas, décimas, the meters used in popular poetry, etc., there is an extensive bibliography and an index. The section on romances contains texts of many that are from Spanish tradition.]

1923. _____. Raíces de la tierra (colección de cuentos populares y tradiciones). Arecibo: Tipografía Hernández, 1941. 242 pp. 23 cm.
[Though concerned principally with cuentos, the volume contains a section, "Modalidades coloniales" (pp. 186-204), which treats satirical and narrative poetry and song — romances, décimas, coplas, pasquines, letrillas, and the like. Few of the texts given are romances, but there are several interesting compositions.]

1924. Coll y Toste, Cayetano. Prehistoria de Puerto-Rico. San Juan: Tip. Boletín Mercantil, 1907. 298 pp. 25.5 cm.
[Torres (ref. 113, p. 34) says: "El Dr. Coll y Toste en Prehistoria de Puerto Rico (San Juan, P. R., 1907), p. 94, dice que al 'Bohique', sacerdote y curandero de la tribu correspondía la educación de los jóvenes indígenas y enseñarles a cantar 'areytos o romances' históricos."]

1925. Coplas cantadas en la gran alborada gibaresca verificada en celebridad del nacimiento de S. A. R. el Príncipe de Asturias. Puerto Rico, 1858. 17 pp.

1926. Deliz, Monserrate. Renadío del cantar folklórico de Puerto Rico. Madrid: Ed. Hispania, 1951. 287 pp. 27.5 cm.
[A collection of children's folklore with texts and music, along with a brief introductory study. The last section of the book, "Romances y romancillos" (pp. 239-287), includes eighteen compositions. Some are

romances from Spanish tradition: Hilo de oro, Las señas del marido (printed with the title, Señora, voy para Francia), Angelina (a version of Delgadina), Mambrú, Blanca Flor, and the like. Some are less well known, if indeed they belong to peninsular tradition. Most interesting is a romance entitled Antonio Olivo (pp. 284-287), which is very similar to Mexican corridos.]

Durán, Gustavo. See entry no. 1286.

1927. Espinosa, Aurelio M. "Romances de Puerto Rico." RH, XLIII:104 (août, 1918), 309-364.

[A collection of romances which were gathered by J. Alden Mason in 1914-1915 (see entry no. 1934). Texts are given for thrity-six poems and each is accompanied by a commentary and notes. Included are compositions such as Delgadina, Las señas del marido, and other will known romances from Spain. The texts of two décimas are also provided.]

1928. González Font, José. Escritos sobre Puerto Rico; noticias históricas, poesías, artículos y otros datos. Barcelona: J. González Font; San Juan: B. F. Sanjurjo, 1903. 198 pp. 18.5 cm.

[Cadilla de Martínez indicates that the work contains some romances, including one in jíbaro dialect, which she prints in full (ref. 1922, pp. 164-165). She says it appears on pp. 140-141 of González Font's work.]

1929. Gordon, Maxine W. "Selections from the Folklore of Vieques, Yauco, and Luquillo, Puerto Rico." JAF, LXIV(1951), 55-82.

[A large body of material from Puerto Rico, including a great deal of popular poetry — décimas, coplas, and the like. However, there are no romances or other narratives.]

1930. López Cruz, Francisco. "La música popular de Puerto Rico." Trabajos y conferencias, Seminario de Estudios Americanistas de la Facultad de Filosofía y Letras (Madrid), Núm. 2 (1953), 57-63.

1931. Malaret, Augusto. "Panorama folklórico de Puerto Rico." UnivCB, III:7 (agosto-septiembre, 1938), 70-82.

[Eleven brief sections about diverse aspects of Puerto Rican folklore. Section IX is called "El canto popular" and section X "Juegos infantiles." While these contain some elementary information of interest to the study of popular poetry, they merely summarize what any fairly well informed investigator would know. The article can be safely ignored.]

1932. Manrique Cabrera, R. "Literatura folklórica puertorriqueña." Revista del Instituto de Cultura Puertorriqueña (San Juan), IV(1959), 4-7.

[Paredes (ref. 91, p. 20) says: "General view of Puerto Rican folklore with special notice give (sic) to the décima."]

1933. Mason, J. Alden. "Porto-Rican Folk-Lore: Décimas, Christmas Carols, Nursery Rhymes, and other Songs." JAF, XXXI(1918), 289-450.

[After an introduction by Aurelio M. Espinosa, who edited Mason's material, the popular poetry collected is divided into these categories: décimas in octosyllabic meter (194 examples), décimas in hexasyllabic meters (37 examples), aguinaldos or Christmas carols (25 examples), nursery rhymes, children's songs, and other popular rhymes (110 examples), and oraciones y cánticos espirituales (7 examples). There are no romances, but some of the décimas are narrative and historical.]

1934. _____. "Spanish Romances from Porto Rico." JAF, XXXIII (1920), 76-79.

[Versions of Las señas del marido (called here La corrida de Catalina), one of Silvana, and one of Delgadina (called here La desgraciada niña). The last two are combinations of verse and prose. The first two have music. At the beginning appears this statement: "The following Romances were collected in Porto Rico by Dr. J. Alden Mason. The music here has been transcribed by Miss Helen H. Roberts. A discussion of the Romances by Professor Aurelio M. Espinosa has appeared in 'Revue Hispanique' (Tome XLIII, 1918)." See entry no. 1927.]

Mendoza, Vicente T. See entry no. 1445.

1935. Plotini, Tomás. "Folklore puertorriqueño." El día estético (Ponce), I(1941):3, pp. 26-28, 30.

1936. "Relación verídica en la que se da noticia de lo acaecido en la ysla de Puerto Rico a fines del año de 45 y principios de el 47 con el motiuo de llorar la muerte de N. rey y señor don Phelipe Quinto y celebrar la exaltacion a la corona de N. S. D. Fernando sexto. Dedícase al señor coronel de los reales exercitos don Jvan Joseph Colomo gouernador y capitán general de dicha ysla. Por vn afectoseruidor suio en 19 de spbre de 1747." Boletín histórico de Puerto Rico (San Juan), Año V:3 (mayo-junio, 1918), 148-192.

[Cadilla Martínez (ref. 1922, p. 116) says with reference to this work: "La primera colección poética que se hizo en Puerto Rico, es de la cuarta década del siglo XVIII. Antes de esa fecha es difícil encontrar pruebas documentales de la existencia de la poesía popular en la isla . . . ." The chronicle in question relates events which occured at the death of Felipe V and the rise of Fernando VI to the Spanish throne. It is in prose with numerous passages of poetry interspersed through it. The compositions are narratives of events or commentaries of various kinds and are written in a variety of meters, though none is in romance and none, except perhaps a copla (p. 182), seems popular.]

Roberts, Helen H. See Mason, J. Alden, entry no. 1934.

1937. Rosa-Nieves, Cesáreo. "El romance tradicional español en Puerto Rico." Revista del Instituto de Cultura Puertorriqueña (San Juan), II(1959):3, pp. 4-7.

[Paredes (ref. 91, p. 59) says: "General review of Spanish ballads found in Puerto Rico and other parts of Spanish America."]

1938. Silva, R. Antología puertorriqueña. San Juan: Imprenta Venezuela, 1928.
[Cited by Cadilla de Martínez (ref. 1922, p. 358).]

"Spanish Romances from Porto Rico." See Mason, J. Alden, entry no. 1934.

1939. Valle Atiles, Francisco del. El campesino puertorriqueño. Puerto Rico: Tipografía de José González Font, 1887. 164 pp. 23 cm.
[The author discusses (pp. 106-110) the poetry of the jíbaro and offers some texts of coplas which are sung in rural areas of Puerto Rico. All are basically cuartetas, though one is an octava formed by linking two cuartetas together.]

EL SALVADOR

The best and, in fact, the only significant study of the popular poetry and songs of El Salvador is the work of María de Baratta. Her <u>Cuzcatlán típico</u>, while lacking organization and unity, is a valuable compendium of information about many aspects of the folklore of her country.

EL SALVADOR

1940. Baratta, María de. Cuzcatlán típico; ensayo sobre etnofonía de El Salvador; folklore, folkwisa y folkway. 2 partes [i.e. vols.] San Salvador: Publicaciones del Ministerio de Cultura (Talleres Gráficos Cisneros), n.d. ("Palabras al lector" in Vol. I is dated 1951). 32 cm.
[This rather remarkable work surveys practically every phase of the popular music, both songs and dances, of El Salvador, with liberal attention to other aspects of folklore. Beginning with pre-Hispanic civilizations and ending with current practices, the author treats musical instruments, songs, dances, costumes, legends, proverbs, pregones, etc. Along with texts there are many musical transcriptions. Though the work is quite disjointed and suffers from this lack of organization, and though it sometimes lacks scholarly principles, it is a most valuable source of information about the subjects treated. Of particular interest to my subject are versions of El venadito (pp. 313-315), the text of the dance of moros y cristianos in romance form (pp. 409-470), versions of El torito pinto ("Echenme ese toro pinto, hijo de la vaca mora") (pp. 481-486), versions of Don Simón (p. 491), some coplas about William Walker (p. 547), a corrido on a trivial subject (p. 550), versions of El piojo y la pulga (pp. 557-559), children's songs which are versions of Spanish romances (pp. 570 ff.), alabados in romance form (pp. 653-654), and numerous coplas.]

1941. Boggs, Ralph Steele. "Contribuciones importantes al folklore general de El Salvador." BBAA, XVII(1954), 1. parte, 112-114.
[Boggs (ref. 13 [1955], p. 20) indicates that this is a survey which covers the years 1941-1952.]

1942. Comité de Investigaciones del Folklore Nacional y Arte Típico Salvadoreño. Recopilación de materiales folklóricos salvadoreños, primera parte. San Salvador: Imprenta Nacional, 1944. 412 pp. 25.5 cm.
[Library of Congress card reads: "'Canciones populares' (without music): V. 1, p. [237]-355. 'Canciones de cuna' (without music): V. 1, p. [357]-362."]

1943. Espinosa, Francisco. Canciones populares. San Salvador: Talleres Gráficos Cisneros, 1941. 40 pp. 18.5 cm. (Folklore salvadoreño, Cuaderno No. 3.)
[A small collection of popular songs of various kinds. There are a few coplas but no romances, corridos, or anything else of a topical character.]

1944. _____, comp. Folk-lore salvadoreño. San Salvador: Talleres Gráficos Cisneros, 1946. 123 pp. 19 cm.
[There are sections on Cantos de cuna, Bombas, Canciones populares, Salvadorismos, Adivinanzas, Apodos, and Nombres indígenas de poblaciones salvadoreñas. The bombas and a good many compositions which appear in other sections are coplas. In all they form a fairly large collection of texts. But there seem to be no romances or romance fragments.]

1945. Espinosa, Francisco, comp. "Folklore salvadoreño: Bombas." RABA, Año XI, Vol. LII:126 (octubre, 1934), 126-136.
[Texts of 140 bombas (coplas) with no commentary whatsoever. Nor are there any data to indicate where they were collected or whether they were found in oral or written tradition.]

Recopilación de materiales folklóricos salvadoreños. See Comité de Investigaciones del Folklore Nacional y Arte Típico, entry no. 1942.

VENEZUELA

The study of Venezuelan popular poetry and song began with the collecting of some texts by A. Ernst and the writing of some essays by Arístides Rojas around the turn of the twentieth century. Next chronologically, José E. Machado dominated folklore studies in Venezuela for a decade or so before about 1930, though with more enthusiasm than scholarly ability. Like Mexico, Venezuela had to wait until the last decade or two for the appearance of some folklorists and literary scholars capable of studying properly the country's rich popular traditions. The high quality of recent work by Juan Liscano, Raúl Olivares Figueroa, Luis Felipe Ramón y Rivera, Isabel Aretz de Ramón y Rivera, and a few other investigators has, however, raised contemporary Venezuelan scholarship in folklore studies to a very respectable level. Not only the literary aspects of Venezuelan popular song and poetry have received attention; the musical characteristics of folklore have also been treated at some length, particularly by Luis Felipe Ramón y Rivera and his very talented wife.

The investigations which have so far been carried out reveal that Venezuela is a rich field indeed for folklore research. Not only romances and corridos are vigorously alive, but a related form, the galerón, which Venezuela shares with Colombia, is also widely cultivated in certain areas. Likewise, décimas and coplas (the latter often known as polos or cantas) are ubiquitous in Venezuela as in most countries of Spanish America.

VENEZUELA

1946. Acosta Saignes, Miguel. "Las décimas de Carlos Rojas." Anales de la Universidad Central de Venezuela (Caracas), XLI (julio de 1956), 113-163.

[The author prints forty-four texts of décimas dictated to him by Carlos Rojas, a worker on a ranch in the Estado Barinas. Forty-three of them are compositions which Rojas recited from memory; one is a composition which he himself wrote. They are of various types and the compiler classifies them as A lo divino and A lo humano, though the latter category has many subheadings. There are also some comments on the décimas in Venezuela and in other areas of America.]

1947. _____. "Introducción al estudio de la gallina en el folklore de Venezuela." TradP, Año IV, Vol. VI:15 (enero, 1954), 29-46.

[Includes several popular coplas about the subject.]

1948. _____. "El maremare: baile del jaguar y la luna." AVF, Año I:2 (julio-diciembre, 1952), 266-282.

[An excellent point of departure for study of this song-dance of Venezuela. The strophes which accompany it are coplas in form. The author not only describes the genre thoroughly and gives many texts, but he also gives bibliography which would be of help toward further study of the maremare.]

1949. Angarita Arvelo, Rafael. "Ilustraciones del romancero castellano; cancionero y romancero venezolano." CV, Año XIII:106 (septiembre-octubre, 1930), 65-93.

[A very interesting study of romances, corridos, and other popular forms in Venezuela. Included are some examples of romances and corridos from the colonial period, the epoch of independence, and later.]

1950. Antolínez, Gilberto. "El hombre de Yaracuy frente a su paisaje y su folk-lore." RNC, VI:46 (septiembre-octubre de 1944), 126-134.

[In a general treatment of the folklore of Yaracuy, the texts of three coplas are quoted.]

1951. Araujo, Orlando. "El folklore en Rómulo Gallegos." AVF, Año I:2 (julio-diciembre, 1952), 323-337.

[Among other types of folklore found in the novels of Gallegos, coplas are the subject of one section of this work. The author quotes several which Gallegos uses and also some commentaries of the novelist about them. Décimas and fulías receive lesser attention.]

1952. Aretz, Isabel. "Cantares populares de Falcón." El Farol (Caracas), Año XVIII:164 (junio, 1956), 20-23.

[The author quotes the texts of a few compositions, including some coplas and a narrative about the death of Christ which is in corrido form, and she publishes some photographs of folk artists.]

1953. Aretz, Isabel. "El canto popular." BIF, I:3 (enero de 1954), 43-51.
[An extremely useful listing of terms used in connection with popular songs. There are definitions of types of songs, manners of singing, types of strophes, and the like. The corrido is listed (p. 48).]

1954. _____. "Documentos de poesía popular." BIF, II:6 pp. 206-212.
[Boggs (ref. 13 [1957], p. 39) says: "Broadside poetic texts about political leaders, often by known poets, from Venezuela."]

1955. _____. "En torno al folklore musical venezolano." BIF, I:2 (noviembre de 1953), 19-24.
[A very useful attempt to classify and to distinguish between the many types of dances found in Venezuela. Most interesting is the fact that corridos and galerones are listed as types of dances under the general heading of joropos. The polo is also mentioned as having been originated, like the galerón and the corrido, by trobadores. Romances, corridos, galerones, polos, and other types are mentioned again in a section entitled "Cantos líricos de parranderos y de troveros."]

1956. _____. "El folklore en los libros de viaje." RNC, Año XX:130 (septiembre-octubre, 1958), 107-115.
[The author has extracted information about folklore from Vol. III of Campaigns and Cruises in Venezuela and New Grenada (London, 1833), known now to have been written by Captain Richard Longeville Vowell though published originally without identification of the author. There are descriptions of singing and dancing and some texts are given in Spanish. None is a romance, but there are some which are based on historical events.]

1957. _____. "Maneras típicas del cantar venezolano." BIF, I:7 (octubre de 1954), 171-176.
[An informative brief description of the different manners of singing popular songs in Venezuela: e. g., canto solista, alternancia de canto y silbido, and the like. Among other types, the galerón, the corrido, and the copla are treated.]

1958. _____. Manual de folklore venezolano. Caracas: Ministerio de Educación, 1957. 220 pp. 17 cm. (Biblioteca popular venezolana, No. 62.)
[An extremely useful manual that contains fine discussions of folklore theory, defines the kinds of folklore that are to be found in Venezuela, and treats the uses of folklore studies in fields such as sociology, literature, and the like. Popular and traditional poetry come in for attention, and the definition of many Venezuelan genres of poetry and song are very valuable. Not many texts are given, but the few there are of corridos, décimas, and the like are of interest. There are also extensive bibliographies.]

1959. _____. "El marmare como expresión musical y coreográfica." BIF, III:2 (julio de 1958), 45-105.

[A masterful study of this Venezuelan dance, it deals with the music, choreography, and literary texts of the verses' which are sung along with the maremare. Several copla texts are given and there is an extremely interesting section on the relationship of some of the latter with the song of Mambrú.]

1960. _____. "El polo. Historia-música-poesía." BIF, III:6 (diciembre, 1959), 227-273.

[Paredes (ref. 91, p. 46) says: "Study of the 'polo,' a Venezuelan folksong form, in its historic, geographic, social, musical and literary aspects. Thirty-three music examples, list of available recordings."]

1961. _____. "Viaje de investigación a la isla de Margarita." BIF, I(1954):5, pp. 101-136.

[Boggs (ref. 13 [1954], p. 19) says: "On dwelling, furniture, dress, occupations, food, arts, transportation, poetry, tales, speech, customs, beliefs, games, music."]

_____. See also entry no. 2072.

1962. Arvelo Torrealba, Alberto. "Glosas al cancionero vernáculo." RNC, I:10 (agosto, 1939), 149-150.

[An unimportant paean to the beauty of Venezuela's popular coplas, along with the wish that they might be more widely appreciated.]

1963. _____. "Las más bellas coplas del cancionero vernáculo." BIBNC, Núm. 42 (abril-junio, 1936), 206-213.

[A floridly written interpretation of five coplas from Venezuelan tradition, which are analyzed line by line by way of explaining their meaning. The galerón and the corrío come in for passing attention, but the author's use of the terms is so vague as to be of little value. There is also superficial treatment of the romance and the appearance of octosyllabic lines in Venezuelan popular poetry.]

1964. Bencomo, Eva R. "Corrío de los animales." OTLV, Año VII:73 (julio de 1945), 13-14.

[Contains the texts without music of a Corrío de los animales from San José de Unare, Venezuela.]

Blaya Alende, Joaquín. See entry no. 171.

1965. Bolívar Coronado, Rafael (Daniel Mendoza). El llanero (estudio de sociología venezolana). Madrid: Editorial América, 1919. 208 pp. 19.5 cm.; also, Caracas: Tip. Cultura Venezolana, 1922; also, B. A.: Editorial Venezuela, 1947. 207 pp.

[A literary fraud, this work was published under the name of Daniel Mendoza with a biographical note about the latter, who was supposedly born in 1823 and died in 1860. Though the deception was exposed (Cf. L. F. Blanco Meaño, Parnaso boliviano, p. 6), the 1947 edition, which

is the only one I have been able to consult, still appears under the
name of Mendoza with no mention of Bolívar Coronado's name. The
work itself contains considerable information about popular poetry
and song, mostly in Chapters III and IV. Most of the texts given are
coplas and seem to be genuine popular literature. One composition
is an interesting historical narrative which is very similar to Mexican corridos in style and tone. The 1947 edition is preceded by José
E. Machado's study, "El gaucho y el llanero" (see entry no. 2023).]

1966. Briceño, Olga. "Música folklórica venezolana." BUPan,
LXXXII:2 (febrero, 1948), 68-76.
[A survey of various types of songs and dances. Some of the types
which are described might be related to romances or coplas, though
this is not clear. The principal value of the article lies in its descriptions of certain genres of folklore such as petronila, fulía, polo, and
others.]

1967. Calcaño, José Antonio (Juan Sebastián). Contribución al estudio
de la música en Venezuela. Caracas: Editorial "Elite," 1939. 128 pp. 16 cm.
[A collection of essays about various aspects of Venezuelan music.
One chapter, "Exaltación y melodía," contains some useful data about
songs (but not romances or corridos) of the period around 1810-1811;
another deals with the tono of Venezuela and describes the way in which
it is sung. There is a musical transcription of a tono.]

1968. _____. "La música folklórica del llano." El País (Caracas), Año III:1, 141 (16 de marzo, 1947), 9-10.
[Boggs (ref. 13 [1947], p. 57) says: "On folkmusic of Venezuelan
plainsmen."]

1969. Cancionero popular. [Caracas, 1945]. [16] pp. 23.5 cm.
[The above entry is copied accurately from the Anuario bibliográfico
venezolano, 1945, p. 31.]

1970. Cancionero popular del niño venezolano (1° y 2° grados).
Caracas: Editado por el Ministerio de Educación Nacional, 1940.
20 pp. 29.5 cm.
[A collection of texts with music of fifteen children's songs. Included
is a version of the romance, Hilo de oro.]

1971. Cancionero popular del niño venezolano; segundo volumen.
Caracas: Editado por el Ministerio de Educación Nacional, 1946. 25
pp. 31.5 cm.
[A second collection of twenty children's songs with words and music. Included are versions of Don Gato, La pulga y el piojo, and a
composition written in décimas, El Perico asado.]

1972. "Cantares llaneros." CV, XI:75 (septiembre de 1926), 361-362; 76 (octubre de 1926), 117-119; 77 (noviembre-diciembre, 1926),
265; 78 (enero-febrero, 1927), 129.

1973. Cardona, Miguel. "Notas sobre el uso del tabaco en Venezuela." BIF, III:1 (marzo de 1958), 3-21.
[Contains a few copla texts related to the subject. They are taken from the well-known collections by Machado, Olivares Figueroa, and others.]

1974. Carrera, Gustavo Luis. "Una nueva versión venezolana del romance de Blancaniña." BIF, III:7 (mayo, 1960), 277-290.

1975. Carreño, F., and Vallmitjana, A. 30 cantos del oriente venezolano. Caracas: Dirección de Cultura; Ediciones del Ministerio de Educación Nacional, 1947. 72 pp. 23.5 cm.
[Contains words and music of thirty folk songs. None is a romance or a corrido.]

1976. Castillo Vázquez, Andrés. Folklore larense; versiones folklóricas larenses. Caracas, 1956.

1977. Celis Ríos, Trino. "Anotaciones marginales; cantares llaneros." CV, Año X, Tomo XXXIII:82 (julio-agosto de 1927), 83-94.
[An attempt to characterize the llanero by studying his psychology as it is revealed in copla texts. The author's conclusions are of doubtful validity, however, since many of the coplas quoted are found in many parts of the Hispanic world and are not, as Celis Ríos apparently believes, uniquely Venezuelan.]

1978. Coll, Pedro Emilio. [Lecture.] CV, Año XIII:102 (abril de 1930).
[Cited by Liscano (ref. 2016, p. 49). He indicates that a corrido text which he prints was taken from the above work.]

1979. "Coplas populares venezolanas." Boletín de cultura "Presente" (Caracas), No. 2 (1941).
[Chase (ref. 25, p. 240) comments: "Folk song texts collected by Juan Liscano."]

1980. "Documentos de poesía popular." BIF, II(1956), 131-141.
[Boggs (ref. 13 [1956], p. 43) indicates that the article contains the texts of four corridos from Apure, Venezuela.]

1981. Domínguez, Luis Arturo. "Aspectos del folklore del estado Falcón." RVF, I:1 (enero-junio de 1947), 91-119.
[A description of many folk customs of the author's home state of Falcón. Though narrative types of popular poetry are not treated, several coplas are given.]

1982. _____. "El polo coriano y sus variedades." AVF, Año I:1 (enero-junio, 1952), 137-152; 2 (julio-diciembre, 1952), 408-411; Año II-III (1953-1954), Vol. II:3, pp. 194-198.
[A collection of 384 copla texts. One section called "Políticos" (pp. 194-195) is composed of topical polos. Many from the early part of the nineteenth century could be corrido fragments.]

1983. Domínguez, Luis Arturo. El polo coriano y sus variedades. Caracas: Imprenta Nacional, 1955. 149 pp. 23.5 cm.

[After a brief study of the polos sung in the state of Falcón, the author offers 643 texts, all octosyllabic cuartetas (i. e., coplas), grouped according to subject matter. There is one section of polos políticos (pp. 66-69). At the end there are some illustrations of musical instruments and a few transcriptions of melodies.]

1984. _____. Velorio de angelito. Mérida, Venezuela: Edit. "El Vigilante," 1955. 52 pp. plus 5 unnumbered lvs. 22.5 cm.; also, 2.ª ed. Caracas: Edición del Ejecutivo del Estado de Trujillo, 1960.

[Treats various customs having to do with pregnancy, childbrith, death, and the velorios. There are a number of cuartetas (i. e., coplas) which are sung at the velorios and also proverbs and other materials.]

1985. Duarte Level, Lino. "Las queseras del medio." Universal-Car, 10 de abril de 1912.

[Grases (ref. 2007, p. 132) quotes some lines from this article with reference to the singing of galerones and coplas by the soldiers of General José Antonio Páez.]

1986. Ernst, Adolf. "Para el cancionero popular de Venezuela." El cojo ilustrado (Caracas), 2 de enero de 1893.

_____. See Lehmann-Nitsche, Robert, ed., entry no. 2008.

1987. Escalona, Isabel María, comp. "Musas campesinas; cantas." OTLC, Año 8:86 (agosto de 1946), 15-16.

[A collection of cantas (i. e., coplas) collected by Isabel María Escalona, Preceptora de la Escuela Federal N.° 3,108, San Miguel, Dto. Jiménez, Estado Lara. She provides texts of twelve cuartetas. There is no commentary of any kind.]

1988. España, Juan. "Folk-lore venezolano: Pragedes el peleador." CV, XIII:105 (agosto de 1930), 419-421.

[A narrative poem about a fight between Pragedes and a Negro challenger, who was defeated. The subject of the poem and its form (cuartetas of octosyllabic lines rhymed abcb with assonance) are basically popular. But while the composition is well written and quite dramatic, the style is artistic and hardly deserves to be called folklore.]

1989. Febres Pobeda, Carlos. Folklore merideño. Mérida: Editorial "Sañirroid." 1950. 34 pp.

1990. "Folk-lore venezolano." CV, Nos. 94 (mayo-junio de 1929), 151-152; 96 (agosto, 1929), 427-429; 97 (septiembre, 1929), 124-127; 98 (octubre, 1929), 276-277; 99 (noviembre-diciembre, 1929), 320-322.

[As Chase describes each of these articles (ref. 25, p. 240), it is apparent that they resemble the items in the series which I have been able to examine personally and which I list in entries which follow. Most of them contain compositions taken from José E. Machado's collection.]

1991. "Folk-lore venezolano: Corridos de Zaraza." CV, Año XIII:107 (noviembre de 1930), 247-249.

[A chaotic collection of strophes which are called corridos and coplas but seem to be thoroughly jumbled as to form, subject, and the like. Even if they were collected and printed properly, most would be of no interest because of their triviality.]

1992. "Folklore venezolano (de la colección del Dr. José E. Machado)." CV, Año XIII, Tomo XLI:101 (febrero y marzo de 1930), 310-311.

[Contains a galerón two strophes long.]

1993. "Folklore venezolano: Desatinos." CV, Año XIII:103 (mayo de 1930), 123-124.

[Some coplas which are based on absurdities, though there are also a few more serious compositions. At the end of the collection the notation: "De la colección del Dr. José E. Machado."]

1994. "Folk-lore venezolano: Gaitas, canto popular maracaibero." CV, VIII:65 (julio-agosto de 1925), 93-95.

[A collection of fifty-three coplas with an introductory note which describes the manner in which they are sung around Maracaibo.]

1995. "Folk-lore venezolano: Glosas llaneras improvisadas en Velorios de Cruz." CV, Año VIII:63 (mayo de 1925), 250-251.

[Two glosas of cuartetas in décimas. Neither is narrative and both are trivial.]

1996. Fombona-Pachano, Jacinto. "Poesía culta y popular de Venezuela." RHM, III:3 (abril, 1937), 185-200.

[Essentially a summary of the production of learned poets from Bello to modern times. The author, however, devotes some attention to the popular poetry of his country and its influence on learned poets. In so doing he touches briefly on the corríos and quotes several cantas (i.e., coplas.]

1997. "Gaitas o cantos populares zulianos." CV, XI:70 (marzo-abril, 1926), 234-235; 71 (mayo, 1926), 139-140; 72 (junio, 1926), 271; 73 (julio, 1926), 104; 74 (agosto, 1926), 234.

[Chase (ref. 25, p. 241) indicates that all these items contain texts of songs from the state of Zulia.]

1998. "El galerón de No. Marcos." CV, X:80 (abril, 1927), 109-110.

[Chase (ref. 25, p. 241) says: "Words to a galerón."]

1999. Gallegos, Rómulo. Canaima. Segunda edición. Barcelona: Casa Editorial Araluce, 1935. 406 pp. 19.5 cm.
[There is a chapter entitled "El corrido del purgüero" (pp. 264-276) which contains a corrido text.]

2000. _____. Cantaclaro. Segunda edición. Barcelona: Casa Editorial Araluce, 1934. 365 pp. 19 cm.
[This novel is replete with texts of popular poetry and song, mostly coplas but including some corridos. See particularly the sections entitled "La copla errante" (pp. 7-19), "El corrido del ahorcado" (pp. 65-79), and "Corridos y contrapunteos" (pp. 147-163).]

2001. _____. Doña Bárbara. Quinta edición. Barcelona: Casa Editorial Araluce, 1929. 392 pp. 19.5 cm.
[There are several copla texts scattered through the novel along with some commentary about coplas and other popular poetry by the author.]

2002. _____. Pobre negro. Tercera edición. B. A.: Espasa-Calpe, 1945. 235 pp. 18 cm. (Colección Austral, No. 307.)
[Contains some texts of popular poetry, particularly in the section entitled "Décimas y fulías" (pp. 89-98). Some of the texts are décimas based on the romance theme of the Doce Pares de Francia.]

2003. _____. Sobre la misma tierra. B. A.: Espasa-Calpe Argentina, S. A., 1944. 234 pp. 18 cm. (Colección Austral, No. 425.)
[There are some texts of popular songs of various types scattered through the volume.]

2004. Gil Fortoul, José. Historia constitucional de Venezuela. Tercera edición revisada. 3 vols. Caracas: Editorial "Las Novedades," 1942. 24 cm.
[The author discusses the songs and poetry of the Venezuelan llanero (Vol. II, pp. 170-172) and he prints a few coplas. There is also a fragment of a corrido.]

2005. González, Eloy G. Curso de folklore. Caracas: Tip. Garrido, 1955. 233 pp. 24 cm.
[Juan de Dios Arias (ref. 730, p. 151) says that González prints here a version of La pulga y el piojo.]

2006. González Bona, C. Trescientas cantas llaneras. 1903.
[Machado (ref. 2019, p. xvii) mentions the work.]

2007. Grases, Pedro. "Galerón en tierra firme." RVF, I:2 (julio-diciembre, 1947), 129-143.
[A discussion of the different meanings of the term galerón as used in Venezuela and Colombia. The author traces the word back to galeón and theorizes on how it came to be applied to popular dance and song. Particularly interesting are some comments in a footnote (p. 133) which deal with the relationship between romance, galerón, and copla.]

2008. Lehmann-Nitsche, Robert, ed. El cancionero popular venezolano; cantos populares de Venezuela recogidos por el doctor A. Ernst (Caracas). Editados por primera vez en la República Argentina por el doctor R. Lehmann-Nitsche (La Plata). B. A.-Montevideo, 1904. 31 pp.

2009. Lira Espejo, Eduardo. "El estado Lara y su riqueza musical." UniversalCar, 19 de enero de 1941.
[Chase (ref. 25, p. 239) comments: "Points out the most important forms of musical expression in the state of Lara, which is one of Venezuela's richest in dance, music and folklore."]

2010. _____. "Expresión musical y popular venezolana." Revista del Caribe (Caracas), Año I:4 (diciembre de 1941), p. 4.
[An unimportant consideration of the Negro and Spanish elements which have entered into Venezuelan folklore. The author merely enumerates for popular consumption some of the genres which show such influences: e.g., fulías, coplas, joropos, corridos, galerones, golpes, décimas, etc.]

2011. _____. "Expresión musical y popular venezolana." Revista del Caribe (Caracas), diciembre, 1941.
[Chase (ref. 25, p. 239) indicates that this article includes treatment of the corrido, the galerón, and many other types of musical folklore.]

2012. Liscano, Juan. "Analogías entre el folklore del Brasil y el de Venezuela: La marujada y el Corrido del marinero." RNC, Año XIII:89 (diciembre de 1951), 45-52.
[The author compares some verses he collected in eastern Venezuela on the Island of Margarita to some romances in Portuguese which come from Brazil, most notably A Nau Catarineta. The first composition he reports consists of two décimas; then he offers two Venezuelan versions of the romance known as El marinerito.]

2013. _____. "Aspectos de la música popular venezolana." Ahora (Caracas), 3 de marzo de 1941.
[Chase (ref. 25, p. 241) says: "Comments on popular Venezuelan music in its Negro, Hispanic, mestizo and indigenous aspects."]

2014. _____. "El cante popular." Acción democrática (Caracas), No. 6 (14 de febrero, 1942).
[Listed by Chase (ref. 25, p. 241).]

2015. _____. "Folklore venezolano." RevMM, III:5 (7 de mayo de 1943), 99-103; reprinted from Boletín del Instituto Cultural Venezolano-Británico (Caracas), Núm. 6 (agosto de 1942).
[A rather poetic interpretation of the psychological aspects of the Indian, Negro, and Spanish elements which have merged to form Venezuelan folklore. The author dwells mostly upon coplas and he gives two texts.]

2016. Liscano, Juan. Folklore y cultura; ensayos. Caracas: Editorial Avila Gráfica, 1950. 266 pp. 23 cm. (Colección Nuestra Tierra, Vol, II.)

[A fine collection of essays on folklore. "Las formas de la poesía popular venezolana" (pp. 25-60) deals with the various kinds of lines and strophes which Liscano has been able to find in Venezuelan popular poetry. Included are sections with examples on coplas, décimas, corridos, and other groups. The sections on the corrido and the décima are very revealing. Particularly interesting is a composition collected from oral tradition, Décimas de elección; muerte de Juan Vicente Gómez (p. 57). It is topical and more like Mexican corridos than the corrido texts the author offers, though one of these (p. 49) is interesting in that it is topical and deals with the violent death of one Pedro León.]

2017. _____. "Lo español en nuestro folklore." Boletín del Instituto Cultural Venezolano-Británico (Caracas), Nos. 11-14 (enero-abril de 1943), 28-51.

[Surveys Spain's contributions to Venezuelan life. Among other things, the author treats romances, corridos, coplas, décimas, etc. He gives a number of texts by way of illustration.]

2018. _____. Poesía popular venezolana. Caracas: Suma, Ediciones al Servicio de la Cultura, 1945. 62 pp. 15.5 cm.

[A small anthology with a brief introduction. Included are 101 coplas, a few décimas, including one about Charlemagne, and three corridos. One of these is a version of El conde Olivos and two are versions of El marinerito. All three of them are true romances in form.]

_____. See "Coplas populares venezolanas," entry no. 1979.

2019. Machado, José E. Cancionero popular venezolano; cantares y corridos, galerones y glosas. Caracas: Imp. El Cojo, 1919. xxi, 251 pp. 19 cm.; also, 2ª edición aumentada y corregida. Caracas: L. Puig Ros y Parra Almenar, 1922. 191 pp. 18 cm.; also, B. A.: Dirección de Cultura, Ministerio de Educación Nacional de Venezuela, Imprenta Balmes, 1946. 177 pp. 17.5 cm. (Biblioteca popular venezolana, Núm. 6.)

[A collection of popular poetry which includes a few corridos, some coplas, and the like. There is an introductory study of Venezuelan popular poetry with mention of some investigators who have treated the subject. Usually, however, necessary bibliographical details are lacking. In the 1946 edition there is an introduction and a bibliographical listing of Machado's works by Alberto Arvelo Torrealba.]

2020. _____. Centón lírico, pasquinadas y canciones, epigramas y corridos. Caracas: Tip. Americana, 1920. xxxv, 244 pp. 20 cm.

[A collection of poetry, some of it popular and concerned with political events of the period of independence. There are a few compositions doubtfully classified as corridos.]

2021. [_____], ed. "Folklore venezolano." BIBNC, Núm. 34 (diciembre 31 de 1931), 118-119.
[As director of the Boletín, Machado prints three songs taken from Campaigns and Cruises in Venezuela and New Granada, and the Pacific Ocean; from 1817 to 1830, anonymously printed in London in 1831 but attributed to Richard Longeville Vowell. The compositions are Canto de las sabanas, Libertad, and Mi general Páez con su guardia de honor. They are not romances, nor are they truly narrative, but they are historical in subject matter. Their tone is anti-Spanish and patriotically dedicated to Bolívar and other heroes of independence.]

2022. [_____], ed. "Folklore venezolano: El 5 de marzo." BIBNC, Núm. 31 (marzo de 30 de 1931), 21-22.
[Contains the text of a historical corrido. The article is unsigned, but Machado as editor of the Boletín was undoubtedly responsible for publishing this text.]

2023. _____. El gaucho y el llanero. Caracas: Tip. Vargas, 1926. 30 pp. 20 cm.; reprinted in entry no. 1965.
[A very superficial essay on the life of the gaucho and the llanero, whom Machado considers kindred types. There is some consideration of their songs and their manner of singing portías or contrapuntos, but the whole is of little importance.]

2024. _____. "Recepción académica." CV, Año VII:56 (abril-mayo, 1924), 30-56.
[A discussion of popular poetry in Venezuela with examples of romances and other folk music of various kinds.]

2025. _____. Viejos cantos y viejos cantores; compilación de varias composiciones, en su mayor parte desconocidas y olvidadas, con notas históricas y literarias. Caracas: Tipografía Americana, 1921. xxviii, 122 pp. 20 cm.
[Concerned with artistic, not popular, poetry, the volume includes some very early décimas which are of interest because they deal with historical subjects. There are also topical poems of other types, including a composition doubtfully classified as a corrido.]

_____. See entries nos. 1990-1995.

2026. Martínez, Marco Antonio. "Notas sobre la idea de alboroto y desorden en Venezuela." AVF, Años VI-VII, Vols. IV-V (1957-1958):5, pp. 7-100.
[A quite exhaustive and well-documented study of words and idioms associated with the subject. A few texts of coplas and other popular poetry, though no romances, are included.]

2027. Matos Romero, Manuel. Improvisadores populares del Zulia: Francisco Cano, Antonio Briñez, Rafael Avila (a) "Titán" y Narciso Perozo; supersticiones. Caracas: Tip. Matheus, 1956. 121 pp. 24 cm.

Mendoza, Daniel. See Bolívar Coronado, Rafael, entry no. 1965.

2028. Monografía de El Tocuyo. Caracas: Junta Pro-Tocuyo en Sus Cuatrocientos Años, 1945.
[Said to contain (Vol. I, pp. 84- 112) the work of Francisco Tamayo, "Datos sobre el folklore de la región de El Tocuyo." See entry no. 2089.]

2029. Monroy Pittaluga, Francisco. Cazorla (encuesta general de geografía social). Caracas: Tipografía Garrido, 1949. 194 pp.
[In this general description of the Cazorla area, there is a chapter entitled "Folklore" (Chapter IV). The author discusses romances, corridos, and bambas (i. e., coplas) and prints the full text of a very interesting corrido entitled En Caracas Joaquín Crespo (pp. 53-55). There are also discussions of musical instruments, velorios, etc. in the chapter.]

2030. _____. "Cuentos y romances tradicionales en Cazorla (llanos del Guárico)." AVF, Año I:2 (julio-diciembre, 1952), 360-380.
[A very important collection of texts collected from oral tradition with useful commentaries. Besides the cuentos, there are the following compositions of Hispanic origin which are grouped under the heading of "Romances": El conde Lirio, Corrido de don Carlos, Las señas del marido, Corrido del marinero, Ricarte y la religión, and Sildana. Under the heading of "Corridos" are: Sobre la muerte de Matías Salazar; Sobre la muerte de Crespo; En Caracas, Joaquín Crespo; Otros motivos sobre Crespo; Corrido del indio Modesto Laya, and Corrido de Ño Ramón. These corridos are of extreme interest because they are close to Mexican corridos in tone and often in form and because some of them date from the nineteenth century. The article concludes with a list of venezuelanismos.]

2031. Montesinos, Pedro. "Dos romances viejos." RNC, Año II:24 (noviembre-diciembre de 1940), 45-53.
[Discusses El conde Olinos and El adúltero castigado. There are Spanish, Venezuelan, and Cuban texts of the former; Spanish and Venezuelan versions of the latter.]

_____. See Olivares Figueroa, Raúl, entry no. 2032.

2032. Olivares Figueroa, Raúl, ed. "Cancionero de Montesinos." RVF, I:1 (enero-junio de 1947), 133-154.
[Olivares Figueroa begins publishing here the Cancionero of Pedro Montesinos, which had been circulating only among a few scholars in mimeographed form. In his introduction the editor points out that the collection contains 2,208 cantas (coplas) and twenty corridos. The date of the original manuscript was 1913, but the collecting was done during several preceding decades. Olivares Figueroa indicates that the collection lacks any organization whatsoever. In this installment there are several hundred texts.]

2033. _____. "Canciones políticas." NacionC, 28 de enero, 1951.

2034. _____. "Cantas amatorias." NacionC, 3 de diciembre, 1950.
[Boggs (ref. 13 [1950], p. 62) says: "Words only of 20 quatrians of folksongs of love."]

2035. _____. "Cantas de pilado." El País (Caracas), 6 de julio, 1947, segunda parte, p. 10.
[Boggs (ref. 13 [1947], p. 60) says: "Verses only of songs sung while corn meal is being prepared, as for arepa cornbread."]

2036. _____. "'Cantas' llaneras de ordeño." OTLC, Año 8:84 (junio de 1946), 17-21.
[After an introductory explanation of the methods used in milking in the Venezuelan llanos and the use of cantas to help quiet the cow, the author gives the texts of twenty-eight cantas (coplas) collected from oral tradition. They are from the states of Lara and Guárico.]

2037. _____. "Cantas margariteñas de 'desconche'." OTLC, Año 8:88 (octubre de 1946), 14-17.
[After describing the work of the pearl seekers who open oysters on the island of Margarita, the author offers the texts of twenty-nine coplas collected from oral tradition which are sung by the pearl seekers as they work.]

2038. _____. "'Cantas' para el 'pilado' de maíz." OTLC, Año 8:83 (mayo de 1946), 20-22.
[After explaining the process involved in the "pilado de maíz," the author gives the texts of seventeen cantas which are sung, especially in the eastern part of Venezuela, to accompany this work.]

2039. _____. "Coplas con alusiones de tipo geográfico." OTLC, Año 8:81 (marzo de 1946), 21-24.
[After examining the Spanish origins of coplas with allusions to geography, the author offers thirty-three texts from Venezuela.]

2040. _____. "Coplas humorísticas." NacionC, 14 de enero, 1951.
[Boggs (ref. 13 [1951], p. 46) says: "Texts only of 24, from Porlamar."]

2041. _____. "'Coplas' o 'cantas'." OTLC, Año 8:80 (febrero de 1946), 6-7, 22-24.
[A brief discussion of the origins of the copla. The article is intended for children and contains thirty-two texts from various parts of Venezuela.]

2042. _____. "Coplillas de San Benito." NacionC, 12 de noviembre, 1950.
[Boggs (ref. 13 [1950], p. 62) says: "Texts of 12 quatrains whose even lines rime."]

2043. Montesinos, Pedro. "Corrido del caballo 'melao' y 'corrío' que empieza 'esta noche canto aquí'." In Folklore de las Américas; primera antología, ed. by Félix Coluccio. B. A.: Ateneo, 1949. Pp. 449-451.
[Texts of two corridos gathered by Olivares Figueroa in Venezuela.]

2044. _____. "Corridos." NacionC, 25 de febrero, 1951.

2045. _____. "Documentación folklórica: Romances coloniales rocogidos en Venezuela." RIPN, Año I:2 (abril, 1944), 151-153; 3 (julio, 1944), 254-256.
[Texts without commentary of Spanish romances which the author has found in Venezuelan oral tradition. There are five texts in the first installment and six in the second. Included are versions of La adúltera castigada, Hilito de oro (two versions), La infantina encantada, Santa Catalina, Don Gato, Delgadina, El marinero, and two romances a lo divino about the nativity of Christ. In each instance the place where the romance was found and the name of the informant are given.]

2046. _____. "Folklore de Nueva Esparta." Nuestra tierra (Caracas), II(1952):14, pp. 18-21.
[Boggs (ref. 13 [1952], p. 30) says: "Descriptive survey of folklore in this state of Venezuela: song verses, food, belief, customs, festivals, games . . ."]

2047. _____. Folklore venezolano, Tomo I, versos. Caracas: Ministerio de Educación Nacional, Dirección de Cultura, 1948. 268 pp. 18 cm. (Biblioteca popular venezolana, No. 23.)
[A large collection of texts of corridos, galerones, décimas, and many other kinds of popular compositions.]

2048. _____. "Folklore venezolano: Cantas margariteñas de 'desconche'." OTLC, Año 8:88 (octubre de 1946), 14-17.
[A collection with introductory commentary of some of the cantas (coplas) which the pearl hunters of the island of Margarita sing as they open oysters. There are twenty-nine cuartetas, all gathered from oral tradition.]

2049. _____. "Folklore venezolano: Cantos de furruco." OTLC, Año 9:89 (noviembre de 1946), 21-23.
[A short discussion of songs sung to the accompaniment of a ferruco around Carnival time or the Día de San Juan. Two texts are given. The second is a version of La pulga y el piojo from La Pica de Maturín, a village near the capital of the state of Monagas.]

2050. _____. "Folklore venezolano: Coplas con alusiones de tipo geográfico." OTLC, Año 8:81 (marzo de 1946), 21-24.
[The author points out that Venezuelan coplas with geographical allusions lack the genuine descriptive character of Spanish counterparts, which really characterize, describe, or otherwise comment upon the salient aspects of a place or the people who live there. He feels, however, that until better ones are discovered or created, it is worth while

to cite textually such of them as are to be found; so he prints here thirty-three cuartetas.]

2051. _____. "Rasgos folklóricos de los estados de Lara, Carabobo y Aragua; lo característico en el folklore oriental." Elite (Caracas), XXVII(1953):1452-1454, 1456, pp. 47-48, 31-32, 33-34.

2052. _____. "Reflexiones sobre la canción de corro en Venezuela." RNC, Año XIII:52 (setiembre-octubre de 1945), 145-151.
[The author notes the general decline of the Spanish canción de corro among Venezuelan children. He reports the presence of a few such songs, however, and gives the text of La viudita, which is a romancillo. He mentions by name Hilito, hilito de oro, Mambrú, Estaba el señor don Gato, and others.]

2053. _____. "Romance de Delgadina; versiones y fragmentos." NacionC, 1 de abril, 1951.

2054. _____. "Romances venezolanos de la vieja tradición española." NacionC, 15 de octubre, 1950.
[Boggs (ref. 13 [1950], p. 62) says: "Words only of 3 Spanish ballads found in Venezuela (Conde Lirio, Martirio de Santa Catalina, and Infantina encantada) with notes of provenience and parallels."]

Ortiz, Fernando. See entry no. 1022.

2055. Ovalles, Víctor Manuel. El llanero; estudio sobre su vida, sus costumbres, su carácter y su poesía. Caracas: Tip. J. M. Herrero Irigoyen, 1905. 209 pp. 16.5 cm.

2056. Pardo, Isaac J. "Viejos romances españoles en la tradición popular venezolana." RNC, Año V:36 (enero-febrero, 1943), 35-74.
[A study of Spanish romances which are still alive in Venezuelan tradition: La esposa infiel, Bernal Francés, Las señas del marido, El marinero, Don Gato, Hilito de oro, Dónde vas, Alfonso Doce, Gaiferos, and others. For a commentary upon this article, see entry no. 2080.]

2057. Pequeñas canturias y danzas venezolanas. Caracas: Edit. Grafolit, 1947. 31 cm.
[A collection of popular compositions with music for piano. One entitled merely Salve is a romance about Joseph and May ("San José pidió posada/para su esposa María . . .").]

2058. Planchart, Enrique. "Observaciones sobre el cancionero venezolano." CV, Año IV:28 (agosto, 1921), 153-167; 29 (septiembre, 1921), 250-257.
[A discussion of popular poetry (romances, corridos, galerones, etc.). There are some texts, including a Venezuelan version of Las señas del esposo.]

2059. Plaza, Ramón de la. Ensayo sobre el arte en Venezuela. Caracas, 1883. 56 pp.
[Calcaño (ref. 1967, p. 87) refers to "aires populares publicados

por Ramón de la Plaza" in this volume. He indicates that the musical transcriptions of the work are unsatisfactory.]

2060. Portillo, J. M. "Cantos populares." BIBNC, Núm. 33 (septiembre, 1931), 71-73.

[Comments on the value of popular poetry in so far as it reveals the true nature of a people. There are many copla texts with commentary on them.]

————. Primer cuaderno de canciones populares venezolanas. See Sojo, Vicente Emilio, ed., entry no. 2085.

2061. Ramón y Rivera, Luis Felipe. Cantos de trabajo del pueblo venezolano. Caracas: Fundación Eugenio Mendoza, 1955. 55 pp. 23 cm.

[The Library of Congress card says: " 'Análisis musical' (p. [21] -52) contains music of 28 Venezuelan work-songs and street-cries (unacc. melodies)."]

2062. ————. "Documentos de poesía popular." BIF, I:7 (octubre de 1954), 186-194.

[A collection of texts of several interesting popular songs. Included are the Joropo "El nuevo gobierno," a golpe, a punto cruzado, a polo margariteño, and some décimas de velorio de cruz. Some of these compositions are related to the romance-corrido and the copla traditions.]

2063. ————. "Documentos de poesía popular." BIF, III:1 (marzo de 1958), 21-25.

[A collection of 65 copla texts without music taken from oral tradition in several states.]

2064. ————. "Documentos de poesía popular venezolana." BIF, I:4 (marzo de 1954), 83-90.

[Some selected texts of various types of folk songs and dances collected by the author and others. Each text is accompanied by a brief commentary. Among other things there is a Corrido del general Horacio Ducharne; a narrative fulía about Jesus (seven décimas which gloss a quintilla); a Pasaje "La Julianita," that is a very personal narrative about a singer's wide travels and experiences; and some Letras que se cantan en el baile de San Pedro, which are coplas with estribillos.]

2065. ————. Una interpretación psicológica del coplero popular. Caracas: Ministerio de Educación, Imprenta de la Dirección de Cultura y Bellas Artes, 1953. 30 pp.

[Boggs (ref. 13 [1953], p. 48) says: "Analysis of the folk soul through its coplas, and how this form of folk poetry reflects the character and attitudes of its singer, with text examples from various parts of Spanish America."]

2066. _____. El joropo, baile nacional de Venezuela. Caracas: Ministerio de Educación, Dirección de Cultura y Bellas Artes, 1953. 92, [40] pp. 24 cm. (Biblioteca venezolana de cultura, Colección "Folklore y Etnología.")
[A superb study of the history and the literary and musical characteristics of the joropo. There is a great deal of attention to corridos and galerones, along with other types of compositions, and several texts with music are given.]

2067. _____. La música popular de Venezuela. B. A.: Embajada de Venezuela, 1951.

2068. _____. "La polifonía popular de Venezuela." RINT, Año I, Entrega 2a. (julio-diciembre, 1948), 168-208; also, B. A.: Impr. Alea, 1949. 46 pp. 27 cm.
[An excellent musical study of part singing of tonos de velorio in Venezuela. In the state of Falcón, Ramón y Rivera and Isabel Aretz de Ramón y Rivera, his wife, found romances sung at these popular fiestas, and he reports here on them (pp. 185 ff.). Besides providing the music of tonos from other areas, the author gives the music of two romances (p. 208), and there is a fragmentary text of one of these (p. 189).]

2069. _____. "Se extingue nuestra música folklórica." BIF, III(1960):3, pp. 295-297.

2070. _____. "El seis." BIF, III(1959):4, pp. 1-38.

2071. _____. "Supervivencia de la polifonía popular en Venezuela." RMC, Año XIII:68 (noviembre-diciembre de 1959), 43-69.
[Gives and analyzes texts and music of a number of tonos. They are glossed décimas and deal mostly with Christ's death, though there are a few about other themes.]

2072. _____, and Aretz-Thiele de Ramón y Rivera, Isabel. "Viaje de investigación a Pregonero." BIF, II(1955), 1-37.
[Boggs (ref. 13 [1955], p. 27) says: "Materials from Táchira, Venezuela, on Christmas tales, songs, beliefs, speech, customs, food, art. . . ."]

Relación muy verdadera de todo lo sucedido en el río del Marañón. See Torres de Mendoza, Luis, entry no. 2096.

2073. Ribas y Ribas, Fidel. Centón, etc.
[Ortiz (ref. 1022, p. 47) indicates that some décimas which he prints, and which Arístides Rojas had published earlier, first appeared in the above work. Unfortunately, the bibliographical entry which he provides gives only the information which I have copied. I have been unable to locate any further data about the work.]

2074. Rojas, Arístides. "Cancionero llanero (de la colección inédita)." El Tiempo (Caracas), 2 de diciembre de 1893.

2075. _____. "El cancionero popular de Venezuela; al Dr. Adolfo Ernst." El cojo ilustrado (Caracas), 15 de marzo de 1893, 100-102; reprinted in Obras escogidas. Paris, 1907. Pp. 402-411; also reprinted in RNC, Año II:19 (junio de 1940), 36-49.
[A superficial and impressionistic attempt to characterize the coplas of Venezuela vis-à-vis those of Spain. Some texts are given and there are some corridos among them. The article is of interest only because of its early date.]

2076. _____. "Cantares; contribuciones llaneras." El Tiempo (Caracas), 7 de octubre de 1893; reprinted in Obras escogidas. Paris, 1907. Pp. 509-510.
[Said to contain popular coplas.]

2077. _____. "Cantos llaneros; contribución del señor Harmann." El Tiempo (Caracas), 9 de diciembre de 1893.

2078. _____. Cantos populares de la revolución.
[Rojas himself (ref. 2079, p. 515) says: "Ya en otro escrito (Cantos populares de la revolución) hemos hablado de las cuartetas que cantaban los soldados llaneros de Boves . . . ." He gives no bibliographical data and I have been unable to obtain information from other sources.]

2079. _____. "Contribuciones al folklore venezolano." In Obras escogidas. Paris, 1907. Pp. 376-517.
[Several chapters reprinted from other sources, the most important being "El cancionero popular en Venezuela" (pp. 402-411). There is discussion of romances, corridos, galerones, and other types. There are texts of songs known as corridos and in several places décimas or glosas about political topics are included.]

_____. See Ortiz, Fernando, entry no. 1022.

2080. "El romance español en Venezuela." RJav, XX:96.
[Said to be a commentary on the article of Isaac J. Pardo, "Viejos romances españoles en la tradición popular venezolana" (entry no. 2056).]

2081. Rugeles, Manuel F. Lo popular y folklórico en el Táchira. B. A.: Publicaciones de la Embajada de Venezuela, 1952. 50 pp. 19 cm. (Publicaciones de la Embajada de Venezuela, No. 10.)
[In surveying many aspects of the folklore of the Táchira region, the author quotes several copla texts. Also, he has occasion to comment upon the lack of a galerón-corrido tradition in the area, though he quotes one text taken from Olivares Figueroa's Folklore venezolano.]

2082. Sánchez Rubio, E. "Cancionero popular venezolano por José E. Machado." BIBNC, Núm. 32 (junio 30 de 1931), 44-48.

[A reprint of an article which appeared in Alma latina (No. 7, 15 de agosto, 1919) to comment upon Machado's book. It is merely Sánchez Rubio's personal reaction to the coplas collected by Machado, with particular reference to those from his native Zulia. He quotes the texts of many of Machado's examples, but in reality he adds very little of value. There is nothing about narrative poetry.]

Sebastián, Juan. See Calcaño, José, entry no. 1967.

Segundo cuaderno de canciones populares venezolanas. See Sojo, Vicente Emilio, entry no. 2086.

2083. Serpa P., Domingo A. "Folklore; del cancionero popular." II:28 (julio y agosto, 1941), 135-139.

[A brief collection of coplas with comments by Serpa.]

2084. Sojo, Vicente Emilio. "Notas y documentos; música folklórica venezolana." AVF, Año I(1952):1, pp. 159-162.

2085. _____, ed. Primer cuaderno de canciones populares venezolanas. Caracas: Editado por el Ministerio de Educación Nacional, Dirección de Cultura, 1940. 45 pp. 32.5 cm. (Biblioteca venezolana de cultura.)

[Some twenty compositions with words and music. Most are merely currently "popular" love songs; none belongs to the romance-corrido or genuine copla tradition.]

2086. _____, ed. Segundo cuaderno de canciones populares venezolanas. Caracas: Editado por la Radio Caracas, 1942. 47 pp. 32.5 cm.

[Chase (ref. 25, p. 240) says: "Contains 20 songs, for voice and piano, some by known composers, others anonymous."]

2087. _____, ed. See also Tercer cuaderno de canciones populares venezolanas, entry no. 2093.

2088. Sucre, Luis Alberto. Gobernadores y capitanes generales de Venezuela. Caracas: Lit. y Tip. del Comercio, 1928. 323 pp. 24 cm.

[Contains (p. 56) the text of perhaps the most important romance about an American subject that has come down from the sixteenth century. It concerns one Juan Rodríguez Suárez, known in colonial Venezuela as "El Invencible Caballero de la Capa Roja," whose escape from prison is narrated in a very fine composition which has the verve and flavor of the best Spanish romances.]

2089. Tamayo, Francisco. Datos sobre el folklore de la región de El Tocuyo. Caracas: Impresores Unidos, 1945. 30 pp. 23.5 cm.; reprinted from the book, Monografía de El Tocuyo, entry no. 2028.

2090. Tamayo, Francisco. "Introducción y bibliografía del folklore del estado de Lara." In Guía económica y social del estado Lara. Barquisimeto, 1952 [?]. Pp. 96-109; also, Barquisimeto: Edit. Continente, 1952. 16 pp.

2091. _____. "Raíces del folklore venezolano; lo español en nuestra poesía espontánea." Cub, I:1 (junio de 1938), 44-45.
[Chase (ref. 25, p. 239) says: "Compares Venezuelan popular poetry in its corrido aspect with the Spanish romance or ballad. Includes an example."]

2092. _____. "Sección folklórica: La fulía." Boletín de la Sociedad Venezolana de Ciencias Naturales (Caracas), VIII:54 (enero-marzo, 1943), 181-184.

2093. Tercer cuaderno de canciones populares venezolanas. Caracas: Taller Gráfico Raúl Santana M., 1943. 57 pp. 32.5 cm.
[The third cuaderno in a series (see Sojo, Vicente Emilio, entries nos. 2085 and 2086). It is not clear from the data I have whether Sojo edited this third cuaderno or not.]

2094. Thompson, Robert Wallace. "Unas páginas de folklore trinitario." AVF, Años VI-VII, Vols. IV-V(1957-1958):5, pp. 207-218.
[An interesting small collection of popular poems, including a few coplas, collected from among the few Spanish-speaking inhabitants, descendants of Venezuelan immigrants, who are still residing on the island of Trinidad.]

2095. Torres Delgado, Silvestre. "Contribución a la bibliografía del folklore de Venezuela; trabajos publicados en el año de 1951." AVF, I(1952):1, pp. 229-232; "Contribución a la bibliografía venezolana del folklore (año de 1952)." AVF, I(1952):2, pp. 463-466.

2096. Torres de Mendoza, Luis, ed. Colección de documentos inéditos del Archivo de Indias, Tomo IV. Madrid: Imprenta de Frías y Compañía, 1865. 576 pp.
[Contains (pp. 267-269) a romance concerning an uprising in Venezuela. It is intercalado in the text of a work entitled Relación muy verdadera de todo lo sucedido en el río del Marañón and dates from about 1550. Gonzalo de Zúñiga is revealed to be the author of the poem (p. 257).]

2097. Tosta García, Francisco. Don Secundino en París. Caracas: Imprenta Editorial de Soriano Sucesores, 1895. 252 pp. 20.5 cm.
[After becoming bored with life in Paris, Don Secundino, the Venezuelan protagonist of this novel, declares (p. 242): ". . . estoy aburrido de tanta música y canciones tontas, de las eternas repeticiones de estos teatros, ya el can can y las piernas desnudas me fastidian, deseo oir el betum, bailar un joropo y cantar un galerón corrido . . . ."]

Vallmitjana, A. See Carreño, F., entry no. 1975.

2098. Vera-Izquierdo, Francisco. Cantares de Venezuela; estudio folklórico. Caracas: Imprenta Nacional, 1952. 133 pp. 23 cm.
[In his introduction the author considers various problems related to Venezuelan folklore. Though he does not pose as a trained scholar, he expresses intelligent views on such matters as the difficulty of distinguishing between corridos and galerones, his inability to detect alleged Negro influence in very much Venezuelan folklore, etc. In a collection of texts, which make up the body of the work, he includes many décimas, though without giving the sources of all of them, a Corrido del Correo de Oro (pp. 63-70), a Corrido de la Revolución de Marzo (pp. 80-91), some coplas, and other types of songs.]

Vowell, Richard Longeville. See Aretz, Isabel, entry no. 1956.

Zúñiga, Gonzalo de. See Torres de Mendoza, Luis, entry no 2096.

THE PACIFIC ISLANDS

Among some of the most interesting vestiges of Hispanic civilization still to be found in the islands of the Pacific Ocean which once were part of Spain's empire are romances and popular or semipopular poems known as corridos. Though clearly related to romance tradition, the latter have suffered fundamental changes in form and even in language so that in the Philippine Islands corridos about old romance and other novelesque themes now circulate in the native Tagalog language of the area.

Though these unique corridos of the Philippines have attracted a modicum of cursory comment on the part of several students of Philippine literature, little is known about the possible survival of Spanish romances or corridos in other areas of the Pacific. A most interesting bit of folklore research by Francisco Ramón Espinosa on the island of Guam suggests, however, that there exists a possibility of fruitful investigation into the romance-corrido tradition of other outposts of Spain's former empire.

THE PACIFIC ISLANDS

2099. Alip, Eufranio M. Tagalog Literature. Manila: U. S. T. [University of Santo Tomás] Press, 1930. xv, 164 pp. 24 cm.
[The author devotes considerable attention to the corridos of the Philippines. Though he gives no texts, he lists (pp. 30-31) the titles of several (about Bernardo del Carpio, the Siete Infantes de Lara, and other legendary figures) and he devotes considerable attention to José Cruz, a literary poet who wrote corridos (pp. 46-47). He also treats the moro-moro plays, which are often based on corridos (pp. 38-39).]

2100. Castillo y Tuazón, Teófilo del. A Brief History of Philippine Literature. Manila: Progressive Schoolbooks, 1937. xv, 467 pp. 19 cm.
[Contains a great deal of information about the corridos of the Philippines and the poets who write them (pp. 125-130, 141-143, and other places indicated in the index under the entry for corrido).]

2101. Corrido o corridong; historias populares en verso. Manila: [various publishers], 1860-1898.
[Palau y Dulcet lists this title with the following comment: "De estos Corrido, o sea la literatura popular de todos los países, se han publicado en Manila, infinidad de ediciones, en tagalo y en panpagno."]

2102. Espinosa, Francisco Ramón. "Folklore español de la Isla de Guam." RDTP, IX(1953), Cuaderno 1.°, 95-125.
[While serving in the U. S. Army in 1945, the author gathered the materials contained in this article: Romance de Valdovinos (known with the title of corrido), Romance de Lucinda y Velardo en la corte del gran sultán, and a Pastorela, a play on the Nativity theme. All these are given textually as furnished to the author in manuscripts written by his informant, José María Cruz.]

2103. Fansler, Dean S. "Metrical Romances in the Philippines." JAF, XXIX:CXI (January-March, 1916), 203-281.
[An interesting discussion of the origins of the corrido tradition in the Philippines and the long narrative compositions in Tagalog which bear the name. All those which are mentioned go back to Spanish sources of the sixteenth century or earlier. Finally, the author prints the complete text of a Corrido at buhay na pinagdaanan nang princesa Florentina sa cahariang Alemania, which he translates as Story of the Eventful Life of Princess Florentine of the Kingdom of Germany. Along with the text in Tagalog, an English translation is provided.]

2104. Manuel, E. Arsenio. "Folk Literature." The Philippines Quarterly (Manila), II:1 (June, 1952), 24-29.
[The author surveys Philippines folk literature with most attention to poetry. He touches on corridos, awits, and other types of ballads and epic poetry. Though the article is only a brief survey, it is of interest.]

2105. Montero y Vidal, José. El archipiélago filipino y las Islas Marianas, Carolinas y Palaos. Madrid: Imprenta y Fundición de Manuel Tello, 1886. xv, 505 pp. 21 cm.

[Contains the following passage (p. 318): "Existen bastantes obras en dialecto tagalo, principalmente diccionarios y gramáticas, escritos por religiosos españoles, y muchas comedias, romances, á que llaman corridos, á que son muy aficionados los indios, pero faltan toda clase de obras de instrucción y recreo."]

2106. Rincón, Manuel María. Romances de ciego. Manila: Tipo-lito-grafía de Chofré y Comp., 1896. xiii, 89 pp. 18 cm.

[A collection of twelve romances written by Rincón about local types in the Rhilippines: the lavandero, the escribiente, the mercader chino, and others. Though they contain considerable popular speech, the poems are basically artistic compositions.]

2107. Santa María, Felixberto C. "Philippine Folk Songs and Ballads through a Changing Culture." SFQ, XXIV(1960):2, 121-134.

[Although none of the songs and ballads here treated (translated from native dialects into English) come from texts originally in Spanish, some of them show definite marks of romance-corrido influences.]

2108. Villanueva, Antonia F. "Dedication to Mary in the Awits and Corridos." Unitas (Manila), XVII(1954), 699-713.

INDEX

"A caza de la música popular," 1141
A las siete palabras del Redentor en la cruz, 1111
A la venida de la expedición española contra el Río de la Plata, 126
Abadía, Julio, 720
Abascal, Carlos, 1331
Acevedo Hernández, Antonio, 491-493
Acosta, José de, 1728
Acosta, Vicente S., 1142
Acosta Saignes, Miguel, 1946-1948
Acuña, Luis Alberto, 721-722
Acuña Escobar, F., 1694
Aguerrevere, A. D., 1
Aguilera, Francisco, 51
Aguirre, Clemente, 1455
Aguirre, Julián, 127
Aguirre y Villar, José de, 1143
Aires bolivianos, 454
Alais, Octavio P., 128-129
Alarcón, Pedro, 1144
Alba, Antonio, 494
"El álbum de aires tradicionales y folklóricos de Chile," 495
Alcevedo López, Santos, 1145
Alcorta, Amancio, 130
Aldava, Fray, 496
Alegría, Fernando, 497
Alip, Eufranio M., 2099
Alix, Juan Antonio, 1066-1068
Allende, Juan Rafael, 499-501, 508, 689
Allende, Pedro Humberto, 498, 502-505
Almeida Portugal, Maria da Glória Rangel de, 1146
Alsina, Adolfo, 131

Altamirano, Ignacio M., 1147-1148
Alva Ixtlilxóchitl, Fernando de, 1433
Alvarez, Juan, 132
Alvarez de Velasco y Zorrilla, Francisco, 723
Alviña, Leandro, 1729
Amador, Armando C., 1149
Ambrosetti, Juan Bautista, 133-134
Ampuero, Galvarino, 506
Amunátegui, Miguel Luis, 507
Amunátegui Solar, Domingo, 508-509
Anaya Monroy, Fernando, 1150
Anaya de Urquidi, Mercedes, 455
Anda, José Guadalupe de, 1151
Andrade, Mariano, 1112
Andrade Coloma, Abdón, 510
Andreu, R., 135
Anfriso, 930-931
Angarita Arvelo, Rafael, 1949
Angeles Caballero, César, 136, 1730-1736
Angulo A., José, 511-512
Antolínez, Gilberto, 1950
Antología de poetas hispanoamericanos, 3
Antología folklórica argentina para las escuelas de adultos, 137
Antología folklórica argentina para las escuelas primarias, 138
Anuario bibliográfico colombiano, 1951-1956, 724
Anuario de la prensa chilena publicado por la Biblioteca Nacional, 513

Anzalaz, Alfredo, 139-142
Aponte, José Manuel, 456
Aprile, Bartolomé R., 143
Aradía, Guillermo, 725
Aragón, Fernando de, 1152
Aramburu, Julio, 144
Araneda, Rosa, 514, 626
Araoz de La Madrid, Gregorio, 145
Araucho, Manual de, 146
Araujo, Orlando, 1951
Arce, Magda, 515
Arce, Margot, 726
Archivo capitular de Jujuy, 386
Arciniegas, Germán, 727
Arciniegas, José Ignacio, 728
Arcos, Dr. (Camilo S. Delgado), 729
Aretz, Isabel, 147-148, 1952-1961, 2072
Aretz-Thiele, Isabel, 149-152
Arguedas, José María, 1153, 1737-1738, 1758
Arias, Juan de Dios, 730-731, 781
Arias Larreta, A., 1739
Arissó, Ana María, 932
Arlt, Gustave O., 1154
Armistead, Samuel G., 1155-1156
Arona, Juan de (Pedro Paz Soldán y Unanué), 1740
Arosteguy, Abdón, 368
Arrom, José Juan, 933
Arróspide de la Flor, César, 1128
Arroyo, César E., 4
Arroyo Ponce, Gamaliel, 1741
Arvelo Torrealba, Alberto, 1962-1963
Arzeno, Julio, 1069
Atl, Dr., 1508
Austin, Mary, 1157-1159
Autenchlus Maier, Olga Francesca, 153, 457

Avellaneda, Félix F., 308
Avila, Juan, 1160
Ayanque, Simón (Esteban Terralla y Landa), 1742
Ayestarán, Lauro, 154-155
Azar, L., 1743
Azara, Agustín de, 156
Azara, Felix de, 156

Bacardí y Moreau, Emilio, 934-935
Bachiller y Morales, Antonio, 936-938
Baez, Jorge, 1720
Baeza, Mario, 516
Bal y Gay, Jesús, 1161
Ballivián y Roxas, Vicente, 458
Balmaceda, Jorge, 517
Balmaceda Toro, Pedro, 518
Baqueiro Foster, Gerónimo, 157, 1162-1164, 1610
Barahona Vega, Clemente, 519
Baratta, María de, 158, 1940
Barbacci, Rodolfo, 1744
Barbieri, Vicente, 159
Barbosa, Manuel, 1165
Barker, George C., 1166
Barker, Ruth Laughlin, 1167
Barras y Prado, Antonio de las, 939
Barreda, Ernesto María, 160
Barriga, Víctor M., 1745
Barriga Rivas, Rogelio, 1168
Barros, Raquel, 520-522
Barros Arana, Diego, 636
Basadre, Jorge, 1746
Batet, Lucas de, 732-733
Batres Jáuregui, Antonio, 1131-1132
Baudouin, Julio, 1747
Bauzá, Francisco, 161
Bayo, Ciro, 5-7, 162-163
Becker, Zahara Z., 164
Béclard d'Harcourt, Marguerite, 1812

Index

Belgrano, Miguel, 165
Bello, Andrés, 8
Beltrán Avila, Marcos, 1748
Beltroy, Manuel, 1749
Bencomo, Eva R., 1964
Benítez, Juan Jesús, 166
Benítez Valle, Manuel, 1169
Berdiales, Germán, 167
Berenguer y Sed, Antonio, 940
Bergaño y Villegas, Simón, 1133
Berggreen, Andreas Peter, 9
Beristáin de Sousa, Joseph Mariano, 1170
Bermejo, Sergio, 1750
Bermúdez de la Torre y Solier, Pedro José de, 1751-1752
Bernal, Dionicio Rodolfo, 1753-1756
Bernal, Rafael, 1171
Berón, Sebastián C., 168-169
Berrien, William, 51
Bertini, G. M., 10
Betanzos, Juan de, 1757
Bibliografía del folklore peruano, 1758
Blanco Amor, Eduardo, 170
Blaya Alende, Joaquín, 171
Boas, Frank, 1172
Boatright, Mody C., 1173-1178, 1344
Boca Angel, Manuel, 1179
Boggs, Edna Garrido de, 1070, 1076
Boggs, Ralph Steele, 11-16, 51, 1180-1183, 1941
Bolívar Coronado, Rafael (Daniel Mendoza), 1965
Bonilla del Valle, Ernesto, 1759
Borges, Jorge Luis, 172
Bork, William, 1616
Borregán, Alonso, 1760
Bosco, Eduardo Jorge, 173
Bose, Fritz, 734

Botero, Juan José, 735-737
Botsford, Florence Hudson [Topping], 17
Braddy, Haldeen, 1184-1185
Brandão, Théo, 18
Brenner, Anita, 1186-1187
Breña Pacheco, Leonor, 1761
Breve Razón del Carro y Loa de Nicolás Rodríguez Juárez (pintor), 1188
Breve recuerdo del formidable ataque del exercito inglés a la Ciudad de Buenos Ayres, 174
Breve Relación del descubrimiento de la Isla de Juaja, 1189
Briceño, Olga, 1966
Briseño, Ramón, 523
Brisson, Jorge, 738
Brown Elsie, 51
Brown, Paul A., 19
Buchanan, Annabel Morris, 1190
Buenahora, Gonzalo, 739
Bulnes, Gonzalo, 1762
Bunge, Carlos Octavio, 175
Burga, Napoleón, 1763
Burgin, Miron, 51
Bustamante, Calixto, 231
Bustamante, Carlos María de, 1191
Bustamante, Manuel E., 1764
Bustamante, Perfecto P., 176
Bustos, Pedro, 524

C. G. V., 1064
Caballero, Jorge Giacoman, 479
Caballero Farfán, P., 177
Caballero Sierra, Abimael, 740
Cabrejo, Miguel E., 1765
Cabrera, Ana S., 20, 178-179, 525, 1192-1193
Cabrera Paz, Manuel, 992
Cabrices, Fernando, 21
Cáceres Freyre, Julián, 180
Cáceres González, ———, 941-942

Cadenas, Pedro de, 1766
Cadilla de Martínez, María, 1920-1923
Caicedo Rojas, José, 741
Calancha, Antonio de la, 1767
Calaveras mexicanas de Chicago, 1194
Calaveras resurrectas, 1195
Calcaño, José Antonio (Juan Sebastián), 1967-1968
Calero, José, 943
Calvete de Estrella, Juan Cristóbal, 1768
Calvo, Mercedes, 181
Camargo, Rafael María, 855
El Camarioqueño, 1015
Camino Calderón, Carlos, 1769-1772
Campa, Arturo L., 1196-1203
Campo, Luzán del, 182
Campo, S. del, 526, 548
Campos, Rubén M., 1204-1212
Canal Feijóo, Bernardo, 183-185
Canción al propio objeto, que concluye con una marcha patriótica, 1031
Cancionero amor y patria, 459
Cancionero anónimo, 186
Cancionero aprista, 1773
El cancionero arequipeño, 1774
Cancionero boliviano, 460
Cancionero chapaco, 461
El cancionero cubano por un "Guajiro" de la Habana, 944
Cancionero de Catamarca. Alternate title of Antiguos cantos populares argentinos, 195
Cancionero de las invasiones inglesas, 187
Cancionero: honor y gloria a los soldados bolivianos, 462
Cancionero 1931, 463
Cancionero moderno, 464
Cancionero patriótico, 465
Cancionero popular, 1969
El cancionero popular, 527
Cancionero popular americano; 75 canciones de las 21 repúblicas americanas, 22
El cancionero popular; colección escogida de cantos, 528
Cancionero popular, con las últimas canciones de moda, 466
Cancionero popular del niño venezolano (1° y 2° grados), 1970
Cancionero popular del niño venezolano; segundo volumen, 1971
Cancionero selecto, 467
Cancionero "Studium," 468
Cancionero tropical, 1137
Canciones cubanas desde "La Bayamesa" hasta las más modernas, 945
Canciones del Ande, 1775
Canciones populares, danzas i zarzuelas, 529
Canciones y corridos sinarquistas, 1213
Candela, Julio, 1776
Cano, Rafael, 188
Cano Vélez, F. Ramón, 189
Cantares de mi patria, 530
Cantares de Vuelta-Abajo, recopilados por un Guajiro, 946
"Cantares llaneros," 1972
Canto a la expedición del señor Barradas, 947
El canto popular, documentos para el estudio del folklore argentino, 190
Canto y baile, 1113

El cantor, 1114
Cantor popular, 1115
El cantor santiaguino, 531
Cantos militares, 532
Los cantos populares de mi tierra, 742
Cantos populares recopilados por un aficionado, 948
Capdevila, José María, 743
Capdevila y Melián, Pedro, 949
Carbonell y Rivero, José, 950
Cárdenas, Fortunato E., 1777
Cardona, Miguel, 1973
Carmona, Antonio, 744
Caro, Víctor, 745
Carpena, Elías, 191-192
Carpentier, Alejo, 951
Carreño, F., 1975
Carrera, Gustavo Luis, 1974
Carrión, Alejandro, 1116
Carrizo, Juan Alfonso, 193-217
Carrizo Valdés, Jesús María, 218
Carta de un soldado a su madre después de la acción de Puerto Caballo, 1071
Cartilla de folk-lore tolimense, 762
Carvajal, Luis Gonzalo, 746-749
Carvalho Neto, Paulo de, 23, 1721-1722
Casá, Agustín Guillermo, 293
Casa, Enrique C. de la, 1214
Casas, Bartolomé de las, 1311
Casas Cordero, Hipólito, 533-534
Cassidy, Ina Sizer, 1215
Castañeda, C. A., 1778
Castañeda, Daniel, 1216-1219
Castellanos, Carlos A., 952
Castellanos, Juan de, 750

Castellví, Marcelino de, 751-752, 769-770
Castex, Eusebio R., 219
Castilla, J. Antonio, 1779
Castilla Barrios, Olga, 753
Castillo, V., 535
Castillo Nájera, Francisco, 1220-1222
Castillo y Tamayo, Francisco del (El ciego de la Merced), 1903
Castillo y Tuazón, Teófilo del, 2100
Castillo Vázquez, Andrés, 1976
Castrillón Arboleda, Diego, 754
Castro, Américo, 220
Castro Leal, Antonio, 1223
Castro Pozo, Hildebrando, 1780
El Catalán Serralonga, 1224
Catálogo de la colección de folklore donada por el Consejo Nacional de Educación, 221
Cavada, Francisco J., 536-537
Cavero, José Salvador, 1781
Cavo, Andrés, 1225
Ceballos Novelo, Roque J., 1226
Celis Ríos, Trino, 1977
Centenario del folklore, 22 de agosto de 1946, 538
Centurión, Carlos R., 1723
Cerón, José D., 1072
Cevallos, P. F., 1138
Chacón, Luis F., 755
Chacón, Rafael, 1227
Chacón, y Calvo, José María, 953-961
Chacón del Campo, Julio, 539-542
El chaqueño, 469
Charlot, Jean, 1228
Chase, Gilbert, 24-26, 36, 51
Chávez, Angélico, 27, 1229
Chávez, Carlos, 1230-1232
Chávez Aliaga, Nazario, 1782

Chávez Orozco, Luis, 1233
Chazarreta, Andrés, 222-225
El chercán; nueva recopilación de cantos, canciones y arabíes, romanzas, etc., 543
El Chonchón, 544
Cielito de Maipú, 226
Cielitos que . . . cantaban los soldados del ejército patriota, 227
Cieza de León, Pedro de, 1783-1785
Cifuentes, Santos, 756
Cincuenta grabados de José Guadalupe Posada, edición homenaje en el primer centenario de su nacimiento, 1234
Cisneros, María Guadalupe, 1235
Cisneros Córdova, E., 1786
Clapier, Pedro J., 545-547
"Claver." "Cancionero poético-musical de Urabá-Chocó," 757
Cobo, Bernabé, 1787
Cobos, Rubén, 1236-1237
Un Colchagüino, 548
Colección de bailes típicos de la provincia de Guanacaste, 924
Colección de canciones y guarachas cubanas, 962
Colección de mulizas del año 1889 a 1936, 1788
Colección de todas las poesías que se han publicado en esta ciudad en elogio del aeronauta don Domingo Blinó, con algunas inéditas, 963
Colección escogida de canciones cubanas, 964

Colección escojida de canciones, décimas y guarachas, 965
Colección general de canciones españolas y americanas con acompañamiento, 28
Colín, Mario, 1238-1240
Coluccio, Félix, 30-31, 228-229
Coll, Pedro Emilio, 1978
Coll y Toste, Cayetano, 1924
Collection Phonothèque Nationale, 29
Cometta Manzoni, Aída, 32
Comité de Investigaciones del Folklore Nacional y Arte Típico Salvadoreño, 1942
Composiciones poéticas de la epopeya argentina, 230
Concolorcorvo (Calixto Bustamante), 231
The Conquest of Peru as Recorded by a Member of the Pizarro Expedition, 1888
La conquista del Perú, llamada la nueva Castilla, 1888
Consejo Nacional de Educación, 137-138
Consejo Nacional de Educación, Comisión de Folklore y Nativismo, 354
Contrapunto entre los famosos payadores, Pablo Vásquez y Gabino Ezeiza, 232
Contreras, Segundo N., 233
Los copihues, nuevo cancionero popular, 549
"La copla política cubana; décimas del año de 1762 acerca de la entrega de la Habana a los ingleses," 966
Coplas cantadas en la gran alborada gibaresca verificada en celebridad del nacimiento de S. A. R. el Príncipe de Asturias, 1925

Index 379

"Coplas de los chinos de Andacollo," 550
"Coplas de nuestro cancionero anónimo," 234
"Coplas del Litoral," 235
"Coplas populares venezolanas," 1979
Corbin, Alice, 1241
Córdova de Fernández, Sofía, 967
Cornejo V., Justino, 1117
Corona Raimundo, Manuel, 968
La coronación de Fernando VII, 969
Cortázar, Augusto Raúl, 236-247
Cortés, José Domingo, 470
Cortijo, A. L., 33
El correo del Perú, 1875
"Corrido de la enamorada," 1242
"Corrido del terremoto," 1243
Corrido o corridong; historias populares en verso, 2101
Corridos and other songs in the Archivo de Bellas Artes, Sección de Música, México, D. F., 1244
Corridos and other types of popular literature which are in the Benjamin Franklin Library, México, D. F., 1245
Corridos, romances, décimas, and other popular verse in the Biblioteca del Museo Nacional, México, D. F., 1246
Corridos and romances in the Biblioteca Nacional de México, D. F., 1247
Corridos and romances in the library of the University of New Mexico, Albuquerque, N. M., 1248
"Corridos de la Revolución," 1249
Corridos mexicanos, 1250
Cossío, J. M. de, 551
Costas Arguedas, José Felipe, 471
Cowell, Sidney Robertson, 1251, 1399
Cuaderno del Taller de San Lucas (Managua), 1695
Cuadra, Pablo Antonio, 1696-1698
Cue Cánovas, Agustín, 1252
Cuéllar, Alfredo B., 1253
Cuervo, Angel, 758
Cuervo, Rufino, 759
Cufré, Angela G. de, 248
Curioso romance en que refieren y declaran unas amorosas quejas, que un galán da á su dama, 1254
Curtis, F. S., 1255-1256
Custodio González, Angel, 636

Daireaux, Emile, 249
Dalevuelta, Jacobo, 1253, 1257-1258
Danneman R., Manuel, 520-522, 552-554
Dantel Argendoña, Elvira, 555
Dávila Garibi, José Ignacio, 1259
"De las costumbres en la poesía," 556
De María, Isidoro, 253
De punta y hacha; payada memorable entre los famosos payadores J. Betinotti y F. Bianco, 250
Décimas populares, 557
Décimas sobre el asesinato cometido del 18 al 19 de enero de 1830, 970
Décimas variadas, 251

Décimas variadas para cantar con guitarra, 252
Declamación hecha en cuartetos contra la francesa perfidia, 971
Delgadillo, Luis A., 1699-1700
Delgado, Antonio I., 1260
Delgado, Camilo S., 729
Delgado, Luis Humberto, 1789
Delgado Vivanco, Edmundo, 34, 1790-1792
Deliz, Monserrate, 1926
Delmotte, J., 1261-1262
Demarest, Donald, 1263
Descripcion poetica de las fiestas con que la nobilissima ciudad de Mexico celebró el buen successo de la empresa contra los otomanos, 1264
Devoto, Daniel, 35
Díaz, Manuel Armando, 972
Díaz, C., Fernando, 565
Díaz Casanueva, Humberto, 558
Díaz del Castillo, Bernal, 1265
Díaz Castro, Eugenio, 760-761
Díaz Gana, Pedro, 570
Díaz y de Ovando, Clementina, 1266-1269
Diccionario de la lengua castellana . . . [de] la Real Academia Española [known as the Diccionario de Autoridades], 1270
Dirección de Educación Pública [del Tolima], 762-763
Disselhoff, Hans Dietrich, 1271
"Dobiarisa," 764
Dobie, J. Frank, 1272-1276
Dobles Segreda, Luis, 925

"Documentos de poesía popular," 1980
Domínguez, Francisco, 1277-1278
Domínguez, Luis Arturo, 1981-1984
Domínguez Camargo, Hernando, 765
Domínguez del Río, T., 766
Don D. M., 973
Don J. M., 974
Donaire Vizarreta, Juan, 1793
Dorantes de Carranza, Baltasar, 1279
Draghi Lucero, Juan, 254
Dromundo, Baltasar, 1280-1283
Duarte Level, Lino, 1985
Duayen, César, 255
Dufourcq, Lucila, 559
Duque, Antonio de J., 767
Durán, Diego, 1284
Durán, Gustavo, 36, 1285-1286
Durán, Sixto M., 1118
Duvalier, Armando, 1287

E. de V., 560
Earle, Henry Edmond, 1288
D'Eça, Raul, 51
Echevarría de Lobato Mulle, Felisa Carmen, 256
Echeverría Reyes, Aníbal, 561
El eco de la guerra, 472
Ellis, Florence Hawley, 1289
Eloy, Rodulfo, 768
Eloy, U. Miguel, 768
Enríquez Córdoba, Gerardo, 769-770
Enríquez de Guzmán, Alonso, 1794
Entregas de poesía popular colombiana, No. 1, 771
Entregas de poesía popular colombiana, No. 2, 772

Entregas de poesía popular colombiana, No. 4, 913
Ernst, Adolf, 1986, 2008
Escalona, Isabel María, 1987
Escandón, Ignacio de, 1795
Escarpit, Robert, 1290
Escoto, José A., 975
Escudero, Alfonso, 562
España, Juan, 1988
Esparza S., Cuauhtémoc, 1291
Espejo, Géronimo, 257
Espinosa, Aurelio M., 37-38, 563-564, 976, 1292-1309, 1927
Espinosa, Aurelio M., Jr., 39
Espinosa, Francisco, 1943-1945
Espinosa, Francisco Ramón, 2102
Estete, Miguel de, 1796
Esteva, Guillermo A., 1310
Estévanez, Nicolás, 1073
Estrada, R., 1134
Evia, Jacinto de, 773, 1119
Exbrayat, Jaime, 774-775
Ezeiza, Gabino, 232, 258-262

F. D., 565
F. H. H., 566
Fabié, Antonio María, 1311
Fabo de María, Pedro, 776-778
La Falange (México), 1312
Falcão Espalter, Mario, 263
Fansler, Dean S., 2103
Farfán, J. M. B., 1797
Farwell, Arthur, 1313, 1409
Febres Pobeda, Carlos, 1989
Fernández, Diego, 1798
Fernández, Horacio, 264
Fernández, Justo, 1799
Fernández, Manuel, 567

Fernández de Oviedo y Valdés, Gonzalo, 1800
Fernández Piedrahita, Lucas, 779
Ferreiro, Pascual, 977-981
Ferrer, J., 1314
Ferreyra Videla, Vidal, 265-266
Figueroa, Elisa, 568
Figueroa, Pedro Pablo, 569-570
Figueroa Fernández, Amelia, 571
Finot, Alfonso, 267
Fletes Bolaños, Anselmo, 1701
Flores Chinarro, Francisco, 1801
Florez, Luis, 780
Fogelquist, Donald F., 1315-1317
Folklore, 1246, 1318
Folklore argentino, proyecto del vocal doctor Juan P. Ramos, resolución del H. Consejo; instrucciones a los maestros, 268
"El folklore de la muerte," 1319
Folklore musical del siglo XVIII, 1802
Folklore santandereano. Tomo I: Coplas populares, 781
"Folk-lore venezolano," 1990
"Folk-lore venezolano: Corridos de Zaraza," 1991
"Folklore venezolano (de la colección del Dr. José E. Machado)," 1992
"Folklore venezolano: Desatinos," 1993
"Folk-lore venezolano: Gaitas, canto popular maracaibero," 1994
"Folk-lore venezolano: Glosas llaneras improvisadas en Velorios de Cruz," 1995

Folk Music of the United States and Latin America; Combined Catalog of Phonograph Records, 40
Folletos de divulgación científica y literaria, 1320
Fombona-Pachano, Jacinto, 1996
Fonseca, Julio, 925
Forero, Manuel José, 782-784
Forte, Vicente, 269, 328
Fortún, Julia Elena, 473
Fraser, Norman, 41
Freire-Marreco, Barbara, 1321
Freitas, Pablo, 453
Frías, Heriberto, 1322
Froebel, Julius, 1702
"El fuego grande del Cayo," 982
Fuente, Nicanor de la, 1803-1804
Fuentes y Matons, Laureano, 983
Furt, Jorge M., 270-274

Gabriel, José, 42
"Gaitas o cantos populares zulianos," 1997
"El galerón de No Marcos," 1998
Galindo, Miguel, 1323-1325
Gallardo, Aurelio Luis, 1326
Gallegos, Rómulo, 1999-2003
Gallop, Rodney, 1327
Gálvez, José, 1805-1806
Gama, Pedro Manuel, 1328
Gamboa, Emma, 926
Gamboa, Fernando, 1329
Gamio, Manuel, 1226, 1330
Gandía, Enrique de, 275-276
Garay, Narciso, 1713
García, Juan Francisco, 1074
García, Nicasio, 572-574, 690

García, Secundino, 1703
García, Serafín, 277
García Bravo y Olivera, R., 1331
García Cubas, Antonio, 1332
García de Diego, Pilar, 43
García Gutiérrez, Jesús, 1333
García Icazbalceta, Joaquín, 1334, 1547
García Rodríguez, José M., 1075
Garcilaso de la Vega, Inca, 1807-1808
Garibaldi, Carlos Alberto, 44
Garibaldi, Verdad, 44
Garibay K., Angel María, 1335
Garrido, Edna, 1076
Garrido, Pablo, 575-576
Garrido Avalos, Cirilo, 577
Garrigó Roque, E., 984
Garzón, Tobías, 278
Geiger, Paul, 45
Gennero, S., 279
Gil Fortoul, José, 2004
Gilbert, A. de, 518
Giménez Rueda, Julio, 280
Gobernación del Tucumán. Papeles de gobernadores en el siglo XVI, 319
Golibart González, Porfirio, 1077
Gómez Carrillo, Manuel, 281
Gómez Leal, Efraín, 1336
Gonzáles de la Rosa, Manuel, 1849
González, Eloy G., 2005
González, Isidro José, 985
González, J. Natalicio, 1724
González, Joaquín V., 282-283
González, Jovita, 1337-1338
González, Pedro, 1809
González, Rafael, 986-988
González Bona, C., 2006
González Bravo, Antonio, 1339
González Casanova, Pablo, 1340-1341, 1496

González Font, José, 1928
González Holguín, Diego, 1810
González Hurtado, Rodolfo, 1342
González Obregón, Luis, 1343
González Tablas, R., 1078
Goodwyn, Frank, 1344-1349
Gordon, Maxine W., 1929
Gorostiza, Manuel Eduardo de, 1588
Gould, Cassius W., 1350
Gras, José, 1351
Grases, Pedro, 46, 2007
Gray, Beryl, 47
Grenón, Pedro, 284
Grijalva de León, Ricardo, 1352
Grillo, Max, 785
Grismer, Mildred B., 48
Grismer, Raymond L., 48
Gronlier, Enrique, 989-991
Grossmann, R., 285
Groussac, Paul, 286
Gruening, Ernest, 1353
Gruesso, José María, 786
Guajardo, Bernardino, 578-579
Guarín, José David, 787-788
Gudiño Kramer, Luis, 287
Guerra, Armando, 992
Guerra, Bernardo de, 580
Guerra P., Misael (Ismael Parraguez), 581
Guerrero, Eduardo, 1354-1357
Guerrero Cárpena, Ismael, 288, 448
Guevara, Darío, 1120-1122
Guevara, Tomás, 582
Guichot y Sierra, Alejandro, 49
Guirnalda criolla, o el ruiseñor de las selvas; gran colección de décimas, 993
Guitar Method with Guitar Arrangements of Spanish-

American Folk Songs of New Mexico, 1358
Gutiérrez, Benigno A., 789-793, 873
Gutiérrez, Juan María, 289
Gutiérrez, Rufino, 794
Gutiérrez de Santa Clara, Pedro, 1811

Hague, Eleanor, 50
Hahn, Bolko von, 290
Handbook of Latin American Studies, 51
Hanke, Lewis, 51
Hansen, Terrence L., 1359
Hanssen, Frederick, 583
d'Harcourt, Marguerite Béclard, 52, 1812-1814
Harcourt, Raoul, 1812-1814
Hare, Maud Cuney, 1360
Haverstock, Nathan A., 51
Hechos del Cap. D. Miguel Velázquez Lorea, 1361
Hediger, Ernest S., 1362
Helfritz, Hans, 1363
Henao, Januario, 795
Hendrix, William S., 1364
Henestrosa, Andrés, 1365-1366
Henius, Frank, 53
Henríquez, Camilo, 507
Henríquez Ureña, Max, 1079
Henríquez Ureña, Pedro, 54-55, 1080, 1367
Hernández, José A., 1815
Hernández, Juan C., 796-797
Hernández, Julio Alberto, 1081
Hernández de Alba, Gregorio, 798
Hernández Cornejo, Roberto, 584
Hernández Crespo, Manuel, 994-995
Hernández Lagos, Julia, 585
Herrera, Antonio de, 1816

Herrera, Carlos Aquiles, 1817
Herrera, Martín G., 1826
Herrera Carrillo, Pablo, 56
Herrera Frimont, Celestino, 1368-1371
Herreros Véliz, Ramón, 586
Herring, Hubert, 1372
Herzog, George, 57
Hidalgo, A. J., 1818
Hidalgo, Bartolomé, 277
Hidalgo, Félix, 291
"Hilarión Pastrana," 905-906
Hill, Gertrude, 1373
Hodge, F. W., 1680
Hölzer, V., 292
Holzmann, Rodolfo, 1128
Horta, Manuel, 1374
House, Guillermo, 293
Hudson, Arthur Palmer, 58
Hudson, W. H., 294
Hudson, Wilson M., 1174-1178
Hurtado, G. Nabor, 1375

Ibáñez, Avelina M., 295
Ibarguren, Carlos, 296-297
"Idea general de los monumentos del antiguo Perú, é introducción á su estudio," 1819
Iglesia, Alvaro de la, 996
Igualada, Francisco de, 799-800
Improvisadores chilenos, 587
Inchauspe, Pedro, 298-299
Inclán, Luis G., 1376
Instituto de Extensión Musical de la Universidad de Chile, 588
Instituto de Investigaciones Folklórico-Musicales de la Universidad de Chile, Facultad de Bellas Artes, 589-590

International Catalogue of Recorded Folk Music, 41
International Institute of Intellectual Cooperation, 1377
"Isabel Villaseñor: homenaje," 1378
La invasión de Cárdenas; romance histórico, 997
Invasión de la Vuelta-Abajo; romance histórico, 998
Las invasiones haitianas, 1082
Iraizoz, Antonio, 999
La isla, 1000
Isamitt, Carlos, 591
Izquierdo Ríos, Francisco, 1820-1823

J. R. V., 1001
Jacovella, Bruno C., 59, 217, 300
Jahn-Ruhnau, Romuald, 301
Jaramillo, Robert, 790
Jaramillo G., Arturo, 801
El jardín cubano; nueva colección de cantos y glosas, 1002
Jáuregui Rosquellas, Alfredo, 474, 480
Jijena Sánchez, Lidia Rosalía de, 60
Jijena Sánchez, Rafael, 61, 302-306
Jiménez Borja, Arturo, 1845
Jiménez de la Espada, Marcos, 1123
Jones, C. K., 62
Jones, Earle E., 592

Keller, Jean P., 802
Kennedy, Stetson, 1379
Kinscella, Hazel, 1636
Kittle, J. L., 1380
Klos, Carlos, 517
Komadina, Tonia Ann, 1381

Krautmacher, Robert, 593
Kress, Dorothy M., 1382

Labardén, Manuel José de, 307
Labastille, Irma, 63
Lafone Quevedo, Samuel A., 308
Lamo Arenas, Ramiro, 803
Lanao Loaiza, José Ramón, 804
Lance, Donald M., 1383
Lances del amor; canciones populares, 1003
Lanuza, José, 309-310
Lara, Jesús, 1824
Larrañaga, Rómulo (El Negro Peluca), 594-597
Larreba, A., 1384
Latcham, Ricardo E., 598-600
Latorre, Mariano, 311
Laval, Ramón A., 601-605
Lavalle, Enrique Richard, 312
Lavín, Carlos, 606-607
Lea, Aurora Lucero-White, 1385-1386
Leal, Luis, 1387-1389
Leguizamón, Martiniano, 313-317
Lehmann-Nitsche, Robert, 318, 2008
Lenz, Rodolfo, 608-611
León, Argeliers, 1004
León, Nicolás, 1390
León Barandarián, Augusto D., 1825-1828
León Mera, Juan, 1124
León Rey, José A., 805-806
Leonard, Irving A., 64-66
Leredo, Pablo, 1391
Lerín, Manuel, 1392
Lescámez, Antón de, 807
Leslie, John Kenneth, 1393
Lesser, Alexander, 1394
Levillier, Roberto, 319

El libro de oro de la poesía mexicana, 1395
Life and Work of the Engraver José Guadalupe Posada, 1396
Lima, Emirto de, 67-68, 808-811
Lira, Miguel N., 1397
La lira andina, 1838
La lira criolla, 1005
Lira Espejo, Eduardo, 812, 2009-2011
La lira popular, 612
Lira popular, 702
Lira popular; colección de cantares populares de Bolivia, 475
Lira popular; ramillete de zarzuelas, canciones, yaravíes, habaneras y serenatas antiguas y modernas, 1829
Liscano, Juan, 1979, 2012-2018
"List of Works of the New York Public Library Relating to Mexico (Language, Art and Folklore)," 1398
"List of Works, in the New York Public Library Relating to the West Indies," 69
Lizana, Desiderio, 526, 613-614
Lizondo Borda, M., 320
Llantos del reino de Chile, 615
Llaverías, Joaquín, 1006
Llorente, Francisco Martín, 992
Lo que canta el pueblo; cancionero popular, 321
Lo que se canta en Chile, 616
Lohmann Villena, Guillermo, 1830-1834
Lomax, Alan, 1399, 1401
Lomax, John, 1400-1401
López, Patricio Antonio, 1402-1404
López Cruz, Francisco, 1930
López de Gomara, Francisco, 1083

López Narváez, Carlos, 813
López Osornio, Mario A., 322
López Peña, Arturo, 61
López y Planes, Vicente F., 131
López Prieto, Antonio, 1007
López Tovar, Manuel María, 1826
Lozano, Pedro, 323
Luce, Allena, 70
Lucero-White, Aurora, 1159, 1405-1406
Lugones, Leopoldo, 405
Lugones, Lorenzo, 324
Luján, Joseph, 1407
Lullo, Orestes di, 325-327
Lummis, Charles F., 1288, 1408-1409, 1680-1681
Lumpkin, Ben Gray, 71
Luna, E. de, 814
Lynch, Ventura R., 328-329

M., 617
M. B., Dr., 1410
M. V. C., 714-715
Macau, M. A., 1008
McCoy, William J., 1411
MacCurdy, Raymond R., 1412-1413
McNeely, John H., 1185
McNeil, Norman Laird ("Brownie"), 71, 1414-1417
Macedo Arguedas, Alfonso, 1835
Macedo C., María Rosa, 1836
Machado, José E., 330, 1990-1995, 2019-2025
Madrid, Miguel Angel, 72
Madueño, Raúl R., 331-332
Madzen, Lorenzo, 618
Major, Mabel, 1418
Malaret, Augusto, 73-75, 1931
Mallo, Nicanor, 476

Mann, W., 76
Manrique Cabrera, F., 1932
Manríquez, Cremilda, 619
Mantecón, Enrique, 1009-1010
Manuel, E. Arsenio, 2104
Marchena, Enrique de, 1084
María, Alcides de, 333
María y Campos, Armando de, 1419-1422
Mariluz Urquijo, J. M., 334
Marín, Abel, 815
Marinas Otero, Luis, 1139
Marino Flores, Anselmo, 1423
Mariño de Lovera, Pedro, 620
Martí, Samuel, 77
Martínez, Domingo, 1011
Martínez, José de J., 1424
Martínez, José Luis, 1425
Martínez, Marco Antonio, 2026
Martínez y Cordero, Eliseo A., 1012
Martínez G. Narciso, 1837-1839
Martínez Moles, Manuel, 1013
Martínez Mutis, Aurelio, 816
Martínez Torner, Eduardo, 1014
Masciopinto, F. Adolfo, 335
Mason, J. Alden, 1933-1934
Massini Ezcurra, José María, 336-337
Matos Romero, Manuel, 2027
Mattfeld, Julius, 78
Maxwell, Allen, 1174-1178
Mayer-Serra, Otto, 1426-1427
Maziel, Juan Baltasar, 338
Mechling, William Hubbs, 1428
Medina, Joaquín R., 817
Medina, José Toribio, 339, 621-623, 1840-1841
Medina Días, L., 1842
Mejía Angel, Carlos, 819
Mejía Baca, José, 1843-1844
Mejía Robledo, Alfonso, 818
Mejía Sánchez, Ernesto, 1704-1706

Index

Los mejores corridos mexicanos, 1429
Melgarejo Vivanco, José Luis, 1430
Mélo, Veríssimo de, 79
Mena Brito, Bernardino, 1431
Méndez, Concha, 80
Méndez Buendía, J. R., 770
Méndez de Cuenca, Laura, 1432
Méndez Plancarte, Alfonso, 1433-1434
Mendia, Ciro (Carlos Mejía Angel), 819
Mendizábal, Miguel O. de, 1435
Mendoza, Daniel, 1965
Mendoza, Eufemio, 1436
Mendoza, Jaime, 477-478
Mendoza, Vicente T., 81, 624, 1388, 1437-1490
Mendoza, Virginia R. R. de, 1490
Menéndez, Enrique, 1029
Menéndez y Pelayo, Marcelino, 82
Menéndez Peña, Hilario, 1491-1492
Menéndez Pidal, Ramón, 83-87, 1493
Meneses, Daniel, 625-629
Meré, Rafael, 820
Mérida, Carlos, 1494
Merino de Zela, Mildred, 1758
Merizalde del Carmen, Bernardo, 821-822
Mexican Folk Music, 1614
Michel, Concepción (Concha), 1220
Millán Maldonado, Amalia, 1495
Ministerio de Educación Pública del Perú, 1845
Miraflores, 1015

Miranda, José, 1496
Miranda, Manuel, 340
Miranda de Villafañe, Luis de, 341, 351
Miró Quesada S., Aurelio, 1846
Moglia, Raúl, 342-343
Molins, W. Jaime, 344
Moncada G., Francisco, 1497
Monge, Pedro S., 1847
Monguió, Luis, 345, 1498-1499
Monografía de El Tocuyo, 2028
Monroy Pittaluga, Francisco, 2029-2030
Monsalve Martínez, Manuel, 823
Montero, Marco Arturo, 1500
Montero y Vidal, José, 2105
Montes de Oca, José G., 1501-1504
Montesinos, Fernando, 1848
Montesinos, Pedro, 2031-2032
Montoya Toro, Jorge, 824
Mora Naranjo, Alfonso, 825
Morales, Ernesto, 346-349, 826
Morel, Tomás E., 1085
Morelet, Arthur, 1505
Moreno, Daniel, 1506
Moreno, Delfino C., 1507
Moreno, Segundo Luis, 1125
Moreno González, Juan Carlos, 1725
Morla Vicuña, Carlos, 351
Morley, S. G., 88
Morúa, Martín de, 1849
Mostajo, Francisco, 1850
Moya, Ismael, 352-353
Muelle, Jorge, 1845
El mulato Taguada, 630
Mundo austral, 763
Muñoz, Diego, 631-632
Muñoz, Lucila, 633
Muñoz R., José María, 634
Murillo, Gerardo (Dr. Atl), 1508

Music of the Gold Rush Era, 1509
Música argentina nativa; cantares y canciones danzadas, 354
"Música, danza y cantos del antiguo México," 1510
Música nicaragüense, 1707
La música popular latinoamericana, 89
Musique et chansons populaires, 1377
Musquiz Blanco, Manuel, 1253

Nápoles Fajardo, Juan C., 1016-1018
Naranjo Martínez, Enrique, 827
Navarrete, Carlos, 1135
Navarro, Alfonso, 635
Navarro del Aguila, Víctor, 1851
El Nego Peluca, 594-597
Nel Ospina, Pedro, 828
Nercasseau y Morán, Enrique, 700
Nettl, Bruno, 90
Nichols, Madaline W., 355-357
Noda, Tranquilino S. de, 1019
Nolasco, Flérida de, 1086-1089
Novo, Salvador, 1511
La nueva lira criolla, 1020
Nueva Relación y Curioso Romance de Diego de Frías y Antonio Montero, 1512
Nuevo cancionero, 479
Nuevo y curioso romance en que se da cuenta de la victoria alcanzada por los españoles . . . guerra de Santo Domingo de América, 1090

Núñez, Evangelina de, 927
Núñez y Domínguez, José de Jesús, 1513-1515
Núñez de Pineda y Bascuñán, Francisco, 636

O. M. S., 637
Obeso, Candelario, 829
Obligado, Pastor S., 358
Obras de eloqüencia y poesía premiadas por la Real Universidad de México . . . el día 28 de diciembre de 1790, 1516
Ocampo, Joseph Gabriel, 174
"Ocho corridos mexicanos," 1517
O'Higgins, Paul, 1652
Olano, Ricardo, 830-831
Olivares Figueroa, Raúl, 2032-2054
Once cantos de México, 1518
Onís, Federico de, 359
d'Orbigny, Alcide Dessalines, 360
Orcillo, Rubén S., 1519
Orea, Basilio, 1520
Ortega, Pompilio, 1140
Ortiz, Fernando, 1021-1025
Ortiz, Sergio Elías, 832-833
Ortiz C., Laurencio, 833-834
Ortiz de Montellano, Bernardo, 1521
Osorio, Juan C., 835
Ospina, Tulio, 836-837
Ospina N., Francisco, 838
Ossa, Peregrino, 839
Otaiza de Estrada, Aída, 638
Otero, Nina, 1522
Otero d'Costa, Enrique, 840-841
Otero Muñoz, Gustavo, 842-843
Otero-Warren, Adelina, 1159

Ovalles, Víctor Manuel, 2055
Oviedo Herrera y Rueda, Luis Antonio, 1852

P. G. C., 1523
Pabón Núñez, Lucio, 844
El Padre Capacho, 1048
Page, Frederick Mann, 361
Palacios, Emanuel, 1524
Palant, ____, 1525
Palma, Athos, 362
Palma, Clemente, 1853
Palma, Ricardo, 1854-1855
Palma y Romay, Ramón de, 1026
Pampa Viejo, Don, 363
Pardo, Isaac J., 2056
Pardo Tovar, Andrés, 845-846
Paredes, Américo, 13, 91, 1526-1535, 1646
Paredes, M. Rigoberto, 480
Paredes, Rómulo, 1828
Paredes Candia, Antonio, 481
Parraguez, Ismael, 581
"Pastrana, Hilarión," 905
Patiño, Víctor Manuel, 847
Pavés P., Francisco A., 639
Paz Soldán y Unanué, Pedro, 1740
Paz y Melia, A., 1536
Pearce, T. M., 1418, 1537-1539
Pedrell, Felipe, 92
Pedrero, Alfonso, 1540
Peguero, Luis José, 1091
Penson, César Nicolás, 1093-1094
Peña, Enrique, 364
Peña Morell, Esteban, 1092
Peñuela, Cayo Leonidas, 848
El Pequén, 488, 501
Pequeñas canturias y danzas venezolanas, 2057

Peralta, Juan Bautista, 640
Peralta y Barnuevo, Pedro de, 1856-1857
Peralta de Gaeta, Juan Bautista, 641
Perdomo Escobar, José Ignacio, 849-851
Pereda Valdés, Ildefonso, 93, 365-366, 1858
Pereira Salas, Eugenio, 642-650
Pérez, V. C., 466
Pérez, Rebeca, Vda. de Nava, 1544
Pérez de Alejo, Miguel A., 1027-1928
Pérez Aragón, Alejandro, 1859
Pérez Arbeláez, E., 852
Pérez de Luarca, Manuel, 1029
Pérez Martínez, Héctor, 1541-1542
Pérez Ortiz, Rubén, 724
Pérez Ramírez, Elías, 853-854
Pérez Vizcaíno, Alfonso, 1543
El picaflor, 651
Piedra-Bueno, Andrés de, 1030
Pimentel y Vargas, Fermín de, 855-856
Pinedo, Manuel D., 1544
Pino, J. J. del, 1860-1861
Pino Saavedra, Y., 652
Pinto, Manuel M., 482
Pinzón M., J. Odilio, 857
Pires de Lima, J. A., 94
Pirotto, Armando D., 367
Pizarro, Pedro, 1862
Planchart, Enrique, 2058
Plath, Oreste, 654
Plaza, Ramón de la, 2059
Plenn, Abel, 1545
Plotini, Tomás, 1935
Podestá, Antonio G., 368
Podestá, José J., 369

Poemas folklóricos y patrióticos; corridos de la Revolución, 1546
Poesía herioca al feliz éxito de la expedición del señor brigadier don I. Barradas, 1031
Poesías populares, 655
Poesías populares, 656
Los poetas del amor y la mujer, 858
Poetas guajiros, 1032
Pogo, Alexander, 1863
Poma de Ayala, Phelipe Guamán, 1864
Pomar, Juan Bautista, 1547
Pombo, Manuel, 859-860
Ponce, Manuel M., 1033, 1548-1549
Ponce de León, José E. (José G. Villa), 1034-1035
Poncet y Cárdenas, Carolina, 1036-1039
Pormenor de las operaciones ejecutadas en Nueva España, 1040
Porras Barrenechea, Raúl, 1865-1867
Portell Vilá, Herminio, 1041-1042
Porter, Carlos E., 657-659, 1294
Porter, Katherine Anne, 1550
Porter de la Barrera, Ricardo, 660-665
Portillo, J. M., 2060
Posada, José Guadalupe, 1551
Pozzi, Leo, 1552
Pradere, Juan A., 370
Praesant, Hans, 95
Prestol Castillo, Fredy, 1095
Prieto, Margarita, 1553
"Primer Congreso Nacional de Poetas y Cantores Populares de Chile," 666

Primer cuaderno de canciones populares venezolanas, 2085
Primera Parte de los Romances del Valiente Francisco Esteban, 1554
Prometheo alegorico, 1555
Puig, Juan de la C., 371
Puig Campillo, Antonio, 861

"Quadretti di folclore messicano," 1556
"Quando volvió vencedor Antequera," 1868
Quesada, Ernesto, 372
Quesada, V. G., 373
Quetzacóatl, órgano de la Sociedad de Antropología de México, 1557
Quevedo, Francisco, 1558-1559
Quiñones Pardo, Octavio, 96, 862-871
Quintero R., Víctor, 771
Quiroga, Adán, 374-376
Quiroga, Carlos B., 377-379

Rael, Juan B., 1560-1562
Ralliere, J. B., 1563-1565
Ramillete de Flores, Quarta, Quinta, y Sexta parte de Flor de Romances nueuos, 667
Ramírez, José F., 1284
Ramírez, Juan Ramón. See Campo, S. del, and Un Colchagüino
Ramírez de Aguilar, Fernando, 1257-1258
Ramírez Plancarte, Francisco, 1566
Ramírez Serna, Gabriel, 772
Ramón y Rivera, Luis Felipe, 2061-2072
Ramos, Juan P., 268-380
Ramos B., Nicolás, 1096-1103

Ramos Espinosa, Alfonso, 1205
Rangel, Nicolás, 1567-1568
Ransom, Harry H., 1344
Raygada, Carlos, 1869
Recinos, Adrián, 1136
Recopilación de los mejores yaravíes y huaynos del Perú, 1839
Recopilación de materiales folklóricos salvadoreños, primera parte, 1942
Recopilación de yaravíes, 1870
Recuerdos de la patria, 381
Redfield, Robert, 51, 1569
Reed, John, 1570
Reindorp, Reginald C., 1571
Rela, Walter, 668
Relación de Doña Blanca, 1572
Relación de la inundación, que hizo el Río Mapocho, 669
Relación del Ciego Toluqueño, 1573
Relación de lo acaecido en Perú desde que Francisco Hernández Girón se alzó hasta el día que murió, 1905
Relación de todo lo sucedido en la provincia del Piru desde que Blasco Nuñez Vela fue enviado por S. M. a ser visorey della, 1871
Relación muy verdadera de todo lo sucedido en el río del Marañón, 2096
"Relación verídica en la que se da noticia de lo acaecido en la ysla de Puerto Rico," 1936
Relación y verdadero romance que declara la inconsiderada y atrevida sublevación . . . en la ciudad de Lima, 1872

Relazión que hizo Butapichún, 670
Reni, Aníbal, 928
Renk, Eldred Joseph, 1574
Restrepo, Antonio José, 872-873
Restrepo, Tomás S., 874
Revollo, Pedro María, 875
Rey, Agapito, 1575
Rey Aguirre, Mariano del, 1043
Reyles, Carlos, 263
Ribas y Ribas, Fidel, 2073
Ricard, Robert, 1576
Richmond, W. Edson, 19
Rincón, Manuel María, 2106
Ríos Franco, Buenaventura, 1577
Rivadeneira, Ester, 671
Rivarola, Pantaleón, 371, 382-383
Rivas, Medardo, 876
Rivera, Diego, 1578
Rivera, Felipe V., 483
Robb, John Donald, 1579-1581
Robe, Stanley L., 97-98
Roberts, Helen H., 1934
Roberts, Sarah Elizabeth, 13
Robledo, Emilio, 877-878
Robledo, Eusebio, 879-880
Rochereau, P. E., 881
Roco del Campo, Antonio, 672-673
Rodríguez, Alberto, 384
Rodríguez, Antonio, 1582
Rodríguez, Federico, 1044-1047
Rodríguez, José (El Padre Capacho), 1048
Rodríguez, Zorobabel, 674-675
Rodríguez Alcalá, Teresa Lamas Carísima de, 1726
Rodríguez Demorizi, Emilio, 1104-1106
Rodríguez García, J. A., 1049
Rodríguez Marín, Francisco, 99
Rodríguez Mira, Pedro, 882
Rodríguez Molas, Ricardo, 385

Rodríguez Moñino, Antonio, 100, 1873
Rodríguez Plata, Horacio, 781
Rodríguez Rivera, Virginia, 1490, 1583-1584
Rojalaga D., Máximo A., 1727
Rojas, Alfonso María, 883
Rojas, Arístides, 1022, 2074-2079
Rojas, Arnold R., 1585
Rojas, Ricardo, 101, 386-388, 409
Rojas Garcidueñas, José, 1586
Rojas Paz, Pablo, 389
Román, Marcelino M., 102
Román Guerrero, Rebeca, 676
"Romance," 1587
[Romance], 1588
Romance a la entrada y ejercicio de fuego que hizo la tropa que volvió de Quito, 1126
Romance en la fiesta con que los Batallones de Lima celebraron la imagen de Ntra. Sra. de Monserrat, 1874
"El romance español en Venezuela," 2080
Romance y corta esplicación de la historia de la estatua de Carlos IV, primera parte, 1589
El romancero; colección de romances, 677
Romancero general (1600, 1604, 1605), 678
Romances del desafío de Oliveros y Montesinos, 679
Romero, Carlos A., 1876
Romero, Emilia, 1845, 1877
Romero, F., 1878
Romero, Jesús C., 1590-1591
Romero, M. J., 884

Romero Flores, Jesús, 1592
Romero de Terreros, Manuel, 1593
Rosa-Nieves, Cesáreo, 1937
Rosales G., F. J., 1708
Rosales y Moreira, Francisco, 1050
Rosas de Oquendo, Mateo, 21, 1536
Rosemberg, Tobías, 390
Ross, Patricia Fent, 1594
Rossi, Giuseppe Carlo, 1595
Rubio, Darío, 1596
Rueda, Soledad Marina O., 885
Rugeles, Manuel F., 2081
El ruiseñor mexicano, 1597
Ruiseñor yucateco, 1598
Ruiz, Bernardino, 484
Ruiz, Eduardo, 1599-1600
Ruiz M., Alberto, 886
Ruschenberger, William Samuel, 680

Saavedra, Alfredo M., 1601
Sabella, Andrés, 681-682
Sáenz, C. L., 887
Sahagún, Bernardino de, 1602
Salado Alvarez, Victoriano, 1603
Salas Viu, V., 683
Salazar, José María, 888-890
Saldaña Suazo, José A., 1107
Saldívar, Gabriel, 1604-1606
Salgado, Luis H., 1127
Samper, Darío, 891-892
Samper, José María, 893
Samuel, S. J., 894
San Joaquín, Sor Tadea de, 669
San Martín, R., 466
Sánchez, Luis Alberto, 1879-1880
Sánchez, Ricardo, 391
Sánchez Escobar, Rafael, 1607
Sánchez de Fuentes y Peláez, Eduardo, 1051-1055

Sánchez García, Julio, 1608
Sánchez Málaga, Carlos, 1845
Sánchez Montenegro, V., 895-896
Sánchez Rubio, E., 2082
Sandburg, Carl, 1609
Sandoval, Luis, 684
Sandoval de Estigarribia, María Jerónima, 392
Santa María, F., 1881
Santa María, Felixberto C., 2107
Santamaría, Francisco J., 1610
Santillán, Fernando de, 1882
Santo de Regla, 1056
Santos, Carlos, 1611
Santullano, **Luis**, 103-104
Sarmiento, **Domingo** Faustino, 393
Sarmiento, **Manuel**, 394
Sas, André, 1883-1884
Schaeffer, Myron, 1714-1716
Schaeffer Gallo, Carlos, 395
Schallehn, Hellmut, 485
Schianca, Arturo C., 396
Schinhan, Jan Philip, 1612
Schmeckebier, Laurence E., 1613
Schuller, Rudolf, 1885
Schwab, Federico, 1845
Sebastián, Juan, 1967
Secretaría de Educación Pública, Sección de Música, 1614
Seeger, Charles, 51, 105-106
Segunda Parte de los Romances del Valiente Francisco Esteban, 1615
Segundo cuaderno de canciones populares venezolanas, 2086
Seibold, Doris, 1616
"La semilla colombiana," 897
Sepúlveda, José Tadeo, 685
Sepúlveda Maira, María Luisa, 686
Sererini, Pedro, 687
Serís, Homero, 107
Serpa P., Domingo A., 2083
Serrano Martínez, Celedonio, 1240, 1617-1623
Serrano Poncela, Segundo, 1108
Shelby, Charmion, 51
Sicramio (pseudonym), 1886
Sierra, Apolinario, 143
Sierra, Florencio de la, 1887
Sifuentes, R. Fernando, 1624
Silva, R., 1938
Silva A., Adolfo, 688
Silva y Aceves, Mariano, 1625
Silva Castro, Raúl, 689-691, 694
Silva Valdés, Fernán, 397-399
Silverman, Joseph H., 1155
Simmons, Merle E., 108, 1626-1631
Simpson, Eylar N., 1632
Sinclair, **Joseph** H., 1888
Sivirichi, Atilio, 1889-1890
Slonimsky, Nicolás, 109
Smith, John T., 1633
Smith, Rebecca, 1418
Soffia, José A., 898
Sojo, Vicente Emilio, 2084-2987
Sordelli, V. O., 400
Sotomayor y M., Ismael, 486
Soustelle, Georgette, 692
Soustelle, **Jacques**, 692
"Spanish Romances from Porto Rico," 1934
Spell, Lota M., 110, 1634-1635
Sperotti Piñero, Emma Susana, 401
Spizzy, Mable Seeds, 1636
Stanley, Daniel D., 1413
Stella, Luz, 899
Stelzmann, A., 1637
Stephenson, Robert C., 1638

Stevenson, Robert, 1639, 1890
Stout, Peter F., 1709
Suannes, S., 111
Sucre, Luis Alberto, 2088
Sundt, Roberto, 693
Suriguez y Acha, Carlos, 402
Surí y Aguila, José, 1057
Swan, Howard, 1640

T. J. C. y P., 1891
Talamón, Gastón O., 403-406
A Tale of Tucumán, 407
Tamayo, Francisco, 2089-2092
Tamayo Vargas, Augusto, 1892-1893
Taylor, Coley, 1263
Taylor, Paul S., 1641-1642
"Teatro callejero nicaragüense: El Güegüence o macho ratón," 1710
Tejada, Valentín, 1109
Tejeda, Luis José de, 408-409
Telégrafo mercantil, 410
Téllez Camacho, Elberto, 900
Téllez Girón, Roberto, 1643
Tercer cuaderno de canciones populares venezolanas, 2093
Terralla y Landa, Esteban, 1742
Terrera, Guillermo Alfredo, 411
Terwilliger, L. Ray, 1058
Testamento de Potosí, 487
Thompson, Robert Wallace, 2094
Tiempo, semanario de la vida y la verdad, 1644
Tinker, Edward Larocque, 1645-1646
El tiple cubano; colección de décimas cubanas, 1059
El tiple cubano; décimas criollas, cantos del pueblo de Cuba, 1060

Tiscornia, Eleuterio F., 412, 901
Tobón, Aurelio, 902
Toor, Frances, 1647-1652
Torquemada, Juan de, 1653
Torre, Manuel, 1654
Torre, M. de la, 1655
Torre Revello, José, 112, 341, 413-414
Torre y Sola, Enrique de la, 1061
Torres, María de Guadalupe, 113
Torres Delgado, Silvestre, 2095
Torres de Mendoza, Luis, 2096
Torres Quintero, Gregorio, 1656-1657
Torres-Ríoseco, Arturo, 694, 1658
Torres Torrente, ____, 903-904
Torri, Julio, 1659
Toscano, Salvador, 1660
Tosta García, Francisco, 2097
Toussaint, Manuel, 1376, 1661-1662
Traversari-Salazar, Pietro P., 114
Trejo Lerdo y Tejada, Carlos, 415
Trelles, Carlos M., 1062
Triumphal pompa, 1663
"El triunfo de la gloria," 1063
"Trovador del Valle," 905-906
El trovador mexicano, 1664
Tuckman, William, 907
Türke, Juan, 695
Tully, Marjorie F., 1665
Tuñón, Fernando, 416
El tuquerreño libre, 908
Twenty-Five Prints of José Guadalupe Posada, 1666

Ugarte, Juan A., 1894
Ugarte y Ch., Miguel Angel, 1845, 1895
Ulloa C., F., 696

Index

Umaña, Salvador, 929
Unamuno, Miguel de, 417
Unanue, Hipólito, 1896
Urbina, Silverio, 1897
Uribe Echevarría, Juan 697
Uriel García, José, 1898
Urquieta, Felipe, 115
Urrutia Blondel, Jorge, 698
Urteaga, Horacio H., 1899
Urueta, Rufo, 909

Valderrama, Adolfo, 699-700
Valdés, Carlos Genaro, 1064
Valdés Rodríguez, Esperanza, 1065
Valdez, Rodrigo de, 1900
Valencia, Reinaldo, 910,
Valenzuela, Inés, 701-702
Valladares Quintana, María Lourdes, 1901
Valle, Rafael Heliodoro, 116-117, 1711
Valle Atiles, Francisco del, 1939
Vallmitjana, A., 1975
Valverde, Sebastián E., 1110
Van Der Voort, Antoni, 1667
Van Stone, M. R., 1668
Vanegas Arroyo, Arsacio, 1669
Vanegas Arroyo, Blas, 1652
Vara Reyes, Víctor, 118
Varallanos, José, 1902
Vargas, Teófilo, 488
Vargas Andrade, Lina, 703
Vargas Osorio, Tomás, 911
Vargas Tamayo, José, 817
Vargas Ugarte, Rubén, 1128
Varias relaciones del Perú y Chile, 1905
Vásquez, Emilio, 1906
Vásquez, Genaro V., 1670
Vásquez Santa Ana, Higinio, 1671-1674
Vega, Carlos, 119, 418-431, 704, 1907

Vega López, Carlos, 120
Vega Miranda, Gilberto, 1712
Velasco, Juan de, 1129
Velásquez, Samuel, 912
Velásquez M., Rogerio, 913-919
Velázquez, Rafael P., 432
Vellard, Jen Albert, 1908
Vera-Izquierdo, Francisco, 2098
Verdadero romance de Lucinda y Velardo, 1675
Verdadero romance en que se refiere un lastimoso caso que le sucedió a una dama, 1676
Vergara Alba, J. Eduardo, 1909
Vergara y Martín, Gabriel María, 121
Vergara y Vergara, J. M., 920
Vial, Román, 705
Vialpando, Roberto L., 1677
Viana, Javier de, 433-434
Viaña, José Enrique, 487
Vicuña Cifuentes, Julio, 706-710
Vidal, Rafael, 1081
Vidal de Battini, Berta E., 435
Vidal Martínez, Leopoldo, 1910-1911
Vidales, Pablo, 711
Vidart, Daniel D., 436
Videla, Heriberto, 437
Vienrich, Adolfo, 1912
Viescas, Ramón, 1130
Viglietti, Cédar, 438-439
Villa, José G., 1034-1035
Villablanca, Celestina, 712
Villafañé Casal, María Teresa, 440
Villafuerte, Carlos, 441
Villalobos, L., 713
Villalobos C., Max (M. V. C.), 714-715
Villanueva, Antonio F., 2108

Villarreal, Concha de, 1678
Villaseñor, Isabel, 1378
"Violeta Parra, hermana mayor de los cantores populares," 716
Vivanco, Moisés, 1913
Vizcarra Rozas, Abraham, 1914-1915
Vowell, Richard Longeville, 122, 622, 1956

Wagner, Max L., 1679
Waldemar, Frank H., 685
Warner, Ralph E., 1658
Waterman, Richard A., 51
Watkins, Frances E., 1680-1681
Webster, Persis Marie Johnson, 123
Wegener, Elena, 717
Weinstock, Herbert, 1230
Whatley, W. A., 1682
Wiesner, L. J., 921
Wildhaber, Robert, 45
Wilgus, A. Curtis, 12
Wilkes, Josué Teófilo, 442-448
Williams, Alberto, 449
Wolfe, Bertram D., 1367, 1683
Wood, Ben D., 1684
Woods, Betty, 1685
Woolsey, A. W., 1686

Works Project Administration, Federal Music Project, 1687-1689

El xarabe loco de Hidalgo y Allende, 1690
Ximénez, Fray Francisco, 124

"Yaraví, versos de la tradición oral," 1916
Yépez Miranda, Alfredo, 1917

Zaffaroni Bécker, Zahara, 450
Zamudio G., Daniel, 922
Zanzig, Augustus D., 125
Zañartu, Sady, 718-719
Zapata Olivella, Delia, 923
Zárate, Belisario, 489
Zárate, Dora Pérez de, 1717, 1719
Zárate, Fidel A., 1918
Zárate, Manuel F., 1718-1719
Zea, F. J., 1000
Zeballos, Estanislao S., 451-452
Zevallos Quiñones, Jorge, 1919
Ziegler, Federico, 453
Zinny, Antonio, 490
Zorrilla, José, 1691
Zuno, José Guadalupe, 1692-1693
Zúñiga, Gonzalo de, 2096

REF
Z
1609
P6S5
#18